The
Disruptor

The
Disruptor

How Vishwanath
Pratap Singh Shook India

DEBASHISH MUKERJI

HarperCollins *Publishers* India

First published in India by
HarperCollins Publishers 2021
A-75, Sector 57, Noida, Uttar Pradesh 201301, India
www.harpercollins.co.in

2 4 6 8 10 9 7 5 3 1

P-ISBN: 978-93-5489-413-8
E-ISBN: 978-93-5489-416-9

Cover design: Saurav Das
Front cover photo: Getty Images
Author photo: Shekhar Ghosh

Typeset in 10.5/14.6 Sabon LT Std at
Manipal Technologies Limited, Manipal

Printed and bound at
Thomson Press (India) Ltd

❶❶◉❾HarperCollinsIn

For AMRITA

The love of my life

From the day she was born

CONTENTS

PART 7: MANDAL AND MANDIR

PART 8: THE LONG GOODBYE

INTRODUCTION

Unlike many others in his family, Vishwanath Pratap Singh had little faith in astrology or palmistry. His father and eldest brother were not only staunch believers but also practised both; V.P. Singh, however, claimed he was never curious about either. 'It was because I found that many predictions turn out wrong,' he said. 'The wrong ones are never remembered, only the correct ones are!'[1] Yet, there was one prediction by their family astrologer, his wife Sita Kumari Singh revealed, which he often recalled in his last years. 'He had forecast that my husband would reach many high positions, but would not last long in any of them,' she said.[2]

It had indeed turned out that way. V.P. Singh's political career advanced at a blistering pace through the 1980s. He became Uttar Pradesh chief minister, Union commerce minister, Union finance minister, Union defence minister and finally Prime Minister—all in the space of a decade. Earlier, he had also been deputy minister—and subsequently minister of state—for commerce from October 1974 to March 1977. But his tenure in each of these offices was short. The first in the commerce ministry, at two years and five months—promoted to minister of state for the last three—eventually proved to have been the longest.

His stint as UP chief minister lasted exactly two years, from June 1980 to June 1982. He was commerce minister for just a year and seven months, from January 1983 to August 1984. His high-profile finance ministry tenure under Prime Minister Rajiv Gandhi again ran for precisely two years, from January 1985 to January 1987, when he was moved to the defence ministry, from which he resigned in less than three months. Finally, his prime ministerial term, starting 2 December 1989, ended in only eleven months.

And yet, in each of his last three positions—as finance minister and defence minister in the Rajiv Gandhi-led Congress government, and Prime Minister in the subsequent Janata Dal government—as well as in the two-and-a-half-year interval when he held no official position at all, some of V.P. Singh's actions changed the course of Indian political history.

<hr />

The best-remembered of these actions is undoubtedly his introduction, as Prime Minister, of 27 per cent reservation in Central government services for the socially and educationally backward classes, or other backward classes (OBCs), identified on the basis of caste. The Indian Constitution, adopted in 1950, seeking to correct the inequalities in Hindu society created over millennia by its caste system, had provided reservations for Scheduled Castes (SCs) and Scheduled Tribes (STs), but not for OBCs. V.P. Singh's announcement, on 7 August 1990, drawing on the recommendations in the report of the Second Backward Classes Commission, chaired by Bindeshwari Prasad Mandal, remains the single-biggest step towards affirmative action in the country thereafter.

At the time it proved hugely controversial, sparking a hysterical two-month-long protest by the upper and intermediate castes excluded from such reservation. This snowballed to a grisly apogee, when young people from these castes began setting themselves on fire, believing that their future employment prospects were doomed—an apprehension that, once OBC reservations were formally adopted in 1993, was found to have been utterly misplaced. Apart from making access to Central government services easier for OBCs—who were greatly underrepresented in them until then—and indeed introducing the term 'Mandalization' into the nation's lexicon as a general descriptor for the attenuation of elitism and consequent increase of egalitarianism in any context, the move also had tremendous political impact.

It accelerated the political consolidation of OBCs across north India, leading them to assert their collective strength in subsequent elections much more forcefully. Its most dramatic effect was seen in UP and Bihar—strongholds of the Congress until then, but where the party drew most of its votes from upper castes, SCs and Muslims, having short-sightedly never courted the OBCs. In every Lok Sabha election until 1984 (barring the 1977 post-Emergency aberration, when it got no seats at all in either state), the combination the Congress had forged enabled it to win the bulk of seats in both states,[3] which, in turn, contributed almost one-third to its nationwide tally, providing it comfortable majorities. The Congress also won most of the assembly elections in both states until 1985, with the same electoral combination.

But once the Mandal Commission's proposal had been introduced by V.P. Singh, the setback the Congress faced in the 1989 Lok Sabha polls—initially thought to be temporary, like that of 1977—turned out to be permanent. Barring one exception in 2009, the party never won more than 10 seats in UP and 5 in Bihar in subsequent general elections; it also never formed the government in either state again. From once being Congress bastions, UP and Bihar are now the party's main vulnerabilities. In the remaining north Indian states too, OBCs have affirmed their importance in elections and played a far greater role in shaping their politics than they did before V.P. Singh's decision.

Detractors of the step have termed it purely political, taken solely due to V.P. Singh's differences with his deputy prime minister, Devi Lal. They maintain that after V.P. Singh sacked Devi Lal from his cabinet and wanted thereafter to isolate him, he enforced the Mandal report's recommendation, thinking it would be the best way to prevent Devi Lal's support group of members of Parliament (MPs) in the Janata Dal from continuing to back him. Undoubtedly, as some of his colleagues at the time have since testified,[4] the timing and abruptness of V.P. Singh's announcement, barely a week after he fired Devi Lal, was dictated by such a strategy. It is another matter that the strategy failed and V.P. Singh's government fell three months later, in November 1990.

Yet, it is also clear, from a series of steps he took as soon as he became Prime Minister, well before his conflict with Devi Lal reached a flashpoint, that V.P. Singh always intended to adopt the Mandal report's main proposal. The announcement could never have been made without this earlier groundwork. Besides, actions have consequences irrespective of the motives prompting them, and the compulsions behind V.P. Singh's move in no way reduce its significance.

❀❀❀

P.V. Narasimha Rao, who became Prime Minister in June 1991, and Manmohan Singh, his finance minister at the time, are rightly credited with ushering in India's economic liberalization by dismantling the Licence Raj that had been built over the past four and a half decades. But they had a predecessor, who sought to move the economy in the same direction, yet who is rarely acknowledged—V.P. Singh.

V.P. Singh's first budget speech as finance minister on the evening of 16 March 1985 was a shocker for many of his listeners (although it had the full support of Prime Minister Rajiv Gandhi), as it substantially reduced both personal and corporate taxes, slashed import and excise duties, and eased considerably the expansion limits that had been imposed by earlier governments on most industrial houses (fearing the creation of monopolies). And while India's dire economic situation in 1991 left the Narasimha Rao–Manmohan Singh duo little choice but to amend policies as they did, V.P. Singh took baby steps when there was no such imperative, having realized that the state's heavy hand on the economy was choking growth.

But the blowback was so strong, not only from the Opposition parties but also from many Congress leaders (who termed it a total surrender to capitalism), that V.P. Singh was forced to revert to the old socialistic pattern in the following year's budget. He tried again with the 1990 budget, alongside new industrial and agricultural policies the year he became Prime Minister, but the precarious nature of his coalition government, as well as opposition from within his own party, stymied his efforts.

How did V.P. Singh square his concern for the poor and disadvantaged—as evinced by his enforcing of reservations for OBCs and his endless harping on 'social justice' in his speeches— with the liberal economic policies he veered towards, both as finance minister and Prime Minister? Was the former only a political ploy, as it is with many politicians? Far from it. V.P. Singh's predilection was apparent long before he entered politics in February 1969, contesting the assembly seat from Soraon, UP—and winning it— and remained well after he had quit politics for health reasons, resigning his seat as MP from UP's Fatehpur in December 1994.

As the third son of one of the biggest zamindars of Allahabad district, Raja of Daiya Bhagwati Prasad Singh, adopted at the age of five by an even bigger zamindar, the neighbouring Raja of Manda, Ram Gopal Singh, V.P. Singh's childhood was one of luxury near unimaginable in the present age. Yet, influenced by Mahatma Gandhi and the freedom movement (India attained Independence while he was in his final year at school), he grew dismissive of personal comforts even in high school; upon discovering that educational facilities hardly existed in the Daiya–Manda region, he started a school there at his own expense in 1952, immediately after he graduated, which functions even today. Post-college, he also joined the Sarvodaya Samaj, the nationwide Gandhian NGO, engaging in shramdaan, or voluntary labour, to build public works. Finally, in a culmination of this bent in 1957, he donated all the agricultural land he had inherited to the Bhoodan movement. Decades later, after his political career halted, even as he was undergoing dialysis for renal failure and chemotherapy for multiple myeloma, he joined protests by slum residents resisting eviction, and by farmers seeking higher compensation for their acquired lands.

What it shows is that all his life, V.P. Singh was spurred by idealism, not ideology. Though close to both the socialist and communist student bodies while at Allahabad University, he does not seem to have been influenced by them the way he was by Gandhi. Thus, when he fathomed that the socialist policies Congress governments had pursued were not really helping the poor, he felt no conflict in discarding them. Indeed, his 1990 budget (as Prime Minister) was an intriguing mix of both liberalizing and welfare measures.

Of greater long-term import for Indian politics than V.P. Singh's effort to open up the economy was the fallout of a parallel drive he launched: even as his policies were bolstering the private sector, he moved to curb corporate corruption. This reflected another dominant strain of his idealism—his obsession with financial integrity. His own was unexceptionable throughout his life, as even his opponents testified, but as finance minister, he tried to impose similar standards across Indian business, unmindful of whether the business owners he was pressuring were Congress party donors. The various enforcement agencies under his ministry conducted so many raids on business houses—sometimes questioning and even arresting venerable industry leaders—that the phase came to be called 'raid raj' and Rajiv Gandhi was finally pushed, allegedly by the industry lobby, into shifting VP to the defence ministry.[5]

V.P. Singh was outraged, not so much by his transfer (though he resented that too) as by Rajiv Gandhi's apparent concurrence with a sustained campaign to malign him by those his ministry's investigations had discomfited[6]—and his outrage ended up making history. His riposte was to start probing defence deals the government had signed before he took over, and he soon stumbled upon an illegal commission of 7 per cent, paid by the German shipbuilding firm Howaldtswerke-Deutsche Werft (HDW) to win a $350-million contract (the cost later escalated to $465 million) to supply four submarines to India. He ordered an enquiry without consulting Rajiv Gandhi, even publicizing his decision through a press release. Rajiv Gandhi reacted with fury, his response suggesting he could well have had much to hide about the deal.[7] Their showdown led to V.P. Singh quitting the cabinet a day later, and the Congress after another three months.

Critics of V.P. Singh have claimed that his campaign to rid Indian business of its many sharp (and worse) practices was duplicitous, in that a good part of the slush funds businessmen generated were out of compulsion to fund political parties, including his own, especially during elections. They have also been disparaging of the HDW deal enquiry he set up for the same reason—if political leaders took kickbacks from defence deals, it was because they had no legitimate means of raising the massive funds elections called for, and since his party had partially funded his election campaigns too, he was himself a beneficiary. V.P. Singh acknowledged their argument but maintained that the solution lay in making political funding transparent.[8] In later life, he would even propose that instead of the oath of secrecy, ministers taking office be administered an oath of transparency.[9]

Remarkably, once he left the Congress, V.P. Singh managed to shed his Congress accoutrements almost instantly and transform himself into an Opposition leader, continuing his campaign against Rajiv Gandhi and the Congress's alleged connivance with corruption—but now unfettered by party loyalty. His effort led to the second of the three big anti-corruption movements waged in the country since Independence. (Jayaprakash Narayan's movement against Indira Gandhi in 1974 was the first and the Anna Hazare–Arvind Kejriwal stir demanding a Lokpal Bill in 2011 the third. In all three cases, the outcome was the same. The incumbent governments against which they were directed lost the next election, but corruption remained as rampant as ever.)

Simultaneously, VP also managed to unite almost the entire array of fragmented Opposition parties, merging some of them to form a new party, the Janata Dal, with himself as its president. With others he made seat-sharing arrangements, thus putting up a united front against the Congress in the 1989 Lok Sabha election. Such unity had been forged only once before—in 1977, in the wake of the Emergency, during which the Opposition leaders had all been imprisoned by Indira Gandhi. It was the palpable fear of being sent back to jail if the Congress won that goaded the Opposition parties to merge to confront her. In 1988–89, there was no such pressing anxiety, and yet V.P. Singh managed, almost single-handedly, to bring about such unity once more and defeat the seemingly invincible Congress—which had won 404 of the 491 seats it had contested in the previous 1984 general election.

V.P. Singh's victory was also historic in that it proved to be the harbinger of an era of coalition governments at the Centre, which would last for the next quarter-century. Political scientists have called it 'a new electoral system—the third since the inauguration of democratic politics (in India) in 1952'.[10] Characteristics of the new system, they have noted, were 'increasing party fragmentation, intensifying political competition, a federalization of national politics ... a relatively stagnant national voter turnout ... and a changing composition of political elites in which lower castes—Dalits and OBCs—gained political representation at the expense of upper and intermediate castes'.[11] The era ended with the 2014 Lok Sabha election, when once again a single party, the Bharatiya Janata Party (BJP) this time, won a clear majority in the Lok Sabha—and which they maintain is a 'fourth phase' where several aspects of the third are being reversed.[12]

No doubt, an unintended side-effect of V.P. Singh's efforts towards political unity—one that his fault-finders make much of—was the fillip it gave to the BJP with its Hindu nationalist credo, thanks to the seat adjustments the Janata Dal worked out with it across several states in the 1989 Lok Sabha election. V.P. Singh agonized over the decision, but finally acquiesced—he knew he could not match the Congress otherwise.[13] The BJP's Lok Sabha seat tally thus rose from just 2 in the 1984 election to 85 in 1989, after which its advance became unstoppable—120 seats in the 1991 general election, 161 seats in 1996 and 182 in 1998, following which, with the help of allied parties, it formed the government at the Centre for the first time (and has continued to do so after the elections of 1999, 2014 and 2019).

However, there were mitigating circumstances. Although the BJP never concealed its sectarian ideology, its image was far less strident prior to 6 December 1992, when its government in UP, through its inaction, allowed the Babri Masjid in Ayodhya to be demolished. Before this happened, both the BJP and its predecessor, the erstwhile Jana Sangh, had always been included in the efforts of the Opposition parties to jointly dislodge the Congress from power. The Jana Sangh was part of all the Samyukta Vidhayak Dal (combined Opposition) governments set up in the north Indian states during 1967–71; in 1977, it merged into the Janata Party and was part of its government; as late as June 1987, in the Haryana assembly elections, the Lok Dal (B) party—which later merged into the Janata Dal—achieved its massive victory in alliance with the BJP. And finally, even if his seat-sharing helped the BJP, V.P. Singh did stand up to the party when it mattered, resisting its first effort to demolish the Babri Masjid in October–November 1990 and sacrificing his government as a result, when the BJP withdrew support.

⬤

For a person who impacted Indian politics as profoundly as did V.P. Singh, his posthumous neglect is a disgrace. Not even a stamp has been issued in his honour, let alone a street or a state-owned institution named after him, even in his native Allahabad. (A Google search threw up just one private college, the Vishwanath Pratap Singh College of Education in Bhind, Madhya Pradesh.) The reason is obvious—his was a political career that riled both poles of Indian politics, the Congress and the BJP, and neither has the slightest interest in commemorating his memory.

But even his inheritors, the heads of the numerous parties that emerged from the Janata Dal—especially Mulayam Singh Yadav of the Samajwadi Party and Lalu Prasad of the Rashtriya Janata Dal, both of whom benefited enormously from V.P. Singh's adoption of the Mandal Commission report—have been indifferent. Having ruled their respective states, UP and Bihar, for years, they could easily have conferred official honours on him, but did not. (V.P. Singh's personal equation with Mulayam Singh Yadav was, in any case, strained.)

On the occasion of V.P. Singh's ninetieth birth anniversary, this biography is my modest effort to redress the imbalance.

Part 1

THE MAKING OF AN IDEALIST

1

'I WAS INSECURE, VERY INSECURE'

Vishwanath Pratap Singh, all of ten years old, sat alone in his room on the upper floor of Aish Mahal, the two-storey mansion in the Civil Lines area of Allahabad (now called Prayagraj) that he had inherited from his late adoptive father. His real father and a host of other relatives and hangers-on were gathered in one of the vast living rooms on the ground floor, but VP had no intention of joining them. He knew they had come to take him away, and he didn't want to leave.

VP was staying with Amar Singh Mathur, a provincial civil service officer in the United Provinces of Agra and Oudh, and his family—or rather, they were staying with him, since it was to him that Aish Mahal belonged. It was late 1941, with the Second World War raging. After the death of VP's adoptive father, the raja of Manda Ram Gopal Singh, earlier that year, his estate had been taken over by the Court of Wards—an institution the British had created for the very purpose of managing the properties of rajas and lesser zamindars who died leaving behind minor heirs. The court had appointed Mathur to look after both the estate and VP. Mathur and his family of seven—wife, two sons and four daughters—had moved into Aish Mahal to do so.

'V.P. Singh became part of our family,' recalled Jagdish Mathur, the younger of Amar Singh's two sons, seven and a half decades later.[1] Mathur, who was five years younger than VP, had only hazy memories of the time. 'He was particularly attached to my mother, Jaijaiwanti, whom he called "Bawua", and two of my sisters, Durgesh and Uma, who were closest to him in age.'

But he remembered that fateful evening well, though the date escaped him. 'My father went upstairs to call him down,' he said. VP was unwilling, but eventually obeyed his guardian. His father, Bhagwati Prasad Singh, also a raja—of Daiya estate, adjoining Manda—beckoned to him, urging him to come into his arms, but VP did not budge.[2] Bhagwati Prasad tried again, with the same result. At this, his cousin, a smaller landlord who had accompanied him, bellowed, indicating Mathur, '*Yeh ladkey ko bhadka diya hai* (This man has instigated the boy to behave this way).'

During his lifetime, VP must have recounted the story several times to his immediate family; his elder son, Ajeya Singh—bald like his father, face rounder, eyes more piercing—easily reeled off the details, including what he claimed were the precise words spoken. 'My grandfather was a tough guy, but he was very soft on children,' he said. 'However, his cousin riled him up. He added, "*Kaise baap ho, apne ladkey ko nahi utha saktey* (What kind of father are you, can't even take away your own son)?"'

At this, Bhagwati Prasad instructed his factotums to pick up VP forcibly and carry him out of the house. 'V.P. Singh, screaming, tried to cling to the chair's armrests, but he was lifted and taken away,' Mathur said.[3]

VP's reluctance to return to his family stemmed from his experiences of the previous five years.

He was born either in the late hours of 25 June or the early ones of the following day in 1931, to Bhagwati Prasad Singh and his third wife, Braj Raj Kanwar, at the raja's two-storey 'mud house' in the hamlet of Vishwanathganj, about 60 km south-east of Allahabad town.[4] (Some claim that his name came from his place of birth.[5]) 'His horoscope says that his birth occurred at the "*ghadi ghanta*", but no one is quite sure what that means,' said Sita Kumari Singh, V.P. Singh's wife. He was the third of his father's five sons and three daughters.

Bhagwati Prasad Singh, born in 1903, was not of raja stock, but hailed from a smaller landowning family within Daiya estate. The previous raja of Daiya, Digvijay Singh, had, however, left a will naming Bhagwati Prasad as his successor, and following the raja's death in 1923, his widow duly carried out his wish by adopting him. Daiya was a mid-sized estate, comprising seventy complete villages and parts of sixty others, paying the British government in the mid-1940s an annual revenue of Rs 40,915.[6] Bhagwati Prasad, tall and fair-complexioned, rapidly grew into his role, managing the estate prudently—unlike some of his neighbour rajas, whose profligacy was legendary—with astrology and shikaar as his favourite pastimes. 'Raja Bhagwati Prasad is a very influential person and has great prestige in the district,' wrote Nurul Hasan Siddiqi, assistant secretary of the Agra Province Zamindar Association in the late 1940s. 'He is very liberal in his treatment of tenants.'[7]

He was also much involved in public affairs, a loyal supporter of the British and a critic of the Indian National Congress. From 1929 to 1945, he was the chairman of the Allahabad District Board (zila parishad). 'I saw his influence when I myself contested the zila parishad elections in 1964–65,' his second son, Sant Bux Singh, who went on to become an MP, recalled years later. 'Everywhere I went, I found hospitals, schools and roads that people said they owed to my father. If V.P. Singh and I entered politics later, the inheritance was from our father.'[8]

Bhagwati Prasad also contested the 1937 provincial elections to the United Provinces assembly from the Jamunapar seat in the district (which post-Independence was broken up into four assembly constituencies), against Congress candidate Ranjit Pandit—Jawaharlal Nehru's brother-in-law, Vijaya Lakshmi Pandit's husband—but was defeated.[9]

Bhagwati Prasad had three wives, by no means unusual for a raja of a century ago. His first wife, Prayag Raj Kunwar, was the daughter of the raja of Bardi Katai (an estate in Siddhi district of what is now Madhya Pradesh); the second was Jayratan Kunwar, daughter of the raja of Bhikampur (an estate near Lucknow); the third, V.P. Singh's mother. Braj Raj Kunwar, like Bhagwati Prasad himself, was not of raja lineage but hailed from a village called Palasi, which was part of the Daiya estate. The year of Bhagwati Prasad's first marriage is not clear, but the other two were solemnized in 1928. 'From what I've heard, the third marriage was not entirely of my grandfather's volition,' said Ajeya Singh. 'He had been betrothed to my grandmother in his pre-raja days. After he'd married twice, the elders of his village suddenly turned up at his doorstep and insisted that he could not break his engagement just because he'd risen in life. So my grandfather married my grandmother as well.'[10]

Pregnancies followed, but Bhagwati Prasad awaited the birth of his children with trepidation. Highly superstitious, he had been told there was a curse on the Daiya family—it did not produce male children, or those born alive did not live long enough to take over as rajas.[11] His adoptive father, Digvijay Singh, had had sons, but they had all died young, forcing him to set down instructions for adoption. (Family lore claims that they were killed in a feud, but there are no details.[12]) Digvijay Singh was himself adopted, being the nephew of the raja before him, Tejbal Singh, who, in turn, was also the nephew of his predecessor, Raja Dhaukal Singh.[13]

A much-trusted pundit told Bhagwati Prasad it was his inherited house on the estate—a huge, sprawling stone-and-brick structure with towering ramparts and four separate aangans (courtyards)— locally called Daiya Palace, that was to blame: It had a curse on it. If his sons were to survive, they should avoid crossing its threshold until they were adults. Accordingly, Bhagwati Prasad had another house built for his family a couple of kilometres away, made entirely of mud, as the pundit had advised, and it was here that the children were born.

At first it seemed that would not be enough. His first wife, Prayag Raj Kunwar, died during childbirth in 1929, along with her male child. But as it happened, later that same year, the other two wives—now designated 'Badi Rani' and 'Chhoti Rani', respectively, in the household—delivered as well. Both children turned out to be male, and both survived. Chhoti Rani was the first into motherhood, giving birth to Chandrasekhar Prasad Singh in June 1929, followed six months later by Badi Rani, whose first son was Sant Bux. Born a year and a half later to Chhoti Rani was Vishwanath Pratap Singh. Badi Rani went on to have two more sons—Har Bux Singh and Rajendra Singh—and three daughters of whom, however, only one, Vimla Devi, survived into adulthood. Not surprisingly, the sons were strictly forbidden from visiting Daiya Palace until they turned adults.

Ajeya Singh remembered that his grandmother had a fiery temper. 'But she would cool down quickly as well,' he said. Sita Kumari recalled that it was Braj Raj Kunwar who ran the household, directing its large retinue of servants. 'Badi Rani was a very simple person, so it was my mother-in-law who was always in charge,' she said. 'She was also older than Badi Rani. She controlled everything at home. She had her own farmlands and managed those too by herself, though she hardly ever stepped out of the house.' Yet, the handicap of living in purdah revealed itself at times. 'I remember we were once being driven somewhere and we passed a jackfruit tree heavy with fruit,' said Sita Kumari.

'My mother-in-law exclaimed, "So that's what a jackfruit tree looks like!" Despite living mostly in a village, surrounded by farms and orchards, she had never seen one before.' Both wives outlived their husband—who passed away in 1974—into the 1980s.

For his first five years, VP lived the conventional life of a privileged child. While at Daiya, he attended a village school, where, writing on a slate with a slate pencil, he learnt the Hindi alphabet from Kaluram, the village schoolmaster.[14] While in Allahabad, he was sent to St. Mary's Convent, a girls' school run by the sisters of the Congregation of Jesus—Indira Gandhi, too, had briefly attended it a few years earlier—which in those days admitted boys as well in the kindergarten classes. 'The boys also had a "tutor guardian" at home, which was quite the fad among wealthy families those days,' said Sita Kumari.[15] By all accounts, the two wives—addressed as 'Badi Ma' and 'Chhoti Ma' by the children—got along amiably, treated their servants well and forbade any distinction between 'real brothers' and 'half-brothers'.

The feudal grandeur VP grew up in encompassed not only privilege but also responsibility. 'One notion I developed was that the people have rights over us,' he said in an exhaustive interview to the Nehru Memorial Museum and Library (NMML), recorded in his last years. 'It is the feudal concept of patronage. If anyone living on the estate had a problem and sought his help, my father felt it was his duty to provide it.'[16]

But all this changed on 11 December 1936, the day VP was adopted by the raja of Manda, Ram Gopal Singh.[17]

Comprising 209 villages and shares in another 187, paying an annual revenue of Rs 106,853,[18] Manda had the largest population among the estates of Allahabad district, much more than Daiya.[19] Both lay side by side, occupying most of the south-eastern portion of the present-day district—the subdivisions of Meja and Koraon today—with their rajas belonging to the Gaharwar clan of Rajputs and claiming a common ancestry dating back to the fifth century.

Fascinatingly, family lore maintains that their most prominent common ancestor was one of the great villains of popular Indian history—Raja Jaichand of Kannauj, who allied with the invading Muhammed Shahabuddin Ghori to defeat Raja Prithviraj Chauhan of Ajmer and thereby aided the Islamic dominance of India for the next six centuries. Chauhan had defeated Ghori the first time their forces clashed at Tarain (Taraori in the present-day Karnal district of Haryana) in 1191, with Jaichand (according to some accounts) supporting him, but Ghori returned two years later to reverse the result—and kill Chauhan—in the second battle at the same spot. This time Jaichand supported Ghori, which may well have made the crucial difference. Muhammed Ghori left behind one of his trusted slaves, Qutubuddin Aibak, to rule Ajmer.

At the time, the different rulers of the kingdoms in India's north-west were forever at war with one another, with alliances constantly shifting, but Jaichand's decision to switch sides and support Muhammed Ghori may well have had personal roots. For Chauhan is also remembered (though the historicity of the incident has been debated) for the most famous elopement in Indian history—with Jaichand's daughter Sanjyukta at some point between the two battles of Tarain.

Jaichand and Qutubuddin Aibak subsequently fell out, and Jaichand, too, was later killed in battle—with Muhammed Ghori returning a third time to support Aibak—in 1194. Family lore— as also the *Gazetteer of Allahabad*, 1928—claims that Jaichand's relatives and nobles fled in all directions, his brother Manik Chand and his entourage moving eastwards and settling down somewhere in the vicinity of present-day Allahabad and Varanasi.[20] Most of the region right up to Varanasi had been part of Jaichand's kingdom, but was then plundered by Muhammed Ghori and his faithful slave.[21]

The exodus is confirmed by historians. As Thomas R. Metcalf writes in *Land, Landlords, and the British Raj: Northern India in the Nineteenth Century*:

> Muhammed Ghori's victory over the illustrious Prithviraj in 1193 not only established Muslim rule in India, it also set in motion a process of migration which slowly spread a new dominant elite across the villages of the central plain. Many bands of defeated warriors fled down the Ganges and southwards ... During the subsequent three centuries these exiles and their descendants ... brought under their control vast tracts of land from the lower Doab [the area between the Ganga and the Yamuna] across Oudh to the Benares region.[22]

The fresh lands they occupied were not uninhabited but ruled by indigenous tribal kings, mostly Bhars and Kols in the Allahabad–Varanasi region, whom the Rajputs fought and largely subjugated. Thus, throughout the 'Muslim period' of north Indian history, while Islamic rulers and their subedars (governors) controlled the key urban centres and their immediate surroundings, in the hinterland it was largely the Hindu Rajput rajas that ran the show (while acknowledging the Islamic king's suzerainty by paying tribute).

A colourful tale, whose historicity again is doubtful, is told about one of the descendants of Manik Chand a few generations later, one Gundan (or Kundan) Deo.[23] A king without a kingdom at the time, Gundan Deo presented himself in the court of Bhar Raja Lorikaditya, who then ruled over the region comprising Daiya and Manda as well as the contiguous Kantit–Bijaipur estate in the neighbouring Mirzapur district and sought employment under him. Lorikaditya, impressed with the royal background Gundan Deo narrated, made him commander of his army. Having won the raja's confidence, Gundan Deo sought his help in getting his three daughters married to royalty, as, he argued, they deserved, given their lineage. Lorikaditya married one of them himself and arranged matches for the other two with the Bhar rajas of Bhadohi (neighbouring Varanasi and now famous for its carpets) and Dalmau (part of the present-day Rae Bareli district). On the night before the next Holi festival, all three daughters poisoned and killed their respective husbands, enabling Gundan Deo to take over the three kingdoms.

Though Metcalf never mentions this particular incident, his account endorses its general outline. He writes:

> In populated areas, the contest for supremacy commonly involved not pitched battles with the indigenous rulers (about whom very little is known), but a drawn-out process of infiltration and subversion by small bands of invaders. Rajput tradition sometimes even represents the clan founder gaining power by guile instead of military prowess. He is portrayed as taking service with an aboriginal chief, or giving him his daughter in marriage; slowly gathering around him his kinsmen and other followers; until at last, on the occasion of a feast when his opponent would be off guard, he would suddenly throw off this dependence, murder his employer and make himself the master of the estate.[24]

More prosaic accounts, however, maintain that Gundan Deo managed to capture the area covered by Manda, Daiya and Kantit–Bijaipur—the region known as Manikpur—during the 'confusion' that followed the first battle of Panipat in 1526,[25] which established the Mughal dynasty in India, and that he never ruled either Bhadohi or Dalmau.

———— ∞ ————

Gundan Deo had two sons, Bhojraj and Ugrasen, and carved up his kingdom between them, allotting Daiya and Manda to the former and Kantit–Bijaipur to the latter. Eleven generations later came the final division, with Raja Mardan Singh allotting Manda to his elder son Prithviraj Singh and Daiya to the younger one, Chhatrasal Singh. But the borders of all three estates remained fluid, with internecine battles often erupting (all rajas had their private armies). Around the turn of the nineteenth century, in particular, Manda saw an expansionist raja named Iswaraj Singh, who attacked Daiya, capturing much of its territory and destroying Daiya Palace. (The existing one was built in stages decades later.)

As the Mughal empire, of which Allahabad was a part, slowly withered away after the death of Aurangzeb in 1707, the town and its surroundings changed hands repeatedly until at last they were taken over in 1801 by the British. Most rajas of the region resisted the British entry and initially withheld revenue payments, but Iswaraj Singh cooperated with the newcomers, even sending his troops to support their battle against the rajas of Bundelkhand along Allahabad's southern border. The Baghels and Bundelas, ruling different parts of Bundelkhand, were subdued within a year and Iswaraj Singh got an additional thirty-five revenue-free villages for his pains.[26]

With most other rajas, the British reciprocated their hostile attitude. Having acquired much of present-day Uttar Pradesh by 1803, barring Avadh (Oudh)—Lucknow and its surrounding districts—they behaved very differently from previous conquerors, who had left the countryside alone as long as they were paid their revenues. Unlike in Bengal earlier, where their permanent settlement encouraged large landholdings, in the North Western Provinces (as UP was called by them), the British set about not only taming the rajas but also demolishing the entire food chain of large landlords and smaller landlords beneath them.

Most of the top British officials, overly influenced by economist David Ricardo's renowned 'theory of rent',[27] regarded the rajas as little more than parasites on the land and preferred drawing their revenue directly from village-level headmen and peasant proprietors. Their land settlements made every effort to marginalize the rajas, especially those who were poor administrators, taking away their right to gather revenue (leaving them just a pension called malikhana), and confiscating unregistered and revenue-free lands granted to them by previous emperors. They hoped, thereby, to relieve the peasants of a big burden and increase agricultural productivity.[28]

It did not work for an obvious reason—the British land assessments were unrealistically high in the first place. 'Almost everywhere these early settlements were based on an exaggerated notion of the resources available to government, and the assessments were sharply enhanced at regular intervals,' writes Metcalf. 'These extraordinarily severe assessments were a product in part of the ignorance of new British Collectors, who were confronted with records of doubtful accuracy. At the same time, however, the British clearly wished to make their new acquisitions pay.'[29] The attempt at rural transformation led instead, as Metcalf titles one of his chapters, to 'Debt, Default and Dispossession'.[30] Peasants and landlords at all levels sold off their lands or abandoned them, unable to pay the revenue being charged.

Thus, for all his bravado and good relations with the British, on his death in 1805, it was found that Manda Raja Iswaraj Singh had mortgaged his entire estate to a banker in Varanasi.[31] Manda's financial condition worsened under his successor, Rudra Pratap Singh, who, in addition, had no appetite for a raja's traditional role, being focused solely on religious scholarship. 'He wrote his own version of the Ramayana, in dohas and chaubolas,[32] in eight volumes,' said Ajeya Singh. 'Many years later, my great-grandfather had them published.' As Manda's debts mounted, the British ultimately reduced the next in line, Chhatarpal Singh, to a malikhana and settled all his villages with resident village communities.[33]

What of the Daiya line of rajas? Among the massive changes the British wrought once they captured the North Western Provinces was also the establishment of an independent judiciary. British-style courts were set up in major urban centres, starting with Allahabad, to which many rajas (and lesser landlords) turned to contest the decisions of British revenue officials—and in a number of cases even succeeded in overturning them.[34] Daiya Raja Dhaukal Singh, however, went to court not against the British but opposing the illegal occupation of his lands by the Manda raja.[35] He got a resounding verdict in his favour—not only were his lands restored to him, but Manda was also required to pay him a heavy indemnity.

The already encumbered Chhatarpal Singh was in no position to do so. Family lore has it that despite their litigation, the two rajas used to attend common family functions. Arriving at a wedding where Dhaukal Singh too was present, Chhatarpal Singh refused to sit down. 'I cannot; there is no place for me to sit,' he is reported to have said. 'Manda is going to be auctioned and all I have will go with it.' At this, Dhaukal Singh promised to tear up the decree in his favour, and never thereafter pressed for the money.[36]

It was not enough to save Manda for Chhatarpal Singh. But then there occurred the seminal event that cleaves British rule in India into two distinct eras—the 1857 Mutiny. Unlike many other north Indian urban centres where rebelling Indian troops took control and held them for months, Allahabad town was liberated for just five days, from 6 to 11 June 1857, before British reinforcements arrived and won it back.[37] The countryside around Allahabad took many more weeks to bring under control and continued to be sporadically attacked by the rebels for over a year.

When the Mutiny began, rajas throughout the North-Western Provinces and Avadh were faced with a life-and-death choice, literally: whom to back, the British or the rebels? In Avadh, which the British had finally taken over only the year before and where they immediately sought to impose the same kind of land settlement they had done gradually across half a century in the North Western Provinces—in effect crushing the rajas—most rajas unsurprisingly backed the mutineers. In the North Western Provinces, despite what they had been subjected to, the rajas' response was much more mixed—many, including those of Manda and Daiya, preferred to remain loyal to the British and sent their armies to fight alongside theirs.[38]

The uprising was quelled, but as is well known, it led to vital changes in British policy towards India, among them, the decision to stop tinkering with land relations. In stark contrast to the past, the rajas of the United Provinces of Agra and Oudh (as UP had by then come to be called) were now validated and given full support (though there were also strict orders to disband their private militias), while those among them, who had helped during the Mutiny, were copiously rewarded. Raja Chhatarpal Singh not only got back all his territories, but his debts—amounting to over Rs 15 lakh on his death in 1864—were also wiped clean, after the government took over the estate for a few years.[39]

The rajas, in turn, remained fiercely loyal right up to the end of British rule. Allahabad town, thanks to its becoming the capital of the state in 1858—and perhaps even more to the Nehru family having its home there—was a focal point of the freedom struggle, but none of the fervour ever reached either Manda or Daiya. Part of the reason was, no doubt, topography. Manda and Daiya were fairly isolated even from the rest of the district. Unlike much of Allahabad, which, being part of the Doab, is highly fertile, Manda and Daiya were, as noted by a later historian:

> ...[P]art of the Bundelkhand hills and physically a salient of Central India jutting out into the Gangetic plain. The rocky Tons hills and dense, swampy forests made all kinds of communication exceptionally difficult ... The instability of

cultivation acted to preserve the ties of lineage and deference ...
It was not until Independence that political impulses from the
town were felt to any extent in this tract.[40]

But this was also because both lines of rajas ruled with fists of iron,
clamping down heavily on nationalist activity. VP's adoptive father,
Raja Ram Gopal Singh, was even said to possess an exceptionally
long shoe, which he used to beat up those he called 'agents of
Gandhi'.[41]

Given his wealth and lineage, Ram Gopal Singh seemed well
qualified for adoptive parenthood, more so when adoption was
quite the norm in childless raja families. (VP's younger brother Har
Bux was also adopted by his maternal uncle, the raja of Bhikampur.)
Born in 1891[42] and educated at Mayo College, Ajmer, Ram Gopal
underwent military training in the Imperial Cadet Corps—now
the Rashtriya Indian Military College in Dehradun. Nurul Hasan
Siddiqi's near-contemporaneous account, *Landlords of Agra and
Oudh*, heaps praise on him, portraying an avid Anglophile:

> He was fond of all outdoor games and was always enthusiastic
> about organising matches and tournaments of football, hockey
> and tennis. He had travelled widely and done a good deal of
> mountaineering in Kashmir. He was a big game hunter and
> his bag included about 15 tigers and 50 panthers ... His chief
> recreations were polo, pig-sticking, billiards and racing. He
> was passionately fond of music and dancing ...[43]

What the account leaves out, however, is that Raja Ram Gopal
Singh was also a romantic. In a setting where women observed
strict purdah and the intermingling of the sexes was impossible,
he fell in love—with a photograph. He had received plenty of
marriage proposals but had rejected them all. Yet this photograph,

which he saw around 1917–18, purportedly of Bhuvaneshwari Kumari, daughter of Raja Kamal Narayan Singh of Khairagarh estate (now part of Chhattisgarh), entranced him. He decided he would marry no one else.

Family elders and other important members of the caste brotherhood were initially agreeable until it was discovered that the Khairagarh rajas belonged to the Nagvanshi clan,[44] which, despite being Rajput, was socially far inferior, having more than a touch of local Gond tribal blood.[45] The same Rajput elders now claimed that the alliance was unthinkable, but by then, Ram Gopal had become adamant. He was the raja—who could stop him? If social ties had to be sacrificed for true love, he was sufficiently steeped in Western romantic fiction to be ready to do so.

He negotiated with the woman's elders and decided on a wedding date, even as fearsome threats reached his ears—that he would be physically assaulted and held prisoner by his caste fellows if he dared to set out for Khairagarh. Khairagarh town lies directly south of Allahabad, about 550 km away, but Ram Gopal resorted to subterfuge, leaving for Calcutta (now Kolkata) by train, with a small, trusted entourage, and then doubling back more than 1,000 km to reach his destination.[46]

But the wedding that followed shattered his life. He found out that Bhuvaneshwari, the woman he had circled the sacred fire with and who had been heavily veiled through the ceremony— as was the custom—was not the girl in the photograph, but her far-plainer-looking elder sister. She was also, Ram Gopal was to discover once he brought her back to Manda, suffering from a terminal disease (whose details are not recorded).[47] The family had been trying for years to get her married off but had failed, and hence resorted to such deception.

Rajputs of the region, true to their word, boycotted Ram Gopal on his return, refusing to dine with him or invite him anywhere. '*Unko jaat sey bahar kar diya* (He was made an outcast),' said

Sita Kumari. The raja made no effort to conciliate his caste fellows, and neither would he forgive his wife and her family. There was no question of getting to know Bhuvaneshwari better or trying to make his marriage work.

Instead, leaving her at his Manda residence, 'Manda Fort', as it is known even today—a behemoth of a structure about 50 km from Allahabad town, with seven aangans (where Daiya Palace has four) and stone ramparts way higher than Daiya Palace's and topped by turrets—he moved himself into his 'club house' next door. 'He was earlier a teetotaller, but now became an alcoholic,' said Sita Kumari. His wife died the following year. 'Her family suggested that he now marry her younger sister, the one whose photo had besotted him, but he refused,' Sita Kumari added.[48] He abandoned all his former interests, stopped caring about his estate, running up huge debts as a result, and shut himself in first in the club house and later at Manda Fort, to drink.

Did Bhagwati Prasad know when, a decade and a half later, still a childless widower and needing an heir for his estate, Ram Gopal Singh sought to adopt five-year-old VP? If he didn't, it points to a shocking lack of due diligence. (The two had become friends despite Ram Gopal being ostracized by the Rajputs, thanks to their common passion for shikaar; they often went on hunts together.) Sita Kumari felt he probably had known. 'For Ram Gopal Singh, it was a means of getting back into the caste, at which he succeeded following the adoption,' she said. 'For my father-in-law, it was a means of reuniting the two families, as they had been in the distant past. In fact, the first choice for adoption, agreed upon by both rajas, was my husband's older brother, Chandrasekhar Prasad Singh. But consent was needed from the British authorities. The then district magistrate of Allahabad vetoed the idea, saying that Chandrasekhar Prasad was already set to be raja of Daiya, and he did not want the two estates amalgamated.'

The next choice was VP, whose horoscope was found to match Ram Gopal's better than those of Sant Bux and Har Bux (Rajendra Singh was not yet born). To this, the district magistrate agreed. Bhagwati Prasad did not inform VP's mother, who is said to have blacked out when she heard the news.[49]

In later interviews, VP could recall few details of the adoption ceremony itself—held at Ram Gopal's Allahabad home, Aish Mahal—except for the presence of a large number of guests, including many British officials, himself clad in silken finery, sitting through a long puja and posing for photographs.[50] What he did remember vividly was the aftermath. Be it at the mammoth Manda Fort or the cavernous Aish Mahal, he found himself completely alone, with servants aplenty to do his bidding but no one to provide warmth or affection—in particular, no mother figure.

'Ram Gopal Singh's father had married four times, and one of his wives was still living at Manda Fort, but she was very old and paid V.P. Singh no attention,' said Sita Kumari. 'He also had a sister—no other siblings—but she had been married off early and hardly kept in touch.'

VP's feelings can be summed up in a line he repeatedly used in interviews describing the period: 'I was insecure, very insecure.'[51]

————

VP knew his life had changed for good. He felt he could take nothing for granted any more and had to work at being accepted, which meant behaving exemplarily all the time.[52] No member of the Daiya family was permitted to meet him. 'I wasn't allowed to meet my natural parents because I was supposed to grow up as a Manda boy,' he said in several interviews. 'My mother wanted to see me, but my adoptive father would not allow it.'[53] Instead, his care was assigned to Ram Gopal's estate manager, at the time a Scot called Captain Cook, and his wife, who lived in the club house next to Manda Fort. The lady proved no mother figure either, keeping her distance from the boy, subjecting him to severe discipline.

In particular, he was required to breakfast with the Cooks and was frequently served a half-boiled egg, whose semi-liquid yolk made him nauseous. The lady insisted he crack the shell himself and consume every bit.[54] The Cooks had one son, but he was much older than VP and had already been sent away to Britain; he was killed in action in the Second World War. 'The only good the Cooks did me was that, having to speak to them daily, my English became fluent,' VP later recalled.[55]

It is not known exactly when—before or after the adoption—Ram Gopal discovered that he had tuberculosis, an incurable disease at the time, and contagious as well. Wisely, he began restricting his physical interaction with young VP to no more than ten minutes twice a day, but that left the boy feeling even more isolated. He had already been taken out of St. Mary's Convent and assigned a private tutor in Manda. He had no playmates, though his adoptive father did buy him an airgun and a camera, both of which he spent much time with.

Apart from Ram Gopal's drinking—which, to his credit, he tried to conceal from the boy, albeit amateurishly—there were also his extreme rages to contend with. One night, VP, for once failing to keep up his exemplary conduct, went off to bed after turning down his dinner. When he woke up the next morning, he found that Ram Gopal, told about it later that night by the servants, had grown so infuriated that he had splashed the dinner all over the dining-room walls.[56] At some stage, to further reduce the chances of infection, Ram Gopal moved VP out of Manda Fort to stay with the Cooks at the club house, but given the boy's feelings for the couple, it was little solace.[57]

After a little over a year in Manda, in 1938, VP, by now seven years old, was suddenly informed that he was being sent to boarding school. This was Colonel Brown's Cambridge School, started by one Colonel William Brown and his wife in Dehradun in 1926. It was the first residential school in a town that went on to become a hub of such schools and is still a thriving institution. As an English-medium residential school for Indians only, it initially attracted mainly the Indian aristocracy—especially the landed gentry—but unlike its counterparts such as Mayo College, Ajmer, or Colvin Taluqdar School, Lucknow, which allowed every student to bring along a troupe of servants, Colonel Brown's school offered no special privileges. Indeed, VP later rated learning to cope on his own without servants as about the only thing he learnt at Colonel Brown's.[58]

He also maintained that he was no happier in Dehradun than he was at Manda, that given his enforced solitude until then, he found it difficult to make friends, and that he never took part in any extracurricular activity. But he also shared memories of pranks he had played, which would have needed the cooperation of other students, suggesting he was not entirely friendless. Once, in severe winter, his friends and he climbed the roof of one of the school buildings and poured water down the chimneys, putting out the fires on which water was being heated below for the boys' baths and inundating the place with smoke. The fire could not be relit that day and most students had to forgo their baths. Another time, his friends and he smeared oil on their dormitory floor and the passage outside, hoping the matron assigned to them would slip and fall while entering.[59] (She did not.)

After a little over two years, in 1940, VP was recalled, as Ram Gopal's health had deteriorated considerably. This time, his adoptive father kept him mostly in Allahabad—not at Manda—where he was enrolled at a leading day school, Boys' High School, set up by the Church of England soon after the 1857 Mutiny had been put down. He stayed at Aish Mahal, once again with only servants for company. Ram Gopal Singh, to pre-empt any chance of infecting him, rarely visited, though he had rented another house close by.

Ram Gopal passed away in less than a year while convalescing in Dehradun. The Court of Wards then took over the estate and appointed Amar Singh Mathur as its manager, as also VP's guardian. Unlike the Cooks, who had lived at Manda, Mathur administered the estate from Allahabad, moving into Aish Mahal with his family. Life changed dramatically for young VP again, because in Mathur's wife Jaijaiwanti, he finally found the mother figure he had been craving. She was extremely affectionate, treating him like one of her own children, and VP, in turn, began doting on her.[60]

It would not last. Unknown to young VP, devious moves were afoot. Some collaterals of the late raja resented this little boy inheriting a vast estate while they got nothing. Three such families went to court challenging his adoption, and his father Bhagwati Prasad began to fear that they might conspire to murder the boy, which would make it easier for them to grab the estate. He shared his fears with the district magistrate and the officials of the Court of Wards, who agreed to provide protection. 'V.P. Singh was one of us, but in some ways he was also different from us,' said Jagdish Mathur. 'We soon got an armed guard in our house, whose only job was to protect him. Also, all the food he ate was tasted by someone else to ensure he was not being poisoned.' But Bhagwati Prasad was not reassured—he now wanted VP back in his own home. However, there was an obstacle. He learnt that Ram Gopal had, in his will, decreed that VP have nothing to do with the Daiya family. The Court of Wards said it was duty-bound to respect this.

A poignant sidelight: During lunch break one day at Boys' High School, VP had an older boy come up to him. 'Don't tell anyone, or we won't be allowed to meet,' the boy whispered. 'But I'm your elder brother.'[61] He was indeed Chandrasekhar Prasad Singh, studying in the same school, as were Sant Bux and Har Bux (Rajendra Singh was still too young to enrol). The brothers began to meet regularly in school, Chandrasekhar, in particular, taking to VP, watching over him closely, buying him ice cream and helping him with his homework. VP came to school in a fancy horse-drawn phaeton, which fascinated Har Bux, who wanted a ride in it. VP feared exposure of their relationship if he obliged but eventually agreed—and got away with the ride without any adults catching on. Later, Mathur was let in on the secret and sportingly allowed VP's brothers to visit him at Aish Mahal.

Yet, these newfound loyalties never dimmed VP's affection for Mathur and his family. He expected to stay with them for years. But Bhagwati Prasad, not one to give up easily, now devised a stratagem—he got officials in the district administration to assign Mathur another position. He then argued with the district magistrate, who headed the Court of Wards, that with his fresh responsibilities, Mathur could no longer take care of VP. Considering the threat to his life, VP needed constant monitoring and should therefore be reverted to his natal family. It still meant disregarding Ram Gopal's will, but he was finally given permission. The adoption was not undone—VP remained under the tutelage of the Court of Wards but was allowed to stay with Bhagwati Prasad.

Another manager must have been duly appointed for the Manda estate later, though VP had no recollection of him. After he was taken away, VP would not meet Mathur or his family again for another decade—his father did not permit it.[62] But at least he was reunited with his mother. Mathur was soon transferred to Meerut and then to Delhi, where he retired in 1950 and died in 1972. His wife outlived him by a dozen years. 'V.P. Singh was away in Bombay the day she died, but he visited us as soon as he got back the next day,' said Jagdish Mathur.

2

'I STUDIED AT THE PACE OF A ROADROLLER, BUT WHATEVER I READ, I INGESTED'

He was an awkward, introverted child, as V.P. Singh himself readily admitted in later life.[1] Political commentators in the late 1980s, when he dominated Indian politics, also noted his wariness about trusting people, which may well have been due to the upheavals of his first ten years.[2] But by no means did these early experiences make him timid.

Bhagwati Prasad Singh was a formidable figure to his children, but that did not deter his son. 'Our father was the typical imperious raja,' reminisced Vimla Devi, VP's sister. 'He loved us all, but we, including the boys, were very scared of him. Whenever he spoke to them, they listened with bowed heads and never answered back.'[3] VP's defiance of his father on the matter of whom he would stay with showed that he was ready to take on authority, even when his position appeared hopeless. Six years later, he displayed similar audacity when he took on his school principal. And unlike the first confrontation, which ended in his abject defeat, this one was roughly a draw.

Though Bhagwati Prasad's four other sons all went only to Allahabad schools—mostly Boys' High School—both he and the district magistrate, for reasons unclear, seemed not to want VP to do the same. The district magistrate was keen on sending him to Doon School, but that did not work out and, after a couple of years at Boys' High School, VP was eventually enrolled[4]—as Bhagwati Prasad desired—in Udai Pratap College, a boarding school in Varanasi.[5]

Udai Pratap College had been started as the Hewett-Kshatriya High School in 1909, named after John Prescott Hewett, lieutenant governor of the United Provinces (1907–12), when it taught up to Class X. It was renamed after its founder Udai Pratap Singh Judeo in 1921, when it added intermediate classes. The 'Kshatriya' in the original name indicated that only boys belonging to the Kshatriya (or warrior) varna, of which Rajputs are a sub-caste, were eligible for admission—a stipulation that continued even after the name was changed.

Founder Udai Pratap Singh was the raja of Bhinga, a mid-sized estate with eighty-nine villages, located in the heart of Avadh, north-east of Lucknow; it paid Rs 91,942 as annual revenue.[6] 'He was a miser and a recluse,' said Ranamata Singh, who was in the same class as V.P. Singh and became his close friend. 'One of my relatives who worked for the raja said that he never donated a paisa.[7] But in his last years, he put practically all his personal savings into Hewett High School.'[8] The school occupies a sprawling 100 acres, and in the 1940s, when VP studied there, had 1,200–1,300 students accommodated in ten hostels.[9]

Udai Pratap Singh's purpose was clear. 'Even wealthy Rajputs did not care much for education those days, especially if they owned land, and the raja of Bhinga wanted to change that,' said Sita Kumari Singh. 'Few Rajputs went to school—it was just not part of our culture. A graduate among Rajputs was rare.' VP always remained a little defensive about having attended a caste-exclusivist school, though obviously he'd had no choice in the matter. 'In those days, every caste set up schools and colleges for its own members,' he said. 'Only upper castes, of course—there was no question of education for the lower castes. But since we were all from the same caste at UP College, there was no casteism. The issue of caste discrimination did not arise.'[10] Post-Independence, with the abolition of caste-exclusivist institutions, UP College was thrown open to all. It also became a full-fledged 'college' soon after, offering undergraduate and postgraduate courses while retaining a high school on its premises.

'To ensure middle class and poor Rajputs attended, Udai Pratap Singh stipulated that fees be low and instruction be in Hindi,' said Ranamata Singh. 'An English-medium school those days would have automatically excluded the bulk of Rajputs.' Not that rich scions were unwelcome. 'Hostel No. 6 was reserved for rajas' sons,' he added. 'Each rajkumar got a room to himself, which he was allowed to share with his guardian, if he brought one along. He was also allowed his own cook. Commoners stayed in shared rooms or dormitories.' (Not Ranamata Singh himself, though—he was the son of one of the mathematics teachers, Rajwant Singh, and stayed with his family in quarters on the campus.)

But even among the rajkumars, young VP was special, because of the threat to his life. The Court of Wards, at Bhagwati Prasad's urging, rented a whole bungalow for him (where he stayed with his servants and armed guards, whose number increased from one to two when he was sent off). Apart from that, he was also assigned a new guardian—one of the staff members, Vijay Shankar Mishra, who taught Sanskrit, Hindi and English. Mishra also moved in with VP.

The bungalow, located on campus, was the one meant for the school principal. When VP joined in 1942, the principal was one Colonel A.W. Long. 'Yet another stipulation of the raja of Bhinga had been that the school's principal always be an Englishman,' said Ranamata Singh. It was empty because the colonel, deputed from the British army, had gone back to serve when the Second World War erupted, while his family had returned to England. (Long never came back.) The then vice principal, Jagdish Prasad Singh, who also taught English, was officiating for him. It was with him, some years later, that VP clashed.

⚬⚬⚬

VP's first year, when he was in Class VII, was difficult. He wanted to blend in with his new surroundings but his circumstances ensured he stood out, embarrassing him dreadfully. The worst feature of his new life was the perennial shadow of his armed guards, who outdid Mary's little lamb by following him to school every day, remaining outside his class all the while he was inside and escorting him back home. He was the only one in the school with such protection. 'One day I wept before my guardian; I made a scene,' V.P. Singh recalled much later. 'I said, "Let the guards drop me outside my classroom, but they should not keep waiting there." I felt so conspicuous! Well, that was allowed.'[11]

Another problem was his continued isolation outside of school hours, for not only did his new guardian impose strict discipline, he also forbade any school friends from visiting VP. Once again, as at Manda, he was alone with his airgun and camera, with 'the sky, nature and my thoughts', as he put it. 'Once studies were over, I was my own companion.'[12] A third complication was the medium of instruction. Hindi was his mother tongue, but all his reading and writing until then had been in English. He had never been a good student, but now his performance worsened.

Then, thanks to two teachers, as he moved into Class VIII, it improved.[13] Who among them, Rajwant Singh or Vijay Shankar Mishra, had the greater influence on him? Both Sita Kumari Singh and Ranamata Singh credit the latter's father, Rajwant Singh, but VP himself plumped for Mishra. 'V.P. Singh

used to be a backbencher; for a start, my father forced him to
sit in the front row in maths class,' said Ranamata Singh. 'My
father took special interest in all students he considered bright,
and besides, he knew V.P. Singh had become my closest friend.
In the Class X school-leaving exam, V.P. Singh topped our class
in maths.'[14]

Sita Kumari, too, maintained that VP had told her that Rajwant
Singh changed his life. 'Mishra was very strict with my husband.
He drew up a timetable for his studies and ensured that he put in
the hours with his books,' she said. 'But a bigger role was that of
Ranamata Singh's father, who coached and encouraged him.'[15] In his
NMML interview, however, VP had no doubt. 'The single-biggest
influence in my life has been my guruji, Vijay Shankar Mishra,'
he said. 'I was a very weak student. But Guruji transformed me
completely.'[16]

Mishra coached VP in almost all subjects, especially the ones
he was weak in, insisting, for instance, that he copy out a page of
Hindi every day. He also added life lessons of a kind that led VP
to question aspects of his feudal tradition. 'Once, I beat up one
of our servants and Guruji forced me to apologize to him,' VP
remembered sixty years later.[17]

Mishra deplored VP's fondness for shooting too. The boy once
downed a small bird with his airgun outside his bungalow, but
just as he retrieved it, Mishra emerged from the front door. There
was a red pillar post box nearby, and in his dread, VP pushed the
bleeding bird inside, under some confused impression that, like
the letters dropped in there, the carcass, too, would disappear.
Mishra's censorious sermon the next day—after the postman,
opening the post box, found the bird and brought it to him, along
with several letters its blood had irrevocably stained—was one
that VP would never forget.[18] It seemed to destroy his appetite for
shooting forever.

Their father being a keen hunter, VP and his brothers had been inducted early into the sport. Sant Bux Singh recalled that early every morning during their holidays, Bhagwati Singh would take his boys hunting in the wilds around Daiya. 'Next, we had to go swimming, and then we had to study,' he added. 'V.P. Singh was a decent marksman—he had shot a tiger, several panthers and stags.'[19]

Vimla Devi, however, five years younger than VP, remembered differently: 'V.P. Singh hated shikaar,' she said. 'He never wanted to go, and if cajoled into it, would deliberately miss his targets while shooting. Sant Bux was the same. But our eldest brother, Chandrasekhar Prasad Singh, loved shikaar and was outstanding at it.'[20] Mishra's pieties may well have changed VP's attitude.

In time, Mishra made an exception to his 'No Visitors' policy for VP—Ranamata Singh was allowed into the house. The boys' daily schedule, Ranamata Singh remembered, consisted of physical training from 7 a.m., followed by breakfast—'usually milk and jalebis'—after which classes were held from 9 a.m. to 4 p.m. 'Thereafter, it was games until 7 p.m., a sandhya puja [evening prayer] and dinner,' he said. 'But V.P. Singh rarely went for games, as one of his "shadows" would follow him to the playground, and he hated that. He would return directly to his house after class. I was not much into sports either, so we spent many evenings together at his house.'

Mishra's coaching would begin after dinner. And with each passing year, VP got better in class, even discovering strengths he hadn't known he possessed. One of them was an exceptional memory. 'I studied very slowly, fully understanding each topic before moving on to the next,' he said about his schooldays. 'I advanced at the pace of a roadroller, but whatever I studied, I ingested. Before exams, many boys would revise their courses—some revised four or five times. I never felt the need to revise.'[21]

But perhaps Mishra's most important contribution to VP's later career was insisting he practise public speaking. 'The first time I tried, my legs were trembling,' VP recalled.[22] He rapidly got better and soon became an outstanding debater, winning 'Best Speaker' awards in the higher classes at both inter-class and inter-school debating competitions. 'He usually won first prize, while I won second prize,' said Ranamata Singh. 'But sometimes the positions were reversed.'[23]

———⊶∞⊷———

VP had his first—albeit fleeting—political experience within months of joining UP College. The year was 1942; the Quit India movement erupted from 9 August, and though Gandhi and the top leadership of the Congress were arrested in the days before it began, demonstrations against British rule—as they had planned—broke out all over the country. One day soon after, a large crowd invaded the UP College campus and exhorted the students to join their protest. Many, including VP—barely eleven, after giving his armed guards the slip—did so, following the crowd to a nearby crossing, where they staged a sit-in. Suddenly, VP felt a sharp tap at the back of his head. He turned to see Mishra glaring at him. He was put on a train and sent back to Allahabad along with his guards that very evening.[24]

But his interest had been sparked and, mainly through newspapers, he began closely following—and even identifying with—Gandhi and the freedom movement. Like many of his generation, he was tremendously impressed by Gandhi, more so after he read My Experiments with Truth in high school.[25] Honesty in his dealings, as well as speaking his mind, became very important to him. He acquired a charkha, learnt to spin and began spinning every day. Impressed by Gandhi's austerity, he started bathing in cold water through the year—even at the height of winter—doing yoga every morning and wearing khadi.

The nationwide surge against authority also strengthened his inherent rebelliousness. In his final year at UP College, the country finally became free, but there was also the Partition. 'The riots during Partition on both sides disturbed me a lot,' said VP. 'But Mahatma Gandhi's readiness to put his life at risk at Noakhali to stop the Bengal killings also overwhelmed me.'[26]

A lot changed for VP in his last two years at UP College, when he was done with high school and entered intermediate. For one, Rajwant Singh departed, taking over as principal of a school in Hardoi, and Ranamata Singh left with him, joining Ewing Christian College, Allahabad, for his intermediate. (Fortunately, Mishra then allowed two other friends—Vijay Singh, the nephew of the school doctor, and Ambika Singh, a newcomer who did his intermediate from UP College—to also enter his bungalow's hallowed precincts.) With Independence, Jagdish Prasad Singh, 'acting' principal until then, was also confirmed in his position. In his final year, VP was made one of the six prefects of the school, who assisted the teachers in enforcing discipline—a distinction usually conferred on the best students in their final year.

As prefect, VP, subject to harsh discipline himself at home, imposed the same on the students. He freely admitted in later life that they were scared of him and there was instant 'pin-drop silence' when he entered the assembly hall or any class.[27] One of the prefects' duties was to check hostel rooms every school-day morning while PT was on, to catch those still asleep or seeking to dodge physical exercise, and subject them to additional exercises— which VP did with zeal in the hostels under his charge. 'I was not looking to be popular,' he said later.[28] Yet, it was this prefecture that started his conflict with the principal.

Student unions are an innate feature of colleges, not of schools. Yet, the anti-establishment mood of 1947 was so strong that the months leading up to Independence saw the students of UP College demand a union, which would take up 'students' issues', whose office-bearers they would elect without interference from the school authorities. Jagdish Prasad Singh generously acquiesced to the demand. Within days, the head prefect, Shiv Shanker Singh, called a meeting with the other five. He told them that he intended to stand for union president and sought their support.

VP was ready to provide it until Shiv Shanker Singh let on that he had the principal's covert support as well, who would also try to influence the other boys to vote for him. The principal's intent to ensure the election of a compliant president, through whom he could control the seemingly independent union, became clear to VP and he said so. 'Why should the principal have anything to do with student union elections?' he asked.[29]

Jagdish Prasad Singh's duplicity made VP furious. Back home, he told Mishra the story, adding that while he could do nothing to prevent Shiv Shanker Singh from contesting with the principal's support and even winning, he wanted to register his protest—and would do so by resigning his prefecture. Given his disciplinarian disposition, Mishra would have been expected to strongly oppose any such step, but curiously, he agreed with VP, even drafting his resignation letter for him, setting out the reason for the step clearly. (Ranamata Singh hinted that Jagdish Prasad Singh was not much liked by either his staff or students. 'He spoke beautiful English, but that apart, my father was much more popular,' he said.) VP submitted the resignation the next day. Now it was Jagdish Prasad 's turn to be furious, as VP stopped performing his prefect's duties. The news reverberated through the school; the students all got to know, and a large number of them insisted that VP contest against Shiv Shanker. In later interviews, VP insisted that this had never occurred to him until then, but at the boys' persistence, he agreed.[30] He won by a landslide.

Jagdish Prasad seethed at the result, but there was nothing he could do about it. Independence followed. Within days, the union raised its first demand—that the portrait of George V, the king of

England and emperor of India until his death in 1936, hanging in the assembly hall, be replaced by one of Maharana Pratap of Mewar, the tallest of Rajput heroes, who had defied the suzerainty of Mughal emperor Akbar in the sixteenth century. With the country now free, Jagdish Prasad had no reason to oppose the demand, but he was not going to oblige VP. He maintained that the school had no spare funds to do so. When asked what a new portrait would cost, he estimated it at Rs 700, which seemed to the boys a wildly inflated figure, given living costs at the time. Unfazed, VP and his friends went around the hostels with a donation box, urging each student to contribute a rupee, and within days handed over Rs 700 to Jagdish Prasad.[31]

Still Jagdish Prasad did nothing about it. George V's portrait remained in place. The boys then decided to hold a protest. But how should they protest? They were averse to boycotting classes, which could easily have been organized. Instead, they decided to boycott the principal at the Krishna Janmashtami celebrations, scheduled for 7 September 1947, which the school had a tradition of holding every year. When Jagdish Prasad entered the assembly hall for the festivities, there were hardly ten boys present. As soon as he left, a large group of boys led by VP entered to perform their puja. They made sure they crossed Jagdish Prasad's path as he was departing, underlining that they were boycotting him, not the occasion. 'Well, after months, a portrait of Maharana Pratap did replace George V's,' said VP.[32]

Jagdish Prasad waited for an opportunity to hit back, and a little later, he got one. As usual, VP was the school's representative at an inter-school debate, which happened to be held in the late afternoon, so he skipped two classes after lunch to prepare for it. To his ill luck, both the classes he stayed away from were of English poetry, taught by Jagdish Prasad. He won a trophy in the debate, but the next morning in class was informed by classmates that Jagdish Prasad had noticed his absence the previous day and

spent 'fifteen minutes at least' haranguing them about it. Soon VP
was summoned to the principal's office and subjected to another
long diatribe. His protests and explanations, pointing out that he
had absented himself only to prepare better for the debate and
had won a trophy too, made no difference. Jagdish Prasad insisted
upon—and finally got—a written apology. But VP went down
fighting. 'I'm sorry for absenting myself from class without taking
official leave,' he wrote (in Hindi). 'But I did so only to enhance the
prestige of our college.'[33]

The mutual antipathy had no further flashpoints. VP passed his
intermediate exams, was placed in the merit list and had nothing
to do with Jagdish Prasad thereafter.

3

'THIS MAN IS SOMETHING ELSE'

The Belan river rises in Sonabhadra district in UP's south-eastern corner, flows west through Mirzapur into Madhya Pradesh and then abruptly turns north into Allahabad. For the last 60 km or so, it moves west through Allahabad, at times marking the border with Madhya Pradesh's Rewa district, before joining the Tons river, which, in turn, flows into the Ganga near Sirsa town.[1] It skirts the grounds of Daiya Palace and flows close to the spot where Bhagwati Prasad Singh's mud house once stood. During his school and college vacations, V.P. Singh's daily routine—once shikaar and the earlier rigorous schedule imposed by his father had been given up—usually consisted of leaving home soon after breakfast to spend the day by the river all alone. He would take a book along and, if they were in season, pluck a few oranges from an orange grove belonging to his family that he passed on the way.[2]

VP had a favourite rock by the riverside he sat on while reading, often with his bare feet immersed in the swiftly running water. The days by the riverside, when he felt 'at one with nature'—as he put it in an interview[3]—clearly meant a lot to him. In his last years in Delhi, when he was not sure he could ever go back, he kept a number of stones collected from the Belan riverbed in his bedroom.

'The waters of the Belan were clear enough for me to see the stones on its bed,' he remembered. 'When the sun's rays fell on them, they shone with a golden light.' He would have his oranges; lunch was brought to the spot by servants; after lunch, he would take a nap and on waking, read again. (Tall, lean and somewhat frail in those days, he had been advised an afternoon nap to gain weight, but this subsequently turned into a bothersome habit, especially during election campaigns, which he could never overcome. Sometimes he would skip lunch just to pre-empt having to nap thereafter.[4] 'When he visited rural areas in his constituency, he always took along a chatai, a pillow and a sheet, which he would spread out to nap on even under a tree,' said Sita Kumari Singh.) He would return home only when daylight began to fade.

His holiday routine may suggest that VP was an avid reader, but curiously, this was not the case. 'He was never much into reading for recreation or pleasure,' said Sita Kumari. It was the spot by the Belan which meant a lot to him, not the books he read there. In his NMML interview, when asked specifically about the books he'd read, VP was able to name only a handful, all of which—with one exception—would have been standard fare for young people of his generation: Gandhi's and Nehru's autobiographies, Munshi Premchand's novels and short stories. 'More than reading, I spent my time thinking,' he said. 'I thought a lot about what I read.'[5]

The exception, however, is significant. VP dwelt on *How to Be Happy though Human* by W. Beran Wolfe[6] in his NMML interview, adding regretfully, 'It's probably out of print now.' His wife confirmed that he had read it several times during his life.[7] Essentially a self-help book, though more substantial than most in its overcrowded genre, its contents, far removed from politics and public life, could well be a pointer to VP's private preoccupations. Beran Wolfe was a practising psychiatrist who translated the works of Alfred Adler—the man who formalized the feeling and coined the term 'inferiority complex'[8]—from German into English.

Much of the book, which is dedicated to Adler, also follows the latter in asserting the universality of this complex, brought on in early infancy through interaction with Brobdingnagian adults, who seem to babies to enjoy so much more power and autonomy than they do.

The complex is either reinforced or attenuated by childhood experiences, Beran Wolfe maintains, and is at the root of every human achievement and every human folly. All aspiration is an effort to compensate for this complex; character and personality are but tools fashioned for this purpose. It is fascinating to speculate on VP's own inferiority complex, what he thought about it as he pored over Beran Wolfe and to what extent compensation influenced his life decisions.

V.P. Singh's search for Adlerian compensation seems to have gone through five phases, in each of which he tried something entirely different; only the last was full-time involvement in electoral politics. Unlike most young people, thanks to his inherited wealth, he was under no pressure to start earning a living and could afford to experiment. The first phase seems to have been to emulate his elder brother Sant Bux Singh. 'In our family, we received intelligence in the same order that we were born,' VP was to say later,[9] but all evidence suggests that even if he thought his eldest brother Chandrasekhar Prasad Singh the wisest of his siblings, it was Sant Bux he bonded best with.

All the books he read by the Belan river came from Sant Bux's extensive library.[10] An aversion to shikaar was only the first of their commonalities. While Bhagwati Prasad was contemptuous of the freedom struggle—'*Lattha hilaye se Angrez na bhag jaye* (Waving flags won't make the British run away),' he would say[11]—Sant Bux supported it, and VP did too. He had already been dazzled by Gandhi's austerity and courage while at school, but returning to Allahabad and joining college, he went further, following Sant Bux.

The Congress had always had a strong reformist faction, which, while campaigning for freedom, emphasized that it was not only freedom from British rule that it sought but also from feudal oppression. High on its post-Independence agenda was abolishing the zamindari system. Sant Bux, the scion of one of the biggest zamindars of Allahabad district, staunchly supported this, and under his influence, VP began to do so too. In any case, being born into a raja's family had brought him only loneliness and embarrassment. Though later he would take a more nuanced view of his feudal background, for many years of his youth and middle age, Sita Kumari remembered him repeatedly saying, 'It's not my fault I was born in a raja's family!'[12]

Thus, from 1948, VP, heir to *the* biggest zamindari in Allahabad, began accompanying Sant Bux on his rural forays, railing against the zamindari system. 'We would go from one village to another, addressing small groups of ten to twenty people,' VP said. The mystified villagers heard them out stoically, mostly keeping their views to themselves.[13] Bhagwati Prasad found it too much of a joke to chastise them,[14] but soon the joke was on him, when the UP assembly passed the UP Zamindari Abolition Act in January 1951.

─────◦◦◦─────

Both Sant Bux and VP attended Allahabad University, the former having joined a year earlier. VP studied philosophy, economics and political science. Established in 1887, the university was the fifth-oldest in the country, after those of Calcutta, Bombay, Madras and Lahore. For many decades—especially during its 'golden period', which a chronicler has bracketed between 1927 and 1957[15]—it enjoyed near-incomparable status in the country. (It declined steeply from the 1970s.)

Its famous alumni from those halcyon days include prominent politicians, bureaucrats, diplomats, judges, lawyers and writers too numerous to name; even its list of famous faculty is imposing. When VP joined in 1948, for instance, its legendary vice chancellor Amarnatha Jha had just retired the previous year, but had been succeeded by the equally eminent Tara Chand, a renowned historian who later became a Rajya Sabha member and India's ambassador to Iran. In VP's philosophy department, the illustrious Ramchandra Dattatraya Ranade—whom Sarvepalli Radhakrishnan was to call 'the greatest philosopher in the country'[16]—had also retired in 1947, though his near-equally esteemed colleague, Anukul Chandra Mukerjee, stayed for another year.

Though he did well enough in his BA exams, missing a first division by just one percentage point,[17] academics does not seem to have occupied VP much at Allahabad University. Beyond naming his subjects, he never discussed them in his interviews relating to that period. What he did emphasize was the role of Sant Bux in his life then, more so because the three older brothers began staying together at Aish Mahal.[18] (There was some initial shock to discover that in the years the house had lain vacant, it had been stripped of all of Ram Gopal Singh's possessions, including the furniture, by corrupt Court-of-Wards officials.[19]) VP also noted that he was delighted to finally get rid of his armed guards, having convinced his father that he was old enough to do without them. The cases contesting his adoption and inheritance, too, had died a lingering death by then.

The high point of VP's first year in college was Sant Bux's election as president of the university's students' union. (No undergraduate—Sant Bux was only in his second year—has accomplished the same feat before or since.) The union had been set up in 1923 with the full support of its British college authorities—Oxford and Cambridge universities had unions, so why shouldn't Allahabad, ran the reasoning[20]—but it had since gone completely out of hand, turning into a hotbed of nationalist activity, vigorously participating in agitations such as the salt satyagraha and the Quit India movement.[21] Yet, strangely, within a year of Independence, Congress influence on the campus had practically disappeared, the main student groups being those backed either by the Socialist Party, the Communist Party of India, or the Hindu-nationalist Rashtriya Swayamsevak Sangh (RSS).[22]

Sant Bux's views were closest to the socialists, but whether he formally joined its students' wing or fought as an independent is not known. What is known is that VP campaigned earnestly for him, leaving home so soon after waking up each day of the campaign that he would often brush his teeth (with a datoon) and have his breakfast—an apple he'd slip into his pocket—en route to the university. The effort paid off—Sant Bux won—though for VP, his victory was slightly marred by what can be called his 'Ashwatthama hata'[23] moment.

Details are scant, but the gist is that a rumour suddenly swept the campus claiming that Sant Bux's rival for the president's post had spat from a balcony upon some girl students seated below. It was a time when such loutish behaviour cost votes. Somehow, VP was aware of what had actually happened and knew that the accusation was untrue. As noted earlier, following Gandhi's example, he made it a point to speak the truth, however unpalatable, at all times, and prided himself on doing so; but on this occasion, since the rumour was to Sant Bux's advantage, he made no attempt to scotch it. But it bothered him to the extent that he admitted it in an interview decades later.[24]

Soon after graduating in 1950, Sant Bux left for Oxford University and later studied law in London, staying away for seven years. But campaigning for him left its mark on VP. He claimed that he never consciously planned to contest student polls, but soon enough, when a challenge was unknowingly thrown at him by a student leader, he responded in the same way he had done earlier to his father and his former school principal. By then, he had graduated and re-enrolled for an MA in philosophy. He narrated to his NMML interviewer,

A senior political leader was to deliver a lecture at the university's Senate Hall and I went along to listen. It was either Acharya J.B. Kripalani or Jayaprakash Narayan or Sarojini Naidu—I can't remember now. The hall was full, so I decided to stand just behind the row of chairs meant for union office bearers. The union's general secretary, who belonged to the RSS's student wing, ordered me to go elsewhere, claiming that the entire area was reserved for the office bearers. I left the hall without hearing the lecture. I decided I was going to get elected to the union, so as to sit on a chair at the very spot where I was not allowed to even stand.[25]

He did it too, contesting and winning the vice president's post in the next election. The RSS had, by then, formally launched its students' organization—the Akhil Bharatiya Vidyarthi Parishad (ABVP), started in 1949—but standing as an independent candidate, informally backed by both the socialists and the communists, VP beat his ABVP rival.

His year as union office-bearer was fairly uneventful. Records of the time reveal only two minor demonstrations—one of them, however, startlingly contemporary-sounding. The ABVP invited the then RSS supremo, Madhav Sadashiv 'Guru' Golwalkar, to the university to address students, which the socialists and communists vehemently objected to. The second protest, however, would never have happened in today's times—so high ran feelings against the United States that the union objected to former US first lady Eleanor Roosevelt's visit in March 1952,[26] despite her record of work on US civil rights and in the United Nations. It may have been due to her support of Israel.

VP never mentioned the protests in any of his interviews. He only noted that soon after the polls, for a month and a half, the union president Kashinath Mishra—later to be a member of UP's legislative assembly—went away from the university for personal reasons, during which VP officiated in Mishra's place.[27] But he added that union-related work took up so much of his time that he gave up his postgraduate studies and enrolled instead for a graduate course in law.

Was it only union activities that took over VP's life? Not so. His real preoccupation at the time can be seen in a couple of austere-looking buildings—one long and single-storey, the other more compact with three storeys—standing at right angles along the edges of a vast field in Koraon town, a tehsil headquarters about 60 km south-east of Allahabad and equidistant from both Daiya and Manda. The triangular arch above the gate leading into the field says in blue lettering, 'Gopal Vidyalaya Inter-College', and then, in much smaller font, 'Established July 1952'.

The school marks VP's second phase of Adlerian compensation, influenced both by the near-absence of formal educational facilities in the Daiya–Manda region and the example of many followers of Gandhi who, after the Mahatma's assassination in January 1948, decided to shun politics and devote themselves to the country's uplift.[28] Considering the dismal educational scenario in the country at the time—the first census after Independence, in 1951, showed the literacy rate at 18.33 per cent[29]—buttressing the government's efforts by setting up private schools in rural or poor urban areas was a priority for them.

'There was only one school in this area before V.P. Singh's, which taught up to Class VIII,' said Koraon resident Prabha Shankar Tiwari, a former block pramukh, who completed high school from Gopal Vidyalaya in 1958. 'Anyone seeking further education had to go to Sirsa, 37 km away.'[30] Tall, square-jawed, narrow-eyed and heavily moustachioed, he marvelled at the change that had since occurred. 'Today, we have more than fifty schools here and four degree colleges.'

VP himself recalled, 'At the time, apart from us brothers, there were only two graduates in all of Daiya.'[31]

The original school was set up a couple of kilometres away, on a much smaller, vacant spot VP's family owned in the heart of Koraon's main market, moving to its present site only in around 1960. Dapper and highly articulate, with a copper complexion and weather-beaten features, Udit Narayan Singh was a student at the old site from Class VIII to Class X. He joined in 1953 and again taught briefly at the new site before going on to start his own schools. 'The school started with classes VI and VII, for which it had obtained government sanction, and added new classes every year,' he said. 'The primary classes were added later—in the same year that Gopal Vidyalaya became a high school.'[32]

Facilities were rudimentary. 'It was just mud huts with thatched roofs, benches and blackboards,' said Prabha Shankar Tiwari. Udit Narayan Singh remembered that the older students even helped in the construction of the huts. 'The mud walls had been built, but it was we who put up some of the thatched roofs,' he said. 'V.P. Singh worked alongside us.' VP also footed the bill for the entire enterprise and, indeed, ran the school for years using his personal funds and donations, until it began receiving government aid. Ranamata Singh, who had, by then, joined the Thomason College of Engineering, Rourkee (now Roorkee)—part of the Indian Institute of Technology (IIT) network today—was among the donors. 'I got a merit scholarship of Rs 10 per month, of which I would send him Rs 5,' he recalled. 'I'd put the note in an envelope and send it by registered post.'

VP taught intermittently at the school for a year or two. 'I remember he taught us English,' said Udit Narayan Singh.

He taught other subjects too, including science, and one of his teaching aids is still remembered.

'Old students tell me he would bring a chemical balance to the school and demonstrate its use,' said Rudra Narayan Bajpai, vice president of the school's managing committee. 'He would show the boys how it could determine the weight of even a single strand of human hair.'[33]

Today, the school has nearly 5,000 students, with classes up to Class XII, and has even added an English-medium section located at a separate site across the road. But beyond a single framed photograph on the wall of Principal Mohammed Shabir Ali's office, there is nothing to indicate that Gopal Vidyalaya was set up by VP.

<hr />

Two important events, unrelated to his Adlerian quest, occurred in VP's life in the first half of the 1950s. First, having turned twenty-one in 1952, he got back his Manda estate from the Court of Wards the following year.[34] Second, in 1955, he got married.

Only after his estate had been restored to him by the Court of Wards did VP return to Manda Fort—for the first time since his adoptive father's death more than a decade ago. Zamindari had already been abolished—he was now raja only in name, divested of all revenue-collecting powers, yet the reception he got was exuberant. 'There were welcome arches along the way, bedecked with flowers,' he recalled. 'I was travelling in an open car, and that was heaped with flowers as well.'[35] In fact, getting back his estate was an occasion for commiseration, not celebration for VP, as Ram Gopal Singh had left behind huge debts—of around Rs 44–45 lakh[36]—which the Court of Wards seemed to have made no effort to ameliorate in the intervening years. 'Much of the debt was accumulated interest,' said Sita Kumari.

On taking over the estate, the government paid VP compensation of Rs 7.5 lakh,[37] according to one account, but the debts were still his to settle. 'There were ninety-eight creditors in all, and my husband located each one and settled with him,' said Sita Kumari. 'He was doing so well into the early 1970s.' She has no idea how he did it but did recall diverting stories he told her about his difficulties. 'Once, he settled with the family of a creditor, who had died,' she said. 'Soon after, the creditor's mistress turned up, saying that she was the one he had been living with and so she deserved some payment as well.'[38]

Sita Kumari was never directly told she would be marrying VP. 'But it was all over the household, and I heard it as well,' she said. 'I did not even see a photograph of his before we were married.' She was the third of eight children, and the eldest daughter, of the raja of Devgarh-Maderia, an estate near Udaipur in Rajasthan (rajas there held the title 'rawat'). She was also the first girl in her family to be sent to school. 'Practically everyone in the family was against it, but my mother and aunt [Lakshmi Singh Chundawat, from Devgarh, later to be both a Congress legislator and a member of Parliament] were determined,' she said.

It was not a day school, but a residential one: Sophia Girls' School in Ajmer, 150 km away, set up by the Mission Sisters of Ajmer in 1919. 'It was a convent school, so I had no special privileges, unlike my brothers who went to Mayo College in the same town,' Sita Kumari recalled. She excelled at athletics, but marriage at the age of nineteen—just after she finished school— put an end to her sporting ambitions. 'I was supposed to be part of the Rajasthan contingent at the All India Olympics [which preceded the National Games] in 1955, taking part in the high jump and javelin-throwing events,' she said. 'But, of course, once I got married, I never went.'

VP acquiesced readily to an arranged marriage—as was the custom then, more so among raja families—but with two caveats. First, he found the custom of grooms inspecting prospective brides with the option of rejecting them distasteful and humiliating for the women, and wanted no part of it. 'If my mother and you are okay with the girl concerned, I'm okay with her too,' he told Sant Bux's wife. 'I think it's very wrong for a man to reject a woman on the basis of her looks.'[39]

Second, he insisted that he would not accept dowry. That led to a delicate moment during the tilak ceremony, which preceded the wedding by a few weeks—the customary gifts Sita Kumari's father, Sangram Singh, heaped on him on the occasion included Rs 50,000 in cash. VP's male relatives—no women are present on the occasion—grew tense, fearing he might create a scene; some of them, especially his father, were already calling him 'paglu' (mad) for his radical views. But VP responded with grace—he took the money quietly and even used part of it to expand his school at Koraon. 'But within a few months after the wedding, he returned the entire amount to me,' said Sita Kumari.[40]

VP set one more condition but couldn't stick to this one. He wanted his beloved elder brother Sant Bux, still away in the UK, to attend the wedding. Sant Bux's response, if any, is not known, but VP kept insisting on waiting until he got back, while the pressure on him to finalize a wedding date mounted. As already seen, VP was no avoider of confrontations, but on this occasion, he preferred flight to fight—he went away to Bombay (now Mumbai), staying with his old school friend Ambika Singh, who had settled there.

It was VP's first visit to the city, and he relished its metropolitan ambience as much as he did his first view of the sea. In his spare time, he read law, which he had been neglecting for months, having found the course utterly boring.[41] 'His eldest brother Chandrasekhar Prasad Singh then followed him to Bombay and persuaded him to come back,' said Anand Singh, Sant Bux's son, who was around five years old then.[42] (He had been born just before Sant Bux left for Oxford.) At some point, soon after his return, VP sat for and passed his law exams.

The marriage was solemnized on 25 June 1955—the date coinciding with VP's birthday—with all the pomp expected of a raja's wedding. 'The bridegroom's party consisted of over a hundred people, who came by train to Udaipur,' said Sita Kumari. 'Almost the entire village of Devgarh went to Udaipur station to welcome them and followed the baraat as it made its way to our house.' What she remembered most vividly of the evening was the smoke. 'They were firing cannons and bursting hundreds of firecrackers outside,' she said. 'Most of the people were outside, but I had to stay in my room. It filled up with smoke to the extent that I was almost choking.'[43] The festivities and rituals went on for much of the night. Sita Kumari departed with VP the very next day. Back in Allahabad, they stayed at Aish Mahal with Chandrasekhar Prasad Singh and VP's mother Brajraj Kunwar, while the rest of the family lived in the old city in a spacious kothi in Muthiganj that Bhagwati Prasad owned.

'Vishwanath has been very lucky in his marriage, my sister-in-law is one of the most devoted and beautiful wives any person can get,' said Sant Bux, soon after VP became Prime Minister. 'She has been of great help to my brother. She has also brought him great luck.'[44] The couple had two sons: Ajeya Singh, born in November 1956, and Abhay Singh, born in April 1959.

⁂

VP's second shot at Adlerian compensation had a dramatic culmination.

Alleviating landlessness was a major concern in the first decade after Independence. The abolishing of the zamindari system helped tenant farmers by ending arbitrary increases in land revenue, ensuring the security of tenure and enabling at least some to turn peasant proprietors; but it made no difference to those with no land at all. In 1951, more than a quarter of those who worked on the land did not own any.[45] At the same time, while the abolition took away zamindars' right to collect revenue, it left their personal lands—often amounting to thousands of acres—

untouched, leading to much debate on whether and how these should be redistributed. (In most states, land ceilings came only in the 1960s.) In Hyderabad state (as Telangana and some of its surrounding areas were then called), an armed communist uprising had begun seizing land forcibly, killing big landlords and inviting brutal police repression in response. It was against this backdrop that the well-known Gandhian Vinoba Bhave decided that he would walk from village to village across the country, appealing to those with excess land to give it up voluntarily.

It was a noble, doomed effort, though in its first years it had some amazing successes.[46] Bhave had the stature to draw an audience wherever he went. Born into a Vadodara-based, middle-class Maharashtrian Brahmin family, spiritually inclined from an early age, he had run away from home to Varanasi when he was twenty years old. Within a year, he joined Mahatma Gandhi at his Sabarmati Ashram and came to be regarded as Gandhi's 'spiritual heir', participating in several agitations and imprisoned for more than five years in the 1940s.[47]

But the zenith of his achievement came well after Independence, with his land-collecting walkathon, Bhoodan. He started with Pochampalli village in Hyderabad in April 1951, seeking to demonstrate an alternative means of land redistribution to the communists' savage methods, where his appeal got him 100 acres. He then moved across the Telangana region to ultimately gather 12,000 acres in fifty days.[48] Over the next eight years, by 1959, when celebrity author Arthur Koestler (*Darkness at Noon*) profiled him, Bhave, then sixty-four, had 'marched the equivalent of the length of the Equator and collected 8 million acres of land'.[49] But this was still way short of the 50-million-acre target he had set himself early on, which he calculated—if judiciously distributed—would solve India's landlessness problem. Besides, much of the donated land was later found to be rocky and uncultivable, while redistribution, too, ran into unexpected difficulties.[50]

Bhave was one of the leaders of the Sarvodaya Samaj—an organization the followers of Gandhi had set up in March 1948, soon after the Mahatma's death, whose guiding motto was serving the people while eschewing political power. It met once a year, and it was after the fourth such meeting, held in a village in Hyderabad, that Bhave embarked on his Telangana odyssey. VP's former associates at Gopal Vidyalaya revealed that from the mid-1950s, he had involved himself in the Sarvodaya Samaj's activities, performing 'shramdaan' (voluntary labour for development).

'The samaj had a centre at Bampur, 40 km east of Koraon, but its activities were all over the Daiya–Manda area,' said Prabha Shankar Tiwari. 'We dug tanks, built roads and performed other services. VP would often visit the Bampur centre.'[51] Udit Narayan Singh confirmed digging tanks in Pasna village, where VP's mother hailed from. VP himself remained prosaic about his activities in those days. 'I tried to dig with a shovel, but by the first afternoon my palms had blisters,' he told his NMML interviewer. 'I felt I would be more useful if I carried bricks or earth on my head instead to the worksite, which I did.'[52]

In 1957 (the exact date is not known), VP participated in a routine two-day Bhoodan camp in Kathauli village, not far from Koraon, a low-key affair Bhave did not even attend. Those at the camp had to do all the menial work together—washing, cleaning, cooking—and sleep on rudimentary wooden takhats, which VP did enthusiastically. 'I did cook, but don't ask me how it got done, or how the food tasted,' he recalled. Lying on his hard bed that night, he thought about all he had heard and took a decision. He said later,

> I consulted no one. I had about 150–200 acres of well-irrigated farmland at Pasna village; I had some other pieces of agricultural land too—and I decided to donate them all. I stood up at the

meeting on the second day and said so. I used to always feel vaguely guilty about owning land.[53]

Returning home to Allahabad, he sent for the tehsildar, seeking a list of all the rural lands he owned in the district, and signed them away to the Bhoodan movement.[54]

Even Bhave sought to dissuade VP from giving up all his land.[55] When they met for the first time at another Bhoodan camp in Bangalore (now Bengaluru) a few months later—which Sita Kumari attended too[56]—Bhave noted that he always asked landlords to donate only a sixth of their land, and urged VP to take some of his back. VP initially refused but was eventually persuaded. However, immediately afterwards he gave away the land Bhave had returned to his Koraon school, which, in turn, leased it to local farmers.[57] The following year, Bhave visited Allahabad and held a public meeting, heaping praise on VP, comparing him to Gautama Buddha. 'Rajputra Siddhartha ne tyag kiya to sansar ka kalyan hua,' said Bhave. 'Rajputra Vishwanath ne jo tyag diya issey bhavishya mein Bharat ka kalyan hoga (Prince Siddhartha's sacrifice proved a boon for the world. Prince Vishwanath's sacrifice will similarly be a boon for India).'[58]

Though VP later made light of his family's reaction to his decision, it is clear that most of them were appalled. Even the most radical of his brothers, Sant Bux, who had just returned from Britain for good and started working with Hindustan Lever (now Hindustan Unilever), claimed to have been 'nonplussed'.[59] But VP remembered it differently. He said later,

> My family knew that I was stubborn and accepted me the way I was. My brothers did not say a word. My mother was upset, I knew, but she could never bring herself to rebuke me. My father said he always knew I was mad, but he accepted it too. My wife has never said a word about it—by God's grace she has always supported me in whatever I have done.[60]

In fact, Bhagwati Prasad's reaction was explosive. 'He kept shouting at my husband, reminding him that he had a wife and child to support, and their well-being should matter more than any political cause,' recalled Sita Kumari. (Ajeya Singh was then a few months old.) 'My husband merely kept staring at the carpet and muttering, "*Jo kar diya, so kar diya* (What's done is done)."'[61]

Bhagwati Prasad was sufficiently alarmed to transfer around 900 acres of his own lands to VP. 'But he made it clear the land was actually for me, for my security and that of the children,' said Sita Kumari.[62] VP responded the same way he had done to his father-in-law's cash gift at his tilak ceremony—he accepted it, but a few years later quietly transferred all the land to the Daiya Charitable Trust, run by his family. (Many landlords, fearing the imposition of land ceiling laws—which were indeed passed in the 1960s—had set up trusts to protect their properties.) Having inherited Manda, he wanted no financial support from Daiya.

His estate gone, his farmlands given away, immersed in debts left by his adoptive father, determined not to take any help from his real family, how did VP manage a living? Sita Kumari maintained she had no idea. 'Whenever I needed money, I asked him for it and he gave it to me,' she said. 'Beyond that I know nothing.'[63] Perhaps the most credible answer came from close friend Ranamata Singh. 'Rajas and maharajas are different from you and me,' he said. 'Even after they've given up "everything", they have enough left over.'[64]

After acquiring his engineering degree from Rourkee, Ranamata Singh joined the Indian army. He remembered VP visiting him in Dehradun in the early 1950s, when he was training at the Indian Military Academy. 'We were driving down a busy Dehradun street, when VP casually gestured out the window and said, "All this belongs to me,"' he recalled.[65]

VP's third Adlerian foray was a passionate—if short-lived—love affair with the physical sciences, physics and chemistry, especially the former.

His elective subjects for his intermediate exam from UP College, chosen for him by his then-guardian Vijay Shankar Mishra, with an eye on his future responsibilities as a raja, had been civics, economics and mathematics. In college he had studied philosophy, economics and political science and, later, law.[66] But he always said later that from high school, he had been fascinated by the sciences.[67] Like many an awed admirer, however, he kept his distance, as though he felt he was not worthy of them. 'I urged him to join the science stream in college like me, but he stuck to humanities,' said Ranamata Singh.[68] Then pure chance helped him get to know physics and chemistry better, and he turned into an obsessive lover.

A few years after VP got married, one of Sita Kumari's younger brothers, Indrajit Singh, enrolled for his intermediate degree in science at Allahabad's Kali Prasad (KP) Inter College. He stayed with the couple at Aish Mahal and VP happened to go through his textbooks.[69] The more he read, the more confident he became that he could handle both physics and chemistry, and that his life's calling was to be a scientist. He wanted to enrol for a bachelor's degree in science immediately at Allahabad University, but discovered that he could not—he had not studied either physics or chemistry for his intermediate. Unfazed, he met the principal of KP College and pleaded with him for a chance to sit for his intermediate exam again in just these two subjects.[70]

The principal, Jalpa Prasad, was cold. 'You may be mad, but I'm not,' he said. 'It's a two-year course; we're already in September; you've never studied physics or chemistry before, and you want to sit for the next exams in March?'[71] VP confirmed this was indeed his intention. 'Let's assume you learn the theory part, which I doubt, but what about practicals? How will you cover the practical classes you've missed?' VP then asked Prasad to give him a couple of months, after which he would be ready to take an entrance test in both theory and practicals. He would take the intermediate exam only if he passed the test.[72]

The principal was still unwilling, but after VP, in his own words, 'pulled a few strings'[73], he reluctantly agreed. VP returned to Aish Mahal and turned one of his rooms into a laboratory, where he carried out the experiments detailed in his brother-in-law's textbooks and journals all by himself.[74] 'He not only passed the entrance test but also, taking the final exam just four months later, got 76 per cent in physics and 75 per cent in chemistry,' said Sita Kumari. 'That's when I first thought—this man is something else.'

Among those especially delighted by VP's new life goal was, naturally, Ranamata Singh. 'Those days I was teaching at the Military College of Engineering in Poona [now Pune], and VP would visit me occasionally,' he said. 'I'd just started, so I had to prepare my lectures every evening. VP would rib me, "What a bore you've become, always studying." I'd tell him, "I'd asked you to study science, but like a fool, you went for arts." That's when he told me that he had done his intermediate in physics and chemistry and was all set to join a B.Sc. course. I suggested he enrol at Fergusson College in Pune, where teaching standards were high and which would also enable us to meet more often. To my surprise, he agreed. He applied, but his case was so singular that the college set up a committee to consider it. It finally granted him admission.'[75]

Fergusson College, though named after James Fergusson, Lieutenant Governor of Bombay Province from 1880 to 1885, was an entirely Indian enterprise. It was set up in 1885 by the Deccan Educational Society (DES)—an offshoot of the nineteenth-century Prarthana Samaj reformist movement—with the intent of imparting Western-style education to Indians. DES still runs over forty institutions, while Fergusson College's distinguished alumni are innumerable—in politics alone, they include renowned freedom fighter J.B. Kripalani; the fountainhead of Hindutva Vinayak Damodar Savarkar; and P.V. Narasimha Rao, who would become Prime Minister seven months after VP resigned. VP brought his family along to Pune and initially gate-crashed Ranamata Singh's residence. 'I remember it was in 1959, because I had gone back to Devgarh for Abhay's delivery and travelled directly from there to Pune when Abhay was just two months old,' said Sita Kumari.[76]

For some weeks, until VP rented a house of his own, it was a tight fit. 'I'd just got married myself and had been allotted what were called "honeymoon quarters" by the army, consisting of just a bedroom and a study, with a kitchen and a bathroom,' said Ranamata Singh. 'VP and his family occupied the bedroom, while my wife and I made do with the study. He was very diligent and studied a lot, despite the distraction of two small sons. It gave me a chance to say to him, "Now you're the bore, always studying."'

But Ranamata Singh was soon transferred out of Pune, returning only in 1962,[77] when VP, having obtained his degree with a distinction—scoring second-highest in his stream at Poona University that year[78]—was set to leave. Both VP and Sita Kumari looked back on their three years in Maharashtra's cultural capital as an idyllic time. They were alone together with their children for the first time in their lives. VP loved the college, particularly impressed by its 'discipline'.[79] Sita Kumari even helped him with his college assignments, especially mathematical calculations.[80] He bought a car, and they took turns to drop Ajeya to school every morning in it. They watched two films a week—usually one Hindi and one English.[81]

But there was a tragedy in the family too during this period, with VP's elder brother Chandrasekhar Prasad's wife falling ill and passing away. Sita Kumari moved back to Allahabad with her sons for nine months to nurse her, and after her demise, temporarily take care of her four young daughters.

The Pune stay also ended badly. By then, VP had decided to become a nuclear physicist. But when he sought to take the Bhabha Atomic Research Centre's (BARC) entrance exam for scientific officers, he discovered that he was overage by just a month.[82] Thenceforth, though he never lost interest in the sciences, his earlier ardour seemed to desert him. Returning to Allahabad, he enrolled for an MSc in physics at the university, where he had later RSS/BJP stalwarts Rajendra Singh and Murli Manohar Joshi among his teachers.[83] But as with his MA in philosophy, he never completed the course.

—❧—

None of his surviving relatives, including Sita Kumari, could recall much of VP's fourth, brief career experiment—trying to become a contractor. All they remembered was that after returning to Allahabad from Pune, he partnered with his younger brother, Har Bux Singh, to build a small dam near Meja, about 40 km south-east of Allahabad city—for the state irrigation department.[84] Through much of the 1960s, he also remained involved with the school in Koraon—getting Vinoba Bhave, for instance, to inaugurate its intermediate section, started in 1965—but he had long withdrawn from its day-to-day activities.

He had several hobbies, however, including sketching and painting, photography and poetry-writing (in Hindi). 'He was quite the photographer in the family, missing from many of our family group photos because it was he who would take them,' said Anand Singh, Sant Bux's son.[85] VP began sketching in school and, during his college years, even attended painting classes in Allahabad. 'We were taught the Bengal school style of watercolour wash painting by one Mr Singhal,' he recalled later.

The process was elaborate. We had to apply very dilute colours which would be hardly visible until quite a few layers had been put. Next day, the painting would be immersed in a bucket of water for five minutes; then drained off by holding one corner. Only after this procedure would we start applying thin washes of colour again. The dip in the bucket and application of thin washes ensured that there were no coarse grains and the colours penetrated deeply.[86]

At his request, Singhal also taught him oil painting, and VP went on to produce a number of oils and watercolours, including one of his favourite spots near the Belan river, which he treasured until the end of his life.[87] But he never seemed to have considered becoming an artist as a career option.

His sons recalled that he had plenty of time for them until he went into politics. Sita Kumari, unhappy with what she felt was a lackadaisical attitude to education among Allahabad's landed gentry, feared for their future if they remained in the city and packed them off to boarding school—Mayo College in Ajmer—very early. 'My mother-in-law was livid, my father-in-law was livid, but I was determined,' she said.

But on their vacations, the sons got their father's full attention. 'I remember two holidays we took, both in Kashmir, which were very enjoyable,' said younger son Abhay Singh. 'I remember going on shikaar with him once. I fired into a shaking bush, and a monkey jumped out! We had two Alsatians, Tiku and Pixie, and he spent a lot of time with them, really spoiling them. But once he joined politics, he had no time for anything else.'[88]

Part 2

LOYALTY DILEMMAS

1

'ONE MAY OR MAY NOT CRAVE WEALTH, BUT EVERYONE CRAVES RECOGNITION'

V.P. Singh's attraction towards the Congress began on foreign soil.

Though never a member of either the Communist Party of India (CPI) or the socialist parties, he had friends in both. He was close enough to some in the former for them to include him in the list of 150-odd delegates from India to the World Festival of Youth and Students in Warsaw, Poland, in 1955.[1] This was a cultural extravaganza held biannually at the time by the World Federation of Democratic Youth, a communist front organization with headquarters in Budapest, to promote 'anti-imperialist solidarity, peace and friendship'.[2] That year it was scheduled from 31 July to 14 August, which meant that VP had to leave for his first trip overseas within a month of his marriage. Curiously, it was his mother who protested, not his wife. 'She had barely entered our household; what could she have said?' said VP about Sita Kumari.[3] Sant Bux Singh had, by then, been away for five years, and his mother feared VP would similarly disappear.

VP assured her he would not and set off by air for Zurich, Switzerland, from where the delegates took the train to Warsaw. 'There was no overt propaganda at the festival, no public meetings extolling communism,' he recalled.[4] All the city was a stage, with about 150 performances held daily, many of them on makeshift street platforms; there were also sporting contests. VP observed, though, that all the flags and buntings of the 114 participating countries could not hide the profusion of bombed-out and machine-gunfire-riddled buildings, still waiting to be restored—a reminder of the horrors the country had undergone during the Second World War.[5] Given the option of returning through either West or East Europe after the festival ended, many in the delegation, including VP, preferred the latter. 'The West one could see any time, but this was a rare opportunity to go behind the Iron Curtain,' he reasoned.[6]

A big crowd and a bigger surprise awaited the delegation as it crossed the Russian border by train and stopped at Brest—now in Belarus, then part of the USSR—200 km east of Warsaw. The members were asked, through their interpreter, to sing '*Awaara hoon*'! They learnt that *Awaara* (1951), screened for the first time the previous September at the first Indian film festival in Moscow,[7] had been an extraordinary success, making Raj Kapoor and Nargis superstars across the country. The band struck up the tune, the interpreter burst into song herself, and VP and his co-delegates had no choice but to follow suit, though they knew only the first four lines of the song and could only repeat them endlessly.[8]

But there was a third Indian superstar in the Soviet Union those days, VP discovered, as the delegation travelled to Moscow and beyond: Jawaharlal Nehru. Nehru had visited barely two months before—a three-week-long trip (state visits appear to have been much longer those days) starting 7 June 1955, during which he was feted rapturously. The crowd at his Moscow public meeting on the concluding day of his visit was so large that the venue had to be shifted from Gorky Park to a football stadium.[9] VP was immensely taken by the influence Nehru had acquired beyond Indian shores. 'Nehru's image in Russia made a great impression on me,' he said later. 'It made me feel that the Congress was the right party to join. It would help me work for the country.'[10] Back in Allahabad, he promptly did so.

With a newcomer's zeal, he began recruiting more members for the Congress, going from village to village in the Daiya–Manda region. Given his raja lineage, it was not difficult. The Congress's joining fee those days was 25 paise—four annas—and soon, VP had literally collected sacks of four-anna coins, which he faithfully brought to the Allahabad Congress office. The reception to his exuberance was cold—with many rajas and maharajas entering the political fray those days, a section of influential members feared that he was preparing to capture the district organization. 'At the time, I didn't even know what "capturing" an organization meant,' said VP.[11] Rebuffed, he temporarily retreated.

Still, his interest had been kindled, and in February 1957— the same year in which he would later give up all his land—he decided, despite the hostility of the Congress's local unit towards him, to campaign for the party. The undivided Allahabad district (Kaushambi was carved out four decades later) had three Lok Sabha seats—Allahabad, Phulpur and Chail. The first two were among the most prestigious in the country; Nehru himself was contesting from Phulpur (as he did in all three Lok Sabha elections he fought), while the Allahabad seat had Lal Bahadur Shastri as the Congress candidate. Shastri, who had acquired national renown for resigning as minister of railways three months earlier—holding himself accountable for a train accident in Madras state (today's Tamil Nadu) that had caused 142 deaths—was fighting his first Lok Sabha election, having been a Rajya Sabha member until then. VP campaigned for both of them, but more intensively for Shastri, since the Daiya–Manda area was part of the Allahabad seat.

When he arrived in Daiya on his campaign trail early in the election, Shastri made it a point to visit Daiya Palace, only to be turned away from the door by Bhagwati Prasad's men. Bhagwati Prasad had clashed with Shastri even when he was district board chairman; his poor opinion of the Congress too had not changed with Independence. 'Why should I support a party that took away my zamindari?' he had said, justifying his rudeness.[12] But that did not constrain his son. 'He did not know Shastri personally then. They met during the campaign,' said Sita Kumari. 'But he was friends with Shastri's son-in-law, Vijay Nath Singh [married to Shastri's daughter, Suman], who had been his junior by a year at Allahabad University.'[13] As expected, both Nehru and Shastri won easily—Nehru by a staggering margin and Shastri by a more modest one.[14]

Both contested and won the same seats in the third general election of 1962 as well,[15] but VP, trying hard to become a physicist at the time, does not seem to have played any role in this election.

—◦◦◦—

Three converging motives seem to have propelled VP towards a full-time political career, once he returned permanently to Allahabad from Poona and abandoned his physicist dreams. The first was the example of his idolized elder brother Sant Bux, who had given up his corporate career and plunged into local Congress politics in Allahabad, while at the same time practising law. The second, he admitted later, was pure egoism. He had resumed his social work and was also trying to earn a bit, and much liked, as he put it, 'sitting in the fields, with the sky and stars above, not caring about what would appear in the newspapers the next day', but he also felt the need to impress people around him. '*Chhavi ki kamzori vyaqti ki antim kamzori hai* (The yearning for a good image is every human being's ultimate weakness),' he said. 'A person may or may not crave wealth, but everyone craves recognition. Even sadhus are unable to overcome this desire.'[16]

The third spur was the realization that the people of Manda had expectations from him that he was not being able to fulfil. They had traditionally turned to their raja in every kind of need, especially for help in dealings with the government, and wanted VP to continue intervening for them, but he lacked the influence to do so successfully. One particular incident affected him greatly. There was a village—which he did not name in his interviews—whose single road had deteriorated to the extent that buses running through it earlier had stopped doing so, bypassing it entirely. Before rajas lost their revenue-collecting powers, the raja of Manda had maintained all the village roads on his estate at his own expense. With the abolition of the zamindari system, this responsibility devolved on individual village gram sabhas, but this village's gram sabha had no funds. 'I took the villagers to the zila parishad office. We went to the Public Works Department, but they both said the road was not their responsibility,' said VP.[17]

District subdivisions—or tehsils—are further divided into blocks, which, in turn, are made up of purwas, and the Manda block comprised fifteen such purwas. Undeterred by governmental apathy, VP organized a fund-collection drive across all fifteen to buy the raw material needed. He also exhorted, and succeeded, in getting each purwa to offer a day's shramdaan. 'It took exactly fifteen days to build the kilometre-long road,' he said. But once the bed of gravel had been laid and tarred, he needed a roadroller to complete the task. Once again, neither the zila parishad nor the PWD was willing to lend him one.

Fortunately, the US-headquartered Catholic Relief Services was running a 'food for work' programme in the vicinity—building roads, digging tube wells, etc.—and VP knew the priest in charge. Father Joseph arranged a private roadroller for him, enabling the reconstruction of the road to be completed. 'I thought to myself that politicians can make a single phone call and get a road built right up to their doorstep for their personal use,' said VP. 'And here we were, knocking on every door to fulfil a genuine need, and the government wouldn't even spare us a roadroller for a day. I decided that I should have some political influence.'[18]

But how would he go about it? VP could have turned to Sant Bux for help, or even to some other Congressmen known to his family, but he decided upon a dramatic gesture aimed at impressing Shastri himself. By then, following the death of Nehru in May 1964, Shastri was India's Prime Minister. The following year, tensions with neighbouring Pakistan peaked—after initial skirmishes in Gujarat's Rann of Kutch in April 1965, Pakistan launched a full-scale attack on India in Jammu and Kashmir at the end of August. In a war lasting twenty-two days through September 1965, the Pakistani army was beaten back and India captured large swathes of territory across the Line of Control in Kashmir, and beyond the border in Punjab. The country was awash with nationalist fervour, hailing the diminutive Shastri as a conquering hero.

Despite his prime ministerial preoccupations, Shastri visited his constituency regularly—it was during a speech at Urwa in Allahabad district in September 1965 that he first uttered his much-repeated slogan, *'Jai Jawan, Jai Kisan'*[19]—and he returned once again at the end of December 1965, including Manda in his itinerary. VP not only played a leading role in organizing the boisterous reception Shastri got in Manda, but also took care to bring along a razor blade in his pocket. When it was his turn to welcome Shastri onstage at the public meeting that followed, he inflicted a cut on his own thumb with the blade and used the blood that trickled out to mark a tilak on Shastri's forehead.[20] It was a Rajput tradition of honouring valour and sacrifice (though Rajputs of yore would have used a sword). Shastri, as VP had hoped, was hugely pleased. Shastri's wife, Lalita, who was also on the stage, would later say that he told her in response, 'This is your fifth son.'[21] (The Shastris had four sons and two daughters.)

In the event, the gambit failed. Within a fortnight, Shastri was dead, felled by a heart attack hours after he signed a historic peace agreement with Pakistan's then President Ayub Khan in Tashkent (now capital of Uzbekistan, then part of Soviet Russia) on 11 January 1966.[22] (The agreement returned all the lands India had captured in the September war.) Still, the razor-blade incident marked the beginning of a long association between VP and the Shastri family. Learning from news reports that Lalita Shastri was keen to encourage rural industry, VP offered her part of his Manda Fort for her work. She set up a trust, the Lal Bahadur Shastri Sewa Niketan, to make khadi garments, matches, candles, soaps and more, whose first centre was started there.[23] The trust still runs a number of such units.

<hr />

The 1960s were difficult years for India, and the results of the fourth general election in 1967 reflected it. Two wars (the first with China in 1962, in which India was badly mauled) and years of successive drought took their toll on the economy. Growth was low, inflation and unemployment high, while food shortages were so acute that during the September 1965 war with Pakistan, Prime Minister Shastri urged citizens to voluntarily 'miss a meal' every week. The euphoria of beating back Pakistan evaporated quickly.

In UP, the situation was worsened for the ruling party due to a bitter, sixty-two-day-long strike of non-gazetted government employees, which was temporarily suspended just days before the election in February 1967. All through the campaign, the employees disrupted Congress public meetings with black flags.[24] People blamed their frustrations on the Congress, which had been ruling uninterruptedly at the Centre and in most of the states since Independence, voting heavily against it. In the first election led by

Indira Gandhi, who had succeeded Shastri as Prime Minister, the Congress's seat tally dropped to 283 (of the 520 contested) from the 361 (of 494 seats in the fray then) won in 1962. In UP, it won 47 of the 85 seats, down from 62 in the previous election.[25]

But for VP, the election was a significant milestone, as the run-up to it gave him an invaluable apprenticeship in the nitty-gritty of fighting polls at the highest level. He already had his university experience behind him and had also worked for Sant Bux when the latter had stood for the zila parishad chairmanship in 1964—the same position his father had held for sixteen years before Independence—and won. 'Many people worked for me during that election, but VP worked the hardest,' Sant Bux would say later.[26]

Then, in 1967, Sant Bux was chosen as the Congress's Lok Sabha candidate—not from Allahabad (where, in a bid to cash in on public sympathy for Shastri following his unexpected death, his eldest son Hari Krishna was given the Congress ticket), but from neighbouring Fatehpur. As he had done when Sant Bux had fought his earlier election, VP immersed himself fully in his brother's campaign, shifting to Fatehpur town—135 km north-west of Allahabad—for nearly a month.[27]

The Fatehpur seat was a relatively safe one for the Congress, with its candidates having won comfortably in both 1952 and 1957. In 1962, however, it suffered a shock defeat, after complacently fielding a complete outsider, B.V. Keskar, who hailed from Poona.[28] The victor, an independent, Gauri (Babu) Shankar Kakkar, was contesting again in 1967, but it was widely held that another independent, Brijlal Verma, stood a better chance this time.

Sant Bux's biggest disadvantage was that he, too, like Keskar, was an outsider—though not from as far away—who barely knew the topography of the region, let alone its people, while both his main opponents hailed from Fatehpur and had fought previous elections there. Countering that was the caste composition of the electorate, with 17–18 per cent belonging to the same Rajput (or Thakur) caste as him,[29] while Verma and Gauri Babu came from other castes. With caste loyalty then, as now, determining voter preference to a fair extent, the bulk of the Rajputs could be expected to not only support Sant Bux, but also, given their dominant status, cajole other castes into doing so.

VP carefully observed the methods his brother and his election managers used. He watched them analyse the voters' list, with names segmented polling-booth-wise; decide which areas to visit and which to ignore, mainly depending on population density; and map out an itinerary. The team bought postcards in bulk, had Sant Bux's photograph and a short vote-seeking letter printed on them and sent them off to all important personages in the constituency. Sant Bux followed it up by personally meeting each individual the letters had been addressed to and seeking their support. With funds limited, expenditure was strictly monitored, and any volunteers expecting payment for their services were asked to leave. With vehicles also limited—most were borrowed from friends—no campaigner was allotted one permanently but had to ask every time one was needed. To prevent their misuse, the drivers were always members of VP's extended family, while every vehicle took along a local guide so as not to lose its way.[30]

While appealing for votes, Sant Bux was not obsequious, clearly spelling out his self-imposed limits. 'My brother was quite a character,' said VP. 'He would openly say in his speeches, "Are you a government employee seeking a transfer from your place of work, and expect me to help you? Are you in trouble with the police and hope your elected representative will come to your aid? Are you embroiled in court cases and expect your MP to influence decisions in your favour? In that case, please—don't vote for me."'[31] VP maintained that he followed the same rules in his own political career as well.

He also admitted to some innocent subterfuge his four brothers and he used during the campaign. The area was vast, with time and vehicles limited. In their door-to-door campaign, each brother took up one of the five assembly segments the parliamentary seat comprised. When they went visiting, mostly in the evenings, each brother—not only Sant Bux—would claim to be the candidate! 'There was no electricity in most of the villages then, so the chances of getting caught were low,' he said. 'We would request the villagers not to raise their lanterns high enough to clearly see the candidate's face, claiming that Raja Sahib could not take the smoke. Our opponents were befuddled as to how "Sant Bux" could meet so many people personally in so short a period.'

The results had Sant Bux Singh beating Brijlal Verma by a convincing 25,000 votes. The incumbent, Gauri Babu, came fourth, behind even the Jana Sangh candidate, who came third. (In Allahabad, Hari Krishna Shastri also won his seat, though narrowly, by just 6,500 votes.)[32]

2

'IF NOT NOW, WHEN?'

While campaigning for Jawaharlal Nehru in Phulpur during the second general election in 1957, V.P. Singh had been sounded out for a Rajya Sabha ticket. Uma Shankar Dikshit (Sheila Dikshit's father-in-law), then a rising Congress politician from Kanpur and close to both Nehru's and VP's family, had asked him if he would be Nehru's representative in the constituency after the polls, overseeing development work, processing complaints and bringing relevant ones to the Prime Minister's notice. If he did his job well, he could expect a Rajya Sabha nomination from the Congress whenever vacancies from UP next arose. VP, with his idealism then at its peak—he would give away all his personal land to the Bhoodan movement later that very year—refused. 'People will say afterwards that I worked for Nehru only because I wanted to get into the Rajya Sabha,' he replied.[1]

Having decided to enter politics, yet still hesitant to take a headlong plunge, VP reconsidered the Rajya Sabha option in 1967–68. A presence in the Upper House, he felt, would give him local influence that he could put to good use, while sparing him the grind of electoral politics, leaving him time for other pursuits. But more than a decade had gone by since 1957 and the opportunity had gone too—the first two Congress leaders he sought help from bluntly told him that he was expecting too much. VP started with Dinesh Singh, the former raja of Kalakanker, an estate in Pratapgarh district (adjoining Allahabad) and a distant relative of his.[2] Dinesh Singh was then Union commerce minister and one of Indira Gandhi's closest advisers.[3]

Dinesh Singh told VP that Rajya Sabha seats were too highly coveted to be offered to political newbies. But he also introduced VP to a rising Allahabad leader, Hemvati Nandan Bahuguna, who, though born and schooled in the Garhwal Himalayas, had made this district his political base.[4] Bahuguna repeated Dinesh Singh's assertion and advised VP to seek a state assembly nomination instead.[5] Against 34-odd Rajya Sabha seats from UP, there were 425 assembly seats—it would be much easier for a newcomer to bag the Congress nomination to one of the latter. Dinesh Singh also pointed out that if he won the election, he could later exchange the seat for one in the Rajya Sabha as his political clout grew.

In the normal course, VP would have had to wait until 1972 for the next assembly poll, since elections to all state assemblies had been held alongside the February 1967 general election. But as it happened, the Congress had fared even worse in the state assembly polls than it had in the Lok Sabha, where it managed to retain at least a slim majority—in the states, it fell short of a majority in eight of the then sixteen assemblies: Punjab, Rajasthan, UP, Bihar, Orissa (now Odisha), West Bengal, Madras (now Tamil Nadu), and Kerala. In two other states, Haryana and Madhya Pradesh, it lost the narrow majority it had won following defections (on which there was no bar at the time). In all these states, the Opposition parties banded together to form coalition governments. But given their disparate ideologies, as well as the pecuniary (and other) temptations on offer to individual members of legislative assemblies (MLAs) to switch sides, most of these governments collapsed within a year, leading to President's Rule and subsequent fresh elections.

In UP, the Congress had bagged 198 of the 425 seats. Falling short of a majority, it initially formed a government with the support of seventeen other MLAs who had won as independents. The number 'seventeen' came to acquire a strange significance as, after the Congress had ruled for just seventeen days, seventeen Congress MLAs switched sides to the Opposition, bringing down the government and leading to an alternative one, with the leader of the defectors, Charan Singh, as chief minister. (It all happened on 1 April, to boot.) Charan Singh had a stellar reputation in UP as the main architect of its Zamindari Abolition Act. Later, during stints as agriculture and revenue minister, he was its chief implementer as well, which earned him the everlasting support of the state's peasantry; he held important ministries in every UP government formed after Independence.

But though he often vied for the position, he had never been chief minister, and that seemed to have bothered him greatly, leading to his unexpected desertion. Yet, as in the other states, the new ministry he formed had perforce to span the gamut of ideologies among Opposition parties, from the right-wing Swatantra Party and the Hindu nationalist Jana Sangh to the socialists and the communists. As a result, the coalition began clashing regularly on policy from the day it was sworn in.

Among the parties in the ruling coalition, the Samyukta Socialist Party (SSP) proved the most obstreperous, making demands such as the abolition of land revenue and its replacement with agricultural income tax, which would be imposed only on wealthy farmers, as also a total ban on the use of the English language in the state. The essentially conservative Charan Singh refused to countenance these, which led to the SSP holding agitations against its own government when he resisted. After repeated threats to resign, Charan Singh ultimately did so in February 1968, leading to President's Rule.[6] When VP met Dinesh Singh, fresh assembly elections—eventually held in February 1969—were already expected.

VP was still tentative about contesting, but Sant Bux helped him make up his mind. 'He returned home from meeting Sant Bux Singh one evening and said his brother had asked him, "If not now, when?"' recalled Sita Kumari Singh.[7] In 1968, VP was already thirty-seven. He decided that he would try seriously for a Congress nomination—but which seat to aim for? The Manda–Daiya area, to which he belonged, was part of the Meja assembly constituency, which, following a delimitation exercise after the 1962 polls, had been reserved for Scheduled Caste candidates.

VP would have to look elsewhere. Despite its poor showing across the state, the Congress had not fared too badly in Allahabad in the 1967 assembly elections—of the 14 assembly seats in undivided Allahabad (i.e., including today's Kaushambi district), it had won 8. Indeed, it had done better than in the previous assembly election of 1962, when it had won only 6 seats. The winners would naturally expect to be re-nominated, so VP crossed those seats out as well.

Advised by his brother and friends, he finally settled on Soraon, though he knew little about the constituency then—it was one of the five assembly segments of the Phulpur Lok Sabha seat, located north of Allahabad town, at the opposite end of the district from Manda–Daiya, which lay in the south-east. He chose Soraon not only because it was a seat that the Congress had lost in the 1967 election—albeit by a margin of fewer than 600 votes—but also since the losing candidate, Sangram Singh (nothing to do with VP's father-in-law), a former freedom fighter, was over eighty years of age and, his advisers believed, unlikely to contest again. In the assembly elections before 1967, Soraon had always been won by the Congress, and was therefore a relatively safe seat.

With the Ganga flowing along its southern edge, Soraon's soil was rich and fertile, unlike that of Manda–Daiya, but in most other respects, it was just as underdeveloped and nondescript. The *Allahabad Gazetteer* of 1928 observed that it was 'an old fiscal subdivision which appears to have undergone very little change since the days of Akbar',[8] and the next four decades had not made much difference either. It had two minor claims to fame—first, during the 1857 Mutiny, Allahabad's best-known rebel, Maulvi Liaqat Ali, after being driven from Allahabad town, had sporadically based himself there, troubling the British with repeated raids for nearly a year.[9] Second, this was the seat from which Shastri had been twice elected to the UP assembly— under British rule in 1946 and again in 1952—before moving to the Centre.

But VP and his friends had misjudged Sangram Singh. Despite his age, he was keen to contest one last time, and even had many senior Congress leaders supporting his candidacy. They included UP's most powerful politician in those days, Chandra Bhanu Gupta,[10] whose tremendous control over the Congress organization in the state enabled him to thrive, even though he did not get along with either Nehru or his daughter.[11] A former freedom fighter, he had been UP's third chief minister, from 1960 to 1963, and had again headed the seventeen-day Congress government formed after the 1967 assembly polls, which fell following Charan Singh's defection.[12]

Gupta's preference was dictated entirely by his main lieutenants in Allahabad district—Mangla Prasad and Muzaffar Hasan, both also former freedom fighters with long prison terms behind them, as well as former UP ministers, and both friends of Sangram Singh.[13] Prasad hailed from Bampur, which housed the Bhoodan centre VP used to visit, and knew VP's family well, but given

Bhagwati Prasad's antipathy to the Congress, relations between them were never warm. Prasad had won the Meja seat in the 1957 poll and been made a minister but had unexpectedly lost in 1962 (Meja wasn't a reserved seat then). He had not contested the 1967 poll, but that in no way reduced his clout.

When a couple of VP's friends, backed also by Bahuguna and Dinesh Singh, suggested his name as nominee for the Soraon seat at the first meeting of the Uttar Pradesh Congress Committee (UPCC) to decide on assembly poll candidates, Prasad vehemently opposed them. He maintained that it was Sangram Singh's 'last wish' to contest this final election of his life, and in view of the veteran freedom fighter's record, it should be honoured. What made matters even more difficult for VP was that Sangram Singh was a highly respected figure, admired for his integrity and personal austerity.[14] The meeting, like all such initial meetings, ended without any decision.

VP, informed by his friends of all that had transpired, didn't know what to do next. 'I'm not going to beg for a ticket,' he told Uma Shankar Dikshit.

'Don't make that blunder,' Dikshit responded. 'In politics, you have to beg all the time. You will get nowhere if you don't.'[15]

He advised VP to get a list of all the UPCC members with their phone numbers, methodically seek appointments and meet them. Trampling upon his pride, VP set about the demeaning task, shifting initially to a Lucknow hotel and later, when he realized that many All India Congress Committee (AICC) members also interfered in the selection process, to Delhi. His children were home for the winter holidays, and he took his family along, booking a room in the five-star Lodhi Hotel. 'But we hardly got to see him once we were there,' said Abhay Singh. 'He was always away.'[16]

'It was the first and last time I have pleaded for a ticket,' said VP later. 'But it was enough humiliation to last a lifetime.'[17] He had to wait long hours in queues to meet the leaders, despite appointments, and even when he got to do so, they were always surrounded by their factotums—there was no privacy in which to raise what he considered a delicate matter. Very few leaders offered any assurances. Instead, he was treated to barbs and homilies.

A senior leader, Kailash Gautam from Aligarh, who used to dominate the UP Congress before C.B. Gupta marginalized him, said, 'Your brother is an MP. Now you want to be an MLA. Does your family want to corner everything?'[18]

The then UP Congress president, Kamalapati Tripathi, responded with a metaphor. 'A new plant cannot grow into a tree overnight,' he said. 'It takes years. So too a political career cannot start overnight. First work for the party for some years; forget about a ticket until then.'

When Fakhruddin Ali Ahmed, then industries minister in Indira's cabinet (later to be President of India), heard that VP had graduated three times over—in the humanities, sciences and law— he quipped, 'These are not qualifications for a politician, they are disqualifications.'[19]

Only towards the end of his rounds did VP realize that perhaps he need not have made them at all. Though most assembly-seat nominees were indeed chosen by the UPCC, those from Allahabad had always, right from the first UP assembly poll of 1952, been decided by the Prime Minister, since all the Prime Ministers until then—Nehru, Shastri and Indira—had hailed from there and had a special interest in the region. None of the men he'd met—and been mocked by—could have got him the Soraon ticket even if they'd wanted to. What was needed was to somehow make his case before Indira.

Yet, how could an unknown aspirant for an assembly ticket meet the country's Prime Minister? Luckily for VP, he had Sant Bux to help him. Having been an MP for nearly two years by then, Sant Bux had built some degree of rapport with her.[20] He took VP with him to her home at Delhi's 1, Safdarjung Road. Indira was just leaving and met the pair at her doorstep. VP, however nervous he may have been, did not fluff his prepared lines. 'I told Indiraji, "I'm new. I cannot claim the ticket on the basis of past performance, because there is no past performance,"' he said later.

'My rival for the ticket has been a freedom fighter. As a human being, he is one of the best. But if we young people don't ask for what we want from the older generation, where else will we go? I admit, you'll be taking a risk if you choose me. I'm a ship, you have to launch it—it may sink or it may sail. All I can say is that I will try to be worthy of your trust.'[21]

Indira heard him out and departed without a word. But at the meeting held soon after at her residence to finalize the last few assembly poll candidates—which Mangla Prasad also attended and during which he brought up Sangram Singh's 'last wish' again—she asserted herself in VP's favour.[22] Her start as Prime Minister may have been faltering,[23] but with nearly three years of rule behind her, she had increasingly begun confronting the old guard in her party and was indeed preparing for a showdown with them. An enraged Prasad stormed out of the house.[24] Indira was not to be moved—Vishwanath Pratap Singh would be the Congress's Soraon candidate.

⸻

Indira's decision sparked the first major resolve of VP's political life—he would remain loyal to her, no matter what. Despite her many controversial actions over the next decade and a half when she dominated Indian politics, VP never wavered. One of his closest associates in his later political career, the dapper and professorial Som Pal, remembered, 'Even in private, even after he had long left the Congress, V.P. Singh would always heap praises on Indira Gandhi's leadership qualities.'[25]

His steadfastness only grew when Indira included Soraon in her electoral-campaign itinerary shortly after VP had been officially named as candidate. To his extreme bad luck, he had a nasty bout of influenza on the very days she spent in Allahabad during her tour, which made it impossible for him to attend her Soraon meeting, or even meet her. A newcomer to electoral politics, an outsider in his constituency and he could not even be present when the Prime Minister was holding a meeting there! He was sure his opponents would fully use the opportunity to trash him, without anyone to counter them—and they did, even submitting a memorandum to Indira, seeking a change of candidate. Unimpressed, she completed her speech and left.[26]

Indira had sealed his candidacy, but it was now up to VP to win the election if he wanted a political career. His chances were not bright. The collapse of the first non-Congress government in the state, barely ten months after it was formed, had no doubt tempered voter enthusiasm for the Opposition parties and reduced hostility towards the Congress, but only by a few shades. Charan Singh, who had defected from the Congress after the 1967 elections, calling his band of supporters the Jana Congress, was the UP Opposition's tallest figure. He had since changed his party's name to Bharatiya Kranti Dal (BKD) and, given his immense popularity among peasants, was rapidly winning support across the state. In Allahabad district, however, the main opposition to the Congress had always come from the socialists, and this continued in the 1969 election.

The socialists would have been even more successful but for the fractious nature of some of their top leaders, which led them to repeatedly come together and fall apart, uniting and dividing the parties they formed. Starting as a breakaway group from the Congress soon after Independence, the Socialist Party (SP) had merged with another similarly inclined party to form the Praja Socialist Party (PSP) in 1952. But following differences over whether to support the Congress occasionally or oppose it implacably, a disgruntled section had split the PSP to revive the

SP once again.[27] Both groups had their pockets of support in UP, though in Allahabad the PSP was much more powerful, winning 6 of the 8 seats (out of 14) that went to the Opposition parties in the 1962 assembly polls. In the mid-1960s, the two parties had come together to form the Samyukta Socialist Party (SSP), even as they were weakened by a large chunk of the PSP going back to the Congress.

More churning led to the PSP breaking away again, but despite the toll such fission and fusion took on both parties' popularity, the SSP had won 3 of the 6 seats the Opposition picked up in Allahabad in the 1967 assembly contest, including the Soraon seat.[28] The SSP's belligerence was mainly responsible for the fall of the Charan Singh government, yet its support in Allahabad remained more or less intact. VP knew that its Soraon candidate, Ram Adhar Pandey, a leading Allahabad lawyer, would be his main opponent—and a formidable one.

As a fellow lawyer, Pandey was a friend of Sant Bux's, dropping in on him occasionally, and thereby knew VP too. They had had one cutting exchange, which VP would recall in his interviews even decades afterwards.[29] Invited to a meal at Sant Bux's one day, at which VP too was present, Pandey had taunted, 'What are you doing these days, VN?[30] You just sit around at home. You should be doing something. People like you should be in politics.'

VP maintained that he replied, 'When there are worthies like you in politics already, what need is there for non-entities like me?'

Pandey's friendship with Sant Bux made no difference in Soraon, however, where, as the election campaign got underway, he launched a fusillade of personal attacks on VP, issuing numbered 'bulletins' about him every few days. All of them focused on VP's lineage, the record of Ram Gopal Singh and rajas in general, and how they had oppressed the people—Dalits in particular—for millennia.[31] His supporters also kept disrupting VP's meetings, raising loud slogans against him, sometimes preventing him from speaking.

'The youth wing of the socialists, called the Samajwadi Yuvjan Sabha (SYS)[32], was notorious for its hooliganism,' recalled Vijay Chaturvedi, who was among the workers VP had taken with him from Manda–Daiya. Big and bearded, sporting a large orange tilak and rudraksh beads, Chaturvedi, now living in Allahabad, said that he had gone along because he hailed from a village close to Manda Fort, and had little to do at the time. He would later become a higher-education-department official in UP and a college principal.[33]

But it was opposition from within his own party that VP had to deal with first. Indira's imperviousness by no means silenced his detractors. At a Congress meeting in Allahabad to introduce the district's candidates in the forthcoming poll, with Bahuguna conducting the proceedings on stage, the announcement of his name drew such loud, rancorous protest from the audience that VP was shaken. The thrust of the outcry was a variation on Pandey's charges—if rajas and maharajas grabbed all the opportunities, how would common people get anywhere? VP was half inclined to withdraw his nomination, and even said so to Bahuguna after the function. Bahuguna assured him that such scenes were common at party meetings preceding elections and that he should not be affected by them.

But how could VP not be, more so when he received news that Sangram Singh had also filed his nomination as an independent candidate? Arriving in Soraon to campaign, an area he hardly knew and where he had expected to depend on local Congress workers, he found that barring a small group at odds with Sangram Singh, all the others, including most of the block-level party presidents, were supporting the rebel candidate. Desperate, he went to Mangla Prasad—though, recalling how strongly Prasad had opposed his political entry and supported Sangram Singh's re-nomination, he was most reluctant to. But he remembered Prasad also telling him, 'If you get the ticket in spite of me, I will support you.'[34] Could Prasad persuade his friend Sangram Singh to withdraw his candidacy?

Prasad, an old-school Congressman, wedded to party loyalty, kept his word. He took VP to meet Sangram Singh and pleaded with him, but the veteran would not budge. On the penultimate day for withdrawal of nominations, VP finally took a desperate gamble— he visited one of Sangram Singh's close associates in Soraon and told him that he was prepared to withdraw from the contest if Sangram Singh wanted. Dramatically, he signed a blank sheet of paper and handed it to the associate—if Sangram Singh desired, he could write out a short letter to the Election Commission above the signature, saying that the undersigned was withdrawing his nomination, and hand it in.

Amazingly, it worked. Sangram Singh was shamed into withdrawing his own candidacy instead. An elated VP met him and suggested that they go campaigning together to show voters they were now united. Sangram Singh refused point-blank.[35]

Still, Sangram Singh's opposition had been effectively neutralized, with the added benefit that some of his volunteers now began working for VP, giving him crucial local support. He had his brothers helping him too, as also a small group of friends and supporters from Manda–Daiya and Allahabad city. For all the debating accolades he had won at school, Chaturvedi was not impressed by VP's oratory at Soraon. 'He had a high-pitched voice those days, somewhat feminine, which does not make for great oratory, but he was fluent in the local dialect and that helped,' he said. 'The SYS activists who kept interrupting his meetings also inadvertently won him voter sympathy.' He also remembered VP's egalitarianism. 'He lived just like the rest of us, eating poori-sabji for breakfast, lunch and dinner, and often sleeping on the floor.'[36]

At Soraon, VP repeated all the best practices in campaign management he had learnt at Fatehpur, shifting permanently to Soraon town until polling day, sending off postcards to all important personages in the constituency and following them up with personal visits; keeping strict control on the few Jeeps and limited funds at his disposal; holding many more padyatras than public meetings. 'The message on the postcards was printed, but every address had to be written out by hand,' recalled Chaturvedi. 'A small group of us spent days just doing that.' Following Sant Bux's example, VP, too, had pamphlets printed and distributed, which spelt out not only what he hoped to do for his constituency if elected, but also what he would not—he wouldn't assist government employees with their transfers or traders with their permits, or try to influence the police or the courts.

But would this be enough? Unlike in Fatehpur, the support of his own Rajput (Thakur) caste made no difference in Soraon—in an electorate of 105,000,[37] Thakurs numbered barely 500.[38] Nearly 50 per cent of the voters belonged to the OBC category, most of them Kurmi small farmers, but also a fair number of Kumbhars (the potter caste), Lohars (ironsmiths), Gadariyas (shepherds) and more. The socialist parties had held a number of agitations supporting small farmers' demands in Allahabad district over the decades, and the Kurmis, as a result, were expected to vote largely for VP's SSP opponent Ram Adhar Pandey.

The second-largest community comprised the Dalits or the Scheduled Castes, around 25–27 per cent, followed by Muslims. VP realized that to win, he'd need the bulk of votes from both. Muslims and Dalits were known to have voted largely for the Congress in previous elections, but even a small section breaking away following some grievance, imagined or real, could spell doom for him. Fortunately, like Mangla Prasad, C.B. Gupta's other right-hand man in Allahabad, Muzaffar Hasan, also believed in party loyalty—he had opposed VP's nomination, but now that VP had bagged it, he was prepared to help. Early in the campaign, he took VP along in his own Jeep and introduced him to all the leading Muslims of Soraon.[39]

It was thus that VP learnt that one of the contesting independents, whose presence in the candidates' list he had ignored earlier, was backed by the Muslim Majlis, a party launched the previous year to promote Muslim interests. With Muslims sharing the general discontent with the Congress those days, the Majlis had been drawing a fair bit of support.[40] If its candidate, Munir Ahmed, took away a sizeable number of Muslim votes, VP knew that his chances would ebb considerably. The Muslim leaders Hasan took him to assured him that they were aware no candidate could win with the support of one community alone, that voting for Majlis amounted to wasting their votes, but some worry remained.

What about the Dalits? VP had been making the rounds of Dalit bastis, as well as sending trusted supporters to Dalit areas that time constraints prevented him from visiting. He believed he was doing well until late one night, around 11 p.m., when, the day's campaigning done, the driver of one of his Jeeps came to see him urgently. He named the trusted campaigner he'd been taking around, and said, 'This man isn't working for you but for an independent Dalit candidate named Ramdhan! The Dalits have decided to use Congress facilities like vehicles and Congress funds, but in fact campaign and vote for their own man, not for you!'[41]

VP was stupefied. If the Dalits deserted the Congress, his defeat was certain. He urged the driver to tell him more. 'Dalits are angry with the Congress,' the driver said. 'They'd wanted Soraon to be declared a reserved constituency so that one of their own could represent it. They're saying former Congress MLAs had promised this would be managed, but it never was.'[42] (Soraon was finally made a reserved constituency in 2007.)

If the Dalits had indeed made up their minds, VP didn't see what he could do, but he decided to try anyway. Despite the late hour, he immediately set off for Allahabad, where he knew a couple of middle-class Dalits hailing from Soraon who worked in the accountant general's (AG's) office. Upon reaching their homes and waking them up, he realized that both of them were aware of the conspiracy—VP seemed to be the only innocent in the election. They said it was too late to do anything, that the Dalits had held a secret panchayat in Soraon and decided to vote for Ramdhan en masse.

'Ramdhan has to withdraw or I'm sunk,' VP said.

'He can't unless the panchayat allows him to,' countered Arjun, one of the two AG office employees.

VP pointed out that Ramdhan could not win anyway with just the Dalit vote—he would only be helping Pandey win by splitting the votes against him. In any case, the Congress was expected to form the next government and it would be better for Soraon's Dalits to have a Congress MLA, who would have better access to Congress ministers.

'But we can't call another panchayat at this stage,' said Arjun. The two men, however, agreed to accompany VP to meet two influential Dalit 'chaudhuris' in Soraon, who made decisions for the entire community—neither of whom VP had heard of until then. Rushing back to Soraon, meeting Chunnilal and Suraj Prasad, the two chaudhuris, in the dead of night, was a revelation for him. 'I realized that it was not simply a matter of a reserved constituency,' he said later. 'Our governments were giving Dalits benefits. But they wanted participation in decision-making. They felt taken for granted.'

That was all very well, but VP had to do something right then to offset Ramdhan's candidacy. He grew impassioned. 'If you want to get me defeated merely because I was born in a raja's family, do so,' he said to them. 'It was not I who decided which family I should be born into. But I've given away my land to Dalits. It is Dalits who cultivate it. It is our deeds we can take responsibility for, not our births.'

The two chaudhuris suggested visiting a third, who lived another 15–20 km away. VP readily agreed, and again had to listen to tales of the Congress's perfidy against Dalits from the new speaker. But he also realized that having got an opportunity to vent their rage before a Congressman, the Dalits' hostility towards the party, and him, was lessening. Finally, as dawn was breaking, the chaudhuris took VP to Ramdhan's house in Soraon. Ramdhan had just woken up and was brushing his teeth. Another long discussion ensued, at the end of which Ramdhan agreed not to contest. The official date of withdrawal was long past, but he would not campaign any more.[43]

There was much suspense during the counting of votes, with neither VP nor Pandey able to establish a clear lead for most of the day. Eventually, in a low-turnout election (only 47 per cent voted), VP got 12,117 votes against Pandey's 10,929.[44] But for the Majlis candidate, who took away 6,217 votes, VP felt that his margin of victory would have been higher. But he was immensely gratified by the result. '*Jitna zindagi mein manga tha, uss election mein ho gaya* (Whatever I could have asked for from life, I got with that election win),' he said.[45]

All the more so, considering the Congress's performance in the district, which proved worse than it had been in the 1967 polls. Of the 14 seats, it won only 5, while the SSP bagged an equal number. (Two other seats went to the Jana Sangh, one to Charan Singh's BKD and one to an independent.) In the five segments of the Phulpur Lok Sabha seat, he was the only Congress winner.

What was truly galling for the Congress in Allahabad was the shock defeat of four of its leaders. Three of the very men who had organized its campaign in the district lost the seats they contested—Bahuguna was defeated in Bara, Mangla Prasad in

Sirathu and Muzaffar Hasan in Pratapur. The fourth unexpected reverse was in the by-election to the Phulpur Lok Sabha seat. After Nehru's death in 1964, his sister Vijaya Lakshmi Pandit had been the Congress candidate in the by-election that followed, and had won easily, holding on to the seat, although by a smaller margin, in 1967. The by-election of 1969 was due to Pandit's very public falling-out with her Prime Minister niece, following which she decided to quit politics. Congress leader and former minister Keshav Deo Malaviya, close to the Nehru family since the 1920s, contested in her place from this seeming party bastion but lost it to the SSP candidate, Janeshwar Mishra. VP's victory shone all the more brightly in contrast.

Across the state, as expected, the Congress fared slightly better than in 1967—winning 211 seats against the 198 obtained two years ago.[46] The figure was still tantalizingly short of a majority in the 425-member House, but independents—seeing clearly which party was set to form the government—rushed to its support, giving it the required majority within days. (The right-wing Swatantra Party, which had won 5 seats, also backed the Congress.)[47] C.B. Gupta, who'd won his own seat in Ranikhet by an underwhelming 800 votes,[48] became chief minister for the third time.

But the big, unexpected success of the 1969 election was that of Charan Singh, whose BKD captured 98 seats, making it the principal Opposition party of UP.[49]

3

'YOU CAN'T FORCE ANYONE TO DO WHAT HE DOESN'T WANT TO'

His job as MLA, V.P. Singh found, had three key performance areas (KPAs)—getting the needs and grievances of his constituents (and sometimes others as well) attended to by lobbying on their behalf within the assembly and outside, either by raising questions in the assembly or pleading with ministers and bureaucrats in Allahabad or the state capital, Lucknow; helping out constituents in other ways, especially resolving disputes among them; and finally, rooting for his party, both within the assembly and outside, performing as directed by party leaders. Each presented singular challenges.

VP lobbied for roads, power connections, irrigation canals, schools in Soraon; his first speech in the assembly dwelt on the need for a road leading to a particular railway gumti (signal cabin) in the constituency. He took many matters directly to the authorities, never bringing them up in the assembly. 'Just as a devotee visiting a temple first worships the main idol and then goes around bowing to the smaller ones, I would start by visiting the minister concerned with my problem, then pay obeisance to the junior minister; next, the department secretary and other bureaucrats; and finally, the senior engineers,' he said. He waited in queues; withstood disinterested and rude responses. 'I always say that an MLA needs to consume a lump of butter every morning so he can roll smoothly along the corridors of power, unruffled by the bumps,' he added.[1]

His biggest triumph in this sort of work occurred within three months of his election. One morning in May 1969, while attending an assembly session in Lucknow as MLA, he learnt from party workers that about 500 farmers from Allahabad had arrived seeking urgent help. They had camped on the lawns of Darul Shafa, a set of government-owned buildings in central Lucknow, where MLAs were allotted quarters. They hailed not from Soraon but from its neighbouring constituency, Kaurihar. VP left the assembly to meet them right away. (He had himself stayed at Darul Shafa initially but then managed to shift into larger and better-maintained accommodation at Royal Hotel, again government-owned and reserved for MLAs.)

The farmers told him that they had been charged by the local police with breaching a canal and diverting some of its waters to their fields. They had had criminal cases lodged against them and been slapped with a fine of Rs 350,000 (an astronomical sum at the time). They frankly admitted their guilt, claiming that their crops desperately needed water, following the failure of the monsoon the previous year. (The mid-1960s saw successive droughts in north India, peaking with the Bihar famine of 1967; though eastern UP was never officially declared a famine area, it was almost as badly affected as its neighbour state.) Kaurihar was among the 5 seats the SSP had won, and they had already approached their own MLA, Ram Pujan Patel, for help. But he had curtly dismissed them with the Hindi equivalent of 'as you sow, so shall you reap'.[2]

VP sympathized with them. They were all Kurmis, a caste that had never voted for the Congress, but he quickly saw in their plight an opportunity to win their loyalty in future elections. He learnt that they had not eaten since their arrival, and immediately sent some of his party workers to buy sacks of jaggery (gur) and puffed rice (lai), which he distributed among them. 'I could not possibly feed 500 people, but I could at least give them gur-lai,' he recalled. He then rushed back to the assembly building and sought an immediate meeting with Chief Minister C.B. Gupta. It was already early evening; the assembly session was over for the day and Gupta was just leaving to inaugurate an art exhibition.

Gupta had opposed VP's MLA nomination, but much like his Allahabad lieutenants, Mangla Prasad and Muzaffar Hasan, did not seem to bear him any ill will. Once VP had won the election, Gupta had welcomed him into the Congress legislators' fold.[3] He suggested that VP accompany him to the exhibition. VP explained the farmers' plight during the drive. 'I told him frankly that the Congress could gain politically if we helped the farmers,' he said later. 'It would also help me establish myself as a local leader.'[4] Gupta not only agreed to help, but also did so in a manner that emphasized VP's role in the assistance.

VP had expected Gupta to call some farmer representatives to the chief minister's office on his return from the exhibition. He was shocked when, in the late evening, a messenger came rushing to him with a message from his wife—Gupta had turned up at his suite in Royal Hotel! He went home post-haste, taking the farmer group's leaders along. After they reached, Gupta passed orders directing the district administration to withdraw the cases against the farmers and cancel the fine.

In his constituency, where he tried his best to spend at least a fortnight each month—the rest of his time was divided between Lucknow and Allahabad—VP often travelled from village to village, recording villagers' problems, driving a second-hand

Jeep whose gearshift he claimed only he could operate. 'Anyone who borrowed it returned it almost at once,' he once said. In that pre-laptop/smartphone era, he used a stash of index cards instead, which he would keep updating. Each card was devoted to a particular department, on which names of villages and their specific problems related to that department were recorded. 'That's how I always had data at my fingertips during meetings with either the Allahabad district administration or authorities in Lucknow,' he said. He hung a notice outside his gate, which said that voters could meet him any time of the day or night.[5]

And they did, often coming with difficulties that stretched his people-management skills. One man once brought along a toddler, claiming that the child had swallowed a coin and he didn't know what to do about it. VP telephoned the district's civil surgeon. 'What's gone in will come out,' the surgeon responded, unperturbed. Another came in dishevelled, with a long tear in his shirt, maintaining that the police were not registering his complaint. VP asked what the complaint was about. The man said that following a heated argument with his wife, she had beaten him up, torn his shirt, taken away his watch and left the house to stay with her parents. He wanted to file an FIR against her for stealing his watch. 'Do you really want to publicize such a matter with an FIR?' VP asked him. 'Why not wait a few days and then get her back from her parents' place?'[6]

But there were also far more critical situations he had to mediate. One such arose in end March 1969, within weeks of his becoming MLA, when the Allahabad district magistrate prohibited the annual tazia procession in Soraon town on the tenth day of Muharram, claiming that it could lead to a clash between Hindus and Muslims. Part of the procession's traditional route was along a narrow track adjoining a Hindu temple, but that track had been blocked by a recent extension of the temple's boundary wall. The only alternative route was through a large field, where, too, a Hindu religious mela was being held. VP, much dependent on the Muslim vote, confronted the district magistrate, insisting that the procession be allowed to cross the field and that he would take personal responsibility to ensure nothing went wrong. The district magistrate refused to reconsider. VP then informed him that the procession would be organized anyway, and that he would lead it—the police were welcome to arrest him. He did so too. The district magistrate blinked; the police left the procession alone and it reached its destination without incident.[7]

Another conflict VP remembered having resolved was caste-related. Traditionally, leatherwork in villages is restricted to Dalits—specifically the Chamar or Jatav caste—and that includes disposing of the carcass when an animal dies. Also, only Dalit women worked as midwives, assisting village deliveries. Much to the outrage of the other castes, Dalits in a particular village— which VP did not name—decided that they would not do either job in future. The other castes responded by refusing to employ Dalits as farm labour in their fields. The Dalits, deprived of their main livelihood source, appealed for VP's help. 'You can't force anyone to do what he doesn't want to,' VP told the villagers at a gathering he organized.[8]

But he also searched for and found an Allahabad-based contractor who collected carcasses to make fertilizer from their bones, and who had trucks and men to do the collecting. He arranged for the contractor to pick up carcasses from this village as well, though naturally, the contractor charged much more than the Dalits had been paid. Finding alternative midwives was more difficult. VP somehow persuaded the Dalits to continue sending their women to carry out deliveries for another three months. He then turned to Gupta for help and once again received support. Gupta got the health ministry to train more women in Allahabad in midwifery so they could be summoned to villages whenever needed.[9]

It was, however, the third KPA that proved the trickiest. VP was ready to follow his leader—but which one? The Congress in UP had been rife with factionalism from pre-Independence times, with every senior politician nurturing his own group among party MLAs and using it to undermine other Congress leaders. The infighting increased markedly after the state's first chief minister, Govind Ballabh Pant—whose fatherly eminence had kept the different factions in check—moved to the Centre as home minister in 1955.[10] When VP entered the assembly, the two main factions were those of Chief Minister C.B. Gupta and Deputy Chief Minister Kamalapati Tripathi—the same man who had used botanical allusions to deter him from contesting—but there were also some smaller ones, such as H.N. Bahuguna's. The different factions made contesting demands on new MLAs, forcing them to opt for one.

This much VP had been prepared for. He had hoped, somewhat impractically, to forge agreeable relations with all factions without fully aligning with any.[11] What happened within months of his becoming MLA, however, made nonsense of such hopes. The Congress party had split a number of times after Independence, both at the Centre and in different states. Charan Singh's departure with sixteen MLAs in April 1967 was only one such instance. But all such departures had been much like branches falling off a giant tree. In 1969, the tree trunk itself split into two, and like every other party functionary, VP had to decide which side of the trunk to grab. All those who chose the other side became political enemies, leading to much embarrassment and awkwardness, since he'd had close personal ties with many of them until then.

In January 1966, Indira Gandhi became Prime Minister following Lal Bahadur Shastri's death, thanks mainly to then Congress president, K. Kamaraj.[12] She had been the Congress president earlier and was minister for information and broadcasting in Shastri's cabinet; even so, at forty-eight, her political experience was far less than that of many senior Congress leaders. When these leaders couldn't decide who among them should be elevated to Prime Minister after Shastri's death, Kamaraj[13] convinced them that Indira's relative youth and feminine charm could be used to draw votes in the general elections next year, while all her policy and administrative moves could be guided and controlled. Only one among the senior leaders, Morarji Desai,[14] disagreed and contested the party leadership against Indira. He lost.

In a little over a year, Kamaraj found himself proved wrong on both counts. The Congress had become so unpopular that despite Indira's tireless campaigning in the 1967 elections—covering 24,000 km in two months and speaking at hundreds of public meetings[15]—it barely managed to retain a majority in the Lok Sabha, while losing in eight of the then-sixteen states. And yet, the poor performance under her leadership did not significantly weaken her, since a number of the senior leaders and their key supporters, collectively dubbed 'the Syndicate' in the press, lost their own seats, while Indira won her first electoral contest—Rae Bareli in UP—by a big margin.[16] Even Kamaraj, who chose to contest the assembly elections in Madras state, was defeated by a little-known student leader.

The Syndicate erred even more grievously in imagining that Indira would ever allow herself to be controlled. As soon as she settled into her job as Prime Minister, she began chafing at its interference. Relations between the two progressively worsened until open conflict broke out over the choice of a new President. On 3 May 1969, the incumbent President, Zakir Husain, died unexpectedly after only two years in office, and the Syndicate decided that the then speaker of the Lok Sabha, Neelam Sanjeeva Reddy, should be the Congress's candidate to succeed him. (The President is chosen by an electoral college comprising MPs of both

Houses of Parliament as well as MLAs of all state assemblies; the Congress, despite its reduced numbers after the 1967 polls, still had enough representatives to ensure its candidate's victory, provided there was no cross-voting.)

Reddy had a worthy record,[17] but with wild rumours circulating that he had been primed by the Syndicate to dismiss Indira once he became President[18]—which he would have the constitutional authority to do—she did not want to nominate him. The Syndicate, however, insisted, and since it had a majority on the Congress Parliamentary Board, which chose the party's presidential candidate,[19] an outvoted Indira was forced to sign Reddy's nomination papers.

Fortuitously for her, there was one more person greatly miffed by the Reddy choice—vice president of India V.V. Giri.[20] In the twenty-two years since Independence, the vice president had always succeeded the outgoing president,[21] and Giri had expected the tradition to be followed this time as well. Named acting president following Husain's death, he resigned in late July to contest the presidential poll as an independent, and Indira decided to confront the Syndicate through him. Though her party was supporting Reddy, she urged MPs and MLAs loyal to her to secretly canvass for Giri.

In UP, Dinesh Singh and H.N. Bahuguna took up the task of meeting individual Congress MPs and MLAs, and urging them to vote against their party's official choice.[22] They met VP too, who needed no convincing. 'Once I learnt what Indira Gandhi wanted, it did not take me a moment to decide who I would vote for,' he said.[23] Besides, Dinesh Singh and Bahuguna had both supported VP's MLA nomination when other Congress leaders had been hostile.

This led to the first of VP's awkward situations. Unlike most other Indira supporters, he did not want to conspire in secret. Chief Minister Gupta was backing the Syndicate—his relations with

Indira had always been frosty—but he had been magnanimous to VP, and the latter decided that, however difficult, he would have to level with him. Gupta was known for his short temper and his use of extremely colourful language when he lost it.[24] His stature and choler made many new Congress MLAs afraid of him.

Gupta had been summoning groups of MLAs to his house to gauge their sympathies, and VP, too, was duly called, along with three other MLAs who had also decided to support Giri. Pure farce followed—one of them flatly refused to go. The other three set off in the car Gupta had sent to fetch them. As the car was passing Lucknow's main railway station, one of them urged the driver to stop, having remembered 'some urgent work', and got off. And then there were two; but at Gupta's doorstep, VP's fellow MLA chickened out as well. 'Where are you taking me?' he said. 'I'm not going.' He departed hurriedly on foot and VP was left to face Gupta alone.[25]

Gupta did not excoriate him, as VP had feared, when informed of his decision. (He may well have already known.) 'Guptaji, you've done a lot for me, but I came to tell you that I'll be voting for Giri,' VP said. 'It is a life-and-death situation for Indiraji, not for you. If she hadn't given me a ticket, you wouldn't have sent a car to bring me here today.'

Gupta harped on the principles of parliamentary democracy VP would be violating. 'Principles matter, not personalities,' he said. 'She only gave you a ticket. I defied the people who gave me birth, my parents, to join the freedom struggle, because I was opposed to foreign rule on principle.'

VP stressed that loyalty was more important. 'If I defy the party, I may be expelled for six years, but if I betray Indiraji, I will not be able to look at myself in the mirror for the rest of my life,' he said. They argued back and forth, with Gupta even tempting VP with an indirect offer of a ministerial position, but the latter was unmoved.[26]

Rampant cross-voting by Congress MPs and MLAs followed in the presidential election held on 25 August 1969. It would still not have been enough to ensure Giri's victory, but with Indira having won over some regional parties as well as the CPI, Giri pulled through by a narrow margin. Much emboldened, the Indira supporters then sought to 'requisition' a party meeting—a demand the Syndicate leaders turned down, as expected—but which led to the group being dubbed the Congress (Requisitionists) in the press, while the Syndicate's flock came to be known as the Congress (Organization).[27] Both factions knew that a complete break was imminent, even as their leaders held rounds of meaningless 'unity talks', and both worked hard to shore up support.

In UP, Bahuguna had long realized that to get sizeable backing for Indira, he needed Deputy Chief Minister Tripathi's group on his side, but Tripathi, though keen to upstage Gupta, dithered at making any firm commitment. Like many others, he wanted to be on the winning side, but at the time it was far from clear which side that would be. 'How to pump some life into that corpse!' Bahuguna once commented in exasperation to VP.[28]

To win over other fence-sitting Congress MLAs, Bahuguna and VP resorted to a clever expedient—they organized public meetings in some of these MLAs' constituencies, which Indira addressed. Most of the MLAs, staggered by the size of the crowd that came to hear her, promptly joined her group after she left. 'She made several trips to the state [UP], and [since she was Prime Minister] I spent state-government money to provide her with security, and helipads for her helicopter to land on,' Gupta said later. 'I worked to bring myself down.'[29]

VP held a meeting in Soraon as well, where he told his listeners that he had decided to support Indira—if they disagreed with his decision, he was prepared to quit as MLA. They did not. On the other side, Gupta, too, tried hard to retain his MLAs by extending to them whatever patronage he could as chief minister, especially after Tripathi finally came out openly in Indira's support.

Eventually, the Syndicate expelled Indira from the Congress on 13 November 1969, only to find that 220 of the Congress's 283 Lok Sabha MPs were on her side. That still left her Congress (R) short of a majority in the 520-member House at the time, but again, as in the presidential election, the CPI and some regional parties came to Indira's rescue, enabling her support to cross the halfway mark and her to continue as Prime Minister.

The break at the Centre reverberated through the country, splitting the Congress in every state into two. In most Congress-ruled states, the chief ministers—irrespective of their stance during the presidential election—now backed the Congress (R) and retained power, albeit with thinner majorities. But in UP, Gujarat and Karnataka, they stayed with the parent Congress. In none of the three states were they able to save their governments. Like VP, more than half their MLAs—although many, unlike him, were induced by a range of blandishments from the Centre—migrated to the Congress (R). In Gujarat and Karnataka, President's Rule was imposed; inexplicably, in UP, it was not, taking political turmoil to greater heights and causing VP another embarrassment some months later.

⸺⸺⸺

Gupta's government in UP fell in February 1970 after 139 Congress MLAs preferred to back Indira. (The party's strength in the UP assembly by then was 219, up from the 211 seats it won in the 1969 polls, thanks to defections; the remaining eighty MLAs stayed loyal to Gupta.) There followed a chaotic scramble by both Gupta and Tripathi to win over Charan Singh, with his ninety-eight MLAs, to form the next government. Tripathi succeeded narrowly, and Charan Singh became chief minister once more, this time in alliance with the Congress (R). But with Indira insisting soon after that Charan Singh return to the Congress, merging his party with it, and Charan Singh rigidly resisting, the alliance remained unstable all through the eight months it lasted.

To strengthen her position in her battle against the Syndicate, Indira had begun, even before the split, to lean ideologically leftward, seeking to stigmatize her opponents as representatives of the wealthy and powerful, while she was all for the poor and the disempowered. Two of her proposals proved terrific crowd-pleasers—the nationalization of banks and the abolition of maharajas' privileges, including their 'privy purses'.[30] She got the Bill related to the first passed easily in both Houses of Parliament—most Opposition parties feared being dubbed 'anti-people' if they voted against bank nationalization—but the second faced considerable pushback.

Charan Singh strongly opposed it, maintaining that taking away privy purses violated a 'solemn promise' made to the maharajas for giving up their powers. The troubled alliance broke when his BKD MPs voted against the relevant constitutional amendment Bill Indira brought. In the Lok Sabha it didn't matter—the Bill still got passed; in the Rajya Sabha, it made all the difference, as the Bill was defeated by one vote. A livid Indira immediately withdrew her support to his UP government.

Though President's Rule was imposed in UP thereafter, the assembly was still not dissolved, which led to Charan Singh now getting together with Gupta to try and form another government, roping in some of the other Opposition parties too. The chief minister chosen to head this unwieldy combination was Tribhuvan Narain Singh[31]—the only person Charan Singh agreed to, after Gupta and the other parties refused to let him take charge for a third time.

T.N. Singh was closely associated with the Shastri Sewa Niketan, which operated out of Manda Fort, and had thus become a good friend of VP. On becoming chief minister in October 1970, he sought VP's support in the confidence motion his government would soon face. But how could VP, who had been championing Indira, agree to support a government of her opponents? 'I had to tell him that if he had wanted my help in any personal matter, I would certainly have obliged,' said VP. 'But my assembly vote was not my own. It belonged to my party and the voters who elected me. It would be dishonest of me to vote in any way other than what my party decided.'[32]

That ended their friendship, though, eventually, with the confidence motion being postponed to March 1971, VP did not have to vote in it at all. For apart from bringing down his UP government, Charan Singh's stance on privy purses had another, bigger fallout—it convinced Indira that she needed a two-thirds majority of her own to get any fresh constitutional amendment she introduced passed. In a great gamble, she had the Lok Sabha dissolved and the country's fifth general election announced for March 1971, a year ahead of schedule. With VP contesting and winning this election too, he had resigned his MLA seat and joined the Lok Sabha by the time T.N. Singh's confidence vote—which he lost, forcing him to step down—was held.

4

'I MAY BE A DHOK (SCARECROW), BUT I DON'T GIVE DHOKA'

It was the poor state of telecommunications in India at the time (hard to imagine now, barely fifty years later) that resulted in V.P. Singh contesting the 1971 Lok Sabha election. He wasn't particularly interested. He still had three years of his five-year MLA term to go; the UP assembly—despite three governments in two years since the 1969 election—had not been dissolved; even if it was later and fresh elections held, he was fairly certain of being nominated by the Congress (R) from Soraon and getting re-elected. (In fact, the assembly ran its full term until February 1974.) Bahuguna, however, wanted him to fight—alone among UP political leaders then, he seemed to lay great store by VP's political influence.

Bahuguna was himself the Congress (R) candidate for the Allahabad Lok Sabha seat, and worried about his chances after his embarrassing reverse in the 1969 assembly poll from Bara. The Daiya–Manda region being part of the seat, he felt that the Congress workers there—many with personal ties to VP and his family—would work harder for him if VP was made the Congress (R) nominee from neighbouring Phulpur. Aware that it was always the Prime Minister who decided the Congress candidates from Allahabad and its surrounding seats, Bahuguna sounded out Indira Gandhi. 'Vishwanath seems to be doing well where he is,' she responded. 'Why do you want to disturb him?'

Bahuguna persisted. '*Aap apne ummidwari ke hisab se soch rahe hain* (You're thinking of your own election, that's why you want him),' she said curtly.[1] When Bahuguna did not reply, she thought he had got her hint and acquiesced.

Though she did not say so, Bahuguna knew that she had another candidate in mind for the Phulpur seat—the Nehru family lawyer in Allahabad, Jagpat Dubey. After VP had turned down the offer to take charge of Phulpur on Nehru's behalf following the 1957 election, this job had been assigned to Dubey, who had been carrying it out faithfully. Indira felt that he deserved some reward for doing so.[2] (Unlike VP, he was never offered a Rajya Sabha seat.) Bahuguna did not care for Dubey, nor would he have benefited in any way from Dubey's candidacy. Unknown to Indira, he suggested running from Phulpur to VP.

'Bahugunaji, *humein chhod deten, hum to seekh rahal hain* (Bahugunaji, leave me out of it, I'm still learning),' VP replied in the local dialect.[3] The Phulpur Lok Sabha area included Soraon, where, in the two years since his election, he had built a network of supporters and workers, but in the rest of the constituency, he hardly knew anyone. He was also worried about the cost of fighting a second election, covering a much wider area than the first, within two years.

'*Paise ke bare mein chinta mat karo* (Don't worry about funds),' said Bahuguna. '*Iss baar party paise dene ja rahi hai* (This time, the party will provide the funds).' (Eventually, the party provided Rs 50,000, inadequate to fight a Lok Sabha election even at the time.) VP departed unconvinced.[4]

As noted earlier, the Phulpur Lok Sabha seat, though once a Congress bastion, had been lost to the SSP's Janeshwar Mishra in the 1969 by-election.[5] Mishra was contesting the Phulpur seat again, his chances seemingly stronger than before, since the SSP this time had teamed up with the Congress (O), Swatantra and Jana Sangh, to put up joint candidates. When news of VP's possible nomination appeared in the local media, Mishra responded with disdain. '*Humse Raja kya ladenge* (Raja [V.P. Singh] can hardly match me),' he told press interviewers. '*Unke to doodh ke daanth bhi nahi aayen hain. Indiraji ko aane do, who humse laden* (In politics, he hasn't even started teething yet. Indiraji should fight me to make it a worthy contest).'[6]

His comment offended VP so much that he decided to accept Bahuguna's offer. Unaware of Indira's plans for the Phulpur seat, he told Bahuguna that he was ready to take on Mishra. Bahuguna, delighted, hastened to Delhi and, taking advantage of Indira's absence (she was away campaigning), persuaded the head of the Congress (R)'s campaign committee to officially name VP the party's candidate from Phulpur right away, without checking with her. With not much time left to file nominations, VP, hearing his name announced over the radio, promptly acquired the needed forms and documents from the local Congress (R) office and completed the contesting formalities. Bahuguna may have hoped that by the time Indira returned to Delhi and found out, the last date for nominations would have passed. But Indira got to know earlier and, incensed by Bahuguna's defiance, promptly dispatched a messenger to Allahabad to direct VP to withdraw and Dubey to file his nomination from Phulpur instead.

The messenger reached VP's house late on the penultimate date for filing nominations. VP was hugely embarrassed to discover that he had unknowingly irked his idol. There was loss of face for him as well in withdrawing his nomination, but that bothered him less. Indira's emissary discovered, however, that Jagpat Dubey, upset at being denied the nomination he was promised, had left Allahabad for Kanpur. Though Kanpur was barely 200 km away, and both Kanpur and Allahabad among the biggest cities of UP, telecommunication links between them were so poor that getting through to Dubey proved impossible.

The emissary departed for Kanpur by the earliest train to meet Dubey, only to discover on reaching that Dubey had just caught another train to Delhi. It was impossible to get him back to Allahabad in time to file his nomination. 'I had decided not to withdraw my nomination until Dubey filed his,' said VP. 'If Dubey didn't return in time, the Phulpur seat would have been left without a Congress (R) candidate. But I prepared all Dubey's papers and waited. He would have just had to sign and file them.'[7]

Dubey never arrived, and VP thus continued as the Congress (R)'s Phulpur candidate. But Indira made her displeasure plain. She travelled around 48,000 km during the 1971 campaign—mostly by air—addressing 410 meetings, surpassing her 1967 record by a wide margin.[8] But despite her family's association with Phulpur, it found no place in her itinerary.[9]

Another embarrassment for VP was his failure to fulfil his end of the unspoken bargain with Bahuguna. He fully intended to get all his family, friends and supporters in Daiya–Manda to back Bahuguna, but to his shock, his own father came in the way. With C.B. Gupta having stayed with the Congress [O], Mangla Prasad and Muzaffar Hasan had done the same, and the Opposition alliance had nominated Prasad as its Allahabad candidate. (Shastri's son Hari Krishna, the sitting MP, who had also stayed with the Congress [O], contested from Meerut.[10]) It was awkward enough having to oppose Prasad, who had backed VP in 1969, despite initially opposing his nomination—though that he could live with. It was worse for him to discover that his father had promised to support Prasad!

Prasad, who had once been MLA from Meja—which included the Daiya–Manda region—had already sought Bhagwati Prasad's help, and the latter, reacting very differently from the way he had when Shastri had come calling fourteen years earlier, had agreed to provide it. VP rushed to Daiya Palace to persuade his father to change his mind. 'I spent a whole day trying to do so, but failed,' he said. 'I remember it was still winter and we sat next to the fireplace, which had a big fire going, and argued endlessly. My father said that he had given his word and would not change it.' In response, Bahuguna loyalists in Phulpur, too, stopped working for VP.[11]

There was nothing to be done about it. VP carried on with whatever support he could muster. He went about his first Lok Sabha campaign the same way he'd done his earlier Vidhan Sabha one—renting a house in Phulpur and living there; sending out postcards to all important personages in the constituency and following them up with personal meetings, focusing on house-to-house visits rather than public meetings. He undertook daily walkathons, since many villages, he discovered, could be reached only on foot. He was pleased to find his track record as an MLA in Soraon appreciated. The Congress (R) workers there told him to focus on the rest of Phulpur constituency—he need not even visit Soraon, its votes were his already.[12]

As the campaign warmed up, it got personal—Janeshwar Mishra called VP a dhok (scarecrow)—not only mocking the latter's lean frame, but also implying that he lacked substance and stature.

'I may be a dhok, but I don't give dhoka,' VP responded. 'In any case, a dhok performs a useful function, protecting crops from birds.'[13] The lanky dhok also displayed more stamina on foot than the somewhat portly Mishra. 'I covered twenty to thirty villages a day,' VP said later. 'I'd get blisters on my feet but I got a doctor to puncture them with a syringe at night, draw out the fluid and bandage them, so that I could carry on the next day. I'm told that Janeshwar Mishra tried to match me, but after a day's attempt, said to his close workers, "I don't care whether I win or lose, I'm not doing this again."'[14]

The way the results turned out, however, VP need not have gone to all the trouble. He had made detailed, area-wise caste calculations and mapped strategies, noting, for instance, that Brahmins who traditionally voted en masse for the Congress in UP might not do so in Phulpur, since Mishra was himself a Brahmin and could draw away some of their votes; or that while the Kurmi and Yadav backward castes would largely support Mishra, their votes could get divided since Charan Singh's BKD also had a candidate in the fray.[15]

None of it mattered. In keeping with the left-wing stance she had adopted soon after she became Prime Minister, Indira had posited the 1971 general election as a battle between haves and have-nots, appealing to voters for a mandate large enough to implement her pro-poor reforms, which parties such as the parent Congress (O), she claimed, were preventing. Referring to the Opposition's grand alliance, she coined a slogan—'*Woh kehtey hain Indira hatao, main kehti hoon garibi hatao* (They say, "Let's get rid of Indira"; I say, "Let's get rid of poverty")'—which proved so effective that the Opposition alliance was decimated.

Her stance resonated so strongly with voters that they rose above caste and other sectarian considerations—even above evaluating the merits or otherwise of individual Congress (R) candidates—and voted in overwhelming numbers for Indira. In the previous Lok Sabha election, the undivided Congress had barely managed a majority, getting 283 of 520 seats. With the split, Indira's support had fallen further to 220 seats. This time, her tally rose to 352, a clear two-thirds majority, while the second-highest tally was that of the Communist Party of India (Marxist) (CPI [M]), which won 25. (The grand alliance of four parties got only 49 seats, with the Congress [O] reduced to just 16.)[16]

In UP, the Congress (R) got 73 of the 85 seats; its allied party, the CPI, won another 3. In Phulpur, VP polled 123,095 votes, nearly 100,000 more than Janeshwar Mishra, who came third and lost his deposit, trailing behind even the BKD candidate, B.D. Singh. In Allahabad, Bahuguna beat Mangla Prasad by a similarly huge margin, triumphing even in the Meja segment—Bhagwati Prasad's backing of his opponent had made no difference. In Fatehpur, Sant Bux Singh, contesting on the Congress (R) ticket, also won by over 50,000 votes.[17]

In contrast, Opposition leaders were mauled, with both C.B. Gupta and Charan Singh, contesting from Nainital and Muzaffarnagar, respectively, losing by wide margins. (Both their parties, the Congress [O] and BKD, won just 1 seat each in UP.) For Gupta, it virtually marked the end of his career, his health failing thereafter. He contested one more election—the next UP assembly poll in 1974, from Lucknow Cantonment—and lost that as well. But whenever he ran into VP in his remaining years (he died in 1980), he would jibe, 'Still clinging to that woman's pallu? You'll never let go of it, will you?'[18]

The by-election to the Soraon assembly seat, held in early 1972 following VP's shift to the Lok Sabha, again forced difficult political choices on him. He found himself opposing—after C.B. Gupta and Mangla Prasad—another Congress elder he knew well and respected, Muzaffar Hasan. Hasan had helped him make initial inroads among Soraon's Muslims in the 1969 assembly election, but when the Congress (O) put him up as its Soraon candidate, VP had no option but to campaign against him. 'It was a dharma

sankat (moral dilemma) for me, but what else could I have done?'
he said later.[19]

Differences over the choice of the Congress (R) candidate
also led to a rift with the man who had backed VP the most until
then—Bahuguna. Their near-annihilation in the 1971 election had
led to much ferment within all the Opposition parties, one fallout
of which was that many second-rank leaders of these parties
quit to join the ruling Congress (R). Almost the entire SSP unit
in Allahabad did so, including, to VP's surprise and dismay, his
principal opponent in the 1969 election, Ram Adhar Pande. Pande
wanted to contest the Soraon seat again, this time on behalf of the
Congress (R), and Bahuguna backed him, claiming that was the
condition on which he had agreed to switch parties.

VP opposed this strongly. He maintained that the Congress (R)
workers in Soraon wanted—and deserved—a local to represent
them, while Pande was a resident of Allahabad city. 'I was an
outsider in Soraon and so is Pande, which is most unfair to the
Congress workers of Soraon, who also have aspirations,' he told
Indira when she summoned him to her Parliament office one
afternoon to discuss the matter. Other UP leaders who were also
present kept rooting for Pande, but VP argued right back until
Indira was convinced. 'If we've promised Pande a position, why
don't we make him a legislative council member instead?' he
suggested. (UP has a bicameral legislature, with members of the
legislative council being elected by different electoral colleges, not
directly.) Indira agreed.

Both Pande and Bahuguna were furious. 'The legislative
council is for has-beens,' Pande fumed when VP ran into him in
Allahabad. (He had already been informed of the party decision
over telephone.) 'Am I finished as an active politician?'[20] But once
Indira had made up her mind, no amount of grumbling was going
to change it. Ramapati Tripathi, a Soraon-based lawyer and close
associate of VP, got the Congress (R) ticket. Pande and Bahuguna

worked hard to sabotage his campaign, even getting a Dalit to stand as an independent candidate to divide the Dalit vote, but it did not work.[21] Tripathi won by more than 2,000 votes, with Hasan coming third, behind the BKD candidate Jang Bahadur Singh Patel.[22] 'My neck was on the line, because Indiraji had taken my side, and it would have been a big embarrassment for her if we had lost the seat,' said VP. 'We had to combat both the Opposition and our own party men.'

5

'I BEGAN MAKING MY PRESENCE FELT'

A Lok Sabha MP has far less to do than a state assembly MLA, V.P. Singh discovered on becoming one. The KPAs of both are similar, but the MP has fewer constituent needs to lobby for, because fewer people approach him or her. Most problems affecting people's daily lives relate to departments under the state's jurisdiction, not the Centre's, and it is to the MLAs, not the MPs, that they largely turn for redress.[1] He did whatever he could for his voters—including getting a unit of the Indian Farmers Fertiliser Cooperative Limited (IFFCO) allotted to Phulpur, mainly because the then managing director, B.B. Singh, was a close friend from Allahabad University—but he still had plenty of time left over.[2]

Initially, most of it was spent understanding his new environs. 'Parliament is an ocean,' he said. 'It took me a year to find my feet.'[3] There were political currents as well as undercurrents, often tugging in different directions. There were lobbies of all kinds within the Congress as well, but he chose not to join any. Personal arrangements had to be made too—he was allotted an apartment at Vithalbhai Patel House on Delhi's Rafi Marg and moved into it with Sita Kumari (both sons were still away at boarding school), buying her a TV (a novelty for Indians in 1971, with broadcasts available only to Delhi residents) when she complained of being lonely. There were also unexpected perks of being an MP, such as an invitation from the West German government for a sponsored visit to their country. VP duly accepted, taking his wife along at his own expense.

With time to spare, as he settled down in Delhi, VP began expanding his areas of interest beyond his constituency and indeed UP, maintaining files of clippings on subjects that interested him and regularly asking questions in the Lok Sabha. 'I submitted starred questions, un-starred questions; I put down my name for short discussions, half-an-hour discussions and all kinds of debates,' he said. 'I began making my presence felt.'[4] His first speech in Parliament in June 1971 had nothing to do with Phulpur or UP, but dwelt on the annual budget that year, praising the finance minister for increasing rates of personal taxation on those earning more than Rs 15,000 per annum.[5]

Overall, VP's first three-and-a-half years in the Lok Sabha were fairly sedate, even as the country went through turmoil. The crisis that had been brewing in neighbouring Pakistan since December 1970, when it held the first general election after its formation in 1947 (having been mostly under army rule until then), reached its apogee within a fortnight of Indira Gandhi's sweeping victory in the March 1971 elections. East Pakistan, denied the autonomy it wanted, declared itself a sovereign, independent country, Bangladesh, while the Pakistani army sought to crush the rebellion, killing and imprisoning thousands. India, too, was drawn in, as an avalanche of Bangladeshi refugees began pouring into the country through its eastern border. Bangladesh-related events dominated the rest of the year in India (among its side-effects was the Soraon by-election's postponement to early 1972), culminating in a fourteen-day India–Pakistan war in December 1971, in which the Pakistani army in Bangladesh surrendered to India, setting Bangladesh free.

The first year following the March 1971 election proved the most successful of Indira's political career. Even Opposition leaders hailed her victory in the Bangladesh war.[6] She used the groundswell of admiration to hold fresh assembly elections in thirteen states in March 1972 (UP, however, was not one of them) and won them all. But thereafter, nothing seemed to go right for her. She tried to make good on the left-leaning promises she had made in the 1971 election campaign—lowering the land ceiling from 40 'standard acres' to 30, imposing higher taxes on the rich, nationalizing the coal industry and general insurance, enacting a law to curb business monopolies and more—but the economic situation continued to worsen. In a repeat of the mid-1960s, there followed three successive years of poor rains, which, combined with the doubling of oil prices at the time by the oil-producing nations, sent inflation soaring.

With Indira trying to wish away her difficulties by encouraging an ambience of sycophancy around her[7] and ignoring mounting evidence of corruption all around, student-led agitations against price rise and corruption began from January 1974. The first was in Gujarat, which coalesced into a demand that the 'corrupt' state government resign and fresh elections be held. After numerous demonstrations, many of them violent, leading to retaliatory police firings and deaths, Indira finally gave in, getting the assembly dissolved. She seemed to have immediately regretted doing so, however, for when a similar agitation arose in Bihar within days of Gujarat being defused, she remained unyielding to the end. Her stance only increased the protests, which grew even stronger after the seventy-two-year-old Gandhian leader, Jayaprakash Narayan, joined the students.

His daring escape from Hazaribagh jail after being imprisoned during the 1942 Quit India movement had made JP, as he was widely called, a national hero. His reputation was further heightened to near-saint stature after his decision—following a few years with the Socialist Party post-Independence—to join Vinoba Bhave's Bhoodan movement, renouncing politics. He now returned to politics to lead the students, claiming that 'the corrupt system' was 'beyond my tolerance'.[8] Opposition parties promptly flocked behind him. While JP held rallies in Patna, Opposition leaders organized a massive one at Delhi's Boat Club lawns on 6 October 1974, protesting Indira's 'misrule'.[9]

It was against this backdrop that Indira, four days later, on 10 October 1974, seeking to shore up whatever support she could, carried out an extensive reshuffle and expansion of her cabinet, changing the portfolios of top ministers, dropping some and inducting new faces, raising its total strength from fifty-seven to sixty. Of the eight newcomers she chose, five were made deputy ministers, one of whom was VP.[10]

For a little-known first-term MP to be inducted into the council of ministers is a huge achievement. But his elevation proved a landmark in VP's life for another reason as well. It led to the first crack in his relationship with the man who had been his mentor and closest political adviser until then—his elder brother Sant Bux Singh.

Whispers about a forthcoming cabinet expansion had been circulating for some time, and many MPs had been lobbying with senior Congressmen to get themselves included. The rumours also claimed that the new inductees would include one MP of the Rajput caste from central or eastern UP. There had been one such earlier, a man who had been among Indira's most trusted confidantes during her first years as Prime Minister. He was the same person VP had first turned to when he had aspired for a Rajya Sabha ticket—Dinesh Singh, the MP from Pratapgarh. Dinesh Singh had successively held the portfolios of commerce, external affairs and industrial development, and had strongly backed Indira in her battle against the Syndicate, but when she reconstituted her cabinet after her stunning 1971 election victory, he was among the seven ministers of the previous cabinet she dropped.[11]

Gossip had it that this was because Dinesh Singh had been insinuating in political circles that his proximity to Indira went beyond merely rendering her political advice.[12] When she found out, she was furious and decided to extirpate him at the first opportunity. (Dinesh Singh always denied having made any such claim, maintaining he was not that stupid.[13]) Three and a half years later, however, with her support shrinking, it was bruited that Indira had decided to soothe any hurt feelings among voters of Dinesh Singh's caste and region by inducting another Rajput from a nearby constituency. With Fatehpur and Phulpur both adjoining Pratapgarh—the first to the west and the second to the south—the two strongest claimants for the vacancy were Sant Bux and VP.

As a second-term MP, erudite and articulate, with many friends across political lines and in the media, and someone who had helped Indira draft speeches on foreign policy in her early years of rule and supported her unstintingly when she had fought the Syndicate,[14] Sant Bux was a far stronger claimant for a ministerial position. He had been lobbying for it too, sending his trusted friend and Congress Rajya Sabha MP, Devendra Nath Dwivedi, to speak to Kamalapati Tripathi, one of Indira's advisers on UP-related matters. (Tripathi had become UP's chief minister after the T.N. Singh government fell, but two years later, in 1973, Indira moved him to the Centre as minister for transport and shipping, replacing him in UP with Bahuguna.) Tripathi, though somewhat miffed that Sant Bux hadn't personally met him to plead his case,[15] faithfully did so. To which Indira replied, '*Unke ek chhotey bhai bhi toh hain* (He has a younger brother too, doesn't he [who's also an MP])?'[16]

When Tripathi, somewhat shocked, responded, 'But he's a novice', Indira retorted, 'I want a novice.'[17]

Why Indira preferred VP to Sant Bux can only be guessed at. Both Mark Tully, the renowned former BBC correspondent in India, and veteran political reporter Janardhan Thakur maintain in their writings on the subject that it was because she considered Sant Bux too independent-minded at a time when she wanted only adulators around her. (Tully's profile of Sant Bux suggests that her assessment was spot-on.[18]) But it is likely that she was also influenced by Dev Kanta Barooah, a senior Congressman from Assam, who had formerly been petroleum minister and had just then become Congress party president, and whom she had grown to trust greatly. Barooah had been much impressed by an intervention VP had made in the Lok Sabha during a short-duration discussion on the oil crisis at the time and had said so to Indira.

VP was no expert on oil or its global politics at the time, but he had picked up a little, following a suggestion from his younger son, Abhay, then fifteen, briefly home for the holidays from boarding school. Abhay, though later to become a doctor, was much interested in the physical sciences in his youth. He attributed his love for the sciences to his father. 'It was he who got me interested,' he said. 'We used to make crystal radios together when I was young.' He was the one who had urged his father to read an article in the monthly magazine *Science Today* (a *Times of India* publication that shut down in 1992), copies of which he'd found piled up at home, almost untouched. 'I came across this article on petroleum and our energy policy, and I knew it would interest him, so I forced him to read it,' he said later.[19] VP remembered Abhay also adding, 'You buy so many magazines, but you hardly read any.'[20]

Obediently, VP did as his son asked. Armed with this knowledge, he put his name down for the discussion on the subject in the Lok Sabha soon after.

He was much surprised when, a few days later, Barooah accosted and complimented him, saying that he had sent VP's speech to his department, whose senior officers had said VP's critique was spot-on. Since then, VP kept hearing that Barooah had been praising him to many, including Indira, showering backhanded compliments, calling him a 'scientific raja' and 'very intelligent for a Thakur'.[21]

On the morning of 10 October 1974, with no inkling of what was to come, VP set out—as he often did those days—on a morning drive in his old Jeep. His wife and he were set to leave for Allahabad that evening and had already told their milkman and their newspaper boy to temporarily stop delivering from the next day. On his way, he spotted Uma Shankar Dikshit's wife out on her morning walk and offered to drop her home. (Dikshit was then the country's home minister. But it was to be his last day as one—in the reshuffle, he was made minister without any portfolio.) She accepted. En route, she said,' Something was decided about you last night.'

She said no more, but VP understood and his hunch was confirmed a few hours later, when he got a call from Indira's private secretary, R.K. Dhawan. Dhawan did not give away anything either, merely asking him to stay at home all day. By late afternoon came the invitation from President Fakhruddin Ali Ahmed—Giri's term had just ended and Ahmed had succeeded him—to the oath-taking ceremony for new ministers at Rashtrapati Bhavan to be held that very evening.[22]

Just before he took his oath, VP was handed a small slip of paper, which said 'Deputy Minister, Commerce'. Following the ceremony—and after VP had faced, for the first time in his life, a barrage of photographers with their popping flashbulbs—he and the other newcomers were met, in a separate room, by Indira, who exchanged pleasantries with them. On the way home, VP found that all the streetlights seemed red to him, realizing later—on reading up—that he was temporarily suffering from 'flash blindness', the effect of too many flashbulbs going off in his face. The next morning, there were no newspapers delivered at home, so to read about his elevation, Sita Kumari had to go looking for a vendor to buy them from.[23]

The same evening, Dwivedi, the friend who had lobbied for Sant Bux's inclusion in the ministry, visited the latter at home. 'The atmosphere in the house was one of mourning,' he told Thakur later.[24]

It was the beginning of a gradual erosion of links between the once-close brothers. 'My father was somewhat overbearing, and I think V.P. Singh resented that,' said Anand Singh, Sant Bux's son. 'He would tell people unpleasant truths to their faces. To V.P. Singh, he was a typical older brother—always advising him, scolding him. I think once V.P. Singh became deputy minister, he felt he had done better in politics than my father, and that their equation should change. My father did not realize it, so V.P. Singh began distancing himself.'[25] In his profile of Sant Bux, Tully maintained that, years later, VP was contrite. 'There was an element of envy [that led to the estrangement], I have to admit, as often happens between brothers,' he said. 'It's the younger brother who envies.'[26]

❧

VP's joy at his elevation was marred by a personal loss soon after—the unexpected death of his father at seventy-one, after having been ill for the past three to four years.[27] Relations between him and Bhagwati Prasad had always been prickly. It is clear that VP deeply resented his 'abandonment'—being given away in adoption to Ram Gopal Singh at the age of five—for which he held Bhagwati Prasad alone responsible. Not only were their politics at odds, but also their lifestyles. 'He [Bhagwati Prasad] had the imperial ways of a raja and did not approve at all of V.P. Singh's efforts to shun ostentation and live simply,' remembered Ranamata Singh. 'He did not approve of me because he felt I was encouraging V.P. Singh to live the way I did.'[28]

Matters were not helped by Bhagwati Prasad's authoritarian parenting, though it was common enough among fathers of that generation. Both Sita Kumari and VP's sister Vimla Devi confirmed the wide distance Bhagwati Prasad preferred to maintain from his children. 'When he spoke, the sons were expected to just listen,' said Sita Kumari. (Traditions were strictly observed—she herself stayed in purdah whenever she visited Daiya and never once met her father-in-law alone, or without 'my ghunghat almost touching my nose'.)[29] Neither was he overly impressed by any of his sons' achievements. 'The family story goes that when my father's eldest brother, Chandrasekhar Prasad Singh, who had become a lawyer at the Allahabad High Court, got his first fee, my grandfather asked him how much it was,' said Ajeya Singh. 'When my uncle told him, my grandfather replied, "That's what I pay each of my cowherds every month."'[30]

Ajeya Singh also recalled a childhood incident during a visit to his grandfather with VP, which continues to baffle him. 'Babasaheb liked to tease children,' he said. 'He asked me, "You want a gun?" When I said I did, he replied, "I won't give you one." I started crying. He then brought me a small gun, which must have been a toy, and I took it from him happily. All the way home from Daiya to Allahabad, my father kept berating me for having accepted the gift. In fact, he later returned it.'[31]

Even so, VP was deeply upset at his father's passing. 'It was the first time I had lost a close family member, and it jolted me,' he said.[32]

6

'CHAPRASIS SALUTE THE CHAIR I OCCUPY, NOT ME'

Elated as he was at being elevated to deputy minister, V.P. Singh remained grounded. His son Ajeya Singh, who had, by then, completed school and was briefly staying with his parents (as minister, VP also got better accommodation, shifting from his one-bedroom apartment in Vithalbhai Patel House to a bungalow at 19, Safdarjung Road[1]), remembered accompanying his father to his office at Udyog Bhavan one morning. Chaprasis saluted VP as he walked along the corridor to his room.

'Who or what do you think they are saluting?' he asked Ajeya soon after.

'You, obviously,' Ajeya replied.

'No,' said VP. 'They are saluting the chair I occupy. They saluted my predecessors and will do so my successors as well. They would not salute me if I wasn't in that chair.'[2]

When department officials asked VP if he wanted the upholstery, curtains or furniture in his room changed, he was genuinely puzzled and said that he wouldn't want to alter a thing—the room was pretty plush anyway. He was told that new ministers usually asked for changes.[3]

VP's interaction with Indira Gandhi remained minimal, more so because deputy ministers were not included in cabinet meetings. His boss was Debi Prasad Chattopadhyaya, a philosophy professor from West Bengal's Jadavpur University turned politician, minister of state with independent charge of the commerce ministry, much liked by Indira. Unlike most ministers, who want to control every department in their ministries, leaving their deputies almost nothing to do, Chattopadhyaya was ready to delegate, assigning VP exports of textiles and agricultural products, as well as all exports to South Asian and Southeast Asian countries.[4] He clarified that there was no need to consult him on any matter related to these departments, as long as they did not involve policy. He also claimed to be travel-weary and sent VP in his place almost every time an overseas visit was required. Thus it was that within a week of his induction, VP found himself travelling to a city that few get to visit even today—Pyongyang, North Korea.

The paucity of connecting flights—he went via Tokyo and returned via Moscow—forced VP to spend a full week in Pyongyang, where he grew increasingly sick of the blatant promotion of the country's supreme leader Kim Il-sung (grandfather of the present supreme leader Kim Jong-un) he was subjected to. It started at the airport itself, where the terminal he alighted at had huge portraits of Kim Il-sung; every factory he was taken to had its miniature model in a glass case, with the path taken by the supreme leader when he last visited lit up with tiny bulbs. 'Every third sentence of every official I met, whether in a speech or in casual conversation, was about the greatness of the supreme leader,' said VP. 'I twice tried to get the official assigned to escort us to discuss personal matters, but both times he somehow brought his supreme leader into his reply. After that, I gave up.'[5]

Did VP see any parallels between the personality cult being promoted in North Korea and what he would witness in India barely eight months later, starting 26 June 1975? Given his awe of Indira, compounded by his gratitude at having been made a minister, any such comparison would have been blasphemous for him. But the similarities surely existed—especially in the manner that All India Radio, Doordarshan and Films Division of India began to promote Indira and her younger son, Sanjay, once the Emergency was declared, as well as in the ubiquitous hoardings that sprang up on street corners, extolling the former's twenty-point programme for the nation's uplift and the latter's five-point one. In the nineteen months until the Emergency was lifted, in March 1977, more than 100,000 people were jailed[6]—including all senior Opposition leaders (barring the communists), starting with JP himself—the press censored and a series of laws passed by a pliant Parliament to restrict individual freedoms.

VP did admit to a vague foreboding the day the Allahabad High Court pronounced its judgment in the memorable case filed against Indira by her main opponent in the 1971 election, accusing her of corrupt electoral practices. It was 12 June 1975, and he had just driven back to Ahmedabad in Gujarat from Jamnagar, when he saw a large hoarding saying that the court had held Indira guilty in the case (albeit on just two counts out of fourteen), annulled her election and debarred her from contesting for six years. He had been in Jamnagar to campaign for the Congress in the assembly election just concluded.[7]

Though the Congress lost the election—the results began trickling forth the same day, 12 June[8]—VP enjoyed his first experience of campaigning in a state other than his own. 'I was much impressed to find that political activity in Gujarat starts only in the evenings, unlike in UP,' he said. 'The earliest public meetings are scheduled for 4 p.m. During the day, people are busy earning a living.'[9] It also meant that he had no problem taking his afternoon nap.

As Opposition demands for Indira's resignation grew following the judgment, she responded within a fortnight by clamping the

Emergency. Given the ministry he held, and his relatively junior position, VP had no role in enforcing it, but he never protested against it either. Being a deputy minister, he was spared the bizarre cabinet meeting Indira held at 6 a.m. on 26 June 1975 to inform her ministers that the Emergency had already been promulgated by President Fakhruddin Ali Ahmed from midnight, 25 June. (Only eight cabinet ministers and five ministers of state attended the meeting.[10] All the others were away, none having a clue that such a drastic step was being considered. VP's boss, Chattopadhyaya, was in Calcutta in connection with Rajya Sabha elections from West Bengal,[11] and VP learnt of the decision from friends.)

VP's initial reaction echoed a popular middle-class response at the time. 'I thought it would have been better if Indira Gandhi had resigned,' he said. 'I didn't like the fact that senior leaders, including JP, had been arrested. But it cannot be denied that government functioning greatly improved. The change was magical. Trains ran on time; government employees came to work on time.'[12]

By December, he began getting reports of policemen abusing their increased powers but does not seem to have done anything about it. 'I heard that policemen in my area had turned extortionists, threatening to lock up people unless they were paid,' he said.[13] December was also the month that Sanjay Gandhi—who turned into a Rasputin-like figure during the Emergency, holding no position of authority but with an uncanny influence over his otherwise inflexible mother—formally joined the Congress's youth wing, shortly before the party's annual convention that year in Chandigarh.[14] Soon, the Youth Congress was overshadowing the party itself, with Indira happily declaring at the next Congress convention (in Guwahati in November 1976) that it had 'stolen our thunder'.[15] One of Sanjay's 'five points' for national regeneration was enforcing birth control, which the states were prodded to relentlessly pursue, and stories of people being forced to get themselves sterilized began pouring in through 1976.

'Sterilization targets were set for each state and some ministers in UP were so anxious to please the chief minister that they persuaded him to treble the state target, knowing this was a programme dear to him,' said VP. 'Then they got their officials to meet the targets set for their ministries at any cost. Whoever came with any kind of complaint or petition to any ministry, or to any police station, was told that unless he got himself vasectomized, he would not be entertained.' The holding of mass vasectomy 'camps' in villages led to many of those sterilized there not getting the post-operative care they needed, resulting in painful physical complications. Stories swirled about minors, unmarried men and elderly men being vasectomized in the overarching bid to meet quotas. In villages, men hid in fields to avoid being rounded up and dragged to the camps; in several UP towns, people rioted in protest, leading to police firings and nearly fifty deaths.[16]

Fresh Lok Sabha elections were due in March 1976, but Indira used her additional powers under the Emergency to postpone them for a year. 'This was the one time I protested to Indiraji, telling her not to extend the term, but to hold elections right away,' VP said. She heard him out, but that was all. 'By March–April 1976, we realized that sterilization was a serious issue,' he added. 'I think, by the later part of the year, Indiraji realized it too.' He quoted Chattopadhyaya—whose proximity to Indira had been growing— telling him in September that she was keen on early elections to 'get out of this Emergency business'.[17] This was at a time when it was increasingly being said that she would defer elections indefinitely, turning her rule into a permanent hereditary dictatorship, where her son would replace her. Such talk increased when, two months later, in November, she extended the Lok Sabha's term for a second time by yet another year.[18]

VP claimed he interacted directly with Sanjay only once all through the Emergency. 'He called me to his office and said that the import duty on an instrument used in laparoscopic surgery was too high,' he said. (Laparoscopy was widely used in sterilization even then.) 'I examined the matter and found the demand perfectly reasonable, so I agreed to it.' They also attended political rallies together across UP but, said VP, 'Sanjay never once spoke to me.'[19] Even Indira rarely sent for him, preferring to deal with Chattopadhyaya. 'I was never part of Indiraji's durbar,' he said. 'She had much smarter people around her. I only met her when I needed some advice, or on occasions like a dinner for MPs she held, or on her birthday, when I would visit her to wish her. I knew she was extremely busy—why take up her time unless it was something very important?'[20]

Indira must have appreciated his work, though, for, in a minor cabinet reshuffle in December, she promoted Chattopadhyaya to full-fledged cabinet minister for commerce, and VP to minister of state. But his tenure proved short. On 18 January 1977, validating Chattopadhyaya's revelation to VP in September but confounding almost everybody else, she announced elections for March, lifted press censorship and released almost all political prisoners. Though he never said so to Indira, VP felt that it was a mistake to hold polls so soon after freeing her jailed opponents. 'We should have released the political prisoners much earlier and given them time to let off steam, work off their bile, get themselves garlanded, and so on,' he said. 'After that, with the Opposition's initial tempo spent, we should have gone to the people, begged their forgiveness for our mistakes during the Emergency and placated them. Only then, after another reasonable time gap, should we have announced elections.'[21]

Within days of their release, pushed hard by JP, the leaders of the four main Opposition parties—the rump Congress (O), which Indira had broken away from; Charan Singh's party, now called Bharatiya Lok Dal (BLD); the Hindu nationalist Jan Sangh; and the few socialists still remaining (most of them had quit the PSP and SSP much earlier, either to join the ruling Congress or

Charan Singh)—accomplished, despite their disparate ideologies, what they had failed to do for years before. Terrified at the prospect of Indira re-imposing dictatorship if she won, they agreed to drop their individual identities and merge into a single party, the Janata Party, and oppose her together. Within a fortnight, the united Opposition was further strengthened by another dramatic turn, as VP's old frenemy Bahuguna also joined it, along with another of Indira's senior-most ministers, Agriculture Minister Jagjivan Ram. Both claimed to have felt 'suffocated' under the Emergency dictatorship, though they had never said a word against it while its draconian provisions were in force.

As a minister from the state, VP was included in the committee formed to decide the Congress nominations to all the 85 Lok Sabha seats in UP. He could thus have contested from any seat he wanted and wondered whether to run from Phulpur again or shift to Allahabad—to which, after all, he really belonged. He asked Sant Bux, with whom his ties had weakened but not completely snapped. 'It doesn't really matter where any of us contests from,' Sant Bux replied. 'Sanjay Gandhi's family-planning drive has ensured that we are all going to lose.'[22] VP eventually settled for Allahabad, where his Janata Party opponent turned out to be not Bahuguna—who had contested and won in 1971, and had chosen Lucknow this time—but his old opponent, Janeshwar Mishra, who, too, had shifted from Phulpur as the Janata Party candidate.

In an early tour of his constituency, VP found Sant Bux's assessment confirmed. (For all his pessimism, Sant Bux, too, contested again from Fatehpur.) 'We wanted to slap the Congress hard this time, but since you are contesting, we may restrain ourselves,' he was repeatedly told.[23] From other constituencies came reports of Congress candidates being asked to show medical certificates testifying that they had been vasectomized if they wanted votes, just as voters had been forced to during the Emergency whenever they sought government help. A desperate

VP, for the first time, even roped in his wife to help him. 'I went from house to house in Allahabad city, accompanied by a group of women Congress workers, seeking votes,' Sita Kumari recalled. 'I didn't have to speak; other women did the talking. I merely did a namaste.'[24]

VP was indiscreet enough to confess his fears about the Congress's prospects to a few party colleagues. One of them tattled to Indira when she came campaigning in Allahabad. She had contracted herpes, had lesions around her mouth and was running a fever, but it was VP's health she enquired about. 'Are you okay? I heard you were feeling weak?' she asked him when they met.[25]

VP got the hint. 'I'm fine, and I'll prove it by getting the highest number of votes among the three candidates we've put up in this district—from Allahabad, Phulpur and Chail,' he said he had replied. (He kept his word.) 'But I must be frank with you. We are facing a tough battle.'[26]

The outpouring of rage against Emergency 'excesses'—a term very popular at the time—expressed through the ballot box exceeded even VP's apprehensions. The Congress failed to win a single seat in UP—the Janata Party got all 85. Indira herself lost her Rae Bareli seat by around 50,000 votes to Raj Narain—the same diehard socialist who had opposed her in the 1971 election and, on losing, filed the case that precipitated the Emergency. Sanjay, contesting from neighbouring Amethi, was defeated by a bigger margin. Janeshwar Mishra avenged his 1971 defeat by polling around 90,000 more votes than VP. Sant Bux was crushed by more than 175,000 votes. Bahuguna won by more than 150,000 votes over his nearest rival, as did Charan Singh from Baghpat by about 125,000 votes.[27]

Countrywide, the Congress crashed to its lowest tally until then—154 seats out of 542, decisively defeated by the two-month-old Janata Party, which won 295.[28] (With allies, its strength went up to 330 seats.[29]) For the first time since Independence, a non-Congress government assumed power at the Centre. Morarji Desai, who had contested the prime ministership against Indira in 1966 and lost, gained the seat at the age of eighty-one. Charan Singh became home minister at seventy-four. VP remained stoic. '*Haar-jeet hoti rehti hain* (There will always be victories and defeats),' he told Sita Kumari when she sought to sympathize.[30]

7

'IF WE SHARED POWER WITH HER, WE SHOULD ALSO SHARE DEFEAT WITH HER'

It was not only the new government—whose leaders she had jailed—that hit out at Indira Gandhi once she lost the 1977 election. Almost all her senior colleagues in the Congress (R) (barring those who had actively helped enforce the Emergency), convinced that she was now a political liability, began speaking out against her too. (None had uttered a critical word against her during the Emergency; some had been among her foremost flatterers.) At the first Congress Working Committee meeting after the defeat, in mid-April, the bulk of members ganged up to expel Bansi Lal, defence minister during the Emergency and one of Indira and Sanjay Gandhi's leading henchmen, from the party, for his 'undemocratic, autocratic and undignified actions' at the time, which 'damaged the image of the party'[1]—a step widely seen as a putdown of Indira herself. As accounts of human rights abuses and corruption scandals during the Emergency began increasingly appearing in the freshly liberated press, every Congress member had to decide whether to join Indira's detractors or her few supporters.

V.P. Singh dithered only briefly. He had problems of his own too at the time, chief among them being homeless in Delhi. He'd had to vacate 19, Safdarjung Road once he was no more a minister. His son Ajeya had graduated and left for London to study chartered accountancy the previous year, but Abhay was at home after finishing school, preparing to take the pre-medical exam. VP was keen to remain in the same house until the exam was held, so that Abhay's preparation could continue undisturbed. But thanks to the Emergency, relations between the new government and members of the old had turned so bitter that his request to extend his stay was turned down.[2]

Having lost the election, he wasn't entitled to MP accommodation either. The family lived with different relatives and friends for short periods. It was while VP was at his wife's aunt Lakshmi Chundawat's[3] home that a senior Congressman remembered catching him just as he was coming out of the bathroom in a towel. When asked whom he intended to back, VP replied, 'I'm still thinking about it.'[4]

But by late April, after attending a few meetings of both camps of Congressmen, VP had made up his mind—Emergency excesses notwithstanding, he would continue to support his idol. He made his reasons clear during a telephone conversation with Karan Singh, the son of the maharaja of Jammu and Kashmir, who had been health minister through the Emergency and thus ultimately responsible for the overreach of the family-planning drive, though, in fact, he had been completely marginalized by Sanjay during the period.

Karan Singh informed him that barring Kamalapati Tripathi and a few others, all top Congress leaders had decided to oppose Indira for her jettisoning of 'basic human values' during the Emergency. 'We should have raised this when we were sharing power with her, and not when she has lost power,' VP replied. 'If we have shared power with her during the Emergency, we should also share defeat with her. If and when she is back in power, we could take up the issue again. But when she is out of power, we should not leave her.' He repeated his view at a meeting in the house of a Congress leader from Kerala, where many spoke against Indira. 'If you had integrity, you should have said all this when the Emergency was on,' he told one of them.[5]

VP and Sita Kumari briefly shifted back to Allahabad, leaving Abhay with friends, but whenever VP was in Delhi—which was often—he would visit Indira. She had moved from the Prime Minister's residence at 1, Safdarjung Road to 12, Willingdon Crescent, from which initially she hardly stepped out, even within Delhi. VP often found her alone and despondent and, on the day Bansi Lal was thrown out of the Congress, in tears.[6] Though they had known each other for years, it was only during this period that he felt he was establishing a rapport with her as he urged her to resume political activity. 'People are angry with you, but you are still in their hearts. Start meeting people, don't sit back,' he advised.[7] Their meetings became more frequent after VP finally decided to buy a flat in Delhi—in south Delhi's Kailash Colony[8]— so that Abhay would have some permanence.

Indira took VP's advice. Her first trip out of Delhi, at the end of July 1977, was to meet Vinoba Bhave, now living quietly at his ashram in Paunar, to seek his blessings.[9] By the following month, she had regained enough chutzpah to visit a critically ill JP in Patna and seek his blessings as well. The second trip's actual destination, however, was Belchi, a village 60 km south-east of Patna, where eleven people, including eight Dalits, had been tied up and shot dead in May. Astonishingly, not a single Janata Party leader had yet visited to commiserate with the victims' families. It was monsoon and the road was so bad—waterlogged in places, non-existent in others—that Indira had to ride an elephant during the final stretch to reach the spot. Her visit re-established her credentials as a champion of Dalits, while the local and Central governments appeared insensitive and Dalit-unfriendly in comparison.

Her third and fourth outings, both in September 1977, were to UP—the first to some western districts, up to Haridwar (now part of Uttarakhand), and the second to her constituency, Rae Bareli.[10] VP accompanied her on the second tour, travelling by overnight train from Delhi. 'None of us in her entourage got any sleep that night because at every station we stopped, despite the lateness of the hour, there were large crowds waiting to welcome her,' said VP. 'When the train began moving to depart, people would keep running alongside on the platform for as far as they could go, reluctant to let her out of their sight.'[11] The public meeting at Rae Bareli was a huge success, with many expressing regret for having voted against her.[12] Rejuvenated, Indira now began travelling all over the country, seeking to win back popular support, making many more trips to UP too, at all of which VP was by her side.

Soon, Indira also tried to reassert her dominance over the Congress party by dislodging its president, Kasu Brahmananda Reddy—home minister during the Emergency—and becoming party president herself. (Two months after the March defeat—and the resignation of the previous president, D.K. Barooah, who took responsibility for the dismal electoral performance—it was she who had supported his elevation to Congress president.) But most of her senior colleagues would have none of it, more so because she refused to distance herself from Sanjay Gandhi or any of the other perpetrators of Emergency excesses. Marshalling her supporters in every state—with VP playing an active role in doing so in UP— Indira then set about splitting the Congress once more, resigning from the Congress Working Committee in mid-December and calling for a national convention of all Congress workers on the first and second days of the new year, 1978.

At the meeting, attended only by her supporters in the Congress, she was unanimously chosen as president of the new party. Thenceforth, the 'R' in the Congress (R) would stand for 'Reddy', not 'Requisitionists', while the new outfit was called the Congress (I), after Indira. Setting up units in each state, Indira made Mohsina Kidwai, a former state minister from Barabanki district whom she was particularly close to, the UP unit's president, while VP became one of the general secretaries.

∽

While in Opposition, for the first time in his life, VP took part in street protests against the government, ending up in jail on three occasions.

The Janata Party government, anxious to punish Indira for the abuses of the Emergency, set up a string of commissions of enquiry to probe its different aspects, but found it extraordinarily difficult to fix responsibility on her. Despite their decade-long rivalry culminating in his Emergency imprisonment, Prime Minister Morarji Desai insisted that penal action against her should be within the confines of the law, and besides, the draconian laws she had used to jail her political opponents should not be used against her.[13] Home Minister Charan Singh, in contrast, believed that her crimes called for 'a trial on the Nuremberg model'[14] and was so impatient to put her in jail that he blundered badly, getting the Central Bureau of Investigation (CBI) to arrest her on 3 October 1977 but on charges so flimsy, the metropolitan magistrate hearing the case against her the next day promptly dismissed them and released her.

Indira made the most of the goof-up, insisting that it was indubitable proof of the witch-hunt the government had launched against her. All through 4 October 1977, even as she was being released, her supporters blocked several of Delhi's streets in protest, which led to the police using tear gas to disperse them in some cases. Among those protesting on Delhi's Parliament Street was VP, where he got his 'first taste of tear gas, which felt like a hundred ants biting all over my face'.[15] Indira's strategists decided that though she was free again, the agitation against the Janata Party government for daring to imprison her should continue. Accordingly, VP proceeded to Allahabad, where he got about 500 volunteers to court arrest along with him.

Dark, burly and sporting a ferocious moustache, Allahabad-based Congress worker Ramesh Pande was among those who accompanied VP to Naini jail, on the outskirts of the city—a landmark location where many freedom fighters, including Jawaharlal Nehru, had been incarcerated in pre-Independence times. 'Prisoners were divided into "A" and "B" categories, where the former got better facilities,' Pande recalled. 'VP was classified among the "A" prisoners, while the rest of us were "B", but he refused the associated privileges barring one, that of a daily lump of butter. He gave it to the cook to add tadka to our watery dal.'[16] Even so, his status as former minister and ex-raja seemed to have set VP apart. Sita Kumari would visit him, taking fruits and home-cooked food with her, which VP promptly distributed among his co-prisoners. 'He didn't seem like a prisoner, the way he was ordering people around,' she said.[17]

VP's own memories of his first incarceration were more sombre. He recalled,

It started with a hunger strike. There was an old man among us protestors, and while we were being driven to the jail in a police van, he kept begging for the van to be stopped, so he could step out and pee. The police accompanying us refused to do so, and the old man wet himself. On reaching the jail, we refused all food unless action was taken against those cops. After three days, some political leaders came to the jail and steps were subsequently taken.[18]

With the comforts he was used to, jail life must have been an ordeal, but VP bore it stoically. 'As an "A" class prisoner, I was entitled to a bed, but I refused it and slept on a concrete platform like the others,' he said. 'Though it was October, it was fairly cold already, and the single blanket issued by the jail of limited help.'[19]

Some memories were plain disgusting. 'The chapatis would have grit in them, which one could feel between one's teeth as one chewed,' he said. 'The trick was to chew just once or twice, and then swallow the lump, or else it became impossible to consume it.' He observed jail staff kneading the flour into dough by stomping repeatedly on it, rather than use their hands. Worst of all were the toilets. 'They were flush toilets, but the flushes didn't work,' he said. 'I threw up the first time I entered one and had to come out immediately. There were different prisoners' faeces piled one on top of another, like a multi-layered cake.' But he still refused bail and spent a week inside.[20]

His second jail stint, for just a day, on 16 March 1978,[21] followed a procession the Congress (I) had organized in Lucknow to highlight the problems of the state's sugarcane farmers. Starting from the city's Begum Hazrat Mahal Park, the procession leaders wanted to make their way to the Vidhan Sabha and present a memorandum to the chief minister but had been told by the police in advance that they would not be allowed beyond the General Post Office in Hazratganj, about a kilometre from their destination. Some of them sought to hoodwink the police and use by-lanes to reach the Vidhan Sabha, while others raised slogans to distract them, following which the police lathi-charged and the crowd responded with stone-pelting. VP considered himself lucky to have escaped being thrashed, but he was picked up by a passing police Jeep and hauled to the district jail on the city's outskirts. 'Usually, political leaders are at the front of any procession, which the police know, and treat them relatively better,' he said. 'But I was somewhere in the middle, since I wanted to be with my group from Allahabad.'[22]

The jail could not cope with the arrival of so many prisoners all at once. 'In some ways, the second stint was worse than the first, because the jail was heavily overcrowded and the prisoners got neither water nor food all day,' Sita Kumari Singh remembered VP telling her.[23] He ate his first morsel following the arrest at 2 a.m. 'Some Congress (I) sympathizer brought loads of poori-sabzi to the jail, which was duly distributed,' he said. In the morning, the jailer informed the protestors that they were free to leave, but VP insisted on staying until he got a certificate discharging him. 'Or else you might call us absconders later,' he reasoned.[24] The lathi charge and arrests had their sequel in the UP Vidhan Sabha the next day, with Congress (I) MLAs interrupting the governor's address in protest, and rival MLAs flinging footwear and paperweights at one another.[25]

VP's third and longest incarceration—for eighteen days— came in December 1978, once again for protesting the arrest and detention of Indira when she was held for a week. This re-arrest followed the Janata Party government's mounting frustration at its inability, once she had formed the Congress (I), to prevent her inexorable political revival. In the nine state assembly elections held in June 1977, three months after the Congress's debacle in the March general election, the Congress had fared just as badly, losing in every state except Tamil Nadu—and that, too, only because it was in alliance with the dominant regional party there, the All India Anna Dravida Munnetra Kazhagam (AIADMK).

But once Indira broke away, her Congress (I) won in two of the five states—Andhra Pradesh and Karnataka—where assembly elections were held in March 1978, less than three months after the party had been formed. More than the Janata Party, it was the rival Congress (R) that was crushed in both states. In a third state, Maharashtra, the Congress (I) did well enough to prevent any of the three main parties from gaining a majority. Eventually, Congress (R) leaders put aside their pride and agreed to a coalition government with the Congress (I).[26]

Janata Party leaders drew consolation from the fact that none of the three states where the Congress (I) had done well was in north India, its bastion, where it had swept the March 1977 election. But the by-elections in May 1978, especially the Lok Sabha poll in Azamgarh in eastern UP in the heart of north India, put paid to the delusion that its support was still intact. In Azamgarh, the Congress (I) candidate was its UP president, Mohsina Kidwai, who beat her nearest Janata Party rival by over 35,000 votes, while the Congress (R) candidate finished a distant third.

VP spent about ten days campaigning for Kidwai, taking charge of one of the blocks. 'I reached Azamgarh town late in the evening to find that all the hotels, state-owned guest houses and dak bungalows had been booked by the government in advance, just to make it difficult for Opposition party leaders to camp there,' he said. 'I spent that night in my car. Next morning, I had to go hunting for a bathroom. Fortunately, a chowkidar at one of the dak bungalows allowed me to briefly use the bathroom of one of the reserved rooms whose occupant had yet to arrive.' Similarly, Indira got no place to stay at first, when she came to campaign. 'But we found private accommodation for her,' he added.[27] There were two other UP by-elections to the Vidhan Sabha at the same time too, and the Congress (I) won them both as well.

Indira's next comeback step was to stand for the Lok Sabha herself in a by-election from Chikmagalur in Karnataka in November 1978, which she won by more than 70,000 votes,[28] despite all the top Janata leaders campaigning vigorously against her, reminding voters of the horrors of the Emergency. But within a month, a Privileges Committee of the Lok Sabha, packed with Janata Party members, held her guilty of having obstructed—back in 1974—officials investigating a case related to Maruti Udyog

Ltd, the auto company Sanjay was then trying unsuccessfully to set up. (It was said to have received numerous undue governmental favours, thanks to his mother being the Prime Minister.) As punishment, after an acrimonious debate, the Lok Sabha voted in favour of stripping her of her newly acquired membership and sending her to jail until the session ended. Accordingly, Indira was imprisoned from 19 to 26 December.[29]

Congress (I) workers responded violently across the country, even provoking police firing, which killed around twenty people.[30] Two of them hijacked an Indian Airlines flight from Calcutta to Delhi, forcing it to land in Varanasi before meekly surrendering.[31] Thousands courted arrest, with VP leading the Allahabad group. 'We were expecting the arrest, so we had more time to plan than on the previous occasion,' he said. 'We got some 4,000–5,000 people to join us.' It was back to Naini jail, where neither the food served nor the toilets had improved one bit. The weather and the overcrowding made it worse. 'We were held from late December into early January, and it was bitterly cold,' said VP. 'This time I'd had a razai [quilt] delivered from home. I'd spread the jail-provided blanket on the concrete platform and wrap myself every night in the razai, but felt cold even then. I'd wake up very early every morning, freezing.'[32]

So many people had courted arrest that the jail ran out of blankets. 'All of us were coughing and some were running a fever too. The jail doctor who came to see us caught the infection from us and was soon coughing just as badly,' said VP. Morale fell. 'By the twelfth or the thirteenth day, many prisoners pleaded they wanted to post bail and leave. We allowed those seriously ill to do so.'[33]

Finally, a magistrate arrived at the jail and released them all. 'V.P. Singh was the last to depart,' said Ramesh Pande, who accompanied him on this occasion as well. 'He stayed behind to ensure there were no problems with anybody's release papers. It showed his character.'[34]

VP's strength of character was also underlined in another unrelated episode that had occurred a few months earlier. In early September 1978, excessive rains led to floods across north India, from Punjab to West Bengal, with all the rivers in spate, killing around 850 people and displacing several million. Many areas in Allahabad (and in Delhi too) went underwater.[35] 'Within days, a team of us Congress (I) workers, led by VP, began going from village to village in the region south of the Yamuna in Allahabad, making extensive notes of the damage that had occurred and reporting to the district administration,' said Pande. 'One day, while crossing the turbulent Belan river on a boat, we were caught in a whirlpool. The boat spun round and round and the boatman couldn't do anything about it. We shrieked and shouted, fearing it was the end. But V.P. Singh remained impassive, seemingly unmoved. Finally, since we were not too far from shore, the boatman managed to fling a rope across, with one end tied to the boat, and people there grabbed it and dragged us out.'[36]

There were minor stumbles too in Indira's renascent to power. Three Lok Sabha by-elections in north India after her Chikmagalur victory all saw the Congress (I) losing, albeit by narrow margins— Samastipur (Bihar) in November 1978, Fatehpur (UP) in early December, and Khandwa (Madhya Pradesh) in February 1979.[37] Fatehpur was a personal embarrassment for VP, since he knew the region well—it was next door to Allahabad, and he'd worked there for Sant Bux in 1967—and was deeply involved in the campaign. (Sant Bux did not contest this time; the Congress (I) candidate was a former MLA from one of Fatehpur's assembly segments, Prem Dutt Tiwari, while the Janata Party put up a local lawyer,

Syed Liakat Husain.) VP remembered the crowds as hostile, memories of the Emergency still fresh among them. 'At one public meeting, people began pelting stones at Indira Gandhi, but she insisted on continuing with her speech,' he said. 'We formed a human wall around her to protect her.'[38]

Ultimately, these setbacks hardly mattered as the Janata Party government imploded four months after the Khandwa by-election. Hailing from UP, where the party had won all 85 seats, and with his influence extending to MPs in neighbouring states as well, Charan Singh had felt from the start that he was more deserving of the Prime Minister's post than Morarji Desai, since he had many more MPs supporting him than did Desai (who hailed from Gujarat, with just twenty-six MPs). (Desai had been JP's choice after the party, unable to decide for itself and reluctant to hold a contest, suggested that JP name the Prime Minister.)

After a series of public spats with Desai on a range of issues—not the least of them being the imperative of speedy and harsh punishment for Indira, where he accused Desai of being tardy—Charan Singh finally quit the government in July 1979 to set up a new party, the Janata Party (Secular), taking eighty (rising to ninety-seven in the next few weeks)[39] of the Janata Party's 295 MPs with him. Desai, losing his majority, resigned.

Blinded by his prime ministerial ambition, Charan Singh then sought to form a government with the support of both the Congress parties—the Congress (R) (now called the Congress [U] after Devraj Urs (who'd taken over as president from Reddy), which had 82 seats, and the Congress (I), which had 72—as well as some regional parties. The same man who, only a year ago, had said that Indira deserved to be 'whipped in public' now wooed her, and she in turn agreed to be wooed, providing him 'outside support' (without joining the government, unlike the other Congress, which did). When an astonished VP asked her why, she merely smiled.[40]

He soon found out. Days after Charan Singh was sworn in, she sought to abolish the special courts that had been set up to try cases related to Emergency excesses as a pre-condition for her party's support. When Charan Singh, the prime mover behind the special courts, baulked at doing so, she promptly withdrew her party's backing, leaving the president little choice but to dissolve the Lok Sabha and call for fresh Lok Sabha elections in January 1980.

VP prepared to contest from Allahabad again but discovered that he had a rival claimant for the Congress (I) ticket—his frenemy Bahuguna, who had quit the Congress soon after the 1977 Lok Sabha elections were announced to protest the Emergency, and teamed up with the Janata Party. He had been minister for chemicals and fertilizers in Morarji Desai's cabinet and finance minister in Charan Singh's, but had sneaked his way back into the Congress (I) weeks before the election and wanted to contest from Allahabad too. Bahuguna had won the seat in the 1971 election, but had shifted to Lucknow in 1977, winning from there as well.

VP was half-inclined to shift to Fatehpur, where, too, he believed he could easily win,[41] until he heard from party workers that Bahuguna had been telling them that after his 1977 defeat from Allahabad, VP was 'finished' there, with no hope of ever winning again. In response, he informed Indira that he would not contest any seat other than Allahabad—if it was denied him, he'd rather not contest at all. 'I was outside Indira Gandhi's house when Bahuguna visited her, carrying a big bouquet of flowers,' said VP. 'But she told him, "Nothing doing."'[42] Since Bahuguna had been born in the Garhwal Himalayas—though his political base had always been Allahabad—Indira insisted that he fight from Garhwal.

Bahuguna wanted tickets for some of his close aides too, who had followed him into the Congress (I), and after much bargaining, Indira and Sanjay agreed to nominate some of them. (Sanjay's was the dominant role in choosing party candidates for UP in this election; in a number of cases, Indira refused to get into details of different contenders for particular seats, telling her party workers, 'Speak to Sanjay.'[43]) Among Bahuguna's men was Ram Nihore Rakesh, who was nominated from the Chail seat in the Allahabad district, dashing the hopes of Dharam Vir, a two-time MLA from one of the assembly segments within Chail and a friend of VP, who had been promised this seat earlier.

VP found Dharam Vir pacing up and down in his room at Delhi's UP Bhavan, furious. He said that since the Congress (I) wasn't giving him a ticket, he had spoken to Charan Singh and intended to fight as the Janata Party (S) candidate from Chail instead. Alarmed, VP took him to meet Sanjay. At the gate of 12, Willingdon Crescent, however, he asked Dharam Vir to wait while he went in.

Chail was a seat reserved for Dalits, and while making Dharam Vir's case before Sanjay, VP pointed out that Dharam Vir belonged to the Pasi community among Dalits, which had largely stood by the Congress even in the 1977 polls when most others, including the dominant Dalit community of the Jatavs (or Chamars), had voted for the Janata Party. He noted that another Pasi hopeful had been denied the Congress (I) ticket from the Sitapur seat and that such exclusion could cost the Congress (I) Pasi votes across the state.

Sanjay's response underlined both his capriciousness and his dominance of the UP Congress (I) at the time. 'The tickets have been decided, but would your friend like to be president of the UP Congress (I) instead?' he asked.

VP was startled—the offer was much better than Dharam Vir could have ever expected. 'Why don't you speak to him yourself? He's just outside, at the gate,' he replied.[44]

Sanjay did, and soon after, Dharam Vir was named president of the UP Congress Committee, replacing Mohsina Kidwai, and gave up all intention of contesting the upcoming poll.

The Janata Party's rule had been marked not only by dissension within its ranks but also widespread unrest—Hindu–Muslim clashes, attacks on Dalits by upper and middle castes (as in Belchi), violent student agitations across campuses (including Allahabad University) and workers' strikes. 'The freedom from dictatorship the new government undoubtedly brought was interpreted by some people as the freedom to do whatever they liked, and that led to chaos,' a Communist Party leader, Atul Anjaan, said later.[45] The relative stability that Indira promised—'Elect a government that works' was her primary campaign slogan this time—together with the division of her opponents' votes between the Janata Party and the Janata Party (S), made her success as sweeping as in 1971. The Congress (I) won 353 of the 492 seats it contested (out of 529 where polls were held), including 51 of UP's 85 seats.[46]

Indira won overwhelmingly from Rae Bareli (as also from another seat she had contested, Medak in Andhra Pradesh), as did Sanjay from neighbouring Amethi. VP, too, won easily in Allahabad—even the combined tally of his Janata and Janata (S) opponents' votes was well below his. Indeed, the trend was clear much before the votes were polled. 'Sarju Pande,[47] who fought on the Janata Party ticket from Allahabad, was a relative of mine,' said Ramesh Pande. 'But he urged me not to ruin my political future by supporting him, but to work for V.P. Singh instead.'[48] Bahuguna, too, won a handsome victory in Garhwal.

Overall, although Charan Singh's Janata Party (S) did not fare too badly in UP, winning 29 of the 34 seats the Congress (I) lost, its nationwide tally was just 41 seats. Desai's Janata Party did even worse, getting a total of only 31 seats.[49] The other Congress, which contested in alliance with the Janata Party (S), won but 13 of the 212 seats it fought, and over the next few years, withered away, with most of its leaders, in ones and twos, trickling into Indira's party.

Part 3

UP AND ITS DISCONTENTS

1

'SINGING PRAISES OF THE LEADER IS PART OF CONGRESS CULTURE'

Uttar Pradesh, the most populous state in the country—low on economic and human development indicators, high on caste and communal tensions, violent crime and corruption—was always notoriously difficult to govern. The political instability that started in the mid-1960s with the weakening of the Congress's hold over the state made it even more so. Between 1971, when V.P. Singh won his first Lok Sabha election and thereafter involved himself more in national politics, and 1980, when Indira Gandhi came back to power, it had seen five chief ministers—three from the Congress and two from the Janata Party—none of whom came close to completing their terms or solving the state's problems.

Given the proximity to Indira he thought he had acquired during her years out of power, VP had been disappointed when he did not figure in the first list of twenty-one ministers[1] she announced on her return as Prime Minister in January 1980. 'I couldn't understand why,' he said later. 'Had I done something wrong? February–March–April passed, and there was still nothing [for me].'[2]

Even so, he was nonplussed—and none too pleased, knowing the challenges he would face—on being summoned to Sanjay Gandhi's presence on the morning of 7 June 1980 and tersely told, 'If you are asked to take over as chief minister of UP, don't refuse.'

Despite the directive and his awe of Indira, he did protest feebly when, the next day, she called him out of a meeting and made the offer. 'I'm not fit for UP politics,' he said.

'Do you think I'm fit for politics at all?' she replied.

VP's honest answer would have been, 'There is no better politician in the country than you.' But he knew that her question was rhetorical—she liked to think of herself as a reluctant politician—and did not object any further.[3]

Indira's decision ended six days of farce that had begun ever since the results of the UP assembly elections became known. Held in end-May, they gave the Congress (I) a resounding win of 309 out of 425 seats.[4] Just as the Janata Party, soon after coming to power in March 1977, had promptly dismissed several Congress-ruled state governments and held fresh polls, winning all but one of them, so too did Indira dissolve nine state assemblies being ruled by the Janata Party—including UP—and held elections once more, with similar results, this time in the Congress (I)'s favour. With many senior UP Congress leaders staying with the Congress (U) and Kamalapati Tripathi already named Union railways minister, the contest for the UP chief minister's position was wide open. Most of the newly elected Congress (I) MLAs were first-timers, little known outside their constituencies.

On 2 June 1980, two groups of these MLAs—along with most of the Congress (I) MPs from UP—gathered in two separate rooms of Delhi's UP Bhavan to debate who the next chief minister should be. One group consisted predominantly of Rajputs (Thakurs), the other of Brahmins. (Brahmin–Thakur rivalry was endemic in the

UP Congress.) The first group—which VP also joined—was led by Sanjay Singh, the elected MLA from Amethi, who was also then president of the UP Youth Congress and one of Sanjay's closest aides. (Ex-raja of the Amethi estate, Sanjay Singh was then married to Garima, VP's younger brother Har Bux Singh's daughter.) Loudest among the members of the second group was Devendra Pandey, MLA from Jaisinghpur in UP's Sultanpur district, whose sole claim to fame was having been one of the hijackers of the Indian Airlines flight to protest Indira's imprisonment in December 1978. Predictably, neither group could agree on who among them should take over.

Suddenly, Pandey convened a press conference, where he declared, 'I want Sanjay Gandhi to be UP's next chief minister.' As in the previous Lok Sabha election, Sanjay had been the final arbiter in the nomination of UP Congress (I) candidates and certainly deserved to be their leader, but whether Indira, clearly grooming him as her successor, would risk allowing him to mount this extremely wobbly stepping stone remained uncertain. Even so, once the proposal was made, neither group dared oppose it; all wannabe leaders promptly withdrew themselves from contention and both groups began collecting MLA signatures in support of Sanjay. MLAs not in Delhi were hastily met and 283 of their signatures obtained. But expectedly, as soon as Indira heard, she told news agencies that there was no question of Sanjay taking up the job.

Undeterred, the MLAs held a legislature party meeting in Lucknow on 6 June 1980 and passed a unanimous resolution declaring, 'This meeting of the UP Congress (I) legislature party elects Sanjay Gandhi as its leader.' Aware of the Prime Minister's view, however, their resolution also added, 'If the services of Sanjay Gandhi are not available to the state, we request Indira Gandhi to appoint any other person.' A number of MLAs and MPs—including VP—rushed back to Delhi with the resolution and met

Indira, only to get an earful. 'Do you want to destroy him?' she asked. 'He has many other important things to do here. I can't spare him.'[5]

Whether Indira always had VP in mind as UP's next chief minister and hence had kept him out of her ministry, or whether, after the Sanjay-as-CM drama, she was persuaded by her advisers, is impossible to tell. VP's name had never figured in media speculation about likely candidates, either before the election or immediately after the results became known. About 250 of the Congress (I)'s new MLAs had not even met him personally before he became chief minister.[6]

What is generally believed is that Sanjay's advisers at the time convinced him that while Brahmins had always dominated the UP Congress, the Thakurs had voted for it in large numbers this time. Considering that the last three Congress chief ministers of the state had all been Brahmins, it would be wise to nominate a Thakur to consolidate the community's vote in the party's favour.[7] Among all the Thakur probables, VP was the only one none of those involved in the decision-making objected strongly to, most likely because he was not identified with any faction in the party, unlike the others. Sanjay Singh, very influential in those days, may well have lobbied for his uncle-in-law too.

Thus, on 9 June 1980, VP was sworn in as the twelfth chief minister of UP, along with a fifteen-member ministry.[8] 'So many people take up jobs they don't want to, because of circumstances, but they do them with full dedication,' he said later. 'It was the same with me.'[9]

It was a personally inconvenient time as well, since his son Ajeya's wedding was scheduled later in the month—to Shruti Kumari, daughter of Pratap Singh, the raja of Gidhaur (in Bihar)—and it would be hard for him to find time for the preparations.[10] The only consolation was that the Opposition had been mauled in the last election and was also badly divided—with just 99 seats across seven parties—which augured a stable government and relative ease in getting fresh legislation passed.[11]

⟋∞⟍

The Congress (I) party workers' propensity to heap exaggerated praise on Indira, which began after her 1971 Lok Sabha victory, grew to nauseating proportions following her 1980 election win. Realizing that she liked sycophancy and that, but for her support, they could never have won their seats, they used every public opportunity to display how much they venerated her. When she made it clear that Sanjay was her chosen successor, similar fawning attention was directed at him as well. VP, too, did not stint in this regard. 'Sanjay is a leader in his own right, and he is my leader too,' he said in one press interview at the time,[12] and 'What would I be without Sanjay?' in another.[13]

At a public rally in Kanpur, he even called Sanjay 'an avatar of Vivekananda'.[14] It helped him politically, giving the impression that he, too, was among Sanjay's confidantes and hence had been chosen as the UP chief minister; many of those made chief minister in the other states the Congress (I) won were indeed Sanjay favourites. In fact, VP usually had to seek an appointment through Sanjay Singh whenever he wanted to meet Sanjay. Decades later, he was to explain, 'Singing praises of the leader is part of Congress culture, and it is one thing to play that game. But when it came to wrong administrative action (as chief minister), I would never do it.'[15]

It is unlikely that Sanjay ever suggested any such action, however, for, within a fortnight of VP taking over in UP, he was dead. VP was in Delhi on 23 June 1980, waiting in the visitors' room for his appointment with Indira at her residential office at 1, Akbar Road—adjoining her 1, Safdarjung Road home—when, around 8.15 a.m., her private secretary R.K. Dhawan rushed past him and entered her office without knocking. He even overheard

Dhawan say, 'Something terrible has happened.' Soon after, Indira, Dhawan and her visitor—another chief minister—rushed out, jumped into a car and drove away, while VP followed in his own car.[16]

Sanjay had gone out for an early-morning spin in a Pitts S-2A two-seater aircraft he had recently acquired, and while trying out some aerobatic loops had crashed it—both he and his co-pilot had died instantly. By the time the convoy of cars reached the crash site, the police and the military were already there. Sanjay's body had been placed in a military truck and covered with a red blanket.

VP watched Indira climb into the truck and lift the blanket partially, stagger a little and clutch at a truck rail, before covering the body again and stepping down. He finally got to meet her in the late afternoon when she came out of the Ram Manohar Lohia Hospital building, where the body had been taken to be embalmed.[17] 'What can one say at such times?' he said later. 'I said, "We understand your pain." She replied, "Rajya Sabha elections will be held in UP at the end of the month."'[18] Four days later, on 27 June, she was back at work.[19]

Sanjay's elder brother Rajiv had been away in Italy with his wife Sonia, visiting her family, when the crash occurred, but returned the same night. Soon, some Congressmen began suggesting that Rajiv take Sanjay's place in the party. On 24 June itself, eighteen Youth Congress members signed a letter to Indira, proposing that Rajiv be made the organization's president.[20] The clamour to induct Rajiv grew louder in the months that followed, as Congress members realized that this was what Indira, too, desired. In August, a crowd of 300 Congress (I) MPs met Rajiv to try to convince him to take over Sanjay's mantle.[21]

VP, too, joined the chorus. In September, he submitted a memorandum to Indira, signed by all Congress (I) MLAs from UP, requesting her to bring Rajiv into the party.[22] At an All India Congress Committee (I) meeting in Delhi in December 1980, he roared, 'Give us Krishna!', recalling the Mahabharata episode in which both Arjuna and Duryodhana seek Krishna's support before the start of the Kurukshetra war. (When Krishna offers them a choice—his entire army for one, and himself, alone and unarmed, for the other—Duryodhana plumps for the army and proceeds to lose the war, while Arjuna chooses Krishna and wins it.)

VP repeated the assertion at a meeting in Amethi—Sanjay's constituency, now vacant—later in the same month, which Indira, too, attended. '[The] people of Amethi have made their choice. Like the Pandavas, they want Krishna—Rajiv Gandhi. If Lord Krishna is with the people of Amethi, resources will automatically follow,' he said.[23]

Rajiv, however, remained reluctant to enter politics—of which he'd had no experience until then—for nearly a year. Finally, he succumbed to pressure and resigned from Indian Airlines, where he had been a commercial pilot since 1967, to join the Congress (I) in May 1981. The same month, he also filed his nomination as its candidate for the Amethi Lok Sabha by-election, held on 14 June.[24] His quiet temperament a striking contrast to that of his brash and arrogant late brother, he never sought to control UP the way Sanjay had, instead assigning his cousin and close friend, Arun Nehru, for the job.

Nehru, a former chief executive with a paints company, had been drafted into the party after Indira, who had contested from two constituencies in 1980—her traditional seat of Rae Bareli in UP and Medak in Andhra Pradesh—decided she would rather keep the Medak seat. But to continue her family's association with Rae Bareli, which had begun with her late husband Feroze Gandhi winning the seat in 1957, she wanted a family member to represent it and chose Nehru, who duly won the by-election from there in November 1980. It was Nehru who handled Rajiv's Amethi campaign, which Rajiv won by a landslide, getting 258,884 of the

275,412 votes cast.[25] VP was pointedly marginalized, told to spend only one day campaigning in Amethi.[26]

However, VP also had other elections to think about, including his own. He had been MP from Allahabad when chosen as chief minister and had to quit that seat and become a member of either UP's Vidhan Sabha or its Vidhan Parishad (legislative council) within six months. He initially joined the Vidhan Parishad, there being no empty Vidhan Sabha seat at the time, but later decided he preferred to be directly elected to the Vidhan Sabha for greater legitimacy. Fortuitously, Tindwari, an assembly segment of the Fatehpur Lok Sabha seat that he knew well, had fallen vacant, and VP chose to contest it. In all, by-elections for 6 Lok Sabha and 23 Vidhan Sabha seats were being held on 14 June 1981, 5 of the former and 8 of the latter from UP, including the Amethi and Allahabad Lok Sabha seats (the latter vacated by VP).[27]

It was during the Tindwari campaign that VP first displayed his flair for theatre. As an incumbent chief minister, funds were no problem for him, but aware of growing public sentiment against excessive expenditure during poll campaigns, mostly of unaccounted 'black' money, he decided to set an example of austere campaigning—and flaunt the fact. 'I didn't risk losing,' he said later. 'I had the biggest attraction going for me, because everyone wants the chief minister to be their MLA. They think he will do a lot for the constituency.'[28] Besides, he had chosen his constituency carefully—Tindwari was Thakur-dominated, just as the Fatehpur Lok Sabha seat was. Finally, he had established such good relations with the Opposition parties that only one of them put up a candidate against him—and a weak one at that.[29]

VP decreed that no cars would be used in his campaign, only motorbikes and bicycles. He was quoted in the local press telling his workers that if he found this order flouted, he would resign as chief minister. He'd do the same, he added, if he heard that they had tried to 'capture' any booths and stamp ballot papers in bulk in his favour on polling day. While visiting his constituency to file his nomination, he chose not to use either the official car or the state government's chopper, but to instead travel by public transport. (It was another matter that his security could not be dispensed with and thus an entire state transport bus was commandeered for his use alone.)[30]

Still, his margin of victory—votes in his favour surpassing Rajiv's in percentage share of the total count[31]—despite his self-imposed constraints, was extraordinary. It was also a riposte to Nehru, who had deemed his theatrics 'stupid'[32] and conducted one of the most expensive campaigns in the country until then at Amethi,[33] even though Rajiv would have won anyway.

───※───

With the Congress winning 4 of the 5 Lok Sabha seats in UP, as well as all the 7 Vidhan Sabha seats it had contested there (the eighth was left to an allied party, whose candidate lost),[34] the by-poll results should have been a celebratory occasion for VP. It was not, all due to the poll in the fifth Lok Sabha seat, which sparked far more controversy than the ones in either Amethi or Tindwari (whose results were widely expected). This was the Garhwal seat, where VP's old mentor-turned-rival H.N. Bahuguna was a candidate.

Bahuguna's second spell in the Congress had not lasted long. As he'd done before the Lok Sabha election, so too, once the UP Vidhan Sabha polls were announced, he demanded a large number of seats for his supporters who had followed him into the Congress, which Indira and Sanjay—far more confident of their popular appeal by then—refused. With their negotiations collapsing, on 19 May 1980, Bahuguna quit the Congress a second time,[35] along with six other MPs, all his supporters.[36] But while doing so, he also made public two letters he had written—the first to Indira and the second to all Congress workers.

The first included a harsh attack on Sanjay's role in the Congress, which he called 'a matter of grave concern because he does not adhere to any ideology and does not hold any position in the party', going on to criticize 'the arbitrary way in which lists for the Lok Sabha and assembly polls were prepared' and 'the reckless ad hocism in constituting party units'. The letter to Congress workers maintained that 'what binds people in this party is not any sense of comradeship, trust, confidence or of working together' but 'a highly subjective and indefinable test of personal loyalty which debases one to the level of a lackey'.[37] Though he need not have, he also resigned the Garhwal seat he had won on the Congress ticket, and said that he would contest it again on his own steam.

Indira was beyond furious. She was still fuming a year later, when Bahuguna, having launched a new party, the Democratic Socialist Front, filed his nomination from Garhwal when the by-election to the seat was announced. 'We were told that Bahuguna had to be defeated,' said VP. 'It was a prestige issue for the Congress.'[38] The Congress nominated Chandramohan Singh Negi, then minister for hill development in VP's cabinet, against him, and launched an aggressive campaign on his behalf. It sent about eighty-five ministers, including many from the Centre and surrounding states, to campaign for Negi, while Indira herself addressed eleven meetings in the constituency.[39]

However, it was still feared that this would not be enough, and on polling day, VP maintained, the police were directed to help Congress toughs capture booths in Negi's favour. Two people were killed and many more hurt as Bahuguna's men resisted; a contemporaneous report called the election one that 'the nation would long remember, marked by political violence, brutality, intimidation of voters and unabashed exhibition of state and money power'.[40]

More than anything else in his long political career, it was his role in the Garhwal by-election that seemed to have troubled VP. Decades later, unasked by his interviewer, he brought up the matter in his NMML interview, awash in mea culpa. 'I was the chief minister; how can I blame anyone else?' he said.[41] He claimed that he had protested when rigging plans were being drawn up, pointing out that they might recoil on the party, which only led to two others—Sanjay Singh and one of his ministers, Veer Bahadur Singh—who were less scrupulous, being given carte blanche to do whatever they wanted.

'People reacted as I had feared, stoning Congress workers from hilltops, so they had to run for their lives,' he said. Chief ministers from neighbouring states were also involved in the campaign, with one of them—Haryana's Bhajan Lal—bringing along both his state police and his hoodlums. 'I was told that Bhajan Lal had sent his men to buy up all the bamboo available in the local market to be used as lathis to frighten away or beat up voters,' VP added.[42]

Bahuguna himself, while trying to run from attackers on polling day, fell and twisted his ankle, which never fully healed. 'Whenever my ankle hurts, I remember you, and hold you responsible,' he told VP later.[43] Naturally, he complained to the Election Commission, both against the booth-capturing as well as the presence of police from another state. The commission, after conducting its own probe, confirmed the latter charge and since the police had been deployed without its permission, cancelled the election. VP claimed that this was what the Congress wanted as well, as it had gathered that despite the booth-capturing, Bahuguna would have won had the votes been counted. 'We pressured the Election Commission to countermand the election, and it was done,' he said.[44]

The re-poll was set for 22 November, but once again, VP received reports from the constituency that Bahuguna would win if it was held. Top UP officials then appeared before the Election

Commission to argue that the situation in Garhwal was 'explosive' and that the state government could not guarantee security if the election was held,[45] leaving the commission no choice but to postpone it again. The Opposition parties protested loudly against the decision in the Lok Sabha and elsewhere, forcing VP to hold a press conference to clarify that his government had not sought the postponement but merely pointed out the limitations of the security it could provide.

The election was finally held in May 1982 with the same contestants, along with assembly elections to four other states. With the Congress making no special effort this time—Indira's temper presumably having cooled at last—Bahuguna duly won by about 30,000 votes.[46] All the while, VP kept defending his government's actions, his public pronouncements totally at odds with his private misgivings.

2

'I THINK I SHOULD BE REPLACED'

Swearing-in ceremonies, with their boilerplate procedure and script, are usually a bore for the audience. Not so V.P. Singh's as UP chief minister on 9 June 1980. For a start, the announcer, UP's then chief secretary Ram Bahadur Saxena, forgot that the chief minister had to take his oath first and straightaway called out the first name in the list of fifteen ministers he had been given.[1] The error was quickly rectified. Much more startling was the response of VP's nephew-in-law, Sanjay Singh. Called to the dais, he announced that he was grateful to have been chosen as minister but preferred to remain outside the government and work for the party, and calmly returned to his seat.

The incident made national headlines, but, of course, it was pure theatre. Its back story dated from the previous night, when VP was finalizing the ministers' list in Delhi. He later claimed that an emissary had informed him that Sanjay Gandhi did not want Sanjay Singh to be made minister. The next morning, VP met Sanjay to confirm, and received the brusque reply, 'Yes, not now', without any reason given. Soon after, VP was met by an anguished Sanjay Singh, who pleaded that to spare him the humiliation of being left out—because of his closeness to Sanjay Gandhi, everyone expected him to become a minister—they should enact the charade of his turning down the job. VP agreed.[2]

Some have speculated that keeping Sanjay Singh out was VP's own idea,[3] both to scuttle a potential rival and avoid being accused of nepotism, but attributed by him to Sanjay Gandhi after his death. This seems unlikely, and not only because it imputes to VP a Machiavellianism he had never displayed before—or, indeed, in his entire career. Considering Sanjay Singh's apparent closeness to Sanjay Gandhi, VP's own fragile status at the time—he was yet to be sworn in—as well as his awe of the Gandhis, it is most unlikely that he would have chosen to cross Sanjay Gandhi by leaving his favourite out of the cabinet. (It is far more likely that differences had arisen between Sanjay Singh and Sanjay Gandhi, which have never been revealed.) On the contrary, knowing that he owed his position entirely to Indira Gandhi, VP continued to genuflect to her throughout his two-year tenure, repeatedly rushing to Delhi—he spent thirty-one of his first hundred days in office in Delhi, for instance[4]—to seek prior sanction for all important decisions before announcing them.

VP justified his frequent visits to the capital. 'If I had merely written letters, I wouldn't have got a single project sanctioned for UP,' he said. 'I'm prepared to go to the North Pole every day if it helps the people of my state.'[5] But he might well have been more obsequious than he needed to. Once, by his own admission, when he showed Indira a list of the names of people he wanted to include during an expansion of his cabinet, she responded, 'Why are you showing me this, Vishwanath? What do I know of these people?'[6]

Another time, when Indira and he were at a public meeting in Agra together, he praised her lavishly in his speech, drawing much cheer from the audience. He hoped that she had been suitably impressed. But soon after the show was over, she said to him, 'What were you saying, Vishwanath? People were clapping a lot.'

It turned out that she had stuffed cotton balls in her ears during the helicopter flight to Agra from Delhi to muffle the noise and never removed them, sitting through the meeting without hearing a word.[7]

VP always insisted he was given 'complete freedom' to choose his ministers, and had done so by drawing up lists of all the major castes and communities, as well as the main regions of the state, and ensuring that most of them got some representation in the cabinet.[8] But as the Sanjay Singh episode and Indira's response to his list reveal, he always took care to seek clearance beforehand too. He carried out around a dozen reshuffles and expansions of his list of ministers during his tenure, eventually accommodating forty-five of them. He dropped only four—two ministers in December 1980 and two ministers of state in August 1981[9]—and all of them after seeking and getting intelligence reports of their corruption. One, a Muslim, was very influential in his community, and his removal could have cost the Congress (I) votes, but he maintained that Indira never once objected.[10]

A sustained effort to stem corruption was one of the hallmarks of VP's term, though press reports at the time—as they are wont to—kept highlighting instances where he had not done enough.[11] In his political career until then, he had already acquired a modest reputation for personal integrity. Favourite press descriptors of him when he was chosen UP chief minister had been 'little-known MP from Allahabad' and 'known for his scrupulous honesty',[12] which grew manifold during his UP rule.

Within a couple of months of his taking charge, the state vigilance department unearthed a Rs 4 crore scam—40 per cent of the state's health budget then—where government hospitals were caught buying either unauthorized drugs or drugs from unauthorized dealers at inflated prices, in return for kickbacks.[13] In his first three months, more than 1,000 government officials were suspended for various kinds of corruption.[14] VP engaged in some dramatics too, carrying out unannounced inspections of government offices and checking their books, and occasionally accompanying the police on their raids on ration shops hoarding items to sell in the black market.[15]

———∞∞∞———

Tall and thin, with striking features, Somansh Prakash was the MLA from Thana Bhavan in Muzaffarnagar district when VP was chief minister and became a close associate of his. 'There were heavy rains in west UP in 1981, due to which water seeped into the pairs (shelters) where the wheat stalks were stored, and damaged them,' he remembered. 'Farmers managed to save much of the crop, but after threshing, it was found that many of the wheat grains had black spots on them. The flour from this wheat would be fine, but private traders refused to accept the grain, while many government collection centres would first reject it but later accept it at a price much lower than the minimum support price the government had announced and the staff there would pocket the difference. When VP visited Muzaffarnagar, I told him about it. He asked if I knew of any centre that was actually doing so, which I did. At his suggestion, the next morning I took him to Jhinjhana town, about 50 km from Muzaffarnagar, travelling in his helicopter, where we caught the guilty staff red-handed.'[16]

VP also sent out a government order the same day, saying that such 'spotted wheat' should not be rejected.

During his Soraon campaign, following the example of his brother Sant Bux, VP had made it clear that if elected, he would not lobby with ministers on behalf of government employees seeking transfers. Many MLAs, however, were not so scrupulous. They revelled in the power the capacity to arrange—or prevent—transfers gave them over government staff, while some even used this power as an illegitimate income source. On becoming chief minister in June 1980, and after an initial round of personnel changes in his administration, VP extended his ethic on transfers across the state—thenceforth, unless there were compelling reasons, transfers would take place only once a year; the next lot in the following June. 'V.P. Singh was always supportive when I went to him with any request,' said Prakash. 'But if MLAs came asking for transfers, he could get very irritated.'[17]

At first, many MLAs did not take his edict seriously. VP remembered an MLA from Ballia district coming to his home at 10 p.m., seeking to prevent the transfer of the officer in charge (thanedaar) of one of the police stations in his constituency. The chief minister bluntly refused—the officer was being transferred as punishment for serious lapses of duty. 'But the man would not leave,' VP said. 'Dinner arrived; he had dinner with me but kept arguing. I finally said to him, "Here we are, chief minister and MLA, quarrelling past midnight, while the man you are lobbying for is probably comfortably asleep under a fan." He said, "It's a question of my honour." I said, "Your honour depends on a thanedaar? I've been an MLA too, but I never needed a thanedaar's support."' The MLA finally departed, fuming.[18]

Another time, when around twenty MLAs barged into his office seeking removal of a police officer in Allahabad, he told their leader, 'You've brought twenty MLAs with you. When you have so much power and influence, you can always get me transferred.'[19]

His obduracy was hardly likely to endear VP to his party MLAs. (They troubled him far more than Opposition MLAs did.) Many complained that thanks to his policy on transfers, government officials in their constituencies no longer took them seriously.[20] Besides, the consensus between the two main Congress (I) factions on his elevation as chief minister did not last long, and both soon began a whisper campaign against him with Delhi leaders, regularly snitching to them about his alleged sins and errors of omission and commission.

'Dissidence' against the incumbent chief minister had by then become a tradition in the UP Congress—at some stage, every chief minister found some among his MLAs lobbying with Delhi for his removal. So did VP. Some friends advised him to form a group of his own to counter the dissidents, but he refused. 'If I form my group, its members will expect undue favours as reward for supporting me,' he said. 'If I grant them, those not in the group and denied similar favours will turn hostile. The group will gradually try to control my decisions. Why should I fall into that trap?'[21]

Both the factions opposed to VP, and now joined in their common endeavour to get rid of him, were led by ministers in his cabinet—the Brahmins by Lokpati Tripathi, health minister, who was Kamalapati Tripathi's eldest son, and the Thakurs by Veer Bahadur Singh, irrigation and transport minister, and Sanjay Singh's partner in crime in sabotaging the Garhwal by-election.[22] Initially, the dissidents, especially their minister leaders, took care not to speak out publicly against VP (for fear of inviting disciplinary action), preferring to plant speculative reports about the chief minister's impending removal in the local press instead. But by mid-1981, they felt they had gathered enough numbers for a few of them to make a written complaint to Delhi about VP's actions and decisions. The complaint, signed by twenty-two Congress (I) MLAs, which even suggested replacements for VP,[23] was leaked to the press as well.

Unlike other chief ministers, who would either disparage the dissidents among their legislators or avoid reporters' questions about them, VP's public response to the leaked letter was unexpected. 'I think I should be replaced,' he said, when asked about it. 'I'm myself a dissident.'[24]

What did he think about his proposed successors? 'They are all quite capable of running the state efficiently,' he replied. But he also worked effectively to neutralize the dissidents, employing disarming tactics at times. When Indira visited Lucknow on

27 July 1981, for instance, and met party MLAs, soon after the dissidents' list of charges against VP had been made public, he began his speech by noting that his very presence would inhibit the MLAs from telling her what they really thought of him. 'So I'll enumerate their complaints against me myself,' he said, going on to discuss each one and rebutting it.[25]

VP survived the onslaught. Luckily for him, the Brahmin lobby had already been weakened, with Kamalapati Tripathi, Union railways minister at the time, developing differences with Indira, which led her to publicly criticize the railways' functioning, and Tripathi to resign as a result. The leader of the twenty-two MLAs who had signed the letter attacking VP, Azad Kumar Kardam from Agra, was said to be close to Arun Nehru, but Nehru summoned and chastised him for doing so, warning that he would be expelled from the party if he continued such activity. All twenty-two MLAs were issued 'show-cause' notices to explain their conduct. 'Far from listening to the dissidents, Indira Gandhi encouraged me to be firm with them,' said VP.[26]

VP went to great lengths in other ways as well to strengthen his image of being impeccably honest.

'Newspapers are routinely delivered at the chief minister's residence at state expense, so V.P. Singh would carry them all to his office when he left home every morning and leave them there,' said Virendra Dixit, a Congressman from Kanpur close to VP, who later became MLA for two terms. 'For private visits, he would use his own car as much as possible, not his official vehicle.'[27]

But VP knew that setting a personal example was far from enough—for a clean administration, what he needed were incorruptible men at the top, and he set about looking for them. 'Having been away from UP politics for years, V.P. Singh hardly knew any UP bureaucrats, but he sent out his spies, both in the bureaucracy and outside, to pinpoint them, and proceeded to appoint only such men in vital departments,' said Manohar Subrahmanyam, who was commissioner, food, under VP.[28]

Thus, Chief Secretary R.B. Saxena, for instance, who had some allegations against him, was soon replaced by Tribhuvan Prasad Tiwari, while Shashikant Bhatnagar, a UP-cadre officer with impeccable credentials, was brought back from Delhi to head the Agricultural Produce Marketing Committee (APMC), a department rife with corruption. For secretaries to the chief minister, VP chose two men acknowledged by all in the bureaucracy as upright and conscientious—Janardhan Pratap Singh and Bhure Lal. Both had an Allahabad connection—J.P. Singh had studied there and knew two of his brothers,[29] while Bhure Lal had been district magistrate there from 1977 to 1979. 'I conducted the 1977 Lok Sabha election in Allahabad, which V.P. Singh lost, but he knew I had been absolutely fair, and maybe that's why he chose me,' said Bhure Lal.[30] He remains full of praise for his former boss. 'He was very upright and willing to listen to criticism about anyone, even those very close to him,' he added.

But there was a flip side to VP's personal honesty—in his keenness to preserve this image, he also shrank from shielding officers who he knew were falsely accused of malfeasance. Three and a half decades later, Subrahmanyam remained bitter about a vigilance enquiry he had to face. 'We used to procure rice in large quantities from millers to be sold at a controlled price,' he said. 'There was a rule saying that the broken-grain content of the rice should not be more than 15 per cent, or else it was paid for at a much lower rate. Since UP was a rice-surplus state, we used to sell some of our rice to the Centre. It happened once that a consignment of about 25,000 tonnes was found to have much higher broken-grain content, around 25 per cent, so the Centre rejected it. We had paid for it already at the higher rate, because of which UP suffered a loss of around Rs 1 crore.'

Rice grains break if millers process the paddy too quickly, or too much at the same time, which they tend to do to increase volumes and thereby profit. It was plain that somebody in the food department had connived with some millers to buy inferior 'broken' rice at the higher rate. 'I pinpointed the man responsible, hauled him up and transferred him,' said Subrahmanyam. 'But V.P. Singh insisted that he deserved more punishment, so he was suspended as well. At that, the man began approaching MLAs and managed to get twenty-five of them to sign a complaint holding me responsible for the rice scam. V.P. Singh knew everything, and yet he agreed to a vigilance enquiry against me. MLAs blamed me during an assembly debate on the subject, but V.P. Singh remained silent.'[31]

Subrahmanyam was exonerated only in 1985. Years later, after he had retired, during a rail journey, he learnt that VP was on the same train and went to meet him. 'I asked him about the enquiry, and he was not in the least embarrassed,' said Subrahmanyam. 'He said it was nothing personal—he got a complaint and sent it along for proper action.'[32]

In the 2017 Hindi film *Newton*, one of the characters rebukes the protagonist for his '*imandari ka ghamand* (arrogance about his own honesty)'. VP seems to have suffered from a similar failing. 'He thought he was the only honest person around and everyone else was a crook,' said Subrahmanyam. 'It made him "*kaan ke kachche*", ready to believe the worst about others. If his friends told him anything adverse about an officer, he would always believe them.'

J.P. Singh remembered an MLA from the area complaining about him trying to influence the vote in favour of certain candidates in the panchayat election in Basti district. 'I was born in Basti but grew up in Allahabad and had no particular interest in Basti,' he said. 'In any case, why on earth would I want to influence panchayat elections? But V.P. Singh took it very seriously and pulled me up.'[33]

Naturally, apart from being perceived as honest, VP wanted to be regarded as effective too. As MLA, MP, deputy minister and minister of state, he had attracted little press scrutiny, but as chief minister he did so every day. Unused to such limelight, he was initially very sensitive to what was published about him. In his book, *V.P. Singh: The Quest for Power*, veteran journalist Janardhan Thakur relates an incident narrated to him by Rajnath Singh, then editor of the Hindi daily *Swatantra Bharat*. Rajnath Singh, having written a critical commentary on the deteriorating power situation in the state, remembered getting a telephone call from the chief minister at 1 a.m.

Woken up from sleep, at first he couldn't place the caller when the voice at the other end said, '*Main Vishwanath bol raha hoon* (This is Vishwanath speaking).' When that had been clarified, VP said he had just read the report, and added, '*Uska ek ek shabd chubh raha hai, main so nahi pa raha hoon* (Every word in your story is pricking me, I'm unable to sleep).' But when Rajnath Singh met VP the next morning, the chief minister simply chatted with him, not bringing up the story he had protested about at all.[34]

J.P. Singh maintained that VP's angst about hostile coverage led him to unduly pamper the press. 'He gave journalists far more importance than they deserved,' he said. 'With some honourable exceptions, the bulk of Lucknow reporters in those days were talebearers, often with agendas more sinister than merely gathering and publishing news, and forever trying to cadge favours from the government. But V.P. Singh listened to them more than he did to bureaucrats.'

VP was also only too ready to dispense favours. 'The practice of allotting government housing to journalists began under him,' J.P. Singh added. 'It was also completely arbitrary. I suggested that some system be set up, some criteria laid down for allotment, which made me very unpopular with the press.'

J.P. Singh's relationship with VP soon soured. 'He had little idea of how UP worked when he started and sought my advice a lot, not only in administrative matters but also political ones,' he said. 'But he had this terrible weakness about his image—he wanted to be well thought of at all costs. If things went wrong, he would never defend me. And after four or five months, I found I was being cold-shouldered, left out of the loop in many important matters.' In a state ridden with caste rivalries, VP was also anxious to appear impervious to caste considerations—in particular, he had a horror of being seen as promoting his own caste's interests. 'Both he and I were Thakurs, and that added to my problems,' said J.P. Singh. 'I was relieved when he transferred me as secretary, local self-government.'[35]

In his political career, VP had always worked hard, but the load on a chief minister staggered him initially. More than a dozen ledger boxes full of files came to him every day. Each file had to be read and an order passed. 'There were so many meetings and other activities through the day that the only time I got to look at the files was after dinner,' he said. 'I found myself working up to 2–3 a.m. every night, but next morning one had to rise at the usual time and start a new day.'[36] (Here, too, he was punctilious about his oath of secrecy. Sita Kumari, who often handled the files, was asked to remove her reading glasses while doing so, to ensure that she would have no idea of their contents.[37])

'After a fortnight, I felt this couldn't go on,' VP added. 'If I couldn't delegate responsibility, I was incompetent. I called a meeting of senior bureaucrats and we made a list of matters that would be finalized at different levels—which should be dealt with by the department secretary, which by the chief secretary and which by the minister concerned. We decided that only the remaining files would come to me. Thereafter, the number of boxes reaching me fell to two per day.'[38]

His post-dinner slog was thus shortened, but not eliminated. 'V.P. Singh was very conscientious about work,' said Subrahmanyam. 'I often got calls from him at 11 p.m. or even later, seeking clarifications on files.' Senior bureaucrats usually had their weekends ruined too. 'Though he worked every night, there were always files left over,' said Sita Kumari. 'So almost every weekend, if he was in Lucknow, V.P. Singh would go off to the government guest house at Kukrail,[39] on the outskirts of the city, where he could work on them undisturbed. And because the guest house had no telephone connection those days, all the bureaucrats whose department files he would be looking at had to be present there as well.'[40] J.P. Singh, however, claimed work also stretched because VP dithered in taking decisions. 'He was inconsistent, would change his mind again and again, except when there was political advantage in a particular decision, in which case he would stick to it doggedly,' he said.[41]

VP took several initiatives as chief minister, including introducing computers in the chief minister's office, which made it easier to monitor implementation as well as catch departments that were fudging figures. 'I'd worked at the Centre, where there was no question of ignoring a ministerial order, but in UP I found my orders often were,' he said. 'I had all the orders entered in the computer and sought a preliminary report on their implementation within fifteen days. Bhure Lal was very diligent in following up.' Soon, VP was able to spot discrepancies. 'The transport department would claim to have bought a certain number of bus engines, or repaired a certain number, and have recorded the cost. But the expenditure on engine oil remained the same,' he said. 'I asked the officers, "How come? Either you are stealing engine oil, or the purchases and repairs were never made."'[42]

VP's concern for the poor had been apparent in his career even before he joined politics, but as chief minister, for the first time, he displayed a particular solicitude for the poorer castes—

the OBCs and Dalits—even as he ignored all demands of his own powerful Rajput caste. OBCs are broadly of two kinds—peasants and 'service providers' (or artisans)—and it is the latter that are worse off, since many of their traditional services have been made redundant by advances in technology. Traditional boatmen, for instance, who comprise the Mallah (or Nishad) caste, are no longer needed once a bridge is built spanning the river they used to ferry people across. 'I gave instructions that Mallahs should be favoured while giving contracts for the supply of sand from riverbanks to government construction sites,' said VP. So too he made a special effort to ensure that landless Dalits allotted land by the government were actually able to take possession and till it, which the powerful castes of the village often prevented them from doing.[43]

Sugarcane farmers faced the perennial problem of sugar mills delaying payments for the cane they had bought, piling up huge arrears. VP forced the mill owners to pay up, threatening to invoke a never-used-before section in the Sugarcane Purchase Act, 1955, which allowed attaching of mill-owner properties for such dereliction.[44] He set up a committee of senior officials, which he himself headed, called 'Kisan Mitra' (friend of the farmer) to keep track of farmers' problems and resolve them.[45] Equally keen to increase private investment in his backward state, he also launched its industrial counterpart called 'Udyog Bandhu' (friend of industry), which those facing bureaucratic hurdles in business could turn to for quick redress. 'Most problems related to licensing, leasing land, power supply and financing,' he said. 'Bureaucrats seemed to delight in hindering new projects, always looking for what was missing in a project proposal so they could withhold sanction, but we made officers explain delays.'[46]

But perhaps VP's biggest initiative was an effort to systemize development planning, so that the least-developed areas got the highest budgetary allocations. (It was quickly undermined by his successor.[47]) He found that no process existed to decide where new roads, schools or hospitals in the state should be built. Requests came from various districts, but ultimately it all depended on the whim of each department's minister and their top bureaucrats. UP then had twelve divisions, made up of thirty-seven districts, which, in turn, were divided into 800 blocks.

VP commissioned a study of every block on thirty-six development parameters, creating an index of development (or backwardness) for each block on each parameter, as well as a composite index for the block. He decided that, from then on, development funds would be allocated to the lowest on the scale in each parameter. If the education department's budget allowed ten more primary schools, for instance, they should be distributed among the blocks that had the fewest primary schools. 'I also decided that 30 per cent of the state's outlay—I wanted a higher percentage but there were hurdles—should be distributed district-wise using the index of development, with the poorest districts getting the most,' he said.[48]

His cabinet resisted strongly. 'The ministers' power to allocate projects was being taken away,' he noted. 'They could no longer visit villages and make grand announcements about new tube wells or roads being built there. It would all be decided according to the index. They could no longer allocate a disproportionate amount of their department funds for their own constituencies, giving out contracts to friends and getting commissions from them.'[49] Unable to have his way, VP made the same suggestion at the next legislature party meeting, where party MLAs enthusiastically supported him. The ministers, sensing the mood of the party, could hardly object.[50] In his cabinet expansion of 16 August 1981,[51] VP added twelve new ministers without portfolios, with each being put in charge of a division of the state to ensure that the new system was properly implemented. He also set up a monitoring committee in each district, comprising its MLAs—including Opposition MLAs—for the same purpose. 'But their job was only to supervise, they had no role in handling funds or deciding the location of projects,' he said.[52]

One consequence of the decision, however, was that VP, too, had to submit to it. Unlike most chief ministers before and after him, who transformed their own constituencies by showering largesse on them while in office, he could do little for either Allahabad or Tindwari during his chief ministerial stint. As his old associate, the retired Koraon school principal Udit Narayan Singh, put it, *'Unke dil mein ilakawaad ya kshetrawaad ya wyaktiwaad nahi tha. Rajya ka kalyan chahte they, desh ka kalyan chahte they* (He never cared about promoting a particular area or person. He wanted the whole state to prosper, the whole country to prosper).'[53]

He recalled being present at a village public meeting in the region that VP was addressing, where one of the listeners shouted out, *'Ka kiye, hum logan ke liye ka kiye* (What have you done for us)?', and maintained that VP replied, *'Kuch nahin. Hum imandari ka nishan bane hain. Jahan jawahan ye garv se kaha, "Hum Meja ke hi hain, hum Koraon ke hi hain." Itna to kahe saket* (I've done nothing, but I've been a symbol of honesty. Wherever I go, I can say with pride, "I'm from Meja, I'm from Koraon").'[54]

3

'IN SENIOR POSITIONS, ONE MUST TAKE RESPONSIBILITY FOR OTHERS' ERRORS'

Crisis upon crisis struck UP during V.P. Singh's two-year tenure, the last one finally overwhelming him. When he took over, inflation was high and kept rising,[1] with sugar and cooking oil scarce. Worse, large parts of the state, including Lucknow, were soon struck by heavy floods, almost as bad as in 1978. The floods lasted for over two months, killing more than a hundred people and displacing hundreds of thousands more.[2] (There was another flood, though not as severe, the following year as well.) Even as the floods were raging, barely ten days after he took over, there occurred an incident that made national headlines, underlining just how tough his new job was going to be, given the state apparatus at his disposal.

On 18 June 1980, four men and a pregnant woman (married to one of the men), travelling from Delhi to their village in west UP in an Ambassador car, stopped at Baghpat town to get a flat mended. A passing policeman—not in uniform—sought to snatch the gold chain the woman,[3] still seated in the car, was wearing, through the open window. Her husband, who was nearby, intervened and scuffled with him; the policeman returned with many more, all of them armed. They began firing blindly at the group, killing three of the four men, including the woman's husband. The woman was then stripped naked on the street and marched to the police station, where she was also raped.[4] When VP sought a report from senior policemen in the district, all of them claimed that the men killed were wanted criminals shot in an armed encounter. Some Congress MLAs of the area, when queried, backed them up.[5]

VP, new to his job, believed them. 'A chief minister has two eyes apart from his own,' he said later. 'One eye is that of his political workers, MLAs and MPs, and the other that of his administration. With that incident, both eyes were deliberately kept shut. Moving with both these eyes closed, nothing could prevent me from falling into a ditch, and I did. It taught me again not to trust people too easily.'[6] He was harsh with the Opposition parties that organized a 'jail bharo' movement in protest, suspecting they were out to get him to compensate for their electoral setback. 'I had been part of a similar movement myself two years ago, and knew how to handle it,' he said. 'Most people courting arrest expect to be released in a day or two. If they have to stay in jail longer, their morale starts to break. The average person cannot afford to sit in jail, even if he can tolerate the dreadful conditions—he has work outside. I refused to release the prisoners for ten to fifteen days. They could always have sought bail and left immediately, but that would have been a loss of face for their party.'[7]

Later, he was contrite. 'I thought about it and wondered if the press, which had also begun a big campaign, was lying,' he said. 'I sent Bhure Lal, who had just joined, to the spot for an honest assessment. He returned and filed a report saying that the episode had indeed occurred. I suspended the policemen responsible and started proceedings against them.'[8]

Hardly had the Baghpat agitation petered out—even the floodwaters had not fully receded—when, on 13 August 1980, the day of Id-ul-Fitr, Moradabad, famed for its brassware, exploded in one of the worst communal riots since Independence. The precipitating incident was the unexpected entry of a pig inside the town's idgah, where thousands had gathered to celebrate.[9] (There was a colony of Valmikis nearby, a Scheduled Caste that reared pigs, but it remains unclear whether a pig had wandered accidentally into the idgah or had deliberately been sneaked in by troublemakers or indeed if there was a pig at all.[10]) Some in the agitated crowd attacked the policemen stationed there. The police first lathi-charged in response and then began firing blindly, leading to a stampede. The eighty-six people killed on the first day included children who were trampled underfoot, as well as three policemen and the magistrate accompanying them, who were stoned to death by the mob.

The usual measures to curb riots were taken, including imposing curfew in the town and arresting hundreds, but the killings—like a lethal virus that seems to have been contained, only for fresh cases of disease to spring up again and again—continued into November, with a total official toll of 284 deaths. After the second major round of rioting, VP visited Moradabad, where he met members of the 'peace committee'—comprising prominent citizens, both Hindus and Muslims—formed to hasten normalcy, and toured the riot-affected areas with them. As he was leaving, the police superintendent informed him that some in the peace committee were, in fact, the ones fuelling the riots.

'Arrest them as soon as I leave,' VP ordered.

Since these were wealthy, influential folk, the arrests caused an outcry, but VP was impervious. 'Better innocents in jail than innocents being killed,' he responded.[11] And yet, the sniper fire between Hindu and Muslim colonies at night did not entirely cease—the random stabbings and arson continued.

Worse, the virus began to spread, with Hindu–Muslim clashes in Bareilly, Saharanpur, Faizabad and Varanasi, and full-scale riots in Aligarh and Allahabad.[12]

VP sought no alibis. In an assembly debate on the riots on 4 September 1980, he maintained that he had no clarifications to offer, that he deserved punishment, and appealed to all political parties to help him end them. It made no difference in Moradabad—the killings continued. By 14 September, after barely three months as chief minister, he was so frustrated that he sent his resignation to Indira Gandhi. 'The party has suffered a big political setback due to the riots,' read the letter, which he made public. 'It would help the party restore its image if the chief minister steps down.'[13] He insisted that he had no personal considerations in mind while offering to quit. 'As when I gave away my land to the Bhoodan movement, I consulted no one before writing that letter,' he told reporters. 'It was a matter between me and my god.'[14] But ironically, the resignation served to strengthen him politically, as Indira turned his suggestion down and, instead, publicly affirmed her faith in him.[15]

There was irony too of a different kind in a step VP backed in December 1980, a month after Moradabad had finally quietened down—the Lucknow district magistrate's decision to ban the Shia Muslims' tazia procession during Muharram. It was not the Hindus who opposed the procession but the Sunnis of the city. The Shias and Sunnis had always had a troubled relationship in Lucknow. Eleven years ago, as the MLA from Soraon, VP had defied a similar edict of the Allahabad authorities, but with the two sects exchanging gunfire at night and burning down each others' homes and shops every now and then ever since Eid that year, he felt he could do little else.[16] The Shias held a procession in protest and the Sunnis attacked that as well, but thereafter, following large-scale arrests, the conflict was contained.[17] VP impressed upon his administration the need for preventive steps, including arrests and curfews while antagonism was still building between communities, rather than after the first clashes had occurred. There were no further riots for the remainder of his term.

But there were other kinds of strife to contend with. Student agitations were numerous and often became violent across several universities—Lucknow, Aligarh, Pantnagar, Allahabad and Gorakhpur, among others—often inviting disproportionate retaliation from the police. In December 1980, for instance, Lucknow University students went on a vandalizing spree after a statue the students' union had put up—of a former student and Janata Party MLA who had been shot dead in Gorakhpur—was forcibly removed by university authorities, prompting police firing in retaliation.[18]

'There were a number of cases when the police fired at students, leading to around a dozen deaths,' said CPI leader Atul Anjaan, who was then president of the Lucknow University students' union. 'We, in turn, made it impossible for V.P. Singh to speak at any student-related function in Lucknow. Finally, he organized a meeting to pay homage to the slain students, which the then director-general of police and the education minister also attended, after which the situation normalized.'[19]

After the students, it was the turn of the teachers. College faculty from all over the state gathered in Lucknow's Hazrat Mahal Park to demonstrate over discrepancies in their pay scales that the education department had been ignoring. This could have been another embarrassment for the government, but it so happened that one of the faculty union office-bearers was Vijay Chaturvedi, VP's old associate from Manda, and he approached the chief minister the evening before the demonstration for a way out.

The demands were not unreasonable, and VP turned the occasion to his political advantage. He arrived unexpectedly at the park the next day just as the teachers had begun shouting slogans against him. '*Hum kahe rahe kuch din intezar kar le, yuh shasan vyavasta hai, yahan sabse samjhe boojhe kaam karu lage* (I was asking [your leaders] to wait awhile; in government, one can only take decisions after understanding everything properly),' he said, using the Bhojpuri dialect, as he often did, to build rapport. '*Abhay hum poora samjhe nahi hain, magar yeh jaan ley ke tomhar logon ka maang hum jonba poori karat* (I haven't yet fully understood [your demands], but let me assure you, they will be met).'[20]

Lawyers of west UP held a prolonged agitation through late 1980 and 1981, paralysing local courts for weeks, demanding a bench of the Allahabad High Court in the region.[21] They noted that travelling to Allahabad, at the eastern edge of the state, was a big inconvenience for litigants. VP agreed with them, but bureaucratic hurdles and resistance from Allahabad's lawyers—who stood to lose clientele—thwarted his efforts to set it up.[22] (Four decades on, there is still no such bench.)

At the end of October 1981, the subordinate jail staff went on strike for over a fortnight, demanding salaries on a par with those of policemen of the same rank. Police personnel had to be hastily drafted in their place to prevent prisoners from escaping. It led to hundreds of jail employees on strike being locked up in the very cells they once guarded, as VP, after examining the state's finances, decided that it could not afford to meet their demands.[23]

Yet another perennial blemish was the state's power shortage, with long daily power cuts, especially during the blazing summer months. In the summer of 1981, a combination of factors—inadequate supply of coal, its poor quality, many generators needing overhaul at the same time, boilers malfunctioning and more—led to the state's power-generation capacity dropping from the available 4,500 MW to about 1,000 MW.[24] For a week, many tier-4 towns remained entirely without electricity. Even Indira, visiting the state in end-June, criticized its power situation. A rattled VP took on the power portfolio himself and systemized the imposition of power cuts to the extent possible, by which district towns (barring the headquarters) and villages would alternately get six hours of power during the day, or eight hours after sunset.[25] Two-hour power cuts were imposed at different times across all localities of Lucknow and other cities, including Mall Avenue, where the chief minister resided.

Unfortunately, just then, Sita Kumari Singh had a virulent attack of herpes, which left sores the size of coins all over her upper body. 'It was hard enough wearing clothes, because the slightest touch of clothing on the sores was agonizing,' she said. 'To top it, it was summer in July and from 10 a.m. to noon every day, there would be no power. There is no real cure for the sores—they just have to dry. Mine took almost six months. I really cursed my husband then. Of course, I complained and he replied, "*Sab jagah hai, yahan par bhi hona hai* (There are power cuts everywhere and so they should be imposed here too). There are people falling ill in other homes too, and they are coping."'[26]

As complaints poured in of influential folk being less conscientious than himself, flouting the schedule and drawing more power than they were entitled to with the connivance of corrupt officials of the UP State Electricity Board (UPSEB), VP resumed his surprise inspections. On one instance, much highlighted in the local press, he took the chairman and chief engineer of UPSEB along from Lucknow in his helicopter, as he visited half a dozen villages across central and west UP. He found that not a single one of the villages was getting even the scant power his schedule had promised. Infuriated, after his last stop at a village in Bulandshahr district, more than 500 km from Lucknow, he flew back alone, leaving the chairman and chief engineer behind to make their own way home![27]

———— ∞∞∞ ————

The challenge that finally led to VP's resignation, and indeed, to which his heavy-handed response sullied his reputation as well, was that of mass murders by dacoits. Banditry in UP has a long history, especially—though not exclusively—in the valley of the Chambal river, which, rising in the Vindhya range in Madhya Pradesh, enters UP in its final stretch in the southern part of the Agra district and joins the Yamuna in the neighbouring Etawah district.

Folklore has it that the first dacoit in this ravine-ridden region, which stretches across large tracts of the adjacent states of Madhya Pradesh and Rajasthan too, was Raja Anangpal Tomar in the twelfth century, after he was forced off his Delhi throne by Prithviraj Chauhan, the same king who had eloped with VP's distant ancestor, Samyukta. With the deep ravines facilitating concealment, Tomar and his men carried out repeated guerrilla attacks on Delhi.[28] Their successors included the terrifying Pindaris and Thugs, who troubled the British rulers no end.[29] The tradition continued well into the first five decades after Independence, until development and improved policing equipment ended it.

Bands of dacoits would loot, extort, kidnap and occasionally kill travellers and residents of villages in the area, but no UP chief minister before VP (or after) had to contend with as many massacres by dacoits as he did. Why so many mass killings occurred only during his tenure remains unexplained. The first of these killings to draw national—indeed global—attention was the one at Behmai village in Jalaun district south of Etawah. On 14 February 1981, Phoolan Devi and her men shot dead twenty-two Thakurs to avenge her rape and humiliation by two Thakur dacoits in the same village seven months ago.[30] (Although Phoolan Devi drew the most media attention those days, due both to her gender and her tragic back story, the biggest and most fearsome gang of the Chambal valley was not hers—that distinction was shared by Chhabiram Pothi [who confined himself mostly to UP] and Malkhan Singh [who ruled the Madhya Pradesh ravines]).

The next mass killing was carried out by a breakaway faction of the Chhabiram gang, led by Mahabir Pothi, which, on 3 May 1981, killed twenty-two Dalits in Kunwarpara village in the Etah district, north-east of Agra, over a land dispute.[31] On 8 August 1981, again in Etah, Chhabiram's gang—rumoured to be 200 strong—battled armed policemen for hours, killing nine of them without suffering a single casualty. On 28 November 1981, a relatively little-known gang led by Santosha Singh and Radheshyam Singh bettered Phoolan's grisly body count at Dehuli village in Mainpuri district, north of Etawah, murdering twenty-four Dalits, because some among the victims had allegedly informed the police of the gang's presence nearby. [32]

Immediately on taking over, when VP asked his UP associates what the state's biggest problem was, they had all highlighted dacoity.[33] Accordingly, his crusade against brigands began in 1980 itself. In that year, according to police records, 983 dacoits were killed against 145 in 1975.[34] Curbing them was much more difficult than catching ordinary criminals, and not only because of the terrain they inhabited. Most gangs were dominated by a single caste and enjoyed the secret support of their caste fellows in surrounding villages, whom in turn they protected. 'Brigands are invariably protected by their caste men almost throughout the valley,' writes M.Z. Khan in his study, *Dacoity in Chambal Valley*. 'This is even in the face of possible police action for harbouring outlaws. Caste men take pride in the exploits and cunning of dacoits and dacoit gangs belonging to their caste group against the police.'[35]

Khan notes that 'caste men' provided dacoits food and temporary shelter, never snitched on them, and kept them informed of police movement.[36] The local term for dacoits—'baaghi', or rebel—was an indication of the esteem they enjoyed. Some of the bigger gangs, influential enough to impact elections, even had discreet political support. Other mundane impediments for the police included lack of personnel (rural police stations usually had just eleven people, at least two of whom would be away every day, bearing witness in court cases); lack of equipment and vehicles (most were provided only bikes, no Jeeps); and plain fear. VP would later say, 'Chhabiram had an open offer for the policemen posted in his area, "Take Rs 5,000 and ignore my presence, or risk your life." Many policemen preferred the first option. They would even mislead the raiding parties.'[37]

After the Behmai carnage, VP further stepped up his drive against dacoits. (Again, as during the Moradabad riots, he offered to resign but was persuaded not to.) A big hurdle to effective policing of the Chambal valley area had been the lack of coordination between the UP and the Madhya Pradesh police—baaghis fleeing the UP police would escape into the adjoining state and vice versa. VP held a meeting with his Madhya Pradesh counterpart, Arjun Singh, in Kalpi in Jalaun district to set this right. They agreed to build watchtowers at the border, ensure that policemen of both states had their wireless sets at the same frequency and formed a committee of policemen from both states to suggest further cooperation measures.[38]

And yet the incidents of mass killings would not stop. VP was so exasperated after the Dehuli slaughter that instead of offering to resign once again, he set himself a publicly announced deadline— he would extirpate all the dacoit gangs in the state in the next thirty days, or quit. Once again Indira intervened, telling him that he was not to resign under any circumstances, while Rajiv Gandhi announced that he had no doubt VP would indeed achieve his objective within the stated deadline. 'My announcement gave an impetus to the police,' said VP. 'They felt, "We stake our lives, now the chief minister, too, has put something at stake."'[39]

The impetus showed. Between 28 November and 28 December 1981, the UP police killed 299 dacoits—including Santosha Singh of Dehuli infamy—and arrested another 1,228.[40] '*Mere haath*

khoon se lathpath hain, par khooniyon ke khoon se lathpath hai
(My hands are bloodstained, but they are stained with the blood
of killers),' VP declared in the UP assembly.[41] Yet, days after he
had taken credit for meeting his deadline, on 30 December 1981,
another ten Dalits, including five women and three children, were
killed by dacoits at Sadhupur village in Mainpuri for reasons that
remain unclear.[42]

Worse, evidence mounted that many of the alleged dacoits
the police had shot dead were not dacoits at all but small-time
criminals and even innocents they had taken away from their
homes, and that many accounts of desperate gun battles in police
reports, which they claimed caused the dacoits' deaths, were
wholly imaginary. These people had all been killed solely to swell
the numbers of slain 'dacoits' and impress superiors. As early as
April 1981, two months after the Behmai killings, five UP Vidhan
Parishad members had written to VP, citing five specific instances
of police encounters with dacoits they had probed and found to
be bogus.[43]

Soon after the Dehuli bloodbath in November 1981, Mulayam
Singh Yadav,[44] then president of the UP Lok Dal, who himself
hailed from Etawah, wrote to UP Governor Chandeshwar Prasad
Narayan Singh, listing 418 cases of such fake encounters and
claiming, perhaps somewhat hyperbolically, that there had been
'5,000 killings by the police' so far. 'Even in the last 100 years, so
many people have not been killed in encounters as during the past
year and a half,' his letter said.[45] Independent investigations by the
media[46] and civil rights groups confirmed the gross overreach of the
police. What made it worse was that a disproportionate number of
those killed belonged to the backward and scheduled castes, which
led to allegations that these castes had been particularly targeted
by upper-caste policemen.[47]

Considering the UP police's record in the Baghpat atrocity or
the Moradabad riots, such excesses were probably inevitable once

they were given overriding powers. 'I was against giving the police a free run of the state,' said J.P. Singh. 'But V.P. Singh had great faith in Naresh Kumar [then inspector general of police, anti-dacoity operations) and allowed him to do whatever he liked.'[48] When the allegations began to mount, VP did issue orders demanding that whenever a dacoit was killed, a report of the incident, along with the deceased's criminal record, should reach his desk by the next morning. He also suspended some guilty policemen, but by then much damage had already occurred.

In comparison, his Madhya Pradesh counterpart Arjun Singh undoubtedly handled his state's dacoit problem far more adroitly (though he never had to face as many massacres as VP), cajoling both Malkhan Singh (in June 1982) and Phoolan Devi (in February 1983) into surrendering to the government. In UP, Chhabiram Pothi, leader of the Chhabiram gang, also wanted to surrender, but the effort ended in a tragic fiasco.

Chhabiram enjoyed exemplary status in the ravines—not only was he powerful, but he was also a Robin Hood figure, sharing some of his wealth with the village poor in the region, especially those from his own Yadav caste, helping them, in particular, with their daughters' wedding expenses. He was also strict about respecting women's dignity and was said to have shot dead a gang member who tried to molest a woman during a raid. But he seemed to have tired of his nomadic, insecure life, for, early in 1982, Congress (I) MLA Satish Ajmani (from Nighasan in the Lakhimpur Kheri district) informed VP in strict confidence that Chhabiram and his gang wanted to surrender. (Such surrenders had taken place earlier, notably in 1960 and 1972, both negotiated by Sarvodaya stalwarts—Vinoba Bhave in the first case and Jayaprakash Narayan in the second; Arjun Singh continued the tradition.) VP sought assurance in writing, whereupon Ajmani brought back a handwritten confirmatory letter from Chhabiram, which also spelt out his terms of surrender, asking for fair treatment and rehabilitation of his gang members.[49]

But everything went wrong after a report on the negotiations with Chhabiram appeared in the local press. 'Police officers raised huge objections,' said VP.[50] They claimed they were close to catching Chhabiram anyway, and any such deal would weaken the anti-dacoity drive. But why VP chose not to overrule them remains unknown. In the UP assembly, Opposition parties, too, demanded that VP make his negotiations with Chhabiram public, and the chief minister had another 'Ashwatthama hata' moment, when he blandly denied any personal negotiations. He asked Ajmani to tell Chhabiram that the deal was off, but Ajmani refused to meet Chhabiram again, fearing for his life if the dacoit felt he had been betrayed. Chhabiram had given away his location in the letter, but VP restrained the police from capturing him and instead insisted that since Chhabiram had trusted the government, he should be given time to get away. Chhabiram did manage to escape, but was killed in an encounter soon after, at the end of March.[51]

❦

Unlike Sant Bux and VP, their eldest brother, Chandrasekhar Prasad Singh, shared their father Bhagwati Prasad's passions—astrology and hunting. 'He was an excellent marksman,' said Ranamata Singh, VP's lifelong friend. 'I once challenged him to shoot a tiny bird on a branch at least 50 metres away. He was reluctant, but when I pressured him, he took an airgun and shot it down unerringly.'[52] He was also the social hub of the family, regularly keeping in touch with all members, bringing them together on important occasions. Starting as a lawyer at the Allahabad High Court in the mid-1950s, specializing in corporate law, he had built an extensive practice before being made a judge—one of the youngest judges at the time—in 1968. After his first wife died young—while VP was studying in Pune—he remarried and had two sons.[53] Two and a half years older than VP, he also repeatedly maintained—after studying his own horoscope—that he would not live beyond fifty-three, a claim no one in the family took seriously, since he was in perfect health.

On 20 March 1982, one day short of his fifty-third birthday, Chandrasekhar Prasad Singh left on a hunting trip to the nearby Shankargarh forest, about 40 km south-west of Allahabad, along with his sons, Ajit Pratap Singh and Vikram Singh, aged fourteen and thirteen, respectively, at the time, and some family retainers, well armed with three rifles. He hadn't been particularly keen on hunting that day but gave in to his sons' repeated pleas. Travelling in an open Jeep, on the way they picked up the former raja of Shankargarh, Mahendra Singh, who was also a relative.[54]

Their day-long trip was fruitless. Returning to Mahendra Singh's residence, they set out again around 8 p.m. This time, deep in the forest, their Jeep had a flat. Close to midnight, after fixing it, they decided to return. At one stage, they had to pass through a forest gate with a low wall on either side, but found their way blocked by a mound of loose stones. As they approached, strong torchlight beams from behind the wall lit up the area. 'There was a gang of dacoits hiding behind the wall,' said Vikram Singh.[55]

Shankargarh is a long way from the Chambal valley, but there were a few gangs in that region as well. One of them—later found to be headed by Jagatpal Pasi, a small-time dacoit whose main operational area was the adjoining Rewa district of Madhya Pradesh—had chosen to target Chandrasekhar Prasad Singh's Jeep. As VP explained,

Dacoits are hungry for weapons. Someone must have informed them that there was a hunting party in the forest with many weapons, and they wanted to acquire them. They did not know they were targeting a judge, or the chief minister's brother. It had nothing to do with my anti-dacoity drive.[56]

Nearly four decades later, Vikram Singh remembered every moment of the fateful encounter that followed. He recalled,

> We went on that trip just after my annual exams. We often went to those jungles. On the way back, my father was driving, with my brother and the driver next to him, while the rest of us were in the back. When the torches shone in our faces, we were unable to see anything because of the glare. Out of the darkness, a voice asked who we were. Then someone—it could have been from their side or from ours—fired a shot. Immediately there were more shots and a regular gun battle began. I got three bullets—one in my arm, one in my thigh and one in the head. But they were superficially embedded, so I survived. Pellets had to be taken out of my skull. It was a narrow escape. But my father and brother were not so lucky.[57]

Most others in the Jeep suffered bullet injuries as well.

The dacoits came up close, inspected them and even seemed to recognize Chandrasekhar Prasad Singh, one of them muttering, 'We made a mistake.' They appeared to have been unnerved, for they did not take the weapons in the jeep, cleared the road and ordered the driver to leave. The injured were taken to a primary health centre in Shankargarh—it had no hospital—which could do nothing for them but advised them to rush to Allahabad. By the time they reached the Swaroop Rani Hospital in Allahabad, both Chandrasekhar Prasad Singh and his older son Ajit were dead.[58]

The first call informing VP came early the next morning, from another Allahabad High Court judge. 'I took the call but on seeing my reaction, V.P. Singh took the receiver away from me and spoke to him,' said Sita Kumari Singh. 'We were in shock; we didn't know what to do. Soon after, Bhure Lal also called, and we told him we already had the news.'[59]

VP left immediately for Allahabad by helicopter. 'The post-mortem was still on when I reached, after which the bodies were brought back to Daiya Kothi in Allahabad. I pressed my head to my brother's corpse. It was a terrible moment,' he said. It also fell to VP to inform their mother Braj Raj Kanwar, who was already ill and had been kept unaware until then. 'I said to her, "Bhaisaab is very ill." She fainted—she may have guessed. I told her everything later, after she was revived. She had to be given tranquillizers.'[60]

Although he kept shuttling between Allahabad and Lucknow by helicopter in the days that followed,[61] VP, sunk deep in depression, found it near impossible to work. Close friends from his Allahabad University days finally gave him a pep talk on the imperative of resuming his duties. Even so, for nearly a year, he could not bear to look at any photograph of his late brother. He even broke down publicly when delivering a speech some months later at a meeting in Banda (a district headquarters 200 km west of Allahabad) to commemorate Chandrasekhar Singh.[62]

The drive against dacoits continued, and VP claimed it had many successes. 'All the "A" category [dacoit] gangs were wiped out,' he said. 'Some were killed, some arrested. I admit I discovered later that there had been some fake encounters, but we took steps to stop them.'[63] And yet, on 28 June 1982, he received the news that there had been not one massacre the previous day, but two— ten people, all of them from a single family of the Yadav caste, had been killed in Dastampur village in the Kanpur Dehat district adjoining Etawah, and another six Dalits in Rampura village of Mainpuri district.

In both cases, the motive was revenge—those murdered had informed the police about specific dacoit gangs, which had then been cornered and their leading members killed. Indeed, the Dastampur family had been responsible for one of the best-known dacoits of the area being eliminated—Mustaqeen, who had helped Phoolan Devi wreak her deadly vengeance in Behmai. The bandits, led by Mustaqeen's brother, Muslim, had even roared, '*Khoon ka badla khoon* (Blood for blood)', before they left.[64]

It was all the more galling since in neighbouring Madhya Pradesh, Chief Minister Arjun Singh had succeeded, barely eighteen days earlier, in cajoling his state's biggest dacoit, Malkhan Singh, to surrender. (The story goes that Muslim had considered surrendering alongside too, but later changed his mind because his brother's death remained to be avenged.) VP had publicly announced his intention of resigning twice before but had not actually done so. After the Dehuli killings, he had set himself a month's deadline to wipe out dacoity entirely and had claimed to have achieved it. He now felt that his continuing as chief minister was untenable. 'My credibility was in question,' he said.[65] He was informed of the killings around 1 p.m.; by 2.30 p.m. he was home.

'Back so early?' Sita Kumari asked.

'I'm resigning,' he replied and went into his residential office.[66]

Then, as now, a chief minister resigning midway through his term, without consulting his party's Central leaders, was unheard of. Indeed, given Indira's complete dominance of the Congress (I) at the time, quitting without her consent amounted to defying her, and thereby wilfully terminating one's political career. In his room, as he was writing out his resignation, VP did pause once to dial her number. Her secretary, Dhawan, answered; VP stayed quiet for a few seconds and then replaced the receiver. 'I realized that if I asked her, and she insisted I continue, and I still resigned, she would never forgive me,' he said later.[67]

He asked himself many questions while writing the resignation letter. 'Will my resignation end the problem of mass murders by dacoits? No ... When Indira Gandhi has entrusted me with a position, do I have the right to throw it away? No.'[68] But there were higher considerations too. He wrote later,

> As a soldier of the party, my duty was clear to me. It was the same as that of the soldier in an army who sees a cannon ball hurtling towards his commander—to throw himself in its path.

There was only one way out for me to save my party from the people's anger that would surely be directed towards it after these two incidents ...[69]

VP sent off his resignation letter to the governor, C.P.N. Singh, through a courier, and proceeded to address a previously scheduled press conference. 'We had prepared to grill him about the massacres,' said senior journalist Pradeep Kapoor, who attended it. 'But he disarmed us completely by saying that he had sent in his resignation.'[70]

Had it been accepted? All the journalists trooped to Lucknow's Raj Bhavan to find C.P.N. Singh perplexed. 'He told us that had V.P. Singh brought the resignation directly to him, he'd have torn it up and asked him to get back to work,' Kapoor remembered. 'But with the decision having already been made public through a press conference, he had no choice but to ask Delhi what to do.' Telephone lines were acting up again—he could not get through to the Prime Minister's office. It is said that Indira finally got to know of the resignation through a news agency ticker. It was her office that called C.P.N. Singh—and advised him to accept it.[71] VP was asked to continue until his successor was chosen.

'If one is in a senior position, one has to take responsibility for errors one may not have personally committed,' VP said later. He recalled Shastri's resignation as railways minister in 1956. 'Shastriji was not driving the engine that derailed.'[72]

Media reactions to his unprecedented resignation were largely positive, though some reports cynically maintained that VP's problems were mounting so rapidly, he would soon have been sacked anyway.[73] Even his estranged brother Sant Bux was impressed. 'My brother is growing up,' he said. 'From a boy who wouldn't say boo to a goose, let alone Indira, he's gone to the man who's challenged her authority—he's committed lèse-majesté by resigning without asking her permission.'[74]

4

'YOU WON'T BE ASKED TO COLLECT FUNDS FOR THE PARTY'

Having resigned without asking Indira Gandhi, V.P. Singh was anxious to avoid meeting her, fearing her wrath if they came face to face. 'I learnt this as a child—if your elders are angry with you, your best strategy is to stay out of their sight,' he said. But his successor—Shripat Mishra, who had been assembly speaker while he was chief minister—was sworn in only on 17 July 1982 (twenty days after VP's resignation, on 28 June), while Indira's schedule for the month, decided earlier, included a visit to Nainital on 4 July,[1] during which the state chief minister had to be present. She was to reach Haldwani by chopper, at the foothills of the Kumaon Himalayas, and travel to Nainital by car. VP awaited her arrival in Haldwani with dread. Many senior UP officials were also present, and a public rebuff, with them looking on, would be mortifying.

He remembered the snub she had delivered Bahuguna once, in the early months of the Emergency, when Bahuguna was UP chief minister. After Indira won the 1971 Lok Sabha poll and the T.N. Singh government in UP fell, defector MLAs backed the

Congress (R) in such large numbers that it soon acquired a majority in the assembly. Kamalapati Tripathi became chief minister but was replaced by Bahuguna two years later. Once the Emergency was declared, however, Bahuguna, too, fell afoul of both Indira and Sanjay Gandhi, and was ousted in November 1975.

Weeks before his removal, with Indira visiting Allahabad, Bahuguna, as well as other political leaders, including VP, had gone to the airport to receive her. They had all lined up as she disembarked from her aircraft. Indira began moving down the line and greeting each one in turn, accepting the bouquets and garlands some had brought with them. But just before she reached Bahuguna, she abruptly turned away and headed for her car.[2]

As it turned out, though, Indira had either not been as enraged as VP had feared, or her anger had abated. Once she arrived in Haldwani, accompanied by two of her ministers, expecting that they would travel in the same car as her, VP was heading for his own, when he heard her command, 'Vishwanath, you come with me.' VP obeyed, fully expecting to be berated during the journey. But Indira made no mention of his resignation at all. The road led through a thick forest on either side, and she began reminiscing about her childhood visits to forests. Relieved, VP talked about his own such visits. 'In Nainital, Indiraji attended meetings, met a lot of people who told her about all kinds of problems they faced, and in every case, she said, "I'll speak to the chief minister about it." She kept my dignity intact,' said VP later.[3]

And indeed, within seven months of his quitting, she gave him what he'd wanted from the start of her term—a place in the Union cabinet. Just before she did so, in early January 1983, she had faced two stunning electoral reverses, losing assembly elections in the states of Andhra Pradesh and Karnataka, where the Congress had never lost since Independence. In the former, a party barely ten months old, the Telugu Desam Party (TDP), set up by film idol N.T. Rama Rao, had trounced hers, winning 202 of the 293 seats;

in the latter, the Janata Party, battered by split after split since 1979 and without any following in the southern states before, had made an astonishing comeback, getting 95 of the 224 seats to the Congress (I)'s 82, and forming a government with the help of allies.[4]

She may well have felt the need to improve her government's image, which VP's induction in the cabinet, with his favourable national reputation following his resignation, would surely help. On 29 January 1983, she reshuffled and expanded her council of ministers, adding two more cabinet ministers and five ministers of state, dropping quite a few incumbents and changing the portfolios of many others. Of the two full-fledged ministers inducted, one was VP.[5] He was given charge of the same ministry where he had been deputy minister and minister of state earlier—commerce. 'I occupied three rooms along the same corridor across a decade,' he said later. 'The first had one window, the second two and the third three.'[6] He quit his Tindwari seat and was elected to the Rajya Sabha.

The seven interim months gave VP a brief respite from the furious pace of his life as chief minister, allowing him time to resume some of his old hobbies, painting in particular. However, keen to demonstrate that his resignation did not mean any tempering of political activity, he spent most of the seven months touring the state, addressing public meetings, starting with west UP.[7] As he'd hoped, he attracted large crowds, enabling him to indicate to Delhi that his resignation had enhanced rather than diminished his political appeal. While on a visit to Ajmer, he fractured a toe and, with his foot in a plaster, had six weeks of enforced rest in Allahabad, during which he painted a portrait of one of his nieces. 'It was the only painting I managed to complete during those months,' he said.[8]

Pleased as he was with his new assignment, VP—familiar with a commerce minister's tasks, having been in the ministry before— had one big worry. But Rajiv Gandhi dispelled it for him. It was Rajiv who summoned him to the Prime Minister's home on the morning of 29 January 1983, hours before the swearing-in, and informed him of his portfolio. VP continued to stare at him without speaking. 'Don't worry, you won't be asked to collect funds for the party,' Rajiv then added.[9]

Relieved that his image was in no danger of being compromised, VP soon began reinforcing it. Alongside felicitations, gifts poured in, welcoming the new commerce minister. Barring inconsequential ones like bouquets, he returned them all. The public sector State Trading Corporation, through which much of the country's global trade was canalized, especially in foodgrains, sent him a new-year diary and an expensive leather briefcase. VP returned the briefcase. 'What I'd really like from you is your balance sheet showing a healthy profit,' he told its chairman.[10]

Compared to his tumultuous time as UP chief minister, VP's eighteen-month spell as commerce minister—barring one four-month phase—was sedate. Once again, he chose his officers with care, making integrity his foremost requirement. Once again, he largely resisted recommendations for transfers and postings, though perhaps less implacably than he had done as UP chief minister. T.S.R. Subramanian, then a joint secretary in the commerce ministry,[11] recalled being summoned by VP and told that a particular officer had to be posted in Geneva as ambassador to the General Agreement on Trade and Tariffs (GATT), the precursor of the World Trade Organization (WTO). 'When I demurred that the officer had no experience in multilateral commercial diplomacy, he told me that these were orders directly from Rajiv Gandhi, which brooked no opposition,' Subramanian wrote later.[12]

But when Subramanian prepared a note reiterating his reservations, VP accepted it. 'Four days later, he returned the note to me, saying, "You are very lucky. He read it and saw your point,"' Subramanian added.[13]

VP's one significant initiative as commerce minister was restarting trade with China, which had stopped entirely after the 1962 border war. 'There were opposing views in the Prime Minister's Office,' he said. 'Some felt that there should be no trade relations until the border issue was resolved, but others, including me, believed that all opportunities should be used to improve relations. We discussed the matter for over fifteen days, and finally Indira Gandhi accepted my view.'[14] The then commerce secretary Abid Hussain[15] visited Beijing, soon leading to trade resumption following an agreement in early 1984.

Other fresh steps were of modest consequence. VP learnt, for instance, that in the global diamond trade, Surat's pre-eminent position as a cutting and polishing centre for small diamonds was being threatened by Israel, whose diamond cutters had better technology. He responded by putting the latest, computerized cutting and polishing equipment in the 'open general licence' (OGL) category of imports, so they could be brought into the country freely. Discovering that the unbridled sale of snakeskin was leading to indiscriminate killing of snakes, which, in turn, had brought about a proliferation of field rats that were eating up more crop than before, he banned their export. Export of processed cashew nuts had fallen because Senegal, which provided India raw nuts in large quantities earlier, had stopped doing so, having set up chocolate factories that now used them. VP got the finance ministry to sanction a subsidy on export-oriented cashew plantations, which led to a boost in indigenous cashew production.[16]

VP instituted a monthly 'open house' in the ministry, at which importers and exporters could raise queries and voice their grievances, which the officers attending had to resolve promptly.

He attended a number of global trade conferences, mostly related to GATT and the UN Conference on Trade and Development (UNCTAD), where he tried hard to rally the developing economies against the efforts of the developed ones to reduce formerly granted trade concessions.[17] But overall, his stint in the ministry was too short for major improvements, with the trade deficit under him even increasing marginally.[18]

Only once was this relatively placid phase of VP's ministerial career rocked—between July and November 1983, when the beef tallow scandal exploded. A Bhatinda-based vanaspati manufacturer was caught mixing imported beef tallow with vanaspati for higher profit; raids elsewhere found more such companies doing the same. Though barely half a dozen instances were unearthed, Opposition parties burst into exaggerated outrage, holding nationwide protests against the government for having allowed the import of beef tallow at all. They claimed that Hindus had been made to unwittingly consume beef, recalled the 1857 Mutiny when Indian troops had revolted over cartridges greased with beef and pork fat, and called this an equally reprehensible affront to Hindu religious feeling. While the import of beef tallow, mainly used in making soap and grease, and its misuse by mixing it with vanaspati, were entirely separate matters, VP as commerce minister found himself the Opposition's main target. Nationwide sale of vanaspati fell by 30 per cent. Even VP's mother, who hardly followed current events, telephoned him. 'She wanted to know if it was safe to use Dalda,' he said.[19]

VP ordered a total ban on every kind of tallow import and then set about finding out how it had been allowed. He learnt that 'mutton tallow' had been imported for industrial purposes since 1964, channelled through the STC, but in 1978, in a bid to liberalize imports, the Janata Party government had removed the STC's import monopoly on a host of items, including 'mutton tallow'. Globally, however, no distinction based on the origin of tallow is made—'tallow' comprises every kind of animal fat, including that of a cow.

To VP's satisfaction, he found that the Congress government had brought 'mutton tallow' back on the canalized list in June 1981, but traders who had contracted direct purchases earlier had continued to import it beyond the ban, in some cases even paying the customs' penalty imposed. The knowledge enabled him to score over the Opposition. 'I went to the House and narrated the facts,' he said. 'The Opposition MPs cheered me. But when I began talking about 1978, they stopped clapping. The next day, newspapers said that I had turned the tables on the Opposition.'[20] Soap makers were hit by VP's ban, but he maintained that it could not be helped. 'If people don't want tallow at all, we cannot allow it surreptitiously in soap,' he said.[21]

But UP claimed VP again as the next general election drew near. The Congress's popularity in the state had slid steeply since he quit as chief minister, and in August 1984—with just four months for the polls—Indira suddenly decided that replacing both Chief Minister Mishra and UP Congress President Sukhdeo Singh would improve the party's standing.[22]

In the five UP by-elections held in December 1983, the Congress had lost three; in three more held in May 1984, it lost two. (In comparison, in the by-elections held while VP was chief minister, the party had won all the Lok Sabha seats it contested—barring Garhwal, which went to Bahuguna—and 10 out of 12 Vidhan Sabha seats.)[23] Worse, 2 of the 5 seats won by the Opposition had been taken by the Rashtriya Sanjay Manch, a new party set up by Sanjay Gandhi's widow Maneka, with whom Indira had a bitter falling out soon after his death, and Indira had taken the reverses very personally.

Indira and her advisers decided that Narayan Dutt Tiwari, then minister for industry in her cabinet, should be the next UP chief minister, and VP the next UP Congress president.[24] But the news was conveyed to the two in a curious fashion. VP was in Bombay for routine meetings when Arun Nehru—still in charge of UP—called him, summoning him back to Delhi by the next flight. 'You have to leave for Vienna right away,' Nehru said as soon as they met. 'But don't tell anyone.' A United Nations Industrial Development Organization (UNIDO) conference was then being held in Vienna, where the Indian delegation was headed by Tiwari. 'We need Tiwari back in Delhi immediately, and you must take his place,' Nehru added, saying no more.

VP noted that he could hardly keep his Vienna visit hidden from his staff, which would be buying his tickets. Nehru insisted that he should. VP obeyed, getting a ticket to London bought for him instead, but with a long layover in Frankfurt. At Frankfurt, he called the Indian ambassador to West Germany from the airport to buy him a ticket to Vienna, as well as get his luggage off the London flight. After all the trouble, on reaching Vienna, he had Nehru calling again, informing him that he would no longer be commerce minister once he returned, and revealing his new assignment. Later, Tiwari told him that he was treated even more cavalierly. 'I landed in Delhi from Vienna and there was a crowd of journalists seeking my reaction to being named UP chief minister, when I didn't even know that was the case,' he said.[25] The purpose of such secretiveness and haste remained opaque to VP.

His new job as UPCC president—again, not one he particularly wanted—was a world apart from the earlier one, but as was his wont, VP gave it his best. He began travelling extensively in UP, streamlining party units across blocks and districts, trying his best to reduce factionalism, assessing the relative winning chances of incumbent MPs and their rivals for party nomination in each of the 85 Lok Sabha seats, soon realizing that the effort was probably too late. 'The general feeling was that the party would not get more than 10 seats in UP,' he said.[26]

The biggest crisis Indira faced in her second stint as Prime Minister was the Sikh agitation in Punjab. The turmoil had many faces, with the moderates among the agitators demanding more autonomy for the state and the redressing of myriad grievances, and the extremists promoting religious fanaticism, with some even seeking a separate Sikh nation of Khalistan. Both the moderates and the extremists, however, seemed to agree on a questionable narrative of Sikh victimhood at the hands of Hindus and the Central government, and of the Sikh religion being under threat, which also briefly attracted widespread support in the community.

The moderates, led by the regional Opposition party, the Akali Dal, held a series of protests starting in the second half of 1980, and also engaged in negotiations with the government over their demands, but could not reach any agreement. The extremists, the most popular of whom was a hitherto unknown preacher, Jarnail Singh Bhindranwale, organized terror strikes, setting off bombs in public places, murdering prominent individuals who opposed them, hijacking a flight and generally wreaking mayhem.

In combating the terrorists, the police found themselves greatly stymied by the fact that most of them had taken refuge on the premises of the holiest of Sikh shrines, the Golden Temple complex in Amritsar, which religious considerations forbade them from entering, and which Bhindranwale and his men gradually turned into an armed fortress. Finally, on 6 June 1984, Operation Bluestar commenced, with Indira setting aside her earlier reservations and sending the army into the Golden Temple to flush out the terrorists and take control. About 250 terrorists were killed, including Bhindranwale.

But as feared, the step also provoked great resentment among the Sikhs, who felt that their holiest shrine had been desecrated. Sikh terrorism was far from wiped out. Around five months later, on the morning of 31 October 1984, two Delhi policemen, both

Sikhs, members of Indira's team of armed bodyguards, sprayed her with bullets as she was walking from her home to her residential office next door. Though she was immediately rushed to the All India Institute of Medical Sciences (AIIMS), there was no chance of her surviving.

VP was in Manda, attending the foundation-laying ceremony of a hospital, when one of the security men accompanying the UP health minister—who was also present—whispered to him that Indira had been 'injured'. 'I was on the makeshift stage, speaking, when someone tapped my back and told me to immediately wind up,' said VP's associate Ramesh Pande, who hails from Manda.[27] Soon after, more details emerged—she had been shot and was in hospital. VP and the health minister, who had both travelled by helicopter from Allahabad, flew back there, and a few hours later, caught the first commercial flight to Delhi. 'We rushed to AIIMS, but by then her body had already been sent for post-mortem,' said VP. The same evening, around 6.30 p.m., Rajiv Gandhi—who had never intended to be in politics and had never held any ministerial position before—was sworn in as Prime Minister.

The abrupt and ghastly manner of his idol and political guru's death must have shaken VP, but in his final interviews he made no mention of his feelings.[28] The killing provoked countrywide frenzy against the Sikhs, leading to thousands of them being attacked and murdered across several cities, often in barbarous ways. In worst-hit Delhi, about 2,500 Sikhs were killed, the army finally being inducted to stop the rioting.

The flood of sympathy for Indira also benefited the Congress immensely in the elections she had been preparing for. Held in late December to 514 Lok Sabha seats (no polls could be held in Punjab, for obvious reasons, or in Assam, where, too, there was turmoil from other causes), it saw the Congress winning 404 of them[29]—a tally higher than it had achieved even at the height of

Jawaharlal Nehru's popularity. In UP, where VP had expected 10 seats before the assassination, it won 83 of the 85 seats, Charan Singh in Baghpat and his party candidate in Etah being the only two to withstand the tide. 'The atmosphere was such that we didn't have to make any effort to win,' said VP. Already a Rajya Sabha member, he did not contest the election himself.

As UP Congress president, VP's was a dominant role in choosing most of his party's candidates from the state. But not for the seat that mattered the most to him—Allahabad. VP had expected a tough contest, since Bahuguna was the main Opposition candidate, having switched from Garhwal to his favoured seat this time. But he was fairly confident that his protégé, K.P. Tiwari—who had the won Allahabad seat in the May 1981 by-election after VP gave it up to become UP chief minister—whom he wanted to nominate again, could stand up to him.

'Tiwari's candidacy had been agreed upon,' said VP. 'Then one day Arun Nehru suddenly said to me, "Tiwari won't be the candidate. We're getting Amitabh Bachchan."' At the time, VP maintained, he was not familiar with the name. 'I asked my wife. She said, "What! You don't know who Amitabh Bachchan is?" I genuinely did not. We used to watch a lot of films at one time, but once I joined politics, I completely stopped.'[30]

Considering that Bachchan had been the top Hindi-film hero for a decade by then; that Indira had been to see him in hospital after his near-fatal accident in July 1982 while shooting for the film *Coolie*; that he, too, hailed from Allahabad; and that his father, poet Harivansh Rai Bachchan, had been a professor at Allahabad University while VP was a student there, VP's unawareness does seem odd. (Bachchan and his parents had been close family friends of Indira and Rajiv Gandhi for years, and Rajiv had persuaded him to make a career switch, contesting from Allahabad.) 'He came to the party office in Delhi after dark, stepping out of his car with a towel covering his face,' VP recalled. 'Even inside the room with us, he at first held the towel in place like a veil.'[31]

It has been suggested, then and since, that VP, fearing a political rival in his party on his home turf, had not been particularly pleased with Bachchan's entry. 'Not at all,' he told his NMML interviewer on being asked. 'But I wanted justice done to K.P. Tiwari, who had been promised the nomination. I wanted an honourable option for him. I suggested that he be made a minister in the UP cabinet right away and guaranteed a ticket in the next UP assembly poll. This was agreed to.'[32]

His enormous fan following made Bachchan a formidable candidate and, fearing that Bahuguna might choose another constituency to contest from if he found out who his opponent was to be, the party kept the superstar's forthcoming candidacy a close secret. 'I cooperated with the effort, ensuring that Bachchan reached Allahabad at 3 p.m. on the last day for filing nominations, just an hour before the process closed,' said VP. 'The nomination was filed at 3.30 p.m. It gave Bahuguna no time to file his nomination elsewhere.' Despite Bahuguna's political stature, the rising gale of support for the Congress might have brought about his defeat anyway, but Bachchan as the Congress candidate ensured he was blown away—getting a mere 109,666 votes to Bachchan's 297,461.[33]

Rajiv's fresh swearing-in as Prime Minister after the elections, along with his new council of ministers, on the last day of 1984, was as chaotic as the first one had been sombre. The full results of the election had been declared only the previous evening, giving him and his advisers such little time to choose ministers that some among them, including VP, could not be informed in advance. One nominee learnt of it indirectly, telephoned the President's office to check, got a confirmation and rushed to Rashtrapati Bhavan, reaching a good ten minutes after the ceremony had begun;

two others, who were not in Delhi, had their names called out to embarrassing silences and had to be sworn in the next day. VP, who attended the ceremony as an onlooker, took his seat in the audience, but was then hastily asked to move to the front row.[34] It was from journalists at the tea party the President held after the swearing-in ceremony that VP first learnt he would be the country's new finance minister.[35] The official confirmation came only the next day, the first day of 1985.

Part 4

RAID RAJ

1

'CLOTHES STITCHED FOR A FIVE-YEAR-OLD CANNOT BE WORN BY A THIRTY-FIVE-YEAR-OLD'

The Licence Raj—the welter of restrictions and protocols that governed business in India from Independence until 1991—was established with the noblest of intentions. An economy sucked dry by colonial rule had perforce to channel its limited resources towards planned priorities and targets; it would have been irresponsible to allow the market free play. But in the decades that followed, the controls turned into growth obstacles, especially with Indira Gandhi's pronounced leftward tilt from the late 1960s. That was when she enacted the Monopolies and Restrictive Trade Practices (MRTP) Act, which, aimed at curbing monopolies, also stifled expansion;[1] and the Foreign Exchange Regulation Act (FERA), which made holding foreign currency or assets legally almost impossible.[2] Additionally, she nationalized the banking and coal industries and, at one stage, raised the rate of marginal income tax, at its highest slab, to 93.5 per cent.

With the economy wilting in the 1970s, small steps to restore the balance had begun during the Janata Party interregnum and continued even during Indira's second stint as Prime Minister in the early 1980s, when she seemed to realize some of her earlier errors. But the most decisive move away from past economic practice (before the raj itself was demolished, starting June 1991) was V.P. Singh's 1985–86 budget. Unlike his mother, Rajiv Gandhi had no special fondness for socialist practices; and VP—despite his close links with socialist and communist parties in his twenties—seemed to have begun to feel the same way. 'Clothes stitched for a five-year-old cannot be worn by a thirty-five-year-old,' he said later. 'It does not mean that the clothes weren't right at the time they were made. Economic policies designed soon after Independence had to change as the country and the world changed.'[3]

Though he began his budget speech by quoting Indira approvingly,[4] it was mainly his one-time idol's excesses that VP's first budget blunted. Between 1977 and 1984, the highest income tax rate had already been reduced to 62 per cent; VP lowered it further to 50 per cent while also raising the income tax exemption limit substantially. He lowered wealth tax from 5 to 2 per cent; corporate tax from 55 to 50 per cent, and abolished both estate duty—payable while inheriting family property above a certain value—and the compulsory deposit scheme (CDS), by which a portion of salary had to be compulsorily kept in a fixed deposit for a given period.[5]

To unshackle private industry, he raised the asset limit, which would make the MRTP Act applicable to a business group, from Rs 20 crore to Rs 100 crore, even though the leading industry lobby, the Federation of Indian Chambers of Commerce and Industry (FICCI), in its pre-budget wish list to the government, had wanted it set at Rs 50 crore. One estimate claimed that as a result, out of the 186 business groups whose companies attracted MRTP Act provisions, 110 would no longer do so.[6] He added to this import-duty and excise-duty reductions on a host of items, abolishing excise duty on the sale of computers and their components, as well as on black-and-white TV sets. At a time when government sanction to close down loss-making companies above a certain size was rarely given, he set up the Board for Industrial and Financial Reconstruction (BIFR), which would help such companies either work out a revival plan or wind them up.[7] He also suggested a discussion on de-licensing certain industries.

Considering the transformation of the economy after 1991, these changes may now seem small, but at the time, VP's 108-minute speech on the evening of 16 March 1985 drew explosive reactions. Free-market proponents applauded; stock prices rose sharply; noted jurist and unabashed free-market enthusiast Nani A. Palkhivala, whose post-budget address at Bombay's Brabourne Stadium was a heavily attended annual event, called the budget 'the best ever in Independent India'.[8] The *Times of India* responded with a front-page editorial, saying that the budget would 'break many of the decades-old shackles on the initiative and enterprise of the Indian people'.[9]

But, equally, there were many who were enraged—and not only the socialist and communist parties, which collectively thrashed it as, in the words of the CPI (M) organ *People's Democracy*, 'promotion of unbridled capitalism'.[10] A large number of Congress members felt the same way, but they could hardly be seen criticizing their own finance minister, more so when he had Rajiv's full support.

Aware of their misgivings, VP himself underplayed the unorthodox aspects of his budget, insisting that they were far from 'revolutionary',[11] denying, in both Houses of Parliament, that there had been any 'departure from the path of socialism'.[12] But the doubters were far from mollified. At the first AICC meeting following the budget in early May 1985—at the usual venue, Delhi's Talkatora Stadium—they objected to the economic resolution VP had drafted, forcing him to remove one sentence in particular—'In the process of continued development, policy instruments relevant to one stage cannot be treated as permanently sacrosanct, nor are they ends in themselves'—and replacing it with several paragraphs reiterating the party's adherence to the 'socialist strategy of development'.[13]

With few revenue-raising options, despite his efforts to curb subsidies, VP's estimated fiscal deficit was the highest ever until then—Rs 3,349 crore.[14] (The actual deficit, revealed in the next budget, turned out even higher, at Rs 4,490 crore, 7.55 per cent of the gross domestic product [GDP]).[15] Inevitably, this led to an increase in prices in the next few months, which finally gave party members, alarmed by his liberalizing bent, the pretext to chastise him openly. The monsoon Parliament session, from the end of July 1985, saw the unusual sight of a number of Congress MPs joining the Opposition to blame their finance minister for the price rise. VP countered them not only in the House, but also with two detailed letters to all Congress MPs, providing tables and charts to show that the price rise in the first quarter of 1985–86 had been lower than in the corresponding period the previous year, and outlining a host of steps he was nevertheless taking to combat it.[16]

Indeed, wholesale price index (WPI) inflation in all twelve months of 1985–86 was a modest 4.4 per cent, the lowest during the 1980s, which saw an average annual inflation of over 8 per cent.[17] Yet, a regular furore over rising prices, rooted almost entirely in the disquiet over VP's departure from traditional economic policy, continued all through his first year as finance minister. Opposition party leaders even united to court arrest in protest when he raised the prices of petroleum products for a second time—having done so once already in his 1985–86 budget—in January 1986. This time around, Rajiv finally stepped in and withdrew his own finance minister's decision. It must have got to VP as his budget for 1986–87 was much more in keeping with those of Indira's time.

In this budget, among other measures, he increased the excise duty on 'luxury goods' such as colour TVs and air conditioners, and raised the allocation for rural poverty alleviation schemes, such as the National Rural Employment Programme, by a massive 65 per cent.[18]

However, even the 1986–87 budget had one innovation that proved far-reaching. VP introduced the concept of 'modified value-added tax' (MODVAT), albeit on a limited number of items, by which the manufacturer obtained 'instant and complete reimbursement of the excise duty paid on components and raw materials',[19] making such duty payable only on the value of the final product. Thus, as he noted in his budget speech, MODVAT decreased 'the cost of the final product considerably through the availability of instant credit of the duties paid and consequential reduction of interest costs'.[20] It was the beginning of the journey towards rationalizing indirect taxes and making them uniform across states, which culminated in the historic Goods and Services Tax (GST) regime from July 2017.[21]

VP's slashing of tax rates in his first budget had prompt, salutary impact. Far from dropping, direct tax collections increased by 22 per cent through the year, with the personal income tax component rising by 36 per cent.[22] In December 1985, for the first time in the country, he announced a 'long-term fiscal policy', valid for the next four years, which reiterated and expanded the government's liberalizing trend. He kept re-examining excise duties, removing anomalies pointed out to him (he learnt, for instance, that while bicycles were exempt from duty, their carriers were not; iron pipes were exempt, but concrete ones not);[23] he began the first full-scale crop-insurance scheme in the country; he allowed companies to provide employee stock options for the first time.

Faced with a growing shortage of steel, he worked towards amending the Industrial Policy Resolution of 1956 to allow new private players in steel production. At a time when the prices of numerous commodities were set by the state, he released a discussion paper questioning whether such 'administered prices' were indeed doing much good.[24] He did his best to counter bureaucratic efforts to subvert well-intended ministerial decisions[25]—instances he later cited seem straight out of the British sitcom *Yes Minister*. At the end of his first year, following an internal appraisal by Rajiv, VP was the only minister to get a congratulatory note for having achieved 95 per cent of his ministry's objectives.[26]

However, for all his efforts to ease business functioning and open up the economy, the GDP growth rate during his tenure remained modest, much the same as in the first half of the 1980s— 4.16 per cent in 1985–86, 4.31 per cent the following year.[27] Similarly, though he kept warning repeatedly against both the growing fiscal deficit and the trade deficit, he was unable to contain either. He was alarmed enough by the rising government expenditure and poor export performance to set up a committee headed by his ministry's banking secretary, Bimal Jalan,[28] to estimate what the deficits would amount to in five years if existing trends continued.

'The committee's report showed that the deficits would be huge,' said VP later. 'Even revenue expenditure might require borrowings, let alone fresh investments.' He made a presentation on the report to the cabinet. 'I said, "1989–90 will be an election year, and we'll have no money to offer anything to voters. Let us apply the brakes now."' He wanted the report discussed in Parliament, but it never was. 'Some people feared that if the report was made public, it would affect our creditworthiness, making foreign loans more costly and compounding our problems,' he said. 'The report was put under lock and key and never mentioned again.'[29]

As the economic meltdown of 1991—when India came close to being declared insolvent, and which forced the radical policy changes that followed—showed, the report had been prescient.[30]

VP pushed for economic liberalization at a time when the term itself was hardly heard in India. He was much more cautious, however, about globalization. Until mid-November 1985 (when a newly inducted cabinet minister was finally given its charge[31]), he also held, alongside finance, the same portfolio he'd had under Indira—commerce. As commerce minister, in mid-April 1985, he announced a new trade policy, valid for the next three years, which mirrored his approach as finance minister—shifting a host of import items from the 'restricted' to the open general licence (OGL) list, reducing import tariffs and simplifying the tariff structure while simultaneously offering more incentives for exports.[32] He continued to make similar policy tweaks for the rest of his term, propelling India further into the global economy. But it was a carefully calibrated opening-up—VP certainly did not support the unrestricted flow of foreign goods or funds into the country. And when it came to trade negotiations at GATT, he stuck firmly to India's traditional position.

GATT was a multilateral effort, begun in January 1948, to lower import tariffs across the world, after many Western countries realized that the high tariffs they had imposed during the Depression years of the 1930s to protect local industries and jobs were, in fact, hindering economic growth. India, despite its early emphasis on self-reliance and restricting imports, had been a founder member of GATT. But its main role during GATT talks—there were eight 'rounds' of such talks, each with a distinct name—had been to resist tariff-lowering measures from being imposed on developing countries and, instead, lobby for various trade concessions for them, insisting that such countries, given the state of their economies, deserved, as the widely used expression at the time went, 'special and differential treatment'.

Across three decades and seven rounds, up to the end of the 1970s, developing countries had managed to extract many privileges and exceptions to their own benefit in world trade, but once President Ronald Reagan assumed power in the US in 1980, his government began pushing back hard.[33] In the eighth and final round of GATT talks in particular—called the Uruguay round, because its first meeting was held at Punta del Este in Uruguay in September 1986—the US sought to expand the scope of GATT beyond a mere easing of trade of select goods, seeking agreements on matters the forum had largely avoided earlier as it was known that many countries did not want them discussed. Agriculture, textiles and services had been left out until then. The US wanted them in, their subsidies and tariffs examined and restricted; it wanted stricter protection of copyrights and patents, freer capital flows between countries and minimum global labour standards—all of which would mainly benefit developed countries while harming the economies of developing ones.

Of these, it was trade in services that the US put the greatest emphasis on at the start of the Uruguay round. US services needed new markets to keep growing, and the government was determined to help find them. In contrast, India, at the time (long before the digital revolution made it the 'world's back office'), had no services to offer that could compete globally. Rather, it feared that if goods and services were linked in any way, developed countries might retaliate against its unwillingness to allow free access to, say, foreign banks and insurance companies, by blocking Indian goods—including much-exported ones such as textiles—from entering their markets. VP fully subscribed to this view. As he put it in his speech at the Punta del Este meeting, 'All kinds of protectionist measures can be brought against us, using the alibi of insufficient opening of the services sector. Can national aspirations be condemned as obstacles to trade? Will vital policies for socio-economic transformation be subject to the vagaries of the marketplace?'[34]

Since GATT was a gathering of sovereign nations, its decisions had to be unanimous—they could not be taken by majority vote. This, in turn, required the US to convince every nation's leadership individually that the agreements it was seeking were also in that country's interest. It sought to do so by alternately hectoring and cajoling and, if that proved insufficient, pointedly reminding countries of the loans and grants it had given them. In his earlier term as commerce minister in 1983-84, VP had already witnessed this strategy first-hand. A favourite US ploy was to hold small closed-door meetings on controversial trade issues, to which invitees would be carefully handpicked. Out of a dozen, about ten would be experts espousing the US viewpoint, while the other two would be key functionaries of countries opposing it. 'The two dissenters would be boxed into a corner and made to feel embarrassed for holding (seemingly) obscurantist views inimical to their own interests,' wrote T.S.R. Subramanian in his memoirs.[35]

Subramanian accompanied VP to Washington for one such meeting in 1984, hosted by Bill Brock, the US trade representative then, but had to remain outside, disallowed from participating. He noted,

> I had briefed V.P. Singh on what to expect in the closed room from which all aides were blocked out. At the end of the meeting, as we were driving back to the hotel, V.P. Singh recounted to me the high-voltage attention applied on him in the pressure-cooker atmosphere. As a result, his opposition could be articulated only in muted terms. Predictably, his implied acquiescence was announced and broadcast to the world as full support for the American position.[36]

At a much larger meeting of global finance ministers with officials of the International Monetary Fund (IMF) and the World Bank in April 1986, again in Washington, VP responded better. Once more, a GATT agreement on trade in services was a major theme, expounded upon in particular by Arthur Dunkel,[37] secretary general of GATT from 1980 to 1993, who was among the speakers at the gathering. After his speech, Dunkel also circulated a report by a seven-member expert committee headed by Fritz Leutwiler, chairman of the Swiss National Bank, strongly advocating a services agreement under the GATT umbrella.[38]

One of the Indian officials at the meeting quietly passed VP a chit of paper, noting that no GATT meeting had endorsed appointing such a committee. VP jumped up immediately and pointed this out. 'I asked, "Is this a GATT report? When was it sought?"' he said later. 'Dunkel was embarrassed. The report was at his personal initiative. His expression was worth watching. I added, "I can also go to a bookstore, pick up a random book supporting my viewpoint and ask this august body to consider it."'[39]

Though the 'Wise Men Report', as it came to be called, was temporarily set aside, the US did not give up. Towards the end of the meeting, listening to the proposed press statement on its proceedings and decisions, VP was shocked to hear a clause related to a possible agreement on trade in services that he had never endorsed. He interrupted immediately, but the meeting's chairman insisted that no further changes to the statement could be made. 'This has all been agreed to,' he said. 'There is a consensus on this.'

'In that case, India reserves its position and will say so to the media,' responded VP.

The chairman pleaded that there was too little time before the scheduled press conference to redraft the statement, but with other developing nations' representatives also chipping in to support VP, he had no choice. The press conference was postponed by several hours while a fresh statement was drafted, which VP and the other dissenters approved of.[40]

At one stage, there were forty-seven developing countries supporting India in its steadfast opposition to any trade agreement on services,[41] but as the US stepped up pressure in the weeks before the Punta del Este meeting in September 1986, their numbers began shrinking. Clayton Yeutter, the new US trade representative who had succeeded Brock, threatened retaliatory action against countries putting 'unreasonable restrictions' on US services' export, while also declaring that the US was considering quitting GATT entirely and working out separate bilateral or multilateral agreements with different nations, if no agreement on services was reached.[42]

Though usually it was the commerce minister who handled GATT negotiations, and VP no longer held that charge, Rajiv preferred to send him as head of the Indian delegation, given his familiarity with its many nuances. Arriving at the scenic resort off the Atlantic coast, VP found that of the four other countries that had formed the core of resistance to a services agreement— Argentina, Egypt, Yugoslavia and Brazil (dubbed, along with India, 'the Gang of Five' [G5] by sections of the US press)[43]—the first three were also wavering. They had all found they had too much to lose by defying the US. Only Brazil stood firm with India.[44]

'We should thank our post-Independence leaders for their stress on economic self-reliance, or else India could never have withstood the pressure,' said VP later. 'A Filipino delegate admitted to me that his country would have liked to take the same stance as India but dared not.'[45]

Though even Rajiv warned him—on telephone—to ensure that India was not 'isolated', VP remained firm.[46] 'You can't play football on a cricket pitch,' he told those who sought to make him change his mind. '"An eye for an eye, a tooth for a tooth," goes the saying—so too should it be "goods for goods, services for services".'[47] Yeutter—leading a seventy-member-strong US delegation to the conference, the biggest among all countries, which set up a row of scrambler phones in an alcove close to the conference hall to keep in constant touch with Washington—met him repeatedly, often impatient and angry. 'He was rude and aggressive, but that doesn't work with me,' said VP. He suggested, instead, setting up a separate global forum on services—independent of GATT—which India would join when it was ready.[48]

VP had his way. The final Punta del Este declaration harped almost entirely on goods, with just four short paragraphs—two of them single sentences—touching on services, saying merely that 'a group of negotiators' was being set up to work out a 'framework' for a global services agreement, which would 'respect the policy objectives of national laws and regulations'.[49]

'It was my happiest moment in the government,' VP said afterwards.[50]

Eight years later, at the conclusion of the Uruguay round—which lasted until 1994—and after much more controversy,[51] the General Agreement on Trade in Services (GATS) was finally hammered out, distinct from GATT but under the aegis of the soon-to-be-formed WTO, which clearly laid down that every country would have the right to decide which of its services it wanted to progressively liberalize, and to what extent.[52]

—⸙—

Given charge of both the finance and the commerce portfolios in early January 1985 (for some months he held the textiles ministry too), with the Union budget to be readied by mid-March and a new export-import policy announced by mid-April, VP had initially assumed that he would soon be relieved of his earlier responsibility of UPCC president. When days went by without any such announcement, he spoke to Rajiv and even proposed a possible successor—Sheila Kaul, second-time MP from Lucknow and Rajiv's aunt. Soon after coming to power in January 1980, Indira had prematurely dissolved nine state assemblies (including UP's) and held fresh elections. All those assemblies were close to completing their five-year terms and another round of elections was due soon. As UPCC president, VP would have to choose candidates for all the 425 UP assembly seats, which would require spending days in Lucknow (if not elsewhere in the state as well), followed by intensive campaigning. Where would he find the time?

Rajiv said that he would consider the suggestion, but a few days later told VP to continue in the position until after the state elections. 'Manage somehow, turn your twenty-four hours into thirty-six,' he said.

VP was not convinced. 'I've already turned my twenty-four hours into forty-eight, and I'm still unable to,' he replied.[53] It made no difference and, soon after, in late January, election dates to eleven state assemblies (two more were added, for different reasons) were announced for early March, with VP still at the helm in the UP unit.

He did his best. As UP chief minister, he had learnt to delegate and did so to the extent possible—but still found himself overburdened. He had just moved with his family into a vast, sprawling bungalow at 1, Teen Murti Marg after becoming finance minister, but initially, he hardly spent any time there. He began living in his office, which he claimed he didn't mind at all. 'The finance minister's office is a vast room, bigger even than the Prime Minister's, with a private bathroom,' he said. 'Every day my wife would send me breakfast, lunch, dinner and a change of clothes.'[54]

Though he did visit Lucknow a couple of times, for the most part, he summoned members of the UP Congress's parliamentary board to Delhi to decide on ticket distribution. He later remembered,

The day's work took up to 9 p.m., after which officers would leave. Then I'd have dinner and from 9.30 p.m. until 1 a.m., I'd meet senior UP Congressmen and ticket aspirants. I'd work on files again until 3 a.m.; sleep from 3 to 6 a.m., and then start getting ready again. I continued that way for about fifteen–twenty days, never once going home.[55]

Even so, it proved inadequate. 'I had to decide not what I would do, but what I would not, where I was prepared to default,' he said. 'I felt I could not compromise on the budget or the trade policy, but some of the ticket distribution could be left to others.'[56]

It led to unhappy consequences for him. One of Rajiv's much-acclaimed efforts in his first year as Prime Minister had been to try to reform the Congress party, weeding out those he called 'power brokers'—men widely believed to be corrupt, some with criminal charges against them, but nonetheless influential—whom both his late mother and brother had tolerated, so long as they delivered votes for the party.[57] Soon after taking over, he had removed some party general secretaries and dropped a few of his mother's favourite ministers from his cabinet, but the most comprehensive effort to cleanse the party was taken during the selection of the 2,543 candidates across eleven states in the March 1985 assembly polls. He sent a set of ten guidelines to the Congress units of states holding elections, emphasizing, above all, that only those possessing a 'clean image'[58] should be considered. While making the final selections from the 6,000-odd shortlisted names sent to him, he sought the help of the Intelligence Bureau to vet their backgrounds.

It led to about 40 per cent of sitting MLAs being denied re-nomination. In UP, exactly 50 per cent—153 of the 306 sitting MLAs—were dropped, including seven ministers.[59] VP, given his own obsession with personal probity, should have been delighted. But he was not, as he felt that the process had been subverted—those entrusted with shortlisting UP candidates had used the opportunity to deny nominations to members of rival factions, 'image' being a secondary consideration. 'Rajiv Gandhi and most of his advisers who took the final call on candidates had few contacts at the ground level, and did not realize they were being misled,' said VP. But he had no time to intervene on behalf of those he believed were unfairly denied. 'I personally knew a number of them,' he said. 'Some may have been the dabang (aggressive) type, but they were not criminals.'[60]

The rejected candidates blamed VP for their omission. Those denied held protests outside the finance ministry. When he visited the Congress office in Delhi, he was surrounded and heckled.[61] This included Kashinath Mishra, the sitting MLA from Ballia on the UP–Bihar border, who had been president of the Allahabad University students' union when VP was vice president, and was a close friend. 'He thought I had denied him the ticket, and our friendship suffered,' said VP. 'He would not believe that I had nothing to do with the decision.'[62]

The fallout was inescapable—many of those denied tickets worked to sabotage the chances of the official Congress candidate, some even contesting as independents. Though the Congress still won nine of the eleven states, including UP, its overall vote share fell by a steep 26.3 per cent from that achieved in the Lok Sabha elections only nine weeks ago. In most states, it did worse than in the 1980 assembly elections. In UP, its seat tally dropped from 306 in the previous assembly to 269; in Allahabad, where it had won 12 of the 14 seats in 1980, it got only 9 this time. Of the 100 rank newcomers given tickets, only thirty won.[63] Reflecting later, VP acknowledged that Kamalapati Tripathi's putdown, comparing a political career to a tree (both take time to grow) when VP himself had first sought a ticket in the 1969 UP assembly election, had been accurate. 'Kamalapatiji was right,' he said. 'A political career is not like a wall, which can be built overnight.'[64]

❧

The candidate-selection process also led to the first meeting between VP and Som Pal, who would become one of his closest political aides in the coming years.[65]

Som Pal hailed from Chhaprauli, the assembly constituency Charan Singh had represented in the early part of his career, and which came to be regarded as his home borough. His father, Raghubir Singh Shastri, had briefly joined Charan Singh's party in its BKD incarnation and was its MP from Baghpat, the Lok Sabha seat of which Chhaprauli is a part, in 1967–71. (Shastri won the seat as an independent, joining BKD well after it was formed.) But except for this short phase, the two, both belonging to the Jat caste, remained rivals for most of their political careers, with Shastri maintaining that Charan Singh had repeatedly let him down.

After Shastri's death in 1982, his family had decided that the rivalry should continue. Accordingly, in the 1984 Lok Sabha polls, Som Pal had sought the Congress nomination from Baghpat, simply to oppose Charan Singh. Indira had been agreeable, since this was a seat the Congress expected to lose anyway and there were few claimants for the nomination. But following her assassination and various later developments, Som Pal chose not to contest.

When the assembly elections were announced soon after, he decided to try again, this time for the Chhaprauli nomination. (Having won the Baghpat Lok Sabha seat in the 1984 election, Charan Singh had made his daughter, Saroj Verma, his party's— now called the Dalit Mazdoor Kisan Party (DMKP)—candidate from Chhaprauli.) Thanks to his father, Som Pal had many political acquaintances, including Congress politicians, but he had never met VP. The Congress leaders he spoke to said they were ready to nominate him—as with Baghpat, no one wanted to contest the seat, and for the same reason—but he needed VP's assent as well. Yet no one was prepared to help arrange a meeting between them.

Som Pal had little time—all nominations would be decided within a few days of the election announcement. He finally remembered a friend who was not in politics and who had claimed that he knew VP well, and approached him for an introduction. 'You don't know the kind of person he is,' the friend replied. 'Ours is a personal relationship. If I start making political recommendations to him, he'll never let me into his house again.'

Discouraged, Som Pal was about to leave when the friend added, 'I'll give you a tip, though—it's the best I can do. V.P. Singh is going to Lucknow tomorrow by the early-morning flight. You could try and catch him en route.' Som Pal consulted Indian Airlines' timetables and found that there were two early-morning flights from Delhi to Lucknow. The friend had no idea which one VP would catch.

Luckily for Som Pal, he had another friend in the Delhi police, a fellow Jat, who was part of the team guarding the airport.[66] He rushed to the airport, met the friend, explained his situation, paid him the airfare to Lucknow and asked him to ensure he got a ticket on whichever flight VP took. The next morning, he was at the airport at 4.15 a.m., well before the first flight was to leave. In the event, VP took the later flight and Som Pal's policeman friend helped him sneak into the VIP lounge, where VP—along with a few UP Congress leaders—was waiting to board. The friend even introduced him to VP.

'I may not be able to defeat Saroj Verma,' Som Pal told VP, 'but because of my family background, my candidature will force Charan Singh to spend a lot more time in Chhaprauli, campaigning for his daughter, than if you choose anyone else. This will constrain his campaign for his candidates in other constituencies.' He recalled VP noting a few particulars about him in a 'pocket computer'— a hi-tech device at the time—he was carrying. There was no need now for Som Pal to travel to Lucknow, but he went along anyway.

Som Pal got the nomination. Pressed though he was for time, VP even campaigned in Chhaprauli, during which they got to know each other better. 'He addressed two meetings in my constituency, and even invited me, a rank newcomer in politics then, to travel with him in his helicopter from the first meeting to the second,' said Som Pal. 'It greatly boosted my image among the people of the area.'

As he had predicted, Charan Singh, rattled by Som Pal's presence as an opponent, spent a full week campaigning in Chhaprauli, much of the time apologizing to village elders for his nepotistic choice of candidate. Som Pal was also right about the result— Saroj Verma won by a modest 4,658 votes.[67]

—◇◇◇—

A couple of months after the election, VP was finally freed of his UP charge, with Mahavir Prasad, a senior Dalit MP from Bansgaon in east UP, taking over.

December 1936: Vishwanath Pratap Singh, five years old, seated on the lap of his adoptive ther Raja of Manda Ram Gopal Singh (sixth from left), posing with guests on the occasion of his option ceremony on the grounds of Aish Mahal, the raja's mansion in Allahabad, Uttar Pradesh.

December 1936: Five-year-old V.P. Singh (centre) with his adoptive father (right).

Manda Palace, V.P. Singh's childhood home after his adoption, 60 km south-east of Allahabad.

1953: V.P. Singh, twenty-two, studes at Allahabad University, at his Aish Mahal home.

25 June 1955: V.P. Singh, twenty-four, on his wedding day, at the residence of his prospective wife, Sita Kumari Singh, in Deogarh, Rajasthan.

31 July 1955: V.P. Singh (second from left), in Warsaw, Poland, participating in the World Festival of Youth and Students. The festival was organized sporadically by the World Federation of Democratic Youth, a communist front organization. V.P. Singh was part of the 150-strong Indian delegation.

1965: V.P. Singh (left) with Bhoodan movement leader Vinoba Bhave (extreme right) at Koraon, 60 km south of Allahabad. Bhave is inaugurating the intermediate section of the school called Gopal Vidyalaya, which V.P. Singh had begun in 1952. In 1957, V.P. Singh had donated all his agricultural land to the Bhoodan movement.

December 1976: V.P. Singh (left) being administered the oath of office as minister of state for commerce in Indira Gandhi's government by President Fakhruddin Ali Ahmed. V.P. Singh first became deputy minister for commerce in October 1974, and was promoted as minister of state two years later.

October 1984: V.P. Singh, then Uttar Pradesh Congress president, with Indira Gandhi at the Congress office in Lucknow. Eleven days later, Indira was shot dead by her own security guards.

16 March 1985: Finance Minister V.P. Singh entering Parliament to deliver his historic 1985 budget. He was finance minister for two years (January 1985–January 1987).

1988: After quitting the Congress in July 1987, V.P. Singh launched the Jan Morcha. His meetings, following his anti-corruption crusade, drew huge crowds, as seen in this rally he is addressing in Varanasi, Uttar Pradesh.

2 December 1989: V.P. Singh being sworn in as Prime Minister of India by President R. Venkataraman at Rashtrapati Bhavan in New Delhi. His government was supported by both the BJP and the communist parties.

March 1990: Prime Minister V.P. Singh meeting Nelson Mandela at Windhoek, Namibia, on e historic occasion of Namibia gaining full independence from South Africa. From left to right: PI (M) general secretary Harkishan Singh Surjeet, V.P. Singh, Nelson Mandela, Winnie Mandela elson Mandela's wife), Sita Kumari Singh (V.P. Singh's wife) and BJP's Atal Bihari Vajpayee.

July 1990: Prime Minister V.P. Singh with USSR Communist Party General Secretary Mikhail orbachev in Moscow. From left to right: Raisa Gorbachev, V.P. Singh, Mikhail Gorbachev and ta Kumari Singh.

Above: 15 August 1990: Prime Minister V.P. Singh addressing the nation from the Red Fort on Independence Day.

Left: V.P. Singh hoisting the Indian flag at the Red Fort earlier on the same day.

2

'THEFT CAN'T BE BUSINESS'

The year 1984 was one of despair for India—the anarchy in Punjab leading to the army assault on the Golden Temple in June; the retributory assassination of Indira Gandhi and the massacre of Sikhs in October–November; the methyl isocyanate gas leak from the Union Carbide plant in Bhopal in December, causing one of the world's worst industrial disasters, killing at least 4,000.

In contrast, 1985 was one of immense, if short-lived, hope. This was mainly because, as noted earlier, Rajiv Gandhi, in his first year as Prime Minister, took several steps that suggested that he was determined to wipe out corruption in politics. But V.P. Singh's actions as finance minister also contributed greatly to the optimism. Not so much because of the new direction he tried to give the Indian economy, but due to a parallel drive he launched against corruption in business, which did not shrink from targeting some of the most venerable companies of the time.

VP's elevation to heading the finance ministry had been a surprise. His predecessor in the job was Pranab Mukherjee[1] (later to be the country's President from 2012 to 2017), one of Indira's closest lieutenants, who got the portfolio in early

1982 and continued to hold it in Rajiv's first cabinet, formed immediately after his mother's assassination. Following the Congress's December 1984 election victory, he was widely expected to be nominated again, but VP was given his job instead, while Mukherjee was excluded from the cabinet. Asked why he took this startling decision, Rajiv replied, 'I thought we needed a change. The finance minister has to be very tough. He can't be goody-goody. I don't think he (Mukherjee) was tough enough.'[2]

VP soon began to display the toughness Rajiv claimed he expected from him. Living up to his reputation for extreme scrupulousness, he started by announcing that while businessmen were welcome to meet him in delegations or attend his 'open house' forums (which were started in this ministry as well), he would never meet them individually. 'I did not have to raise funds for the party, so I could do what I wanted,' he said later. 'When he gave me the job, Rajiv Gandhi knew I was incapable of raising funds.'[3]

For his clean-up drive, VP needed officers as firm and upright as himself and, as in his previous positions, set about finding them. Among his notable appointees was Vinod Pande, whom he had first met in his earlier stint in the commerce ministry. VP had been much impressed by his rectitude, and now made him revenue secretary. (It helped that Pande, too, hailed from Allahabad, was a well-regarded novelist and poet [apart from his day job], and shared VP's father and late elder brother Chandrasekhar Singh's passion for astrology.)[4] Another was Bhure Lal, who had been his secretary when he was UP chief minister and whom he now made head of the Enforcement Directorate.

VP also set up a new department, the Central Bureau of Economic Intelligence, purely to gather information on economic crimes. He announced a reward scheme for teams that unearthed illegal assets during raids, offering them 20 per cent of the confiscated assets' value. He hoped this would deter them from taking bribes, letting off those found owning unexplained assets—

and indeed this scheme enabled some of the team members to earn more than their cumulative salary of the past ten years.[5]

But he knew that there were also officers sunk too deep in corruption to be swayed by departmental rewards. He began weeding them out, focusing on the senior ones, scanning their records, seeking feedback from select retired officers and following up relevant media reports. In a burst of initial enthusiasm, in mid-February 1985, he sacked the chairmen of three leading public-sector banks—Central Bank of India, Punjab National Bank and Bank of Baroda—along with some of their other top officials.[6]

Though he gave no reasons, it was widely speculated that this was because Central Bank and Punjab National Bank had provided insufficiently secured loans to companies owned by the flamboyant London-based businessman Rajinder Sethia, who had, by then, acquired the tag of being 'the biggest bankrupt in Britain's history'.[7] (Sethia, then absconding, was arrested in Delhi a month later and spent over two years in Tihar jail.) Bank of Baroda was alleged to have been less than vigilant in a cheating case. But the dismissed London-based general manager of Punjab National Bank, Amarjeet Singh, challenged his removal in court, which, while not reinstating him, admonished the government for its action and ordered payment of compensation.[8]

Thereafter, VP abandoned firings and stuck to transfers, shifting officials he was distrustful of to humdrum corners of their departments, which offered no scope for corruption. (Some even faced CBI raids.[9]) The churn was particularly vigorous in the income tax, and excise and customs departments, where the graft was rife and revenue collections had been falling well short of targets in past years. By the time he was done by mid-July, every fourth officer at and above the level of commissioner in both departments had been transferred, including all the commissioners of income tax, three of the seven members of the Central Board of Direct Taxes, and six of the seven on the Central Board of Excise and Customs,[10] starting with its chairman.[11] In his capacity as commerce minister, following a bungled deal in which the United Arab Emirates rejected a large consignment of rice the State Trading Corporation had exported, VP removed its chairman and the director responsible for exports.[12]

Of the income tax commissioners transferred, eight were sent as instructors to the National Academy of Direct Taxes, Nagpur, where freshly inducted members of the Indian Revenue Service are trained before assuming field duties. Rajiv objected at first to this, not because such teachers were hardly the role models new entrants to the service deserved, but as it would require creating commissioner-level positions at the academy, which was staffed by officers of lower rank. 'You keep saying ministries should cut expenditure,' he pointed out to VP, 'but you are increasing it in your own ministry.'

'Every department, like every household, needs to invest in waste bins to keep it clean,' VP replied. 'This move will ultimately earn the government a lot of money.'[13]

Soon after, a delegation of about twenty-five MPs stormed into VP's room, protesting on behalf of one of the eight commissioners, but VP responded to them as he had done in transfer-related matters while he was UP chief minister—he told the MPs that they were welcome to try and get him removed as minister but that he would not change his order. Eventually, seven of the commissioners resigned, with only one joining the National Academy in Nagpur.[14]

Raids by the law enforcement agencies of the finance ministry—especially by the income tax and excise and customs departments, the Enforcement Directorate and the Department of Revenue Intelligence (DRI)—increased as soon as VP took over, with more of them being conducted in the first three months of 1985 than in all of 1984.[15] Bhure Lal remembered VP's early instructions. 'He told us that we could raid whichever individual or company we chose, that no one was sacrosanct and that we need not even inform him beforehand, but that our homework had to be thorough before taking any step,' he said.

How did he do his homework? 'I needed intelligence, which could only be obtained through informers,' he said. 'I had my network of informers—how else would I know anything?'[16]

Among his first raids was the home of Ahmedabad's biggest textile tycoon, Mrugesh Jaikrishna, owner of Sri Ambika Mills, one of whose couriers had been caught at the Bombay airport with a suitcase full of US dollars. This led to further raids—jointly with a DRI team—on a host of cubbyhole shops in Bombay's Agripada area that were found to be fronts for a flourishing illegal market in foreign exchange.[17]

At first, VP seemed to proceed industry by industry. In February 1985, he began with real estate, where charging unofficial premiums on every property sale was (and remains) commonplace, raiding a large number of Bombay-based developers.[18] He moved on to diamond merchants and gold jewellers, who were accused of evading customs duty on their imports and excise duty on their sales; he got after the leading cigarette makers in the country for evading excise duty; he targeted Bombay film producers, also notorious for black-money dealings, raiding the likes of Gulshan Rai, N.N. Sippy and Subhash Ghai.[19] The same business forums that had been rhapsodic about his 1985 budget began to complain loudly, both about the raids and the wide publicity given to the charges against the raided even before they had been proved in court—but VP was nonchalant. 'I've not yet started moving,' he told *India Today* in September 1985. 'I've only turned the ignition on.'[20]

The next twelve months proved that he'd meant it. His two-year tenure in the finance ministry saw about 6,000 raids, with 100,000 premises being searched and about half a million people interrogated,[21] in a wide-ranging clean-up drive dubbed 'Operation Ketu' by his department. Apart from the numbers, which were unprecedented in Indian history, it was the stature of some of the industrial groups and companies investigated that shocked—the then globally renowned engineering-goods-making Kirloskar Group, the paper- and glass-manufacturing Thapar Group, the two-wheeler and three-wheeler behemoth Bajaj Auto, the Tata-owned air-conditioning heavyweight Voltas, the Hindustan Lever-owned tea brand Lipton India, and the Indian subsidiary of global shoemaker Bata, among others. The Kirloskar and Thapar companies were both charged with violating foreign-exchange rules; Voltas and Bata India with evading excise duty; Lipton with overpaying overseas advertisers in return for kickbacks;[22] and Bajaj Auto with pocketing an unofficial premium from the sale of its scarce autorickshaws.[23]

As the raids mounted, so did the volume of business owners' protests, but VP was implacable. 'The culture of business has to change,' he said. 'We're after tax evaders, not business. Our whole policy package, including reasonable tax rates, was designed to promote the growth of a healthy private sector. But theft can't be business.'[24]

Public sentiment overwhelmingly supported VP, all the more because unlike raids of the past, which were often undertaken to intimidate businessmen supporting the rivals of the ruling party, his were all-encompassing, free of political bias. An *India Today* poll ranking the top leaders of the time—the results carried in its 31 August 1986 issue—found VP a surprisingly close second to Rajiv. (No other Congress leader matched them; the next four places all went to chief ministers of Opposition-ruled states.) 'V.P. Singh has given people the confidence [to think] that honesty does pay, and that the dishonest will be brought to book. Now, for the first time, corruption is not being looked upon as a fact of life,' wrote one of the respondents.[25]

There was some disquiet, however, over the severity of treatment of some of the heads of the raided companies. The first such case was that of Kapal Mehra, chairman of Orkay Silk Mills, a polyester yarn manufacturer and rising company at the time. Mehra was jailed for eighteen days in November 1985, with DRI officials opposing his bail application five times before they finally relented. Orkay was charged with under-invoicing the polyester chips it had imported from a Japanese company to evade import duty, with DRI officials even travelling to Tokyo to obtain documents that showed that the company had paid the full amount due, while claiming to Indian customs that it had managed a discount. 'The law is for all and does not recognize your address,' said VP in response to the criticism.[26]

But the second such case invited even more flak. On 6 December 1985, Enforcement Directorate officers raided the Pune home of the eighty-two-year-old chairman of the Kirloskar Group, Shantanu Laxman Kirloskar, early in the morning, hauled him to the police station and questioned him until 3 a.m. the next day. Bhure Lal, who had flown to Pune to supervise the operation, however, insisted that his team's conduct had been unexceptionable. 'Kirloskar may have been eighty-two, but he was quite fit,' he said. 'Actually, I treated him with a lot of respect. I explained the case to him and he understood. I said, "I'll have to arrest you, but when you seek bail, we won't oppose it." But eventually we only questioned him—he was not arrested. Later, he sought anticipatory bail, and we did not oppose it.'[27]

VP, too, seemed contrite afterwards. 'I learnt about it in the afternoon and telephoned Bhure Lal,' he said. 'I said, "Why police station? Why don't you question him at home?" He said that when he suggested it to Kirloskar, he was told, "Now that you've brought me to the police station, finish the matter here itself."'[28] What made it worse for the ministry was that a Pune court eventually exonerated the company of any wrongdoing, though VP later insisted that it was only because he could not get a crucial document from Hamburg, West Germany, in time.[29]

'I put the fear of God into industrialists and V.P. Singh supported me all the way,' said Bhure Lal. 'Companies began conducting mock raids at their offices to ensure no incriminating pieces of paper would be found if they were ever raided.'[30] Among his arrests was a man little known then, but instantly recognizable today—Vijay Mallya, then barely thirty, who had taken over United Breweries (UB) following the unexpected death of his father two years earlier. 'I arrested him at the Bangalore airport as he flew in from Calcutta,' said Bhure Lal. The UB Group was arraigned for allegedly breaching both the FERA and the MRTP Act.[31]

The arrest and overnight detention of Lalit Mohan Thapar, chairman of the Thapar Group, the fifth-largest conglomerate in India at the time, on 4 September 1986, brought even greater blowback than Kirloskar's prolonged questioning. Thapar was Delhi-based and knew several leading politicians and bureaucrats well. The matter was raised in Parliament; the Prime Minister's office also sought an explanation.

But in this case, VP and Bhure Lal came out triumphant, as five weeks later, on 17 October 1986, after much discussion between the Enforcement Directorate and Thapar's lawyers, Thapar tendered a written apology, accepting fourteen of the eighteen charges framed against his companies, while the Enforcement Directorate agreed to drop criminal charges.[32] 'By and large, I feel there were no excesses during our investigations and said so in my Parliament speech on the matter,' said VP later. 'I submitted proof showing why the probes were sought. Many of those who complained later sought my pardon in writing.'[33]

From mid-1986, VP even got after companies that deferred paying excise dues by contesting them in tribunals or courts. Pointing out that Rs 3,700 crore of revenue was thereby being withheld from the government, he got the cabinet to endorse an economic boycott of all companies with excise dues of over Rs 5 crore—no more industrial licences, permits to increase capacity, sanctions for fresh share issues or loans from financial institutions for them until they paid up. His cabinet colleague N.D. Tiwari—whom Rajiv had brought back as industries minister in September 1985, after his second stint as UP chief minister—argued strongly that industrial development could not be held hostage to revenue collection, but VP had his way. He prepared and released his blacklist of 400 such companies soon after, which included TISCO (now Tata Steel), ITC and Hindustan Lever.[34]

What prompted VP to embark on such a crusade, almost as relentless as his drive against dacoits as UP chief minister? Rajiv's early emphasis on a clean government may have been the trigger, but VP persisted in his cleansing efforts all through his tenure, well after Rajiv—realizing the contradictions arising from this—had abandoned his own. Surely VP knew that much of the black-money private business generated was to surreptitiously fund political parties, especially during elections, and excessive zeal in unearthing it could embarrass his own party?[35] As both UP chief minister and commerce minister, he had sought to reduce corruption, but never as relentlessly as he did while he was finance minister.

Some have claimed that he was prompted by the largely negative political response—including within his party—to his 1985 budget; he wanted to correct any perception that he was partial to private industry, which, in the socialistic ambience of the time, could be ruinous for his political future. (When former US Secretary of State Henry Kissinger visited India in February 1986, VP refused him an appointment, despite being advised to meet him by the Prime Minister's Office. It was said that he was worried that such a meeting, just before his 1986 budget was due, would be used by his critics as further proof of his pro-capitalist, pro-US bent.[36])

Asked about it, VP's reply, however, suggested that his sole motive was to leave a lasting imprint as finance minister. He said,

In Hindu mythology, Brahma is the god of creation. How many temples are devoted to Brahma? I think there is one at Pushkar, but that's it. How many temples worship Rama or Krishna? There are innumerable. It is because they fought and overcame evil. I decided that I too should fight corporate evil.[37]

There was one more leading company VP targeted during his clean-up drive, but in this case, it cost him his job and changed the course of his political career. Reliance Industries was already a business superstar by the time he became finance minister in 1985. Set up by the redoubtable Dhirubhai Ambani—the son of an impecunious schoolteacher in Junagadh, Gujarat, who couldn't afford to send him to college[38]—it had, in just eighteen years since its launch in 1967, become the third-biggest company in the country in terms of revenue (after the two venerable Tata-owned companies, TISCO and TELCO, started decades earlier). It also had the highest net worth and net profit among Indian companies.[39]

Starting with overseas trade in numerous commodities, later specializing in the yarn trade alone, Reliance had since expanded into textile manufacturing as well, setting up the country's most advanced textile mill in Naroda, Gujarat, and a giant polyester filament yarn-making factory in Patalganga, Maharashtra, buying the technology from the US chemical giant DuPont de Nemours. It was also, at the time, building a plant to manufacture purified terephthalic acid (PTA), one of the ingredients used to make polyester fibre, at Patalganga, again with technical support from DuPont.

Reliance was also justly renowned for having galvanized the Indian stock market ever since it went public in 1977, drawing into its fold innumerable first-time small investors through its adept use of a financial instrument rarely employed by Indian companies before—the convertible debenture. Between 1979 and 1984, it had issued four 'series' of partially convertible debentures of progressively increasing amounts, which, thanks to its ever-rising stock price, were all wildly oversubscribed.[40] Once the convertible part was turned into shares, the company had so many shareholders that its annual general body meetings were famously held at Bombay's Cooperage football stadium and, on one memorable occasion, at the vast Cross Maidan in the city, to be able to accommodate the thousands attending. Between 1980 and 1985, the number of Indians owning shares increased from less than a million to over four million, of whom more than one million held Reliance shares.

In that era of strict controls, business houses had to network extensively with relevant ministries, both at the Centre and in the states, for licences and permits, but it was widely whispered that Reliance did so much more effectively than most others. At times, even national policy bore an imprint of Reliance's influence.[41] Thus, for instance, although forty-four companies had applied for licences to manufacture polyester filament yarn, Reliance was initially the only one granted it.[42] (Two others, Orkay Silk Mills and JK Synthetics, were allowed smaller capacities later.) Again, soon after Reliance's factory was commissioned, the government imposed anti-dumping duty on imported polyester yarn—in addition to the high customs duty already existing—thereby helping Reliance's product compete better on price.

Further, in September 1984, Reliance was given permission to convert even the non-convertible part of its four debenture series into shares, enabling it to retire a substantial amount of debt as well as increase its equity base. Encouraged, Reliance issued its fifth or 'E' series of similar debentures in October 1984, and an 'F' series in mid-1985, for much larger amounts than the first four.[43]

The first indication that VP's entry had reduced Reliance's influence in the finance and commerce ministries came in May 1985. One of Reliance's rivals in the polyester trade—as old and venerable a company as Reliance was young and brash—was the 1879-founded Bombay Dyeing and Manufacturing Co., which had just completed setting up a plant to make dimethyl terephthalate (DMT), which could be substituted for the PTA that Reliance was set to manufacture to make polyester fibre.

While the import of DMT was difficult, with the item being on the 'restricted' list, that of PTA was not. Indeed, Reliance had been bringing in large amounts of PTA ever since it launched its polyester-manufacturing units; its own PTA plant was still more than a year from completion. At a time when VP was generously liberalizing imports, shifting numerous items from the 'restricted' to the 'open general licence (OGL)' list, Bombay Dyeing, to expand the market for its own product, lobbied successfully to get PTA moved the other way—from the 'OGL' list to the 'restricted'.

Evidently, Bombay Dyeing's lobbyists had scored over Reliance's. Certainly, Reliance had the option to buy DMT from Bombay Dyeing for its polyester manufacturing instead of importing PTA, but to use DMT as raw material, it would have had to make major changes to its manufacturing plant, apart from absorbing a sizeable rise in input costs. But Reliance, too, responded with panache—it was revealed soon after that in the forty-eight hours before the change was made, the company had opened letters of credit with a number of banks to place orders importing more than a year's supply of PTA, enough to meet its needs until its own PTA plant got going.

It was clear that either informers in the ministry had tipped it off about the decision in advance, or the letters of credit had been opened after the ministry's order but backdated with the connivance of bank officials, or both. Departmental enquiries were ordered, and though their results were never made public, three senior officials from at least one of the banks involved—Canara Bank—were suspended soon after.[44]

All at once, reports also began appearing in the media rubbishing the use of DMT to make polyester fibre, calling it an obsolete method as compared to the more modern one employing PTA. Other reports ran down the quality of the DMT Bombay Dyeing was producing. Soon, a bitter media war erupted between Reliance and Bombay Dyeing, with many publications blatantly backing one or the other, hurling accusations that went well beyond their polyester market rivalry.

The most important of these was a series of more than a dozen investigative reports in *The Indian Express*—the second-highest selling newspaper in the country at the time (after the *Times of India*). Beginning in March 1986 and continuing through the year, it made such serious charges of fraud against Reliance that no finance minister—let alone VP, by then well into his anti-corruption crusade—could have ignored them. *The Indian Express* was then still headed by its founder, the formidable Ramnath Goenka, eighty-one at the time, immensely respected for his resistance to press censorship during the Emergency ten years ago.

Reliance had just then sought permission to convert the non-convertible portion of its 'E' and 'F' series of debentures into equity shares, just as it had done with its previous four series. The first four *Indian Express* reports discussed the scheme threadbare and concluded that sanctioning the change 'risked destroying the whole principle behind the distinction between convertibles and non-convertibles … [N]o one will bother with convertible issues if this is allowed as a general practice.' One of the reports also pointed out that many obscure investment companies had taken bank loans at 18 per cent interest to buy the debentures, which offered only 13.5 per cent, and wondered what lay behind this seeming abandoning of business sense by both banks and investors.[45]

Subsequent stories revealed that dubious overseas companies, registered in tax havens such as the Isle of Man and the British Virgin Islands, had invested substantially in Reliance, and speculated on who actually owned them.[46] An August 1986 *Indian Express* report made the further sensational charge that Reliance had imported much greater capacity for its polyester fibre-making factory at Patalganga than it had officially declared, surreptitiously bringing in a 25 MW power plant too, avoiding import duty of more than Rs 100 crore.[47] It went on,

> We know of watches, radio recorders, videos, popular consumer durables sneaking into India. But we had not so far come across anyone trying to smuggle in large factories ... If huge steel structures ... can be smuggled into India, why not guns? Tanks and missiles even? [Also] doesn't the Enforcement Directorate want to know where Reliance got the foreign exchange to pay for these?[48]

The reports were written, not by any *Indian Express* staffer, but by Swaminathan Gurumurthy, a Madras-based chartered accountant whose firm handled *The Indian Express*'s tax returns. 'One day in May 1985, when I met Ramnathji at his penthouse in Mumbai, he had a file in his hands,' recalled Gurumurthy, currently an independent director with the Reserve Bank of India (RBI). 'He asked me at the top of his voice, "Guru, who owns *Indian Express*?" I told him he did. He said, "No, Ambani owns it." Then he showed me the file, which had clippings of several articles and editorials that had appeared in either *Indian Express* or its sister publication *Financial Express,* directly or obliquely supporting Reliance's position on various policy matters against its business rivals.' Goenka wanted Gurumurthy to probe Reliance's finances and activities, and submit a report to him. 'He told me, "We have to fight this monster together,"' said Gurumurthy.[49]

Gurumurthy admitted that he had known nothing of the polyester business when he had started, but with the help of a couple of experts he was introduced to, he quickly learnt.[50]

'I produced a three-volume report on Reliance's fraudulent activities and thought my work would end with that,' he said. 'But when Ramnathji saw the explosive facts I had unearthed, he decided *Indian Express* should launch a campaign against Reliance. We took some of the senior editors of the paper into confidence, but found they were unwilling to write on the subject.' Their reasons were genuine enough. Some said it was too specialized for them, while others were unwilling to associate with an investigation they had not themselves carried out. 'Ramnathji then insisted that I write the reports,' said Gurumurthy. 'It was a call of destiny for me, as it turned me into a celebrity writer within months.'[51]

Gurumurthy did more than write his reports—he also met ministers and officials to apprise them of his findings. 'V.P. Singh was the first person I met in the government,' he said. 'Ramnathji arranged the meeting.' Contrary to VP's image at the time of a rampaging wrecker of private industry, Gurumurthy found him Hamlet-like. 'He struck me as an honest man, but not sure of himself,' he said. 'He was always hesitant and highly image-conscious. What mattered, however, was that he was unapproachable for the powerful Reliance lobby.'[52]

VP's first step, on 10 June 1986, was an outright ban on all conversion of non-convertible debentures into shares, although an 'in principle' assent for such conversion of Reliance's 'E' and 'F' debentures had already been given. Reliance's share price slumped; the market price of the two debenture series dropped by nearly 50 per cent. Following an 'open house' some weeks later with the texturizers of polyester yarn, VP also rescinded the anti-dumping duty on polyester yarn the previous government had imposed.

VP went on to order an RBI enquiry into the role of banks in funding purchases of the 'E' and 'F' debentures. The central bank's interim report in July maintained that its guidelines had been violated by nine banks while lending to newly formed companies to invest in Reliance debentures, but the final report in October hedged its findings, failing to establish any specific wrongdoing. In contrast, the customs and excise department's probe into the smuggling of excess capacity at Reliance's polyester yarn-making plant vindicated Gurumurthy, estimating its capacity at 55,000–63,000 MT, though it had been licensed only 25,125 MT.[53] (It also found the power plant Gurumurthy had written about, but Reliance insisted that it was a gift from DuPont, thrown in free with the imports, and thus should not attract import duty.) In February 1987, the department imposed one of its heaviest penalties until then on Reliance.

There remained, however, the matter of how Reliance had paid in foreign exchange for the additional machinery it imported, as well as its links with the mysterious Isle of Man and British Virgin Islands companies. 'V.P. Singh put me on to Vinod Pande and Bhure Lal, both spotlessly clean officers in the ministry,' said Gurumurthy. Bhure Lal and Gurumurthy began working closely together, both separately visiting London for enquiries, but neither could unearth much. Gurumurthy, who had even met a couple of private detective agencies while in London, suggested the Indian government engage one.

Bhure Lal agreed. 'How do we get financial information from overseas except by using a detective agency?' he said later. 'Indian laws don't matter there. Our embassies are useless in this regard and, in fact, hostile. They claim such investigations could spoil our relations with the host countries.'[54] He sought Vinod Pande's permission to do so, who, in turn, asked VP. At first, the finance minister demurred, but later gave a wary go-ahead. 'I told Pande that the Indian government would not pay any fee,' said VP later. 'The agency must meet its own expenses. But if it found anything illegally squirrelled away, if the government gained financially, we would pay our usual 20 per cent reward.'[55]

The agency Bhure Lal and Gurumurthy chose was the US-based Fairfax, started in 1983 by Michael Hershman, a former

US military intelligence officer.[56] 'It was a friend of Goenka's in the US who recommended Hershman,' said Gurumurthy. 'It is normal for US professionals, including lawyers, to work on the basis of a success fee—they are paid only if they deliver. When Hershman said he was interested, I asked him to come to India and meet Bhure Lal.'[57]

Hershman did; following a first meeting in Delhi in mid-November 1986, Bhure Lal visited the US in late December for further meetings. (He also went to the DuPont headquarters to ask questions about Reliance but got very little.) Hershman sought Indian government authorization for his investigation, which was duly given. 'It is true Gurumurthy recommended Fairfax, but we did our own due diligence too, and found that Fairfax had impeccable credentials,' said Bhure Lal.[58]

Gurumurthy maintained that until September–October 1986, Rajiv had been supportive of his Reliance probe. 'After I gave V.P. Singh a note on the implications of Reliance's non-convertible debentures being converted, he spoke to Rajiv Gandhi (on the telephone) in my presence and got his approval for banning the practice,' he said. A long-time close aide of the Gandhis, Mohammed Yunus, whose Willingdon Crescent house Indira had stayed in after losing power in 1977, met Gurumurthy and Goenka a number of times while the reports on Reliance were being published. 'Yunus told us to be in Delhi in the first week of September as Rajiv Gandhi wanted to meet us before leaving for a non-aligned countries' meeting in Harare,' said Gurumurthy. 'But the promised meeting never took place and thereafter Yunus, too, stopped communicating with us.'[59]

What changed Rajiv's attitude to Reliance and Ambani can only be guessed at. Hamish McDonald, in both his biographies of the Ambanis, *The Polyester Prince: The Rise of Dhirubhai Ambani*[60] and *Ambani and Sons: The Making of the World's Richest Brothers and Their Feud*, which also includes Mukesh and

Anil Ambani's lives in its ambit, recounts 'a wonderful story, still widely told in Bombay and New Delhi, that at their first meeting, Dhirubhai bluntly told Rajiv that he was holding a huge amount of funds on behalf of Rajiv's late mother and wanted to know what to do with the money. Apocryphal or not, it became part of India's political folklore because it fitted with Dhirubhai's reputation for both brazenness and keen judgement of character.'[61]

The Mani Ratnam-directed film *Guru* (2007), which saucily mixes fiction with fact to tell Ambani's life story, suggests the same—only, in this case, the protagonist tells the 'nephew' politician that his late 'uncle' had left money with him and wonders whether to return it or send it overseas for safekeeping. But McDonald also adds, 'Undoubtedly, Dhirubhai used the meeting to outline his big plans for industrial expansion and how these would fit into Rajiv's vision of a high-tech India.'

Whatever the reason, Rajiv's changed view had unhappy consequences for VP, Gurumurthy and Bhure Lal.

3

'I WAS NOT OUTMANOEUVRED BECAUSE I WAS NOT MANOEUVRING'

A recurring feature of V.P. Singh's political life was that of friends turning foes, which, in turn, forced upon him painful loyalty choices. It started when Indira Gandhi split the Congress and formed the Congress (R), which he supported—while most of those who had helped him as a rookie politician remained with the Congress (O). They included Mangla Prasad and Muzaffar Hasan, both heavyweights of Allahabad politics at the time, who had generously backed him despite their early reservations about him; as well as former chief minister C.B. Gupta. It happened again with H.N. Bahuguna, but for whom he would never have been chosen Congress candidate for either the Soraon assembly seat in 1969 or the Phulpur Lok Sabha seat in 1971. It happened with his friend T.N. Singh after the non-Congress parties briefly made T.N. Singh UP chief minister. It happened with his elder brother Sant Bux Singh, who had been VP's lodestar while he was growing up. But his most dramatic and bitter reversal of relations was with Rajiv Gandhi.

When Rajiv began as Prime Minister, the mutual trust and respect between him and VP was immense. A minister of state at the time noted in his memoirs, 'The first three months gave some indication of the functioning of the Rajiv Gandhi government. V.P. Singh, as finance minister, was the favourite. In cabinet meetings, he sat to the right of the prime minister ... (We) ministers of state were at a loose end.'[1] In the months that followed, the two remained close, both tolerating each other's angularities. Trying hard to curb expenditure, for instance, VP found Rajiv's weakness for announcing initiatives without considering their financial implications trying, but always accommodated him.

Soon after taking over, Rajiv declared that he would announce a new education policy; he made good on his promise in May 1986. 'Just before the announcement, my officers told me that under the new policy, 6 per cent of GDP would be allocated to education,' said VP. (Until then, the allocation had always been 3–3.5 per cent of the GDP and remains so three and a half decades later.) He added,

> We don't spend 6 per cent even on defence, how could we do so on education? I asked Rajiv Gandhi, 'Are you really going to announce this?' He said he was. I said, 'I'm your finance minister, but this file never came to me. How can you announce it without discussing with me first?' He said, 'Okay, I'll send you the file.' I got the file, but the same evening the announcement was made.[2]

VP admitted that he used some statistical jugglery to show that the 6 per cent promise was being kept. 'Rajiv Gandhi went to Kashmir and announced a Rs 1,000-crore special package for the state,' he recalled. 'He went to Punjab and announced another Rs 1,000-crore package for Punjab. I said, "Where will the money come from?" Well, the Prime Minister had given his word, so the money was somehow found.'[3]

Similarly, despite the protests of businessmen and, indeed, many Congress leaders, Rajiv, until September 1986, wholeheartedly backed both VP's liberalizing efforts and his campaign against economic crimes. 'I could never have taken the steps I did but for the Prime Minister's support,' said VP.[4] Rajiv may well have been uneasy about VP's raids—'The problem is not the raids themselves, but perhaps the manner of the raids, the level of the people doing the raids, the people whom they are raiding,' he had said in a newspaper interview as early as March 1986, soon after the arrest of Orkay's Kapal Mehra and the questioning of the aged S.L. Kirloskar[5]—but he made no attempt to curb them.

He did, however, suggest that VP reduce his aloofness towards business leaders. The latter duly complied, attending many more business gatherings thereafter than before, even occasionally meeting individual businessmen.[6] At Rajiv's behest, VP also provided a way out for those who wanted to pre-empt penal action by admitting to their crimes. In August 1986, he announced a scheme—lasting until the end of the calendar year—by which companies that had cheated on import or excise duties could pay up and avoid prosecution. In November, he announced a similar amnesty scheme, valid until the end of the financial year, for those who had stashed assets overseas, violating the FERA.[7]

Rajiv did not retaliate even when VP ignored his nudges while deciding on the award of business contracts. In at least two cases, the company denied was the Italian oil and gas equipment giant Snamprogetti (later acquired by another Italian firm, Saipem), whose chief India representative then, Ottavio Quattrocchi, was a close friend of Rajiv and his family. The first was a contract to build the 1,750-km-long Hazira–Bijaipur–Jagdishpur (HBJ) gas pipeline, for which a consortium led by Snamprogetti competed, but which was eventually awarded to a rival consortium led by French firm Spiecapag. As VP recounted,

> Rajiv Gandhi phoned and asked me to meet Quattrocchi. I agreed. We spoke. I sent the representation Quattrocchi had given me to my ministry officials, but they still felt Spiecapag's bid offered better terms. I sent the file to Rajiv Gandhi with the officers' comments. He phoned again and said to me, 'There are lobbies at work in your ministry.' I told him he was welcome to remove me if he felt that way. Well, he did not overrule me; he signed the file too.[8]

In the second instance, VP withheld consent for the import of machinery from Snamprogetti for a fertilizer plant owned by the then (still undivided) Birla Group in Rajasthan, on the grounds that no global tender for the purchase had been floated. He said,

> I felt that the government would be releasing precious foreign exchange, so a global tender was necessary to make the deal transparent. The parties concerned complained to Rajiv Gandhi that I was holding up the country's development. I told him, 'Had they floated a global tender, the machines would have been here by now.' As it happened, soon after, the development finance institution financing part of the purchase sent us a telegram saying Snamprogetti had sold the same equipment to Bangladesh for Rs 100 crore less than we were paying, so I was vindicated.[9]

The first hint that VP no longer enjoyed Rajiv's unstinted backing came in the form of a magazine article questioning the cornerstone of VP's politics—his personal integrity. In early September, the Hindi weekly *Ravivar* carried a cover story on the alleged malpractices of the Daiya Charitable Trust, set up by his parents and brothers, claiming that the man who sought to root out corruption from

Indian business was himself not personally clean. Though zamindari had been abolished in UP soon after Independence, the zamindars' personal lands had initially been left untouched. But in January 1961, the state enforced the UP Imposition of Ceilings on Land Holdings Act, by which family holdings were restricted to a maximum of 40–128 'standard acres', depending on the quality of the land and the size of the family.[10] As the legislation became imminent, many rajas and lesser zamindars—some of whom owned thousands of acres—sought to bypass it by setting up charitable trusts and transferring most of their lands to these. The story maintained that VP's family had done the same, starting the Daiya Charitable Trust in June 1959, and that the avowed aims of the trust—to start a school and a free hospital and, later, an agricultural research centre—were never fulfilled.[11]

But even this hatchet job had to concede that save a single transaction, VP had had nothing to do with the trust. Adopted at the age of five by the raja of Manda, his relations with his biological father forever prickly, he had always remained aloof from the Daiya estate's financial dealings. The sole exception—which the story made much of—was in 1968, when he transferred about 1,000 acres to the trust. What the story did not mention was that these were the very lands his father, fearing for his son's future, had given him after VP donated his own lands to the Bhoodan movement, and VP had merely returned them. He had always wanted to do so,[12] but perhaps only after he had paid off the bulk of his adoptive father's debts did he feel secure enough to take the step.

In any case, his family's ploy did not help its cause. Realizing that many zamindari families had taken the same route, Bahuguna, while chief minister in 1975, got an amendment to the Land Ceiling Act passed, which said that lands held by trusts set up after May 1959 would not be exempt from it. Accordingly, most of the trust's lands were acquired by the state, some of them going to the

UP forest department and the rest being distributed to landless peasants. VP's brothers then petitioned the district court, seeking higher compensation for their forest land, claiming that there were many more trees—with valuable wood—on it than had been counted. The court agreed (after ordering a recount of the trees) and increased their compensation amount from about Rs 25 lakh to Rs 47 lakh. By then, VP was chief minister of UP, but despite this, the state government contested the district court's decision in the Allahabad High Court and later the Supreme Court, only to have the increased compensation upheld both times. The *Ravivar* story suggested that the revised tree estimate was fraudulent and that VP, as chief minister, had influenced the state's counsel to present a weak case, so that the government lost.[13]

It was a thin, far-fetched allegation, with no proof of any such subterfuge, but the Opposition parties in the UP Vidhan Sabha made much of it, harping on it for days, moving an adjournment motion against the Congress state government on the matter. The sinister aspect of the controversy, however, was that although Rajiv soon issued a statement, maintaining that he had 'complete faith' in VP's integrity, there were suggestions in the local press that it was some UP Congressmen who, at the behest of their Delhi leaders, had provided *Ravivar* most of the information in the story, as well as spurred the Opposition to move the adjournment motion.

But VP's response was also curious. Instead of seeking a governmental or judicial enquiry, he wrote to six leading Opposition MPs[14]—of his own choosing—that he was ready to 'subject himself' to their scrutiny in the matter, because he had 'faith in their fairness'. 'I know I can weather this attack because the weapon being used against me is falsehood,' he said.[15] He explained later that he had done so because he felt there was no point in a judicial enquiry, as the Supreme Court had already ruled on it.[16] But the suggestion, which many termed a 'gimmick',[17] was irregular, and the concerned MPs turned him down.

The next inkling of Rajiv's changed attitude was far more direct. On 17 September 1986, he attended a FICCI meeting in Calcutta, at which the then FICCI president, Rama Prasad Goenka,[18] sharing the dais with him, deplored the 'raid raj' that had been unleashed in the country. Goenka, renowned for his successful takeovers of numerous companies, had been particularly close to Indira—so close that he was jailed by the Janata government along with her in October 1977, and raided repeatedly while it was in power.[19] In his speech, Rajiv made no effort to rebut Goenka and, indeed, speaking to reporters later, maintained that the recent arrest of L.M. Thapar had not been 'as per my guidelines'. Learning of his reaction, VP—more than 16,000 km away in Punta del Este at the time, defending India's position at the GATT conference (see Part 4, Chapter 1)—was disturbed enough to return to the country immediately after the talks ended, cancelling his scheduled visits to a couple of Caribbean island nations.[20]

The third indication came at a meeting between Rajiv and VP in the third week of October 1986, a day before the Prime Minister carried out a sweeping reshuffle of his cabinet. Rajiv asked VP to suggest a 'good' full-time external affairs minister, as the then incumbent, P. Shiv Shanker, also held charge of commerce. VP innocently complied, proposing some names, not realizing that Rajiv wanted him to volunteer for the job and give up finance. 'He approached me in such a roundabout fashion,' he said later, laughing. 'Had he been open about it, I might even have agreed.'[21] However, in the reshuffle, though six ministers were dropped—including Rajiv's once-closest associate, his cousin Arun Nehru, with whom, too, his relations had suddenly soured—VP was left untouched. (N.D. Tiwari, until then industries minister, got external affairs.)[22]

The fourth signal was the most ominous. Even as VP authorized various probes into Reliance Industries' finances and activities, the CBI, in early December 1986, began investigating how

Swaminathan Gurumurthy had obtained some of the information used in his reports on Reliance, claiming that it came from confidential files of the Director General of Trade Development (DGTD), and that by publishing it, he had violated the Official Secrets Act, 1923. On 21 December 1986, the CBI even raided Gurumurthy's Madras office. Considering that Gurumurthy was working closely with the finance ministry at the time to nail Reliance, it clearly indicated that other arms of VP's own government were out to undermine him.[23]

———— ❧ ————

By late 1986, the early optimism over Rajiv had largely vanished. The Congress had lost most of the assembly elections held after its March 1985 wins; many of its chief ministers were performing poorly, sparking dissidence and street protests; Punjab still burnt, with terrorists back in control of the Golden Temple; serious differences had cropped up between Rajiv and President Zail Singh; Hindu–Muslim tensions were rising across the country; and a hasty intervention in neighbouring Sri Lanka's civil war had backfired. By October, and especially after his meeting with Dhirubhai Ambani, Rajiv seemed to have become convinced that VP was trying to take advantage of his difficulties and upstage him, using the raids to indicate to voters that VP's efforts to eliminate corruption were more sincere than Rajiv's. He wanted VP out of the finance ministry, but was hesitant to unilaterally remove him, given VP's growing popularity, thanks to the raids. Once VP refused the external affairs ministry bait, Rajiv began looking for a suitable opportunity to justify the ouster.[24]

It came in January 1987, following an unexpected misunderstanding with Pakistan. Though the two countries had fought three wars since Independence, India–Pakistan relations during the 1980s had remained fairly placid. Trade between the two countries had grown, as had the frequency of cultural exchanges and cricket matches. The previous month, however, the Indian army had begun conducting, in the Rajasthan desert, the biggest military exercise it had ever done until then, called Operation Brasstacks,[25] to which a panic-stricken Pakistan, fearing an attack, had responded by amassing its own troops along parts of the border.

In the third week of January 1987, VP, who had caught a viral fever and was recuperating at home, was intrigued to find himself summoned to the defence ministry headquarters to take part in a meeting to discuss the situation. He knew nothing of defence, had never heard of Operation Brasstacks before the meeting and had been to Pakistan only once—a year ago in January 1986—on a routine visit, reciprocating an earlier visit to India by his Pakistani counterpart.[26]

With reports of VP's impending removal from the finance ministry having appeared in newspapers, he quickly guessed why he had been called, but was unprepared for the degree of distrust in him that Rajiv—to whom he had once been so close—displayed at their meeting. Since falling ill, VP had not shaved, and Rajiv's first reaction on seeing him was, 'Oh, you really are ill!' He had obviously thought that VP was sulking, staying away from his office to protest his possible removal as finance minister. 'I found it strange,' VP said later. 'Would any minister feign illness to avoid work, like some part-time domestic servant?'[27]

His suspicion was confirmed the next day when he was asked to join a small group to brief President Zail Singh on the matter. On 24 January 1987, as he'd expected, Rajiv directed him to take over defence, relinquishing finance.[28] Until then, the Prime Minister himself had held defence, with a minister of state to help him, but he now maintained that much of the current crisis had been caused by the minister of state's ineptitude[29] and that such an important portfolio required 'a strong, full-time' minister.[30]

Media reaction to VP's policies, especially his raids, had been mixed, but the response to his transfer from finance was uniformly supportive of him. 'The Lobbyists Win' was the headline of the *Indian Express*'s editorial on the subject,[31] while *India Today* noted that VP was leaving behind 'a reputation as finance minister that will be almost impossible to equal'.[32] Opposition leaders, too, were sceptical of the ostensible reason for his transfer, with one of them telling VP in Parliament that he did not know whether to congratulate him or offer condolences.[33] Even VP made little effort to hide his real feelings. He expressed no pleasure at his new assignment, merely declaring to the media, '*Neta ka hokum sar mathe par* (I bow to my leader's orders).'[34] With an aide of Rajiv, who sought to console him, he was much more frank. 'Look here, I'm committed to him because of his mother,' he said. 'She gave me so much that I do not even need a ministry from him. He could have sent me anywhere. In this case, defence is as good a place as any.'[35]

With Republic Day just a day away, VP realized that the service chiefs would be tied up the next day (which was also a Sunday) overseeing arrangements for the parade. He got to work immediately, first clearing crucial finance ministry files, then seeking a detailed briefing from the service chiefs that very night, getting home well past 1 a.m.[36] The border crisis with Pakistan was easily resolved over the next fortnight, with Pakistan's foreign secretary, Abdus Sattar, visiting Delhi and both countries agreeing to a phased de-escalation. Indeed, normal relations were restored so quickly that by late February, Pakistan President Zia-ul-Haq was in Delhi to watch an India–Pakistan cricket match.

Though he always denied it, there were clues enough to indicate that VP resented Amitabh Bachchan's entry into politics, fearing his Allahabad turf threatened by Bachchan's enormous popularity—

independent of the party organization—as well as his proximity to Rajiv (see Part 3, Chapter 4). When he went to Allahabad as UPCC president during the 1984 Lok Sabha election campaign, for instance, he had initially refused to call on Bachchan, maintaining that as a newbie candidate, Bachchan should call on him. VP later changed his mind and visited him anyway.[37] After the election, as finance minister, trying hard to reduce the fiscal deficit by curbing expenditure, he was cool to Bachchan's pleas for more Central funds for Allahabad's development.[38]

With allegations of black-money transactions rampant in the film industry, once VP's anti-corruption drive began targeting celebrities, speculation soon started about whether he would strike at Bachchan as well. One magazine editor even asked VP about it, claiming that while 'many film stars were being raided' for concealing their real incomes, 'the biggest star of them all' had been spared.[39] 'When have I raided film stars ... when I do, you'll see whether we spare anyone or not,' VP replied.[40] (He never did—he raided some film producers at the start of his tenure, but never actors.) With foreign exchange outflows strictly regulated by the FERA those days, he did, however, send notices to a few actors who had participated in a stage show organized by Bachchan in late 1986 at Madison Garden, New York—but not to Bachchan himself—asking how they met their expenses.

There was speculation, too, about whether VP was using his powers as finance minister to sift through Bachchan's tax returns, looking for inconsistencies, hoping thereby to besmirch him. No evidence supporting this has ever emerged; yet Rajiv—his attitude to VP already much changed following VP's Reliance faceoff— somehow became convinced that VP was trying to smear not only Bachchan but also, by association, him.[41] It all began after Bachchan's younger brother, Ajitabh Bachchan, who owned a successful pharmaceutical business in Bombay, suddenly relocated to Montreux, Switzerland, in August 1986.

Given the controlled economy of those times and the Bachchans' vast wealth, there was inevitable gossip—never probed, never proven—that the Bachchan brothers had transferred a chunk of their funds illegally into Swiss banks. Months later, Ajitabh Bachchan's own comments in a magazine interview made the matter murkier, for while he maintained he'd got a job in Montreux, he would not name his employer. He also claimed not to own any assets outside India,[42] yet the *Indian Express* revealed that the apartment he was living in was registered in his own name.

By the time Bhure Lal, returning from the US after having signed on Fairfax, filed his report to his boss, Revenue Secretary Vinod Pande, VP had already been shifted to the defence ministry. In mid-February 1987, the new minister of state for finance, Brahm Dutt,[43] asked VP if he had indeed sanctioned engaging a foreign detective agency. VP confirmed that he had done so verbally, then called for the relevant file and set down his consent in writing. Soon after, Rajiv also summoned him to ask the same question, demanding to know specifically if the agency had carried out any investigations in Switzerland. VP said that it was unlikely, but only Bhure Lal would know. Rajiv summoned Bhure Lal, who emphatically denied it.[44]

Bizarre developments followed. On 11 March 1987, Bhure Lal was transferred out of the Enforcement Directorate with immediate effect. The next day, late at night, the CBI raided Gurumurthy a second time, as also some offices and properties of *The Indian Express*. This time Gurumurthy was arrested, with the CBI claiming to have unearthed two letters, both with the Fairfax letterhead, purportedly written by Hershman's deputy at Fairfax, Gordon McKay, to Gurumurthy. Their contents were extraordinary. The first, dated 20 November 1986, acknowledged receipt of a vast sum of money—in US dollars!—and sought still more, promising, in turn, to apprise Ramnath Goenka of 'the progress made on source of funds for [the] purchase of Swiss properties of Mr Bachchan'.[45]

No such payment to Fairfax had ever been contemplated by *The Indian Express*, let alone made; it was the finance ministry that had hired Fairfax under its 'rewards scheme', not Gurumurthy. Both VP and Bhure Lal also repeatedly stressed that it was Reliance Industries' overseas dealings Fairfax had been assigned to probe, not those—if any—of the Bachchan brothers. The second letter, which was undated, sought details of Ajitabh Bachchan's 'non-resident Indian' status, as available in Reserve Bank of India files, as well as, inexplicably, India's rice exports to the erstwhile Soviet Union!

Media attention at the time focused exclusively on the first letter, whose contents had been leaked. Containing expressions such as 'expedite end results', and peppered with incorrect use of the definite article, it had plainly been composed by an Indian with limited English, and McKay promptly called it out as a forgery, saying it was 'preposterous' to think that he could have written it, even had its contents been factually correct, which they were not. Simultaneously, there were also startling reports—never confirmed by either of the Bachchan brothers—maintaining that a mysterious individual, claiming to represent Fairfax, had, in fact, turned up at Ajitabh Bachchan's Montreux home and questioned him about his finances! Who this individual was, and why he did so, was never established, though VP later squarely accused Reliance of having sent an imposter in a bid to scuttle the probe into its own overseas dealings.[46]

Meanwhile, Gurumurthy had to spend ten days in custody explaining himself, repeating ad nauseam that he'd never received either of the two letters, while every time he tried to focus on the charges he'd made in his reports on Reliance, his interrogators diverted their questioning. Who forged the letters was never investigated, let alone established, though it was obvious that their source was someone well aware of the inner workings of Congress politics at the time, the fraught relationship between Rajiv, Amitabh Bachchan and VP, as well as the finance ministry's effort to use Fairfax to nail Reliance.

Gurumurthy had no doubt how the forgery was carried out—the perpetrators had photocopied the Fairfax letterhead and McKay's signature from actual letters McKay had written to DuPont enquiring about its deals with Reliance. If proved authentic, the letters could have turned the charge against him from violating the Official Secrets Act to espionage—passing on sensitive information to a foreign detective agency—which would have denied him bail and earned him a long jail sentence if found guilty. But Gurumurthy quickly convinced those interrogating him of the truth. 'They were honest and professional officers,' he said. 'On the first day of questioning itself, they realized that they were wrong in arresting me. When they showed me a photocopy of the [first] letter, I said that I had never received it and asked to see the original. They asked me about Fairfax and Hershman. I told them the facts.'[47]

Yet his incarceration kept being extended, as there were senior CBI officers anxious to please Rajiv by establishing his guilt.[48] Thrice subjected to a lie-detector test, Gurumurthy refused to reveal how he had obtained information about Reliance from confidential government files, claiming journalistic immunity from naming sources. 'The officers asked me if I was investigating people close to the Gandhi family,' he said. 'I told my lawyers this and they brought it up in court, which hit media headlines and had the Opposition parties roaring.' Years later, a member of the CBI investigating team, Yashwant Malhotra, even wrote to him, almost apologizing. 'I always admired your fortitude, courage and integrity,' he said in an email in 2016. 'I hope you found us fair, in spite of all pressures.'[49]

Even after his release, Gurumurthy's harassment continued. 'I faced security issues, direct and indirect threats,' he said. 'For almost two and a half years [until the government changed], I could barely sleep three to four hours a day. There were more than 300 prosecutions launched against the *Indian Express*. The government kept probing my tax returns but found nothing.' The CBI did not pursue the information he had provided on Reliance to its conclusion. 'I served in the CBI until 1991, after which I opted to return to my home cadre in disgust, mainly because our strong chargesheet against Reliance Industries was not allowed to be filed in court, thanks to the powers that be,' Malhotra added in his mail to Gurumurthy. 'I resolved never to work with the CBI again.'[50]

The arrangement with Fairfax naturally stood abandoned, but that the agency had been engaged at all was far from forgotten. On 31 March 1987, the matter was discussed in the Rajya Sabha following a notice from some Opposition MPs. VP fully expected the government to defend engaging Fairfax. 'I hadn't even gone to Parliament that day, as the matter no longer concerned me, but in my Parliament office I happened to switch on the system to listen to its proceedings,' he said.[51] He was shocked by what he heard, since he recognized the voice speaking. He was being personally pilloried for the Fairfax appointment and not by any Opposition MP but by a Congress member, that too, a friend and mentor— Dinesh Singh.

Dinesh Singh, the former raja of Kalakanker estate in the Pratapgarh district, was the first person VP had approached for help when he had decided to enter politics (See Part 2, Chapter 2). He was also the one whose later exclusion from the cabinet had led to VP being inducted in it (See Part 2, Chapter 5). He had defected to the Janata Party when it came to power in 1977 but returned to the Congress after the Janata government's collapse, where, though given a Rajya Sabha nomination, he had been ignored by both Indira and Rajiv. 'He wanted to become a minister again and this was the price he was asked to pay,' said VP.[52] (Dinesh Singh was indeed made minister for water resources in February 1988.)

Dinesh Singh expanded on the same charges the CBI had made against Gurumurthy, levelling them instead at VP, claiming Fairfax had links with the US's Central Intelligence Agency (CIA) and that recruiting it had been a dangerous conspiracy to 'prepare a political case against the government' and harm the country. 'The finance minister was doing something behind the back of the prime minister which would embarrass the prime minister,' he said. 'He would present it [later] to the prime minister as a kind of blackmail.'[53]

With three major spying operations having, in fact, been busted in the past few years—the Larkins brothers' case in late 1983, and the Coomar Narain and Rama Swarup cases in 1985[54]—the allegations may not have sounded as absurd then as they do now. By the time VP reached the Rajya Sabha, Dinesh Singh had finished, but other Congress MPs followed him, making the same accusations. They had obviously all been primed in advance to attack him. Not one Congress MP rose to defend VP.

'You've plunged a dagger in my back,' VP observed quietly to Dinesh Singh.

'What else could I have done?' Dinesh Singh replied.[55]

But Rajiv wasn't done yet. In their speeches at different forums and in press interviews, select Congress MPs, led by Dinesh Singh, continued to vilify VP. Within days of the debate, Rajiv summoned a meeting of the Cabinet Committee on Political Affairs (CCPA)—which included VP—to declare that he wanted a judicial commission to enquire into Fairfax's appointment. VP made a futile effort to point out that foreign detective agencies had been engaged by the government several times in the past as well,[56] but no one listened. Instead, as other committee members endorsed Rajiv, he slowly realized that like the parliamentary debate before, this, too, was a set-up to corner him.

He was reminded of his school principal Jagdish Prasad Singh, who, furious with him for having contested (and won) the school union election against his wishes, had berated him for skipping a couple of classes, deliberately ignoring that he had done so only to practise for an interschool debate (which, too, he had won). So too Rajiv, enraged for reasons he would not admit, kept harping only on the pitfalls of engaging a detective agency overseas, pointedly overlooking that it was done to ferret out corporate corruption.[57] As VP recalled,

> I told Rajiv Gandhi, 'The Rajya Sabha debate is over—why rake up the matter again? You'll only provide a fresh opportunity for people to say all kinds of things.' But he was adamant. He said, 'No, Amitabh (Bachchan) has been mentioned, that involves me too, I want my name cleared and only a judicial enquiry can do so.'[58]

A cabinet meeting followed to decide the terms of reference of the commission. These included finding out who authorized engaging Fairfax and why, what information it had been given and what it had provided, whether any payment had been made to it and if the country's security had indeed been compromised.

'I met Rajiv Gandhi before the meeting and pointed out to him that it was the letter purportedly written by Fairfax to Gurumurthy that had started the controversy,' said VP. He added,

> I wanted a probe into that letter included in the terms of reference—whether it was genuine or not, how it came to light, and so forth. Rajiv Gandhi assured me it would be, but he made no mention of it at the cabinet meeting. I raised the matter at the meeting, but he did not say anything. Later he told me, 'I'll look into the letter myself.'[59]

He never did. The commission, comprising two sitting Supreme Court judges—M.P. Thakkar and S. Natarajan—was heavily criticized in the media through the eight months that it functioned, not only for its skewed terms of reference but also the way it went about its job. It barred the media from its hearings and refused to question Gurumurthy or even call him as a witness.[60] It gave Bhure Lal, in particular, a hard time, summoning him initially while he was ill and on leave, giving him no time to consult office files and prepare himself. Bhure Lal remembered:

> Natarajan was the quiet sort, but Thakkar had this habit of exploding in rage and shouting. I fast on Tuesdays, eschewing solid food, and one Tuesday, despite knowing this, they kept questioning me past 9 p.m. Finally, I said, 'May I have a cup of tea?' Well, that was allowed.[61]

The commission's report, in early December 1987, revealed no new facts. It predictably indicted VP, Vinod Pande and Bhure Lal for violating departmental procedure in appointing Fairfax and endorsed the fantastic claim that doing so had endangered the country's security.[62]

Not that it mattered, as by then, the political landscape had changed drastically. On 9 April 1987, furious at having been framed, VP had struck back.

———— ✿ ————

Although India's armed forces are one of the largest in the world, its defence manufacturing capacity is modest. In the 1980s, this was even more so. Most of its military hardware came from overseas. Global arms sellers in India (as elsewhere) worked through agents, who were paid handsome commissions on successful contracts. It was widely believed—though never proven—that these agents, in turn, paid part of the commissions in the form of illegal kickbacks to the decision makers who facilitated the contracts. In October 1985, still awash with idealistic fervour, Rajiv, at the time holding the defence portfolio too, announced a ban on employing defence agents, maintaining that future arms deals would be negotiated directly by the government with the seller.[63]

In late 1981, with Indira back in power, India had contracted to buy four Type 209/1500 SSK submarines from (West) Germany's Howaldtswerke-Deutsche Werft (HDW) for about Rs 350 crore (the cost later escalated to about Rs 465 crore). Two of them had already been delivered and paid for by the time VP took charge as defence minister, with him attending the formal induction of one, INS *Shishukumar*, into the Indian Navy on 16 February 1987. The purchase of the other two—which were to be assembled at Mazagon Docks in Bombay—was still being negotiated.

VP's fixation with curbing expenditure, developed as finance minister, may have carried over into the defence ministry, for soon after taking over, he messaged J.C. Ajmani, the Indian ambassador in Bonn, West Germany, suggesting that HDW be asked for a discount on the remaining submarines. In his coded telex reply, Ajmani maintained that HDW had refused to consider it, with a senior company official telling him that it was not possible as HDW had already paid 7 per cent commission to an agent to facilitate the first deal and was committed to paying the same for the second one too.[64]

Though the contract was signed well before the ban on defence agents, VP felt that since deliveries were made after the announcement, paying the commission was a violation of government policy. The telexed reply arrived on 24 February 1987,[65] and it is not clear when VP actually saw it, but it was only on 9 April 1987—the Fairfax uproar having erupted in the interim, starting 11 March 1987—that he asked Rajiv about it, requesting

him to stay back for a bit at the end of a cabinet meeting.
He said later,

> The same telex message had gone to the Prime Minister too,
> but I felt I should apprise him personally as well. He did not
> reply. I was surprised. I was expecting some sort of guidance
> from him about what to do next. I waited; he still said nothing.
> I thought, 'I can't cross-examine the Prime Minister. I've told
> him—I've done my job.'[66]

Returning to his room, VP called in the defence secretary and
asked him to start an enquiry. Not only that, he made the matter
public. 'I didn't give any details,' he said. 'The press release just
said that the defence ministry had ordered an enquiry into a deal in
which information had been received that 7 per cent commission
was paid to an Indian agent.'[67]

It must have been obvious to VP that Rajiv did not want the
matter pursued, that he probably knew much more about it than
he had let on and that any enquiry would embarrass him. It was
an opportunity to avenge the humiliation VP was being subjected
to and he took it, though he surely realized that it amounted to
confronting the Prime Minister and that his continuing in the
cabinet thereafter would be difficult. 'I knew there would be
pressure not to hold the enquiry, so to counter it, I announced
it in the press,' he said. 'I felt thereby the pressure would be less.
I also sent the file ordering the enquiry to Rajiv Gandhi. He saw it
the following day.'[68] By then, the news had already appeared in the
morning's newspapers.

Amid a predictable clamour by Opposition MPs, the Lok
Sabha that day witnessed the extraordinary sight of the home
minister, Buta Singh, fearful of further revelations, appealing to
the Speaker not to let the defence minister make a statement on
the matter.[69] While the ruling-party members attacked their own

defence minister, Opposition MPs supported him. When he was finally allowed to speak, VP merely stated that the information about the enquiry was correct.

He was soon summoned by Rajiv, who had not attended the day's proceedings. VP recalled,

> He was red-faced with fury. He said to me, 'How do you know what the telex says is correct?' I said, 'How do I know it is incorrect? It has come through proper channels; it was in code; it had no errors of grammar or logic. I've no reason to disbelieve it.' He asked, 'What will be the result of your enquiry?' I said, 'I don't know, but if your order on defence agents was violated, setting one up was my duty.' He said, 'Why would HDW tell us? It must be paying so many heads of state to buy its products. If it started revealing names, it would have to shut down.' I grew slightly annoyed at this. I said, 'Keeping HDW going is not my responsibility.'[70]

Predictably, later in the day, both at a CCPA meeting and a full cabinet meeting that followed, VP was excoriated by a number of others present for ordering his enquiry without the Prime Minister's consent.[71] He sat through them impassively, and by the end, if he had any hesitation left about resigning from the cabinet, a meeting with Sant Bux Singh convinced him. The brothers had grown apart, and VP was surprised by Sant Bux's call, saying he wanted to visit him at home. Instead, VP went to see him. 'You can't go back on the enquiry without ruining your reputation as a crusader against corruption, so you have only two alternatives,' said Sant Bux. 'Either you stay on and allow yourself to be thrown out, or you search your heart, and if you think you have it in you to be prime minister, resign in good time.'[72]

VP waited a day. He did not want to create a crisis at an important function scheduled the next day, 11 April 1987—the annual award of the President's gallantry medals—where the defence minister plays an important role. Rajiv, too, attended the tea party at Rashtrapati Bhavan that followed. 'We met; I knew it was my last day in office,' said VP later.[73]

Back home, he wrote out a two-line resignation letter: 'In view of the serious differences of perception between us, I do not think it is proper for me to continue in the cabinet. I am, therefore, submitting my resignation.' Having sent away his official car, as he usually did after work, he requested his younger son Abhay, who was at home, to drive him to the Prime Minister's residence. Rajiv was out to dinner, so he submitted the letter to an aide. The next morning, following a brief meeting at noon, Rajiv accepted the resignation.[74]

With VP out of office, the enquiry into the HDW contract was soon aborted. ('Just as a submarine is underwater, so is the enquiry,' VP observed some months later.[75]) The press remained divided on the resignation. For instance, the *Indian Express* predictably indicted Rajiv: 'No Prime Minister has confirmed the worst allegations and suspicions about his probity as Rajiv Gandhi has by his conduct ... The decision to force V.P. Singh out removes all doubt.' The *Times of India* maintained that VP deserved what he got: 'There cannot now be the slightest doubt that V.P. Singh was out to undermine Rajiv Gandhi's position, leaving him no choice but to remove him from the government.'[76]

Others argued that by quitting, VP had acknowledged political defeat, that with it, he was giving up on his moves to challenge and possibly replace Rajiv as the Congress's—and the country's—leader. VP vehemently denied that he had ever had any such plan. 'I was not outmanoeuvred because I was not manoeuvring,' he said.

<hr />

Alongside his political setback, VP also suffered a personal tragedy—his mother Braj Raj Kanwar died in May 1987. His relations with her, unlike those with his father, had always been close and uncomplicated. She ran her large household and her farm efficiently, but due to her cloistered existence—always in purdah—her worldly awareness was limited. When VP first became a minister, for instance, in October 1974, she had been far from pleased. *'Sune hain, tu Indira Gandhi ka naukar ban gaye* (Heard you've become Indira Gandhi's servant)?' she had asked when they had met some days later. 'Why? Give up the job. You don't need it.'[77]

When she underwent a major surgery in 1967, from which she took long weeks to recover, VP, then yet to enter politics, sat up many nights caring for her. 'I'd look after her during the day and he at night,' said Sita Kumari Singh. 'That was when, staying up nights, he began writing poetry again.'[78] (The collection of poems, to which he kept adding over the years, was finally published in book form as *Ek Tukda Dharti, Ek Tukda Akash* [A Piece of Earth, a Piece of Sky], three decades later.) In 1985, when she fell seriously ill once more, he was already finance minister and unable to spare as much time, though Sita Kumari was always with her. 'I went to Allahabad; my mother was unconscious and on oxygen— her nose and lips had turned blue,' VP remembered. 'I asked the doctor if I should shift her to Delhi, but he said, "If it were my mother, I wouldn't trouble her anymore."'[79]

Instead, VP prayed. 'Despite the many ups and downs in my life, I've prayed only three times, and this was one of them,' he said. 'I've never prayed for anything related to my career, party or government. Maybe I didn't feel any of them were worth praying for.' (The two other occasions were first, when Sita Kumari had a near-fatal medical complication in 1974, with her intestines getting tangled—'There was no ultrasound those days, only X-rays; the doctors opened me up and were shocked,' she recalled;[80] and second, during a visit to Kedarnath with his wife soon after Chandrasekhar Prasad Singh's death—'I prayed that wherever my brother might be, his soul was at peace,' said VP).[81]

Miraculously, his mother recovered. 'In a week she was better and, later, I brought her to Delhi, where she stayed with me for some months,' said VP. 'But she did not like living in Delhi. She wanted to be in her village, where the women she'd known all her life would come to see her, where they would make achar (pickles) and badi (lentil balls) together.'

But the 1985 illness had ruined her health, though she lived for two more years. 'Even after her recovery, she was in and out of hospitals,' said Sita Kumari. 'Doctors in Allahabad were not sure what was wrong. They felt it was something to do with her heart. She kind of just withered away.' Shortly before she died, she asked for VP. 'The doctors told me that she was remembering my husband and that I should call him over,' said Sita Kumari. 'He came to Allahabad and met her. The next day, she was much better. She said, "*Bhaiya* (she used to call him Bhaiya) *aaye they na* (He was here, wasn't he?)?" She recovered and we brought her home. But she was soon in hospital again.'[82]

Part 5

'DESH KA TAQDEER HAI'

1

'I'M GOING TO DIG IN AND FIGHT'

Rajiv Gandhi's response to V.P. Singh's resignation was contradictory. On the one hand, the personal attacks by Congress members on VP, begun by Dinesh Singh in Parliament on 31 March 1987, increased, with a couple of MPs in particular—K.K. Tewari and Kalpanath Rai—going ballistic. 'American imperialism has found a quisling in V.P. Singh,' was one of Tewari's milder remarks.[1] At its next meeting, the Congress Working Committee's resolution charged VP with 'a grand design of destabilization', seeking 'the country's balkanization' and attempting to 'undermine the morale of our defence forces'.[2] Thirty MPs signed a statement accusing him of 'immoral conduct' in appointing Fairfax.[3]

The apogee was reached at a big Congress rally on 16 May 1987 at the Boat Club grounds in Delhi.[4] 'I advised VP not to attend it, but he insisted on going,' recalled Som Pal. 'I drove him there but waited for him in my car.'[5]

VP presumably felt that being a Congress MP, his absence from the meeting could be used to further malign him. On a blazing hot day, with a towel wrapped around his shaved head—following his mother's demise—VP sat in the front row of listeners to hear himself being indirectly jeered at by the Prime Minister. '*Aaj hamey yaad rakhna hai kaise hamarey beech se Mir Jafar uthey they, Jaichand uthey they, Bharat ko bechney ke liye, Bharat ko kamzor karney ke liye* (Today we should remember how a Mir Jafar[6] rose in our midst, a Jaichand rose in our midst, to weaken the country),' Rajiv thundered in his speech. '*Unko hum kararey jawab dengey* (We'll give them a fitting reply).'[7] Jaichand purportedly being VP's ancestor (see Part 1, Chapter 1), the implication was clear. VP left the venue soon after.

On the other hand, Rajiv also sent emissaries to VP's home, urging reconciliation. A cabinet minister, a top bureaucrat in the Prime Minister's Office, and VP's old mentor Uma Shankar Dikshit all visited him separately, claiming that Rajiv was keen on meeting him to resolve their differences. Dikshit, by then in his late eighties, arthritic and leaning heavily on his walking stick, had suddenly been plucked out of his gubernatorial position by Rajiv in mid-1986 and made an AICC office-bearer. He was the most persuasive of the three. 'I'm quite sure Rajiv Gandhi isn't neck-deep in the HDW payoff,' he said, according to VP's later recount. 'He is nose-deep. But what else did you expect? Black money is as crucial to the functioning of a political party as this walking stick is to me. Without this walking stick, I can't even go to the bathroom. You were trying to take away Rajiv Gandhi's walking stick.'[8]

'There was nothing I could really say to that,' commented VP, 'except that political funding needed to be transparent.'[9]

He even agreed to meet Rajiv twice, but both meetings ended badly. At the first meeting, in the Prime Minister's Office, VP brought up the sustained slander campaign against him. 'Day in and day out, people like K.K. Tewari and Kalpanath Rai are calling me a CIA agent,' he said. 'I know they are only loudspeakers, and the mike feeding them is located in this room.'

Rajiv denied it strongly. 'Our party people are very angry with you,' he said. 'I'm trying to control them.'

'Look, we must stop playing games with each other,' VP responded. 'You've forgotten I've worked this Congress machine with your mother, and I know its every nut and bolt. None of this could have been said without your clearance. You call me a lousy, incompetent minister—I'm okay with that. But I'm not willing to accept being called a traitor. I'm going to dig in and fight.'[10]

The second meeting, late in the evening of 22 May 1987 at the new prime ministerial residence, 7, Race Course Road (now called Lok Kalyan Marg).[11] was worse. 'I remember the date because we had a double celebration planned that day,' said Sita Kumari Singh. 'Abhay had just got his postgraduate degree in medicine and it was also my granddaughter Adrija's (the younger of Ajeya Singh's two daughters) third birthday. We reserved a table for dinner at the India International Centre, but my husband did not show up until well after 10 p.m. and seemed very upset when he did.'[12]

At their meeting, Rajiv accused VP of having deserted Indira Gandhi after her 1977 Lok Sabha defeat and of staying away from the May 1978 Azamgarh by-election, which Mohsina Kidwai contested as the Congress(I) candidate and unexpectedly won, whereas VP had spent a week in Azamgarh campaigning. VP was finally provoked to counter, 'How would you know who was with your mother then and who wasn't? If anyone was missing around her then, it was you.'[13]

The meeting ended with VP storming out. 'As far as you are concerned, Vishwanath is dead,' he said dramatically. 'I'm leaving carrying my shroud.'

'No, no, sit down. What are you getting angry about?' said Rajiv, but VP did not wait.[14]

A last emissary arrived—*Dainik Jagran's* proprietor, Narendra Mohan—to suggest that VP could return as finance minister if he made up with Rajiv. VP turned down a third meeting. 'I feel

insulted by the proposal that I should return as finance minister,'
he replied. 'Rajiv Gandhi thinks he can throw me a crumb and I'll
succumb. It shows he does not understand me at all.'[15]

Even so, at the time, VP seemed to have had no idea of what he
would do next. In his first statement after quitting, he sought to
counter the charge that he had been trying to overshadow Rajiv
with an extraordinary declaration that he was later unable to
stick to. 'Of late, there has been a rumour campaign saying I'm
overambitious. To nail this lie, I hereby declare I will not hold
office in government in future.'[16] For the first few weeks after
his resignation, he eschewed all contact with Opposition leaders,
claiming that he remained a loyal Congressman. Ajeya Singh, by
then an investment banker with Citibank in New York, remembered
reading about the attacks on his father in the US press and asking
him about them during a long-distance telephone conversation.
'What kind of lallu (wimp) is this Rajiv Gandhi, who can't even stop
these fellows from saying all kinds of things about you?' he asked.

'Don't you dare say a word against him,' VP replied. 'Rajiv
Gandhi is my leader.'[17]

<hr />

'*Unke sitare itne buland they* (His stars were so strong),' Anand
Singh, Sant Bux Singh's son, said wistfully about his estranged
uncle VP.[18] Whether this was true of VP's entire political career can
be debated, but undoubtedly, on 16 April 1987, just five days after
he had resigned over alleged kickbacks in the HDW submarine
deal, he had an extraordinary piece of luck—the Bofors scandal
broke. Swedish radio made the sensational revelation that at least
Rs 6.6 crore (SEK 33 million) had been paid as commissions in a
Rs 1,437-crore deal to buy 410 155-mm howitzer guns that India
had signed with Swedish armaments manufacturer Bofors AB in
March 1986. A subsequent enquiry by the Swedish National Audit
Bureau estimated the commissions at Rs 64 crore (some later

estimates were even higher),[19] all of it paid into coded accounts in Swiss banks.[20]

The Bofors deal was more than three times the size of the HDW one; unlike the latter, which had been finalized before the government order outlawing commission agents in defence purchases was passed, the former was signed well after. The government's defensive reaction to the revelations, its initial unwillingness to start investigations and the subsequent conduct of the investigation it was forced to initiate—which seemed bent on shielding rather than outing the commission agents—as also further exposés in newspapers such as *The Hindu* and *The Indian Express*,[21] emphatically vindicated VP's decision to probe the HDW deal and helped him immensely in the campaign he shortly launched against Rajiv.

When Som Pal met VP at his residence on 13 April 1987, the morning after his resignation had been made public, and travelled with him to Lucknow the same evening, he found the latter strangely hesitant to take any further step. 'I felt he did not have the confidence to take on Rajiv Gandhi,' he said. 'I told him, "You have no idea how highly you are regarded. You should go out and see how people feel about you. You are as popular as Mahatma Gandhi was in his time."'[22] Still VP hesitated, but the 16 May 1987 Boat Club meeting seemed to have been a watershed moment for him. Santosh Bhartiya, a leading journalist then, who was so taken by VP that he temporarily quit the profession to join him, becoming another of his close advisers, remembered, 'If Rajiv Gandhi had not uttered that line about Jaichand, V.P. Singh would not have started touring the country. He told me so himself. He saw that epithet as a challenge.'[23]

But with so many Opposition parties already around, none of them capable of individually beating the Congress in national elections, VP saw little point in starting another. Instead, as he had done after resigning as UP chief minister in 1982, he began travelling, addressing meetings arranged by Congress front organizations, associations of government employees, farmers, teachers and the like. The only difference was that after his earlier resignation, he had confined himself to UP, but this time he went all over the country, discovering, to his surprise, that there were plenty of organizations eager to give him a platform, that Som Pal may not have been exaggerating too much. But he still kept away from Opposition party forums and spoke with caution, harping on the need for 'value-based politics' (the expression soon became one of his favourites), of bringing back to the country wealth illegally stashed by Indians abroad, without expressly criticizing either Rajiv or the Congress.

VP particularly remembered a meeting in Gaya, Bihar, organized in the third week of June 1987 by two Congress MLAs of the state, who had their own grievances against the then Bihar chief minister Bindeshwari Dubey. VP recalled,

> They had called the meeting in their personal capacity. There were no posters advertising it. Yet on our way to the meeting ground, we found large crowds waiting for us at every crossing. I'm used to crowds; there was always a crowd around me when I visited my constituency. But I had never had such massive crowds welcoming me before. For the last kilometre or so before the meeting ground, there were so many people around us that the driver of the Maruti van I was travelling in could hardly drive. The vehicle was simply pushed along.[24]

By then, VP had also begun networking with other once-powerful Congressmen, who, too, for different reasons, had fallen foul of Rajiv. Three of them became close political lieutenants in his drive against the Congress, along with Som Pal and Santosh Bhartiya. The first was Arun Nehru, Rajiv's corpulent cousin and once his most trusted associate. Made minister of state for home in October 1985, he had been widely regarded as the most powerful person in the cabinet next to the Prime Minister. But his aggressiveness also provoked much resentment in the party, leading to his being dropped from the cabinet a year later and ignored thereafter. Earlier, as the AICC general secretary in charge of UP, Nehru had been domineering and peremptory towards VP during the latter's stint as UP chief minister,[25] but VP seemed to have decided early on that in his hunt for allies, he was not going to be choosy.

The second was Arif Mohammad Khan (governor of Kerala at the time of writing), a former president of the Aligarh Muslim University students' union and first-term MP at the time, who had resigned as minister of state for power from Rajiv's cabinet following differences over a raging controversy then—on whether Muslim ex-husbands paying long-term maintenance to their divorced wives was in keeping with Quranic decrees. Delivering its judgment in a celebrated case in April 1985,[26] where a sixty-two-year-old mother of five, Shah Bano Begum, had sought such maintenance, the Supreme Court ruled that it was. With conservative Muslim groups opposing the judgment, Rajiv had asked Arif Khan to defend it in the Lok Sabha, which he had duly done. Khan quit the cabinet when, a few months later, as Muslim opposition grew, Rajiv changed his mind and, without even informing Khan, had a Bill introduced in Parliament to nullify the court's decision.

Khan was flayed by his co-religionists for taking the position he had and, once he'd resigned, shunned by Congress members as well. 'Within a few days of my resigning, Congress MPs started avoiding me, including some who I'd thought were personal friends,' he said. 'So, when a couple of people—whom I'd rather not name—approached me saying V.P. Singh wanted to meet me, I warned them, "I'm persona non grata in the party already and I don't want to embarrass him." But they persisted, so I did. Of course, I knew him from before—we were in the cabinet together and he was such a fine gentleman at a personal level.'[27] With VP's fifty-sixth birthday close—on 25 June 1987—Khan decided to hold a party for him at his home, to which he invited Arun Nehru as well. The party, much covered in the media, which was also invited, became the first indubitable proof that Rajiv's opponents in the Congress were coming together.

The third was Vidya Charan Shukla, notorious for his heavy-handed suppression of press freedom during the Emergency, when he had been information and broadcasting minister. Much promoted by Indira then, he later lost favour with Rajiv for encouraging dissidence against his home state Madhya Pradesh's chief minister, Arjun Singh, and was dropped from the cabinet.

'A common friend said that V.C. Shukla, whom I had known for years, wanted to see me,' said Som Pal. 'When I met him, he said that he wanted to join V.P. Singh and it was up to me to fix a meeting. I broached the subject with V.P. Singh. He said, "*Nahi, Som Pal, unki to chhavi bahut kharab hai* (No, he has a very poor image)." I said, "*Arun Nehru se bhi kharab hai* (Is it any worse than Arun Nehru's)? He carries much influence in Madhya Pradesh. Who else do you have from there?" After two or three heated discussions, he agreed. It was my single-handed achievement.'[28] VP had clearly decided not to be choosy.

So high was VP's stature at the time that, despite such dubious colleagues, the first public meeting all of them addressed together—at Haridwar, on 15 July 1987—was a bigger success than the one at Gaya.[29] 'The president of the union of Bharat Heavy Electricals Ltd (BHEL) at its Haridwar unit, Brijpal Singh, was a friend of mine,' said Som Pal. 'The union was affiliated to the Indian National Trade Union Congress (INTUC—the Congress's trade union arm), and since V.P. Singh was still avoiding Opposition forums, I approached Brijpal to organize a public meeting and he agreed.'

Short of funds, he remembered being worried about organizing a decent-sized cavalcade of cars that would set out from Delhi for the meeting. 'I telephoned whoever I thought could help, hoping to manage around fifteen–twenty cars,' he said. 'When we set out in the morning, our cavalcade comprised 171 vehicles. V.P. Singh was with me in the car I drove. More joined us on the way and by the time we reached Haridwar, we were around 300 vehicles.' The weather worked against them, but that, too, did not matter. 'The rains were late that year, but that day it poured,' he said. 'Yet no one left the meeting. All speeches were delivered to a sea of umbrellas. There were at least 30,000 people present, amazing for a town the size of Haridwar then.'[30]

Back at the Haridwar Circuit House, where they would spend the night, VP and his men heard on the Doordarshan news broadcast that even as they were addressing the meeting, Nehru, Arif Khan and Shukla had been expelled from the Congress for 'anti-party activity'.[31] The bulletin said nothing about VP. There followed long confabulations that night and the next morning on how VP should react. 'Most of those present felt that VP should not resign from the Congress in protest, but I maintained that he should,' said Som Pal. 'I told VP, "Politics is a matter of showing grit and decisiveness at the right time. If three of your senior colleagues have been expelled and you still don't react, *aapke saath kaun lagega* (who will join you)?" Ultimately, VP decided he would resign.'[32]

Som Pal feared that if VP waited until he returned to Delhi, he might be prevailed upon to change his mind. 'I told him, "Your resignation should reach the press before you reach Delhi," and he agreed,' he said. On the way back, they stopped for lunch, as scheduled, at Somansh Prakash's home in Muzaffarnagar. 'After lunch, VP said to me, "I'll need to use your bedroom for a while,"' said Prakash. 'I knew he had this habit of taking a post-lunch nap and had a bedroom ready for him. But he had more on his mind. He said, "Look, I'm going to bolt the door from inside. Make sure I'm not disturbed. I need to write a letter. When I'm done,

I'll open the door myself."[33] There were indeed two calls from senior Congress leaders, but Prakash repeated VP's instructions to them and refused to put them through.

This time, VP resigned from both the Congress and the Rajya Sabha. 'The action against them [Nehru, Khan and Shukla] was undemocratic and dictatorial,' his letter to Rajiv said. 'It proves Congressmen can be politically hanged without any hearing or show-cause notice. Even Nathuram Godse [Mahatma Gandhi's assassin] was given a fair trial. If you persist in this, you can treat this as my letter of resignation.'[34]

The letter was quickly typed, cyclostyled and distributed to news-agency stringers in Muzaffarnagar. On reaching Delhi, Som Pal also personally delivered copies to all the important newspapers.

Rajiv did not accept VP's resignation, but four days later, decided to expel him from the Congress. 'Since the letter had been composed at my house, I was expelled as well,' said Prakash.[35]

<hr />

Rajiv's relations with President Giani Zail Singh had been uneasy even before he became Prime Minister. Zail Singh[36] had been chief minister of Punjab in the 1970s and Union home minister before being made President in 1982. But as Punjab slipped into chaos in the early 1980s, Rajiv and his close aides became suspicious of his role as home minister in propping up the extremists.[37] Later, though he was the country's President, he was not informed in advance of Operation Bluestar.[38]

With Zail Singh away on an official visit to Yemen the day Indira was assassinated, some of Rajiv's men had even suggested that the vice president swear him in as Prime Minister, unsure whether Zail Singh—given his disaffection for Rajiv—would raise constitutional objections to the hasty procedure if they waited for him to return. Eventually they did wait, and Zail Singh complied at once, claiming that he had already made up his mind on the flight back to do so.

Zail Singh later maintained that he began feeling slighted within days of Rajiv's taking charge. 'After three or four days, it was a Sunday when I sent for Rajiv Gandhi, but my secretary was informed by the prime minister's secretary that he would call on me in a couple of days and he wanted me to rest on a Sunday,' he wrote in his memoirs later. 'But he never came and in the following days and weeks I realized he had started avoiding me.'[39]

Soon Rajiv's visits to Rashtrapati Bhavan, scarce to start with, stopped entirely. The convention of the Prime Minister briefing the President before and after every foreign visit was abandoned; moreover, permission for Zail Singh's own visits overseas was withheld. K.K. Tewari—the same MP who would later call VP a US quisling—alleged in the Lok Sabha in mid-1985 that Zail Singh had hosted two Sikh extremists at Rashtrapati Bhavan. (The charge was never established, but though Zail Singh protested, Tewari was never admonished by Rajiv.) The President was completely excluded from the efforts Rajiv made to quell the Punjab unrest, including his signing of the Punjab peace accord with Sant Harchand Singh Longowal, the head of the agitating Sikhs' moderate faction, in July 1985, or the decision to hold elections in the state soon after. Zail Singh's speech on the eve of Independence Day in 1986, already recorded by All India Radio and Doordarshan while Rajiv was abroad, had to be reworked after the Prime Minister read it on his return and demanded that several parts be changed.

In the last six months of his five-year term ending July 1987, as Rajiv's popularity began dipping drastically, Zail Singh hit back. It started with a letter he wrote to Rajiv on 9 March 1987, rebutting his claim in Parliament a few days earlier that all was well between them, which was also leaked to the press. As Rajiv's troubles increased further, with VP's resignation as defence minister in April, the Bofors-related charges emerging and the Congress's crushing defeat in assembly elections held in Haryana in mid-June, it began to be widely rumoured that Zail Singh was consulting legal opinion to see if the President indeed had the constitutional right to dismiss the Prime Minister. If so, he needed a credible alternative to replace Rajiv immediately, and rumours claimed that he had zoomed in on VP.[40]

In his memoirs, Zail Singh strongly denied ever having had any such intention.[41] But the press reports persisted, and VP's last interviews also claimed that he had been sounded out.[42] At first, he was approached through intermediaries led by V.C. Shukla, with whom he had just teamed up, thanks to Som Pal. But VP was clear that whatever his differences with Rajiv, the dismissal of a popularly elected Prime Minister was just not right. 'I'll fight him face to face; I'm not going to stab him in the back,' he told all those who discussed the matter with him.[43]

Later, VP maintained, Zail Singh, too, personally summoned him. He remembered,

> We did not sit in any of the Rashtrapati Bhavan rooms, which Zail Singh said were all bugged, but went into his garden. He said, 'You're not agreeing. You should agree to be the prime minister. I'll dismiss Rajiv Gandhi. You take the oath and become prime minister.' I said, 'Gianiji, I can't do that because I don't think it is right, my conscience won't allow it.' The matter ended there. He never asked again.[44]

Eventually, Zail Singh quit quietly once his term ended on 25 July 1987.

—❀—

The Congress's attacks on VP had so far been verbal. Once he was expelled from the party, they also turned physical. The most serious of these was in Delhi, while he was on his way to a dinner being hosted by a friend, a professor at St. Stephen's College, and briefly stopped his car to greet a group of young men, one of them holding a garland, who he thought wanted to felicitate him.[45] He narrated later,

> When I went for public meetings, I always took precautions, but this was a private dinner, so I was not expecting trouble. But I had a personal security officer with me, who was very alert. He pulled away the garland as it was being put around my neck. It had a wire enmeshed among the flowers, which the man garlanding me must have intended to tug and try to choke me. When that ruse failed, the group attacked the car with stones and petrol-filled bottles.[46]

Som Pal, who was driving, somehow managed to pull away. 'The men shoved bundles of grass beneath the car and tried to set them alight,' he said. 'I honestly don't remember how I managed to drive off,' he said.[47] Once they were inside the professor's home, the group attacked again. A number of other Delhi University professors had also been invited to the dinner, and the driveway was full of cars and two-wheelers. VP recalled,

> They burnt the scooters outside, smashed the car windows and began banging on the front door. We heard gunfire. I went up on the roof. Somehow, they managed to break open the front door and enter. They asked for me and began thrashing the living room when told I was not there. They left, threatening they would be waiting for me outside. But by then Som Pal had phoned the police. They arrived shortly and arrested the boys.[48]

Many them turned out to be affiliated to the National Students' Union of India (NSUI), the Congress's student arm.[49]

There was a second heinous attack as VP was travelling by car from Lucknow to Unnao, 65 km to its south-west, to address a rally there. This time he had a large convoy with him, but his attackers were also more in number and better armed. As he recollected in his interview,

> Some of our volunteers on bikes, who had gone a little ahead, returned saying they had been attacked by a large group with lathis, and when they were rushing back, fired upon. One of them had a serious injury on his leg. We were not sure whether to continue our journey or not, but we also realized that if we got cowed down, the same pattern would be repeated to prevent our future meetings. Our people were unarmed, but they collected stout tree branches and stones to use as weapons. As expected, we were assaulted, but our boys retaliated. They even caught some of the attackers and beat them up. Later we learnt that the man behind it all had a murder charge against him but had been told the charge would be dropped if he stopped our rally.[50]

In UP, in particular—whose chief minister by then was Veer Bahadur Singh, the same man who had spearheaded the attacks on Bahuguna on polling day in Garhwal in June 1981—efforts to disrupt VP's meetings, or prevent him from reaching the venue, became almost routine. There were always Congress workers waving black flags when he spoke or trying to disrupt his speech by sloganeering against him. At times, as in Lucknow and Gorakhpur, his rallies were denied permission; at others, flights he had to take to address them were mysteriously cancelled, or trains he travelled in developed engine snags and stopped moving, only to start again when he left by a car his men could hastily organize.[51]

En route to a meeting in Lakhimpur Kheri, VP was struck by a stone on the forehead and began bleeding. On his way to a Kanpur meeting, he was warned by the district's police chief not to take the route he had planned—along which welcome arches had been erected for him—as there were reports of a sniper aiming at him from one of the rooftops. Arriving at the grounds where he was to address the rally by an alternative route, he found that half of it had been deliberately flooded the night before. At a number of his rallies, snakes would be let loose amid the audience, leading to near-stampedes.[52]

The slander campaign against VP also continued unabated, with many being pressured to join it. Late one evening, Sant Bux, who had been ignored by the Congress for years, was surprised to find himself summoned by a senior cabinet minister. When they met, the minister—well aware of the brothers' estrangement—flourished a document, urging him to sign it, assuring him of a Rajya Sabha seat if he did. The gist of the document was that Sant Bux knew of secret accounts VP held in Swiss banks. 'If you want to fight Vishwanath, you have to do so politically,' Sant Bux said and departed, his career in the Congress thereby effectively ending.[53]

As it turned out, both the verbal and the physical attacks—much publicized in the press—only served to boost VP's popularity and further discredit the government. The crowds at his rallies kept swelling, which delighted but also worried him. 'One felt good, of course, but there was also the anxiety of living up to expectations,' he said. 'If people think of you as a god, you must have the capacity to grant boons, or how long will they keep thinking that way?'[54]

2

'ISKI TO BAHUT HAWA HAI'

The Opposition parties had been badly mauled in the January 1980 Lok Sabha elections. In the next one, in December 1984, with the outpouring of sympathy for Rajiv Gandhi after Indira Gandhi's assassination, they fared even worse. 'After this election, there will no more be an Opposition,' Rajiv had famously said during the campaign, and the results almost proved him right. The Janata Party, following its government's collapse in July 1979, had splintered many times, but its main remnants were three—the shrunken Janata, Charan Singh's DMKP and the BJP, a regrouping of the members of the erstwhile Bharatiya Jana Sangh. The three contested 508 of the 514 seats where polls were held in 1984, and won only 15. They had fared a little better in the assembly elections to eleven states held in March 1985, but the Congress had still won nine of them, the exceptions being Andhra Pradesh and Karnataka, which had Opposition party governments even before the polls.

Rajiv's dipping popularity over the next two and a half years had kindled the hopes of all three Janata remnants of making a comeback, but until VP joined them—except in one state—they had failed to make any impact. After the March 1985 victories, until mid-1987, Rajiv lost seven assembly elections in a row, but the winners were mostly regional parties—as in Punjab and Assam—or the CPI(M) in Bengal and Kerala. The exception was Haryana, where, in June 1987, a breakaway group from Charan Singh's party—which, by then, had reverted to its earlier name of Lok Dal—partnered with the BJP and nearly obliterated the Congress, winning 76 of the state's 90 seats and reducing the Congress to just 5.[1]

All these parties, both national and regional, had been trying, ever since the January 1980 defeat, to forge a united front against the Congress and present a credible challenge at the national level, even holding a number of 'conclaves' to discuss this. But given their disparate ideologies and their leaders' quarrelsome temperaments, their efforts had gone nowhere. An August 1987 poll by *India Today* found that if Lok Sabha elections were held right then, the Congress—despite Rajiv's corroded image—would still win 323 of the 543 seats, because Opposition votes would be split.[2] (Indeed, far from uniting, one of the parties, Charan Singh's Lok Dal, had split further, one unit led by Charan Singh's son Ajit Singh [hence called Lok Dal (A)], and the other by Bahuguna [and thus called Lok Dal (B)]). It was the Lok Dal [B] that won the Haryana election.[3])

Even so, the Rajiv–VP clash greatly boosted the Opposition's morale, bringing urgency and focus to its unity efforts as its leaders realized that it had battered the Congress's image and could benefit them electorally. But their response to VP joining their ranks—once out of the Congress, he abandoned his earlier aloofness towards Opposition parties and began actively courting them—was mixed. Some welcomed him, aware of how popular he had grown and that any alliance with him could only help them. But there were also those who were wary, precisely because of VP's popularity, fearing that in any unified party or front they might build, they would have to yield overall leadership to him.

They resented being overshadowed by a man who, until recently, had been a leading figure of the very party they were opposing—one who, moreover, had supported the Emergency and indeed thrived during it, rising from deputy minister to minister of state while they were being imprisoned and harassed.

The first to unreservedly welcome VP—even announcing that he be projected as the Opposition parties' prime ministerial aspirant—was also the man mainly responsible for the Lok Dal (B)'s stupendous victory in Haryana—the formidable Devi Lal. Big and bellicose, Devi Lal had an impressive record as a freedom fighter and peasant leader;[4] his organizational skills had enabled the Lok Dal (B) (which he joined once the Lok Dal broke up) to remain a force in Haryana, even as all the other splinter groups of the Janata Party floundered badly in the rest of the country. The Lok Dal (B)'s popularity rose further from mid-1985 (while that of the Congress plummeted) after Rajiv signed the Punjab accord, Devi Lal having managed to convince Haryanvis that the concessions to neighbouring Punjab made in the accord were blatantly unfair to their state. The poll results reflected voter fury at the sell-out.

Devi Lal was Som Pal's uncle by marriage—his younger sister, Parameshwari, was Som Pal's mother-in-law. 'V.P. Singh was already in touch with some other Opposition leaders, and it was decided among them that I should be the one to talk to Devi Lal, who had just then become Haryana chief minister for the second time,' said Som Pal. 'I went to Chandigarh to meet him, but he disappointed me utterly. He said, *"Kya bekar ki baat kar raha hai? Kaun V.P. Singh–P.P. Singh? Congress ka aadmi tha. Delhi mein sarkar ab main hi banaoonga* (What nonsense is this? Who's this V.P. Singh–P.P. Singh? He used to be in the Congress. I will be the one forming the next government in Delhi).' Som Pal spent all day in Chandigarh trying to convince Devi Lal that a partnership with

VP would help his entry into national politics, speaking to him late into the night—but to no avail.[5]

Returning to Delhi the next day, he avoided VP. 'I used to meet him daily, but now I stopped out of embarrassment,' he said. 'I had been so confident, and I had failed. But two days later, as I was stepping out for my morning walk, the phone rang and it was Devi Lal. "*Kya kar rahe ho* (What are you doing)?" he boomed over the phone, before saying that he was visiting Delhi and wanted to dine with me. During dinner, at Delhi's Haryana Bhavan, he said, "*Tu woh jo tazveez leke aaya tha, theek lag rahi hai mujhe* (I agree with the suggestion you had given me)."

Som Pal asked what had happened to make him change his mind. He said, '*Arrey bawley, maine ek dozen se zyada CID ke aadmi bheje Dilli mein, west UP mein, Haryana mein ... Iski to bahut hawa hai. Tu uski aur meri baat karwa de* (You idiot, I sent more than a dozen men from Haryana's CID (Criminal Investigation Department) to Delhi, west UP and Haryana to check out this fellow ... There is a strong wind in his favour. You arrange my meeting with him).'

The meeting duly transpired the next day, where VP and Devi Lal agreed to hold the first three of their many public meetings together—all in one day—on the Punjab–Haryana–Rajasthan border, all of them close to Chautala village, from which Devi Lal hailed.[6]

Among Opposition leaders hostile to VP, the most prominent were his old adversary Bahuguna and the Janata Party President Chandra Shekhar (who went on to briefly succeed VP as Prime Minister). His troubled past with VP had embittered Bahuguna, who felt betrayed by a man whose political career he had nurtured; he remained especially sore about the Garhwal by-election of 1981, when he had been injured on polling day running away from Congress goons. 'I have a scar on my foot to remind me of that day,' he would say. 'I see V.P. Singh's face in that scar.'[7]

As he was president of the Lok Dal (B), his animus led to another schism in the party, since Devi Lal ignored him, openly rooting for VP. Initially, Bahuguna's supporters boycotted all of VP's public meetings, including those on their common home turf Allahabad, but many of them eventually shifted loyalties to Devi Lal, especially after Bahuguna, diagnosed with cancer in late 1988, passed away in March 1989.

Chandra Shekhar's hostility proved more durable. He had been VP's contemporary at Allahabad University, pursuing an MA in philosophy, closely involved with the socialist group among the students, though there is no record of any interaction between them. He entered politics almost immediately afterwards, joining the Socialist Party—where he met and became a lifelong fan of Jayaprakash Narayan—then moving on in the early 1960s, like many other socialist leaders, to the Congress. He had strenuously backed Indira Gandhi's socialist policies—heading a group of young MPs who called themselves 'Young Turks'[8]—and greatly helped her in her battle with the Syndicate.[9]

He ran afoul of Indira, however, when, following JP's agitation, he urged her to reconcile with him; during the Emergency, she expelled him from the party and locked him up along with the Opposition leaders. While other leaders clamoured to become ministers once the Janata Party won the 1977 elections, he preferred to be made its organizational president. But the collapse of the Janata effort seemed to sour him, as he clung tenaciously to his position for the next eleven years, even as his party shrivelled following repeated splits, ruthlessly stamping out all leadership challenges.[10] The Janata Party had only one success after its mid-1979 implosion, unexpectedly winning the assembly elections in Karnataka in 1983 and again in 1985, but Chandra Sekhar even resented the popularity of Karnataka Chief Minister Ramakrishna Hegde[11]—the man largely responsible for the Janata's victories in that state—and tried hard to encourage dissidence against him.

No doubt he saw his own chance of becoming Prime Minister—if ever the Congress was dislodged from power at the Centre—recede in direct proportion to VP's rise. 'We need an alternative to Rajiv Gandhi, and not a substitute,' was among the many uncharitable remarks he made about VP. 'I'm not swayed by "leaders" created by the press.'[12] (Not surprisingly, to counter Chandra Shekhar, Hegde joined Devi Lal in ardently championing VP.)

In late September 1987, Devi Lal organized yet another Opposition conclave at Surajkund in Haryana, 40 km south-east of Delhi, attended by twenty-two leaders—including VP—representing sixteen parties. It was the first time VP was attending such a gathering of the Opposition, and the formidable hurdles to Opposition unity were soon clear to him.[13] For one, Chandra Shekhar and Bahuguna emphasized that they would never accept VP as the leader of any united party or front. For another, the regional party representatives present made it clear that only a united front was feasible for them—merging into a larger national party would only dilute their state identities and weaken them.

Two other obstacles were apparent as well, not from those who came to the conclave but by their significant absence. Not all parties had been invited. Though the ideologies of the Lok Dal (A) and Lok Dal (B) were much the same, Charan Singh's son and Lok Dal (A) President Ajit Singh was missing because Devi Lal could not stand him. Again, the communist parties, the CPI and the CPI (M) boycotted the meeting—they would not attend any event at which the BJP, which they regarded as communal and opposed to minority interests, was present, let alone join any alliance that included it.

VP maintained later that for the first few months after leaving the Congress, he hadn't still decided whether to continue with his movement against corporate and political corruption or to confront Rajiv electorally. Greatly inspired by Mahatma Gandhi and JP—both of whom led mass movements without ever seeking positions of power—he claimed he was initially more inclined towards following their path. 'I wanted to wage a struggle, not form another party, which would only lead to further fragmentation of the polity,' he said.[14]

Initially, he didn't even launch an organization. When he did, soon after the Surajkund conclave—on 2 October 1987 (on Mahatma Gandhi's birth anniversary)—with a low-key inauguration on the lawns of his 1, Teenmurti Marg residence,[15] it was called a 'forum', not a political party; its constitution expressly forbade those with political-party affiliations from becoming executive members.[16] Jan Morcha, as the forum was called, held its first public meeting in Mathura a few days later, drawing a huge crowd, with 10,000 volunteers joining it right there.[17] 'But with the political support I began getting, things changed,' VP said later. 'I felt it could be channelled into a real democratic alternative to the Congress, which would be a contribution to the country.'[18]

The decision was not taken easily. For one, as the MPs and MLAs supporting him pointed out, under the anti-defection law passed in 1985, they could all be disqualified from Parliament for joining a party other than the one on whose ticket they had been elected. More crucially, the fate of the Janata Party a decade back was a sobering reminder of the pitfalls of hastily cobbling together a united Opposition front or party. Many in VP's own Jan Morcha recalled the Janata example, the loudest objectors to any merger with other parties being Ram Dhan, a Dalit MP from Lalganj, UP, who had been made its convenor (he was earlier part of the Young Turks group with Chandra Shekhar and, like him, had been imprisoned during the Emergency), and Arif Mohammad Khan. 'I told V.P. Singh, "These Opposition people want us because, unlike them, we have credibility,"' said Arif Khan. 'We join them and within a year our credibility will be finished too.'[19] But with the Lok Sabha polls barely two years away, VP felt that he had no option.

The large crowds at his meetings notwithstanding, he was well aware that without a nationwide organization with workers in every district, their numbers would not automatically translate into votes. He remembered Kamalapati Tripathi's admonition about political careers being like trees, which could never spring up overnight. 'If we want to walk alone, we should forget about the forthcoming Lok Sabha election and set our sights on the next one, five years later,' he said.[20] Not many in the Jan Morcha— where the distinction between 'forum' and 'party', blurry from the start, soon disappeared—were ready for that. Another alternative, that of persuading top leaders from the entire gamut of Opposition parties to join the Jan Morcha along with their followers, severing links with their earlier parties, was also considered and rejected, since it would result in every party splitting further, thereby only helping the Congress.

Once he had made up his mind to pursue unity, VP began doing so with zeal, tackling the fissures he had observed at the Surajkund conclave as best he could. Deeply sensitive, he was mortified by the statements of Chandra Shekhar and Bahuguna contesting his right to lead the Opposition, and insisted that he'd never wanted to lead in the first place. 'I've made it clear I'm not in the running for Prime Minister,' he declared at a press conference.[21] 'It would be a national disaster if I became Prime Minister,' he told an interviewer.[22] He agreed with the assessment of the regional parties that they were better off forming a united front rather than merging into a single party.

The other two problems were intractable, and though VP realized that they could eventually be the undoing of any united Opposition,[23] he pressed ahead, ignoring them. He was convinced that to dislodge Rajiv and the Congress from power, he needed to marshal every section opposed to them and even if some of these sections could not stand one another, he was not going to choose between them. He would have to make them realize that power could only be achieved by coming together, ignoring their differences. 'When contradictions cannot be resolved, they have to be managed,' he noted.[24]

Thus, well aware that Devi Lal would resent the move, he agreed to forge links with Lok Dal (A) chief Ajit Singh. Both Devi Lal and Ajit Singh belonged to the Jat caste, dominant in Haryana and west UP. 'Devi Lal's influence was immense, but it was restricted to Haryana and we knew that for support from west UP, we needed Ajit Singh,' said Som Pal.[25] Arranging a meeting was not difficult— Ajit Singh had already been seeking one. 'He was trying through my son Abhay's father-in-law, Anand Singh, the raja of Mankapur, and also a Congress MP,' VP said. 'Anand Singh would repeatedly remind me. I kept him waiting for three months, but eventually agreed to meet.'[26]

Som Pal, despite his old rivalry with Charan Singh's family, also pitched in to persuade Ajit Singh. As expected, Devi Lal was furious when, some months later, a delegation of Opposition leaders that came to meet him at Pinjore Gardens near Chandigarh, where he was temporarily staying, included Ajit Singh. 'Why have you brought that fellow along? He is nothing but a saudagar (wheeler-dealer),' he said to VP. But he was eventually placated.[27]

Sustaining the support of both the BJP and the communist parties proved even more difficult, because VP's natural instinct conflicted with what he believed was a political imperative. His secular outlook—acquired through long years in the Congress and, before that, his association with socialists and communists—made him recoil from the BJP's pro-Hindu agenda; he also knew that any alliance with the party could cost him the backing of the communist parties as well as of Muslims disenchanted with the Congress (who might well revert to voting for the Congress, considering it a lesser evil). But humbling Rajiv being his main aim, he felt he could not do without the BJP. 'I was not really in favour of allying with the BJP,' he said later. 'But given the situation and recalling that Jayaprakash Narayan had also taken the help of the Jana Sangh during his movement, I followed suit.'[28]

Yet, he could never bring himself to admit this at the time— he preferred to duck and feint whenever questioned about it by journalists. Som Pal felt that if VP had clearly explained his purpose, the Left and the BJP could have been reconciled to jointly support him from the start, since their areas of influence did not overlap—the BJP's mainly included the north Indian states and the Left's was restricted to West Bengal and Kerala. 'I was not happy about V.P. Singh's evasiveness,' he said. 'I would have preferred him to say openly that we were taking the BJP's help because we wanted to rid the country of the Congress's corruption, nepotism and insensitivity. But it was not in his nature to answer difficult questions in a straightforward way. He liked to elude direct replies.'[29]

However, his actions confirmed his all-embracing intentions— while calling the Left his 'natural allies', he also attended functions hosted by RSS-affiliated organizations and even addressed a few public meetings jointly with BJP leaders.

No doubt, on one count VP was disappointed—belying his hopes, only fifteen Congress MPs (which included Arif Khan, Arun Nehru and V.C. Shukla) joined him. When Zail Singh was considering dismissing Rajiv, it was estimated that around 200 Congress MPs were so unhappy with their Prime Minister that they would back the successor he chose; yet, when VP left the party, hardly anyone followed him. In the UP assembly too, though a large number of MLAs owed their nominations to VP—he had, after all, been UPCC president during the last elections in March 1985, though owing to his other preoccupations he couldn't give candidate selection the attention it deserved—only eighteen,[30] including just one minister (his nephew-in-law Sanjay Singh, who had finally been made minister by VP's successors as chief minister in UP) eventually joined him.

Even in Allahabad, some of the men he had mentored, such as K.P. Tiwari and even Ramesh Pande, preferred to stay put in the Congress. 'V.P. Singh thought that a large number of Congressmen would follow him out of the party, but I always doubted it,' said Som Pal. 'I told him, *"Congressi ko satta mein rahne ka adat hai. Usme kisi aadmi ki apni haisiyat nahi hai* (Congress people are used to being in power. They have no standing of their own). If you are waiting for them to join you, you're wasting your time."'[31]

<hr>

Shortly after the controversy around Ajitabh Bachchan owning an apartment in Montreux, Switzerland, broke, Amitabh Bachchan resigned from the Lok Sabha, citing no reasons. In the months that followed, however, strong rumours were heard claiming that both he and Rajiv felt he had been impetuous, considering there was no definite charge of corruption against him, and that he intended to re-contest from Allahabad whenever a fresh poll was held. Since his departure from the Congress, the tenor of VP's speeches had also changed, becoming much more critical of Rajiv—whom he would hardly name earlier—and particularly targeting Bachchan.[32]

When by-polls to seven Lok Sabha seats, including Allahabad, were announced for 16 June 1988, VP sought the support of all Opposition parties to stand as their common candidate against Bachchan. Barring one exception,[33] they eventually acquiesced. 'I thought it worth contesting as the issue (of corruption) would then be sharply focused upon as an adjunct to our campaign,' he said.[34]

But finally, Bachchan did not contest. With no Congress candidate officially announced and the rumours louder than ever, VP waited until the last day for filing nominations—indeed, until the last two hours before the deadline—before completing his own formalities. Soon after he finished came the anti-climax—

the Congress candidate at last arrived to file and it turned out to be Sunil Shastri, the third son of former Prime Minister Lal Bahadur Shastri. (Ironically, Shastri, who had been minister of power in the UP cabinet, had resigned his position to protest Chief Minister Bir Bahadur Singh's many slanderous comments on VP—he and Sanjay Singh had been the only ministers to object. Many had expected that, like Sanjay Singh, Shastri, too, would quit the Congress to join VP, but he had not.)

Shocked and embarrassed, all the more because of his close ties with the Shastri family—whose Shastri Sewa Niketan still operated out of his Manda residence—VP declared that he would withdraw his candidature; he had intended to contest against Bachchan alone. But other Opposition leaders refused to let him, noting that it would leave the Allahabad poll without an Opposition candidate.[35]

As he'd done in the last election he'd fought—from Tindwari for the UP Vidhan Sabha—VP decided that his would be an austere campaign, eschewing four-wheel vehicles while canvassing. In Tindwari, as incumbent chief minister, confident of winning, he had hardly campaigned, but this time he did so aggressively. At first, he even refused to use posters and loudspeakers, but midway through the campaign realized that this was proving too big a handicap; Som Pal, who owned a small printing press in Delhi then, remembered hurriedly printing thousands of posters and trucking them to Allahabad.[36]

Early each morning, clad in a white kurta-pyjama, with a white bandana covering his rapidly balding pate to protect it from the fierce May–June sun (the temperature often crossed 45-degree Celsius), VP, fifty-seven at the time, would set out, riding pillion on an Enfield Bullet motorbike, with a host of volunteers on their own bikes surrounding him, deep into the countryside, returning late at night. There were mishaps but VP remained unruffled. Associate Udit Narayan Singh recalled his bike once skidding and toppling over. 'We were a convoy of around fifty bikes, with V.P. Singh somewhere in the middle, travelling from a village called Hardaon to another called Basaha when it happened,' he said. 'It was my fault and it led to a pile-up; I saw V.P. Singh flat on his back on the road, as his bike had skidded too. I was most embarrassed and tried to avoid him at the next meeting. But he called me and reassured me, "*Hamare chot-wot nahi lagi, dukhiya ka* (I'm not hurt; are you upset)?"'[37] Using motorcycles not only made for a good spectacle in an election that had drawn tremendous media interest, but also enabled VP to reach backward rural areas his Congress rival's cars and Jeeps could not.

Top Opposition leaders, including those of both the BJP and the communists, and even Chandra Shekhar and Bahuguna, campaigned for VP; so too did the Congress have its own battery of bigwigs rooting for Sunil Shastri. Recalling Lal Bahadur Shastri's purported remark that VP was his 'fifth son', some in the press depicted the contest as a modern-day Mahabharata, an epic battle of brothers[38]—but it was, in fact, a one-sided contest, with VP winning by more than 110,000 votes.

Realizing that Shastri was losing, state Congress leaders even sought the district administration's help to rig the election,[39] but to VP's luck, the district magistrate, Prabhat Chaturvedi, proved exceptionally upright and refused to cooperate.[40] With fresh disclosures about Bofors commissions in *The Hindu* in late April 1988 contributing, corruption remained the overriding theme of the poll, caste considerations being swept aside. VP triumphed in all the five assembly segments of the seat, doing better overall in the rural areas than in the urban. As a fallout, Bir Bahadur Singh lost his job,[41] and was replaced by N.D. Tiwari, who took over as chief minister of UP for the third time.

There was only one grey lining to this burst of sunshine for the Opposition—Jan Morcha colleague Arif Khan refrained from canvassing for VP. It emerged that VP had never asked him to, for fear that his very presence, given his support of the Supreme Court judgment in the Shah Bano case, would lose him Muslim votes. Instead, he invited Syed Shahabuddin, a former diplomat and Janata Party leader, who had led the agitation against the judgment, to address some of his meetings in Muslim areas.

'No one asked me to stay away, nor did I need an invitation to campaign for V.P. Singh,' said Arif Khan. 'I was planning to do so anyway. But one evening, after having spent hours with me discussing the nitty-gritty of our Allahabad election strategy, I learnt he had gone directly to Shahabuddin and sought his support as well. A person present at their meeting informed me that Shahabuddin told him, "You'll have my full support if you keep Arif Khan out of the campaign." Once I heard that, I decided not to go to Allahabad.'[42]

The rumpus saw VP widely accused of pandering to Muslim fundamentalists, and he really had no answer to the charge, though he seemed to have reconsidered the repercussions of Shahabuddin's support soon after seeking it. When Shahabuddin arrived in Allahabad, Janardhan Thakur notes in *V.P. Singh: A Quest for Power*, '... [I]t was as though he was quite unwanted; he went to Muslim areas all the same and did his best to mobilize votes in favour of Singh.'[43] Arif Khan remained furious and, after the election, threatened to quit the Jan Morcha. 'I still regret succumbing to pressure from various Opposition leaders and friends and staying back,' he said. 'They said, "*Arif Bhai, agar aap iss waqt alag hue toh V.P. Singh ki credibility khatam ho jayegi. Abhi mahaul ban gaya hai. Abhi zahar ko pee lijiye* (Arif Bhai, if you separate now, it will destroy V.P. Singh's credibility. The situation is ripe [for our success]. Please swallow this insult for the time being)," and I agreed.'[44]

Even before the Allahabad by-election, VP had embarked upon a three-tier unity pattern for the Opposition parties. First, he wanted the national Opposition parties with broadly centrist ideologies— the Jan Morcha, the Lok Dal (A), the Lok Dal (B), the Janata Party and the remnants of the Congress Indira had left behind, now called Congress (S)—to merge into one.[45] Next, he looked to forge a united front of this merged entity with as many regional parties as possible, keeping the regional parties' identities intact. Finally, he hoped for this omnibus front to have seat adjustments before the election with both the BJP and the communists in their respective strongholds, avoiding any formal alliance.

'I knew we needed to form a coalition, given the heterogeneity of the forces supporting us,' he said. 'At the same time, a coalition of too many parties would have lacked credibility, so the centrist parties had to merge.'[46] In less than four months after his Allahabad win, against seemingly impossible odds, he accomplished the first two steps. Even the third was managed, albeit partially, just before the general election.

The first proved far more difficult than the second and, indeed, the united front was launched before the merged party. This was due not to any differences between the merging parties over ideology or programme, which were minor and easily sorted out, but because any merger leads to a shrinking of the number of executive positions available in the new entity, compared to those that existed before—while the five parties had five presidents, for instance, the new single party could have only one. Every leader wanted to ensure that his influence (and that of his close followers) increased in the new party, while that of his rivals diminished.

The only way to reassure each leader that his importance would not be compromised (even if his designated position was) was through endless discussions, and VP engaged in them tirelessly, taking up the task in addition to his innumerable public engagements all over the country. Stern and unbending during his stint as finance minister, he now revealed an unexpected capacity for compromise and accommodation. 'He was always a hard worker, but after he left the Congress, he became completely obsessed,' said Sita Kumari Singh.[47]

All Opposition leaders endorsed the ultimate goal of uniting against the Congress, but in practice, Chandra Shekhar and Bahuguna (and their proxies) used a variety of stratagems to hamper VP's efforts—making statements critical of his abilities and utterances, reneging on assurances, leaking likely decisions prematurely to the press (and thereby sabotaging them), trying to lure away members of other parties involved in the merger and delaying crucial meetings on flimsy pretexts. But VP—no novice in politics—ably aided by Devi Lal, Hegde and a few others, countered them, foiling their moves as best he could.

As a first step, a four-party front comprising the Jan Morcha, the Janata Party, the Lok Dal (A) and the Congress (S) was formed in early December 1987—the Lok Dal (B) stayed away, with Devi Lal still unwilling to countenance the presence of Lok Dal (A)'s Ajit Singh in any alliance. Chandra Shekhar agreed to include his Janata Party in the front but soon after, in March 1988, his party merged with Ajit Singh's Lok Dal (A), thereby increasing his bargaining power within the front vis-à-vis VP.

The Allahabad by-election in June, held along with six other Lok Sabha by-elections, showed clearly the gains possible from Opposition unity, giving it a fresh impetus—the Congress, which had held all 7 seats earlier, lost the 4 where it faced a single, common Opposition candidate. In a little over a month, at a crucial meeting on 22 July 1988, the Jan Morcha, the expanded Janata Party (including Lok Dal [A]), the Lok Dal (B) and the Congress (S) agreed to form a single party called Samajwadi Janata Dal. It happened so suddenly, after months of bickering, that it sounded too good to be true—and it was.

Within a day, VP faced a revolt in his own ranks. Convenor Ram Dhan, who had always opposed the merger, declared that he would continue the Jan Morcha.[48] (Arif Khan, though still sceptical of the merger's long-term prospects, went along with the consensus.) The Lok Dal (B) also split, with Bahuguna refusing to join, but the bulk of his workers, led by Devi Lal, did.

Some members of the other merging parties raised objections as well, while Chandra Shekhar's Janata Party, in particular, kept repeatedly postponing the executive meeting required to endorse their merger. One of the participants in the 22 July 1988 meeting prematurely released the provisional list of office-bearers of the proposed new party, which named VP as its president, leading to another furore. The deadline of 15 August 1988, set for sealing the merger, could not be met. A fresh deadline for 11 October 1988 (Jayaprakash Narayan's birthday) was set and somehow kept, though disagreements continued right up to the morning of the new party's inauguration.

It led, among other changes, to a contraction of the name earlier chosen, 'Samajwadi Janata Dal' to 'Janata Dal', as Devi Lal suddenly developed an aversion to the term 'Samajwadi', or socialist.[49] 'Chandra Shekhar insisted on "samajwadi" being retained, while Devi Lal was equally adamant that it not be,' said VP. 'We were in Bangalore, where the public meeting to announce the new party was to be held that very evening. The plenary session was to follow the next day and here we were, still arguing about the name of the new party. Finally, Chandra Shekhar relented.'[50]

VP was confirmed as president of the new outfit, with Devi Lal as chairman of its parliamentary board and Ajit Singh its secretary general; Chandra Shekhar refused all office. In his speech at the inaugural public meeting, he even explicitly declared that agreeing to VP becoming president did not amount to accepting him as his leader. 'There is a difference between a president and a leader,' he stated.[51] VP did not let the insult go unanswered. In his speech, made after Chandra Shekhar's, he said, 'Chandra Shekharji may not consider me his leader, but I have always considered him mine, since he is my senior in politics. As for being made president, I have been given a responsibility, and I will fulfil it as best I can.'[52]

The united front with the regional parties had already been set up by then with far less ado. Three parties, all of which were historically opposed to the Congress—the TDP in Andhra Pradesh, the Dravida Munnetra Kazhagam (DMK) in Tamil Nadu and the Asom Gana Parishad (AGP) in Assam—agreed to join the others to form the National Front, with TDP Chief and Andhra Pradesh Chief Minister N.T. Rama Rao (NTR) taking much of the initiative of bringing them all together, considerably easing VP's burden.

An eleven-member presidium to head it was formed with minimum fuss, with NTR as chairman and VP as convenor, and all the seven participating parties represented. NTR was keen to accommodate the BJP too—which was eager to join—but VP kept it out. '"Brother, what is the harm?" NTR said to me,' VP recalled. 'I said, "Brother, if we take the BJP, our support will reduce. Right now, both the Left and the BJP are broadly with us. If we include the BJP in the National Front, the Left will find it difficult to back us."'[53]

3

'POLITICS IS A VERY UNCERTAIN PROFESSION'

The Bofors scam, breaking five days after V.P. Singh resigned as defence minister on 11 April 1987, gave his campaign against the Rajiv Gandhi government its turbocharge. For the next two years, periodic revelations of fresh details of its payoffs kept sustaining the campaign's momentum. And just as the strife within the newly formed Janata Dal was turning tragi-comic, making VP the butt of innumerable press cartoons, Bofors again came to his rescue.

VP's plight was pitiable as, after inaugurating the party at the Bangalore meeting on 11 October 1988, he sought to choose the Janata Dal's office-bearers, consulting and trying to please every faction leader but failing. In trying to accommodate every leader's suggestions, he put together a jumbo organization—ten general secretaries (the party's constitution allowed four), twenty-two members of the parliamentary board (the constitution had set eleven), along with a 138-member national executive, which included a twenty-two-member steering committee.[1] Yet, as soon as he announced his list in early December 1988, Ajit Singh exploded, claiming that Devi Lal's erstwhile Lok Dal (B) had better representation than his Lok Dal (A), while Chandra Shekhar accused VP of 'undemocratic functioning'.[2]

Within a few days, just as VP was holding his first press conference to introduce the new office-bearers, five senior party members—all of them close to Chandra Shekhar—held another one, announcing that they were quitting the Janata Dal to revive the Janata Party because President V.P. Singh was 'ideologically incoherent, politically incompetent and authoritarian'.[3] Another round of quarrels broke out over the next few months around appointments of the heads of different state units and, this time, six members of the parliamentary board—all Ajit Singh supporters— quit to protest the choices.

The worst confrontation was in Bihar, where his party refused to accept VP's choice of party president—a respected social activist, Acharya Ramamurthi—preferring, instead, a Chandra Shekhar acolyte, Raghunath Jha. VP, in turn, sacked Jha, leading to a confrontation with Chandra Shekhar, where Devi Lal had to play peacemaker. The Janata Dal had inherited just two state governments—the Lok Dal (B)'s in Haryana and the Janata Party's in Karnataka—and both were hit by internal crises.[4] Though the Haryana government wobbled and survived, the one in Karnataka collapsed towards the end of April 1989, with President's Rule being imposed in the state.

Yet all these squabbles were temporarily forgotten with the release of the Comptroller and Auditor General's (CAG's) report on the Bofors gun purchase on 19 July 1989. It proved to be another indictment of the deal, claiming that the evaluation of competing offers before finalizing the contract had been flawed, that the guns were chosen in undue haste after insufficient field trials, and more. Opposition MPs began shrieking in both Houses of Parliament that having been censured by a constitutional authority, Rajiv Gandhi ought to resign. When the latter refused to, in a stunning, coordinated exercise masterminded by VP and NTR, the entire

Opposition (barring a few) resigned en masse—both BJP and communist MPs having been persuaded to follow the example of their National Front counterparts.

The CAG report reinvigorated the Opposition, keeping its spirits high right up to the Lok Sabha election four months later, at the end of November. Not even the numerous little mutinies that broke out between different factions of the Janata Dal over the distribution of tickets could dent it. (Assembly elections in UP, Andhra Pradesh and Karnataka were also called.) VP resumed his hectic touring—which had dwindled for a few months after the Janata Dal was formed as he struggled to resolve its internal spats—collecting crowds as impressive as before. His party's campaign predictably focused on Bofors and corruption but also emphasized VP's own probity and spartan ways, with '*Raja nahin, faqir hai/desh ka taqdeer hai* (He is not a king, he's an ascetic/he is the nation's destiny)' becoming its most popular slogan.

However, the bickering had permanently shrunk VP's expectations. From hoping to create a long-term, secular, democratic alternative to the Congress, he had begun to fear that he was merely repeating the Janata Party's 1977—to be followed by its 1979. 'I knew the Janata Dal would fail and split up again,' he told his NMML interviewer. 'It became clear to me that such politically contrasting groups could not stay together. I had no illusions.'[5]

⚬⚬⚬

The Rajiv Gandhi government responded to VP's rising challenge in several ways—some salutary, some shocking. Often charged by his critics with having a single-point agenda in his speeches—the need to curb corruption—and ignoring all else, VP had gradually expanded his catalogue of concerns, including in it the need for electoral reforms, especially making the funding of elections transparent. To neutralize him, the government, in December 1988, introduced its own set of such reforms—though they left the all-important matter of funding untouched—the most important of them being lowering the minimum voting age from twenty-one to eighteen. It introduced a comprehensive rural-employment scheme, the Jawahar Rozgar Yojna; it sought to empower panchayati raj institutions, giving them constitutional status and transferring certain subjects—and the funds earmarked for these—exclusively to them.

At the same time, its defamatory campaign against VP touched new creative heights, targeting not only him but his closest family members, his wife Sita Kumari and elder son Ajeya.[6] A pliant Opposition MP—one of those who had quit the Janata Dal and revived the Janata Party (and refrained from resigning from the Lok Sabha when the bulk of the Opposition MPs did)—released 'documents' purporting to show that VP had received $1 million from a CIA front organization in New York called Committee for the Free World, but the very next day, both the US embassy in Delhi and CIA sources in Washington rubbished the charge, calling the documents—which some newspapers had reproduced—forged, pointing out laughable errors in them.[7]

Next, Home Minister Buta Singh declared in Parliament that after VP gave away his lands to the Bhoodan movement, Sita Kumari, in a fruitless effort to get them back, had moved the Allahabad High Court claiming that her husband was insane, had spent time in a mental institution and, hence, his decision should be annulled. VP challenged Buta Singh to produce any court record to this effect, which he was unable to.[8]

Much more devious planning went into the framing of Ajeya Singh. He was accused of having opened a bank account, with VP as nominee, in the tax haven of Basseterre, the capital of Saint Kitts and Nevis—a country comprising two tiny islands in the Caribbean Sea—in September 1986 (when VP was still finance minister) and operating it until February 1988, when it was closed and the balance of $21 million (Rs 35 crore at the time) withdrawn. Specific details were provided, including photos of his printed account statements clearly displaying the bank's name (First Trust Corporation Ltd), his account number (29479), as well as his and his father's signatures. Strangely, it was a Kuwaiti newspaper, *Arab Times,* which had never shown any interest in Indian politics earlier, that broke the story at the end of August 1989. It was immediately picked up by leading Indian newspapers. A former managing director of the bank, George Maclean, also surfaced in London to confirm the charge.[9]

Ajeya Singh's relationship with his father had always been delicate. Having taken school lightly, he had fared so poorly in his school-leaving exams that he could not qualify for admission in any Delhi college. And with Allahabad University in the 1970s almost permanently closed thanks to student agitations, he finally joined Kanpur University as a private student for his B. Com course. 'If you can get even a chaprasi's job without my help, I'll be relieved,' VP had told him at the time. The remark rankled sufficiently for him to turn serious about his career once he left for London to study chartered accountancy in 1976, where he cleared his exams at the first attempt. 'I discovered I had an aptitude for numbers, I understood them,' he said. Moving to the US, he worked with several leading financial institutions, including Citibank, before the accusation erupted, leaving him shaken. He had never been to St. Kitts, let alone opened an account there.

'What should I do?' he asked his father over the telephone.

'Come back to India and clear your name,' VP replied.[10]

By then a non-resident Indian with a US green card, Ajeya was under no compulsion to do so but he did, returning to Delhi on 11 September 1989. In response to an order from the Enforcement Directorate, he made his list of overseas assets—of around $140,000, acquired over thirteen years of living abroad—public. Though wild charges against both him and VP continued to be made in both Houses of Parliament[11]—where they were never rebutted, as most Opposition MPs had resigned by then—and in newspapers supportive of Rajiv Gandhi, claiming that the $21 million in the account came from bribes VP had taken while he was finance minister, the Enforcement Directorate never seriously pursued them, perhaps aware of their spurious nature. On the contrary, Ajeya's return to India enabled the Janata Dal to score a strong political point, contrasting his response with that of Ajitabh Bachchan's, who, similarly charged with dubious foreign transactions, had preferred to stay away.

The unexpected publicity he got led Ajeya to even consider an alternative career in Indian politics, egged on by some senior Janata Dal leaders, who claimed, given his father's popularity at the time, that he would easily win if he contested a Lok Sabha seat in the coming election. But VP wouldn't hear of it. 'You're in a good place, stay there,' he said. 'Politics is a very uncertain profession.'[12] Ajeya did briefly remain behind, however, to help his father in the election.

Ajeya was not the only relative who sought a Janata Dal ticket in the 1989 Lok Sabha election. Sant Bux Singh, after years in political hibernation, did the same. Too embarrassed to ask VP, he approached Devi Lal instead through his good friend BBC's India correspondent Mark Tully. 'For the only time in my BBC career, I deserted the role of observer to become a participant in Indian politics,' wrote Tully later. 'I felt there was nothing wrong in trying to help a friend who I knew would never be in a position to do me a favour, nor would he do one if he could.'[13]

Sant Bux wanted his old seat, Fatehpur, which he had won in the 1967 and the 1971 Lok Sabha elections but lost in 1977, and Devi Lal assured he would help. But a few days later, he called Tully over to Haryana Bhavan. 'What sort of man is this V.P. Singh who would cut his own brother's ticket?' Devi Lal asked. 'He has not only cut Sant Bux Singh's name, he has taken Fatehpur for himself. At first, when Sant Bux Singh's name came up in the discussion, he said, "Let's think about it", but eventually it became clear he was not going to have his brother's name in the (candidates') list.'[14]

VP maintained that he had both a grouse and a compulsion. Sant Bux had remained a Congress member until then, never uttering a word in his brother's support during his campaign against the Rajiv government. He later said,

> I felt his asking for a Janata Dal ticket at the last moment was not fair. If he wanted the ticket as my brother, he should have been with me during our movement. If he wanted it as a politician, he should have been part of the Janata Dal. He never shared our difficulties. But now he wanted the benefit of our impending victory. Had I given him the ticket, it would have been sheer nepotism.[15]

Besides, as Devi Lal also told Tully, despite having won the Allahabad Lok Sabha seat by a big margin just seventeen months earlier, VP had already decided that Fatehpur—dominated by his Thakur caste men—would be a safer bet for him than heterogeneous Allahabad. Being the Janata Dal's main vote-getter, he would have to campaign for other party candidates across the country, with little time to spare for his own seat. 'Fatehpur was one constituency I knew we could win even if I didn't visit it at all, and I needed one such,' he said. 'Every day of campaigning counted.'[16] (His old rival-turned-colleague, Janeshwar Mishra, against whom he had contested twice before as a Congress candidate, beating him in Phulpur in 1971 but losing to him in Allahabad in 1977, got—and won—the Allahabad seat.) But this led to the final break between the brothers—they rarely spoke thereafter.

Fatehpur presented another personal embarrassment for VP. The sitting Congress MP, who had won in 1980 and 1984 and was contesting for a third time in 1989, was another of Lal Bahadur Shastri's sons, his eldest, Hari Krishna. Again he was clashing with the Shastri family, but he claimed that he gave Hari Krishna Shastri fair notice. 'I'd told him through his brother Sunil Shastri a month and a half ago to change his constituency if he wanted to,' he said in an interview then. But Shastri denied it, calling VP a liar.[17] As VP had anticipated, he won by 121,000 votes,[18] a slightly bigger margin than in Allahabad, despite spending just a day in Fatehpur campaigning.

But there were severe bumps along the road to victory, starting with his nomination. Like all leading politicians, VP waited until the last permissible day to file it, intending to fly from Delhi to Kanpur early morning and drive down to Fatehpur, about 80 km south-east. But soon after his flight took off, it returned to Delhi, following a bomb scare aboard the aircraft. Hours passed with no sign of it intending to take off again, and VP, growing increasingly frantic, even considered at one stage giving up on Fatehpur and filing his nomination from the nearest UP constituency—Ghaziabad, on Delhi's outskirts.[19] 'We made a big fuss and were finally asked to board again,' said Ajeya, who was accompanying his father. 'But no other passengers joined us—we were the only ones on the plane. Again we protested, having grown very suspicious by then, and finally a few more passengers entered.'[20] He remains convinced that the bomb threat was faked. They made it to Fatehpur barely before nomination-closing time.

VP soon left Fatehpur for his countrywide election tours, returning only on polling day, leaving Ajeya behind to oversee the campaign. 'I had a tough time because both the district magistrate and the superintendent of police were totally hostile, openly supporting the Congress, refusing to meet me whenever I went with a complaint,' Ajeya said. 'Their attitude changed dramatically after the election.'[21]

A local BJP-RSS leader was unexpectedly shot dead, allegedly by Muslims, leading to sharp communal polarization.[22] 'Our Janata Dal candidate for the Fatehpur assembly seat, Liaqat Ahmed, came to see me in the dead of night, saying Muslims of Fatehpur town were terrified, expecting an attack by Hindu mobs anytime,' said Ajeya. '"*Aap kahein to unko bandook dilwa dein* (If you agree, I can get them guns to protect themselves)," he said to me. I said, "Nothing doing. Hindus will protect Muslims." I got our Hindu Janata Dal workers to do so.'[23]

⸻

VP had achieved the historically unprecedented step of uniting the entire spectrum of Opposition political parties against the Congress. He should have been exultant, but he was not—and not just because of the fissures in his own party. The final steps to his rainbow coalition were the seat adjustments the Janata Dal had to enter into with both the communist parties and the BJP. While the former was smooth, the latter proved tormenting for him, even though the communist parties had tacitly agreed to support him despite the BJP's presence, and despite him seeking and obtaining sanction for the same from Muslim leaders unhappy with the Congress.

'I was not so naive as to link up with the BJP without consulting the Muslims,' he said. 'I told the Muslim leaders that elections have been announced, but my party is not entirely ready. I said, "I've built my home's walls but not the roof as yet. It's started raining, so what should I do?" The Muslim leaders said I should build the roof with whatever I could get. They said I could use the BJP's help or whosoever else's, but I should defeat the Congress.'[24]

But he still agonized—and with reason. He had, in the early months after leaving the Congress, addressed some RSS-backed forums as he tried to build public opinion against Rajiv, but had soon become more circumspect, mainly due to the growing communal divide in the country and the RSS–BJP's role in fomenting it. The Fatehpur rumble was not an isolated incident; on the contrary, it was trivial compared to some of the other riots that had been occurring over the past three years. The latest was in Bhagalpur, Bihar, which began even as seat-sharing talks with the BJP were on at the end of October 1989 and continued through the campaign, and which led to over a thousand people being killed. Most of the riots—though not all—had been sparked by an agitation the BJP had decided to support, one that was to poison Hindu–Muslim relations in the country for the next three decades—the Ram Janmabhoomi–Babri Masjid stir.[25]

Among the many organizations spawned by the RSS—including the BJP and the ABVP—was the Vishwa Hindu Parishad (VHP), launched in August 1964 to expressly 'consolidate and strengthen Hindu society; protect, promote and propagate Hindu values'.[26] The VHP engaged in diverse activities, such as converting tribals in remote areas from Christianity to Hinduism (it was called ghar wapsi, or homecoming), but it remained little known until it began this particular agitation in 1984, demanding that a temple be built at the precise spot in Ayodhya where Lord Rama was purportedly born. What stood there at the time was a mosque, the Babri Masjid, built in 1528 by Mir Baqi, an army commander of the first Mughal emperor, Babur, whom he had made governor of the Avadh region of UP, in which Ayodhya lies.

Hindus of the area claimed Mir Baqi had built the mosque after demolishing a temple to Rama that had stood there earlier, and in December 1949—two years after India became independent—they smuggled idols of Rama and Sita into the mosque in the dead of night and began worshipping them round the clock, unwilling to budge. The mosque was thus effectively turned into a temple, with the local administration refusing to force the worshippers out. Aggrieved local Muslims had moved the court to get their mosque back, where the matter remained pending.

It was a local dispute, largely ignored by all except those directly involved, until the VHP decided, decades later, to make it a national one. Stirring up buried Hindu historical memories of the Islamic conquest of India, the contested, difficult past of Hindu–Muslim relations, including the demolition of hundreds of temples by Islamic rulers, they succeeded spectacularly. As Hindu sentiment in favour of removing the mosque and building a temple at Rama's birthplace rose, so did Muslim fervour against any such step, stoked greatly by the setting up of the Babri Masjid Action Committee, which began a counter agitation—led by the same Shahabuddin who had campaigned against the Shah Bano judgment and in favour of VP during his 1988 Allahabad election.

It was this growing Hindu–Muslim divide that was causing the riots. The one at Bhagalpur, for instance, followed the VHP's move, in several towns, to hold 'Ram Shila Pujans'—processions carrying 'consecrated' bricks for the building of the proposed Rama temple. Bhagalpur's Muslims refused to allow the procession, with horrifying consequences.

Most political parties, including the Congress and the Janata Dal—unwilling to lose either Hindu or Muslim votes—had taken the position that the court would decide the matter, or that Hindu and Muslim leaders should reach a settlement on it, withdrawing the court cases, and that, until then, the status quo should continue. In contrast, the VHP wanted to embark immediately on demolishing the mosque and building a temple, claiming it was a matter of faith, beyond legal purview. The RSS's various organizations being semi-autonomous; the BJP, too, at first echoed the other political parties.

After its inglorious performance in the 1984 Lok Sabha poll, when it was reduced to just 2 seats, the BJP had even briefly considered moving away from its pro-Hindu stance, modifying its ideology to match that of the centrist parties—without whose help it felt it could never come to power—proclaiming such goals as

'Gandhian Socialism' and 'Integral Humanism'. But by 1989, it realized that the VHP had served it a vote-winner it had been short-sightedly ignoring. The BJP's resolution at the end of its national executive meeting at Palampur, Himachal Pradesh, in June 1989, forcefully backed its sister organization's demand for the first time.

VP was greatly dismayed. 'We were all shocked (by the resolution) and wondered how we could have anything to do with the BJP after this,' he said. But he also took the BJP's explanation during their seat-adjustment talks at face value. 'I asked the BJP leaders and they said "it [the Ayodhya issue] does not figure in our election manifesto",' he said. '"We've expressed our moral support for it in the preamble to our manifesto, but it is not included in the manifesto itself."'[27]

Eventually, VP left it to each state unit to decide whether it wanted the BJP's cooperation. In most states, the adjustment was partial—the Janata Dal and the BJP fielded common candidates in some seats, while contesting against each other in others. In UP, which had assembly elections too, Janata Dal and BJP candidates clashed in nearly 100 of the 425 assembly seats. In Maharashtra, where the BJP unexpectedly chose to ally with an even more stridently pro-Hindu regional party, the Shiv Sena, VP decided that no seat-sharing was possible.

During the entire campaign, he remained at pains not to endorse the BJP, refusing to speak at any public meeting that displayed the party's flags. 'In Agra, the BJP had held a meeting at the very ground where I was to speak,' he recalled. 'It had put up flags and posters that it was refusing to remove.' (The BJP was backing the Janata Dal candidate for the seat, Ajay Singh.) 'I insisted that the BJP flags go, and only then would I speak,' he added.[28]

He was similarly stubborn in neighbouring Mathura and Aligarh. 'In Mathura, after the BJP workers refused to remove their flags from the stage that had been built, I insisted on a separate stage,' he added. 'I waited until a new one was constructed, and only then spoke. It delayed my schedule by several hours. In Aligarh, BJP workers were so angry with me, they stoned my car.'[29]

The other major problem was the paucity of funds—especially compared to the Congress's unlimited supply, made worse by VP's horror of involving himself in the grubby task of fund collection (given that most of it had to be 'unofficial'). '*Party ke paas koi paisa nahin tha, aur V.P. Singh kisise milne ko taiyaar nahi they* (The Janata Dal had no money, and V.P. Singh was not willing to meet any donor),' recalled Arif Khan. 'I would tell him, "XYZ is giving us Rs 5 lakh. If you meet him, he will gladly give Rs 20–25 lakh." But he never would.'

Yet money was always needed. 'He used to send me people with these little slips of paper, on which he had written, "Please give him Rs 50,000," or "*Inka Rs 1 lakh intazam kar dijiye* (Arrange Rs 1 lakh for him),"' Arif Khan added. 'From where would I arrange it? Still, I did what I could. I shared whatever had been given to me for my own election campaign with others.'[30] (Arif Khan contested and won the Bahraich Lok Sabha seat.)

On the use of brawn and firearms too, the Janata Dal, hard as it tried, could not match the Congress. On the polling days of 22 and 24 November 1989, attempts at rigging—alongside efforts by opposing party workers to prevent it—saw widespread violence across the north Indian states, with about seventy-five people being killed,[31] especially in Haryana, where Devi Lal had raised a private goon squad called the Green Brigade, as well as in UP and Bihar, where the Congress was far better equipped. VP himself was fired at while inspecting polling booths in Fatehpur, but escaped unhurt.[32] In nearby Amethi, however, his nephew-in-law Sanjay Singh—who was also a candidate in the assembly election—tried to intervene in a gun battle and ended up as a target.[33] He had to be flown to Bombay and thereafter to London for the surgeries he needed to recover.

The results of the 1989 elections were confounding. In a personal triumph for VP, in this first election campaign he had ever led, his party, for all its internal dissensions, performed outstandingly. In UP, in the Lok Sabha election, it notched up 54 of the 85 Lok Sabha seats, with another 8 going to the BJP and 3 to the communist parties; in Bihar, it got 32 of the 54, with 8 more seats for the BJP and 5 for the communists; in Rajasthan, along with the BJP, it won all 25 seats, the Congress failing to get any. (In the UP assembly election, it nearly achieved a majority on its own, getting 208 of the 425 seats.)[34]

The only disappointment was Karnataka, where it could win only 1 of the 28 seats (and lost the assembly polls too), mainly because the discontents who had broken away from the Janata Dal and revived the Janata Party had their strongest base in Karnataka and, contesting against the Janata Dal, split the vote against the Congress. Still, in all, the Janata Dal won 143 of the 244 Lok Sabha seats it contested—nearly 60 per cent.

But it was badly let down by the regional parties it had allied with to form the National Front—the TDP, the DMK and the AGP—parties that were already running state governments and were widely expected to sweep their respective states. NTR, chairman of the National Front, had been chief minister of Andhra Pradesh for nearly seven years, but seemed to have been so taken up with strategizing to oust Rajiv in Delhi that he failed to hear the growing grumbles against his own government. Of the 42 Lok Sabha seats in Andhra, his TDP won only 2, the rest going to the Congress. (The party was trounced in the state assembly elections as well.)

In neighbouring Tamil Nadu, the DMK had won the assembly polls convincingly less than a year ago, but failed to win a single one of the state's 39 Lok Sabha seats this time, all of them going to the rival alliance of the Congress and the AIADMK. In Assam, following a resurgence of internal disturbances, no polls were held.

The three parties thus added a grand total of 2 seats to the National Front tally, raising it to 145. 'Barring once, we Janata Dal leaders were never invited to campaign in the southern states, so we left it to the regional parties, but they failed to deliver,' said VP.[35]

Though the Left parties did much better than in 1984, especially in West Bengal, they too were mauled in Kerala, ending up with a nationwide total of 52 seats. Indeed, the voting in all the four southern states (Andhra Pradesh, Tamil Nadu, Karnataka and Kerala) strongly backed the Congress—completely contrary to the trend in the north—enabling the party to reach a tally of 197 seats, the highest among all the contenders. But the figure remained well short of a majority, as did the National Front–Left's combined total, also touching 197 seats. The difference was made by the BJP, which—with the impetus of the Ram Janmabhoomi movement—performed magnificently, rising from its 2-seat tally of 1984 to 85, and which readily agreed to back the National Front government without joining it. (The Left parties similarly provided 'outside' support.)

—❧—

But who would be Prime Minister? The choice should have been obvious, yet for three tantalizing days, from 28 November 1989—when all the results were announced—to 1 December 1989, when VP was finally elected leader of his parliamentary party, it often seemed that he might not be. The main hurdle was Chandra Shekhar's dogged refusal to endorse him, which could not be ignored, since a large block of MPs from the erstwhile Janata Party owed him their nominations and would support any decision he took.

Early on, at a meeting to discuss the matter, he had stated bluntly, 'Vishwanath, if you are contesting, I am contesting.'[36] Such a contest for leadership had been held before—in 1966, Morarji Desai had stood against Indira Gandhi and lost. But Chandra Shekhar knew that VP would never take up the challenge—he would not be seen coveting the job. Indeed, another major reason for the delay was VP's own diffidence. Ever since he had left the Congress, he had been repeating that he never wanted to hold a position of power again, and he remained consistent for those first three days.

Some have claimed that his reluctance was a sham. Yashwant Sinha, for instance, a senior Indian Administrative Service (IAS) officer-turned-politician,[37] who was then very close to Chandra Shekhar, claimed in his autobiography, *Relentless*, that VP's sole intent was to mislead Chandra Shekhar and lower his resistance. He recounted an incident,

> He [V.P. Singh] telephoned me to come to his place, saying he had important matters to discuss ... [I reached] only to find the drawing room, where we generally met, ringed by lights and cameras. I was asked to wait as V.P. Singh was in the middle of an interview with the BBC. The interview was soon over and out walked Mark Tully. He told me ... Singh had said he would not accept the post of Prime Minister ... As we were to find out later, this had merely been a ploy to lead everyone up the garden path, only for him to strike a hammer blow at the end.[38]

But it was not only to Tully that VP expressed his reluctance—he said so to other journalists as well.[39] Given his obsession with his image, it is highly unlikely that he would deliberately have lied, knowing that his lie would be caught within days. Inder Kumar Gujral, who was not allied to any group in the Janata Dal, expressed a view very different from Sinha's in his own memoirs, *Matters of Discretion*.[40] He wrote,

> V.P. Singh had adopted an enigmatic posture saying he did not wish to 'shoulder responsibility of high office'. I asked V.P. Singh about his position. He told me he was not sure if 'such a ramshackle government would survive as he felt it would

only attract more muck', as a result of which it would become difficult for him to preserve his hard-earned prestige and the reputation of the party. According to him, 'It is a question of retaining my credibility. Minus that I too would look like Rajiv Gandhi.'[41]

Indeed, if VP was dissembling, he was doing so even before his own family. Ajeya Singh, who returned to Delhi only on the morning of VP's swearing-in—he had taken a diversionary route back from Fatehpur, visiting the family deity at the Vindhyavasini temple on Mirzapur's outskirts and then spending a day in Lucknow—was startled when asked by his mother to shave and shower immediately to attend the occasion. 'I thought you said you were not going to accept the Prime Minister's position,' he told his father.

'I had to,' VP replied. 'The party would have broken up otherwise.'[42]

Even supporters of Chandra Shekhar would later acknowledge that public sentiment was overwhelmingly in favour of VP—and no one else—becoming Prime Minister. In his book, Sinha recalled the experience of his friend and fellow Chandra Shekhar supporter, Digvijay Singh,

> He had gone to a paan shop in New Delhi's Janpath with a few friends. The paanwala must have guessed from their conversation they belonged to the Janata Dal and asked casually, 'Who is going to be your prime minister?' Just to test him, Digvijay Singh replied, 'Devi Lal.' The paanwala immediately snatched the paan he had already offered him and shouted, 'In that case, go eat your paan somewhere else!'[43]

The name Digvijay Singh mentioned was not a random choice— it was Devi Lal that Chandra Shekhar had decided to promote as an alternative when dozens of leaders from the Janata Dal, the BJP and the communist parties visited him, imploring him to reconcile to VP. Though struck by malaria just as the results were being declared and confined mostly to bed, Chandra Shekhar met Devi Lal's eldest son, Om Prakash Chautala, and urged him to convince his father to agree, knowing Devi Lal's age (seventy-five at the time) and status in the party would make it impossible for the other leaders to openly turn him down.

Chautala[44] had his own reason for enthusiastically consenting. At fifty-five, he'd also been in politics for years; was widely regarded as Devi Lal's political heir; and was impatient to take over as Haryana chief minister, which he could only do if Devi Lal vacated the position. He succeeded. Though Devi Lal had been the first Opposition leader to publicly endorse VP as his candidate for Prime Minister, he now began lobbying for himself for the job. Chautala organized for busloads of supporters from Haryana to reach Delhi and demonstrate outside Haryana Bhavan and elsewhere, demanding Devi Lal be elevated.

Devi Lal's decision caused consternation in the party, including among former members of his Lok Dal (B)—for reasons rather unflattering to him. Som Pal claimed that he was absolutely candid with his uncle-in-law when he met him in his suite at Haryana Bhavan. 'Mamaji, it would be a matter of great happiness if a family member became Prime Minister,' he maintained he told him. 'But running the country is not the same as running a state. You don't have the capacity.'[45]

Among Devi Lal's long-time associates was Sharad Yadav, who had been with him in the Janata Party, Lok Dal (B) and, subsequently, Janata Dal and who would shortly be appointed textiles and food processing minister in VP's cabinet. But on the question of Devi Lal becoming Prime Minister, he said he was equally clear. 'Devi Lal visited me at home the day before the leader was chosen,' he recalled. '"Everyone wants me to be the Prime Minister," he told me. I said, "That wouldn't be right." I explained as best as I could. The next day, we travelled in the

same car to Parliament, where the crucial meeting to choose the
leader was to be held in Central Hall, and again I urged him not
to stake his claim.' But why? 'The Prime Minister's position is a
very important and responsible one,' said Sharad Yadav. 'Unme
prakriti nahi thi (He didn't have it in him).'[46]

In fact, by then Devi Lal had changed his mind—though when
and why he did so remains unclear. He had a long meeting with
Arun Nehru that morning but what transpired between them is
not known. The crucial meeting to set the stage was held at Orissa
Bhavan in the early afternoon. VP later recounted,

> There were a number of leaders present, including Devi Lal and
> Chandra Shekhar. Almost all of them wanted me to become
> Prime Minister. Then Devi Lal said to Chandra Shekhar, 'I want
> to speak to you alone.' They went into another room. I don't
> know what they spoke about, after which Chandra Shekhar
> left. Then Devi Lal said he wanted to speak to me alone. He
> took me aside and said, 'You have to save my honour.' I'm
> repeating verbatim what was said, hiding nothing.[47]

Devi Lal claimed that his impending candidature for the top job
had been discussed so widely that he would lose face if it turned
out to be mere speculation. 'I thought this old man has helped
me so much, so I agreed,' added VP. 'He said, "Let my name be
proposed as Prime Minister first. I'll refuse and then you can take
my place."'

Typically, VP demurred. 'I told him, "Why should you refuse?
You become the Prime Minister." Devi Lal said, "No one but you
should be the Prime Minister. People will beat us up otherwise."
I said, "Chaliye, theek hai (Okay)."'[48]

Was VP aware that Chandra Shekhar had not been told?
He insisted he was not.[49] But Chandra Shekhar was clearly
hoodwinked. When Yashwant Sinha, who was overseeing
the arrangements for the meeting at Central Hall, asked

Chandra Shekhar who should preside over it, the latter replied, 'Ask Vishwanath.' '"But he is a candidate in the election. How can he preside over the meeting?" I asked,' Sinha writes in *Relentless*. 'Chandra Shekhar's reply left me even more baffled. "*Woh* candidate *honge tab na* (That's only if he is a candidate, right?)?"'[50]

Sinha intuitively still decided not to, assigning the job to the senior Maharashtra leader Madhu Dandavate (who would be finance minister in VP's cabinet) instead. Dandavate asked for nominations, at which VP proposed Devi Lal, which Chandra Shekhar quickly seconded. With no other nominations, Dandavate declared Devi Lal elected.

There was shocked silence in the hall. The news was promptly leaked to the journalists waiting outside. News agencies, local and global, flashed the message that Devi Lal was India's next Prime Minister. But within ten minutes, frantic follow-ups were being sent out to 'kill earlier story',[51] as Devi Lal, keeping his word to VP, upended it. Standing up, he declared, '*Mujhe Haryana mein tau kehte hain. Yahan bhi tau hi rahna chahta hoon. Main apna naam wapas leta hoon aur mananiya V.P. Singh ka naam tazviz karta hoon* (I'm addressed as "tau" [father's elder brother] in Haryana. I want to remain "tau" here as well. I hereby withdraw my name and propose V.P. Singh's instead).'[52]

Ajit Singh seconded it, and with no other names being suggested, Dandavate declared VP elected. Chandra Shekhar stormed out of the hall, not hiding his feelings even from the journalists who accosted him outside, thrashing VP. Even VP conceded later, in classic understatement, 'I don't know what had transpired in the discussion between Chandra Shekhar and Devi Lal, but whatever it was, Chandra Shekhar looked very upset.'[53]

Part 6

CRISIS PRONE

1

'I DO WHAT I HAVE TO'

Some people are said to be accident-prone—V.P. Singh seemed crisis-prone. Both as UP chief minister and as Prime Minister, he was hit by many more unexpected crises than others in the same positions over much longer tenures. His victory had dislodged the mighty Congress from power, which had won four-fifths of the Lok Sabha seats in the previous general election and had once seemed invincible. He had formed India's first minority government at the Centre, its first coalition government at the Centre,[1] supported, incredibly, by both the communist parties and the BJP.

It was a fantastic feat, but he had no time to savour it. Elected leader of the Janata Dal parliamentary party on 1 December 1989, he was sworn in as Prime Minister (along with Devi Lal as deputy prime minister) on 2 December, and named the rest of his cabinet on 5 December 1989. Kashmir politician Mufti Mohammad Sayeed was appointed the country's home minister. On 8 December 1989, Sayeed's daughter, Rubaiya Sayeed, was kidnapped in Srinagar by Kashmiri terrorists.

It was the Punjab insurgency that had dominated the 1980s, with Jammu and Kashmir a distant second, and VP was caught completely unawares. 'No one expected it,' he said later. 'Nothing like it had happened before.'[2] He had no experience of dealing with terrorism and little of Kashmir—and it showed. Apart from holidays in the 1960s before he joined politics, his only visit to Kashmir had been earlier in 1989 with Mufti Sayeed, when he had addressed a rally in Anantnag and spent a night there, coming away with the impression that the people of the state had much the same aspirations as those in the rest of the country.

'On the way to Anantnag, we had to stop due to a landslide and while waiting for it to be cleared, I spoke to the locals,' VP said. 'One of them pointed to a muddy pond nearby and said, "See how dirty the water is? That's the water we drink. Central funds come to Srinagar for the state's development but never reach us."' The sizeable crowd at his meeting further misled him. 'People welcomed us,' he said. 'If they were hostile to India, would they have done so?'[3]

In fact, separatist feelings in Kashmir were already rivalling Punjab's and would soon overtake it—the state's worst years were just beginning. No doubt it had been a troubled region ever since Partition, when the Hindu maharaja of this Muslim-majority, formerly princely kingdom initially sought to remain independent, refusing to join either India or Pakistan. Kashmir's independence lasted only over two months, however, as in late October 1947, thousands of armed infiltrators from Pakistan invaded, seeking to capture the state, at which its maharaja hastily signed a treaty acceding to India, enabling the Indian army to intervene and drive the infiltrators out. (Two of the five broad regions of the state, Gilgit and Baltistan, however, remained under the infiltrators' control and have since been under Pakistani occupation.)

Though the maharaja was soon deposed and a popular government installed, the Kashmiri desire for independence remained, with Sheikh Abdullah, its first chief minister, who dominated the state's politics for the first three and half decades after it joined India, repeatedly pursuing it through diplomatic channels. As a result, Abdullah spent more than two of those decades in jail. In his last years, however, he seemed to give up on his self-determination dream for Kashmir. He signed an accord with Indira Gandhi in February 1975 that restored him as chief minister, and convincingly won the election held thereafter in July 1977. On his death, in September 1982, his son Farooq Abdullah succeeded him both as head of his National Conference party and as chief minister, and proceeded to win the next assembly election too.

But with peaceful efforts to secure Kashmir's independence abandoned, insurgency replaced them, leading to sporadic killings and bomb explosions in the region through the early 1980s. These incidents, as well as Farooq's growing closeness to Opposition parties in other states—he attended their unity conclaves and even organized one in Srinagar in October 1983—led to Indira conspiring with a chunk of his party MLAs, encouraging them to separate and form another party. Once they did, in August 1984, Farooq, having lost his majority, was dismissed, and the breakaway party—headed, interestingly, by Farooq's estranged brother-in-law Ghulam Mohammad Shah—installed in power with Congress support. But such machinations only served to bolster the secessionist insurgency, reinforcing the growing Kashmiri belief that India did not care about democracy in their state.

After he became Prime Minister, Rajiv Gandhi decided to make amends, withdrawing Congress support to G.M. Shah in March 1986, restoring Abdullah as chief minister after a brief spell of governor's rule and teaming up with his National Conference to contest the next election, held exactly a year later. The secessionists had, by then, been emboldened to form a number of political parties too, which came together as the Muslim United Front (MUF) against the National Conference–Congress alliance.

It was widely held that the National Conference–Congress combination would have won the March 1987 elections

comfortably, but in their panic, fearful of the MUF forming
the government and embarrassing the Centre with separatist
demands thereafter, the two parties used the administration to
blatantly rig the elections.[4] As a result, MUF candidates won
only 4 seats in the 76-member assembly, the alliance getting 66.
Not surprisingly, the state's conduct of this infamous election won
the insurgents immense public sympathy, with many former MUF
workers joining them. With Pakistan's avid support—it provided
weapons and arms training to a growing stream of volunteers,
who now clandestinely began going back and forth across the
Line of Control (LoC) between the two countries—the insurgency
advanced rapidly from then on, aided too, claimed his critics, by
Farooq's inept governance.

Starting his political career in the National Conference, Mufti
Sayeed had moved to the Congress in the mid-1960s and risen
to become its Kashmir unit's chief. He had rebuilt the party after
its crushing defeat in the 1977 assembly election—when Sheikh
Abdullah got 46 of the 76 seats while the Congress got 11. Sayeed
grew his political base through his implacable opposition to the
Abdullahs, father and son, harping endlessly on their alleged
corruption and high-handedness as chief ministers. He played a
crucial role in Indira's dismissal of Farooq's government, hoping to
become chief minister himself, only to be disappointed.

Two years later, when Rajiv decided to ally with Farooq, Sayeed
was, naturally, devastated. Though Rajiv tried to console him by
moving him to Delhi as tourism minister, he quit the Congress
and joined the Jan Morcha in late 1987. In the 1989 Lok Sabha
election, he preferred to contest from Muzaffarnagar in UP as the
Janata Dal's candidate—and won easily, thanks to the upsurge in
VP's favour.

VP choosing Sayeed for the all-important position of home
minister—a surprise, since many weightier Janata Dal leaders had
wanted the job—had nothing to do with Kashmir but was aimed

at consolidating his Muslim support, to underline that though his government was dependent on the BJP for survival, the BJP did not influence his actions.[5] Neither he, nor Sayeed seemed to have realized that the latter's family in Srinagar—wife, three daughters and a son—would need immediate security.

Mufti Sayeed's youngest daughter, Rubaiya, twenty-three, a medical intern at a Srinagar hospital, continued attending work unescorted, using public transport. The kidnappers took advantage of this lacuna, realizing that abducting the home minister's daughter would bring them instant global recognition, which it did.[6] From the day Sayeed became home minister, they began following her. Two days later, they stopped the minibus she had taken to go home in the late afternoon after her hospital shift, and took her away in a waiting car. A telephone call to a local newspaper said she had been abducted and demanded the release of five jailed terrorists in exchange for her safe return, threatening to kill her if the government refused.

The government's unpreparedness, coupled with Sayeed's desperation to free his daughter at the earliest, led to VP's first big setback as Prime Minister, while also giving the Kashmir insurgency a turboboost. The kidnapping had occurred on a most inopportune day for the government—Chief Minister Farooq Abdullah, Chief Secretary Moosa Raza and the Intelligence Bureau's Kashmir head Amarjit Singh Dulat (the last two of whom later published their accounts of the event) were all away. All three hastened back to Srinagar, but in their absence, for the first forty-eight hours, nothing was done about rescuing the girl. 'We put all the intelligence agencies to work, but they couldn't get anything,' said VP.[7]

Bitter differences over how to respond to the abductors' demands arose. Farooq knew well that with his old enemy as home minister, and the home minister's daughter's life at stake, his government could be dismissed if the rescue was botched, more so because he was in coalition with the Congress, the National Front government's main political opponent. Yet he insisted that terrorist blackmail should never be entertained, while Sayeed clamoured to meet their demands right away. VP was initially neutral, but at the end of a long cabinet meeting on 10 December 1989, which stretched into the early hours of the next day, he agreed with Sayeed. 'After much debate, the Prime Minister decided, shocking as it seemed then and even now, to meet the demands of the abductors to get Rubaiya freed,' wrote I.K. Gujral in *Matters of Discretion*.[8]

Farooq still held out. 'Farooq ... asked for a written directive from the Prime Minister himself "if he wishes to establish any contact with the abductors",' Gujral wrote.[9] Different members of the government continued to work at cross purposes—while Dulat and Moosa Raza managed to locate and meet the father of one of the kidnappers, who hinted that freeing just one of the five terrorists named by the kidnappers could be enough to secure Rubaiya's release,[10] Mufti Sayeed, having begun parallel negotiations with the kidnappers through other, unofficial intermediaries, readily agreed to release all five.

Two ministers, Gujral and Arif Mohammad Khan, were then dispatched from Delhi to Srinagar in the early hours of 13 December 1989 to force Farooq to accept Sayeed's deal. But while Gujral had been attending the CCPA meetings in Delhi to discuss the kidnapping, Arif Khan—holding the ministries of power and civil aviation—was not part of the CCPA and was never briefed. 'I had been fast asleep when I was woken by a call from Arun Nehru around 2 a.m., saying I had to go to Srinagar immediately along with Gujral,' he said later. 'I left home at 4 a.m., and we took off on a special plane around 5 a.m.'[11]

The winter of 1989 was one of north India's coldest, and both men were shivering as they alighted in Srinagar's sub-zero temperature. They were driven directly to Farooq's home.

There was an element of black comedy in the discussions that followed, with Arif Khan strongly opposing setting free the jailed terrorists, unaware that Farooq was being pressured by VP to do just that. 'Farooq repeated that he was against releasing the terrorists and I agreed with him strongly,' said Arif Khan later. 'I said the problem would escalate if the government surrendered. Farooq began staring hard at me. *Agar mujhe Delhi mein bata diya hota kisliye hamey bheja ja raha hai, to main jata hi nahin* (Had I been told about the purpose of our visit in Delhi, I wouldn't have gone).'[12]

But surely Gujral knew? '*Gujral ekdum chup* (Gujral was absolutely silent),' said Arif Khan. In his account of the meeting in his book *Kashmir: The Vajpayee Years*, A.S. Dulat, who also attended it, was more scathing. 'Whatever Farooq would say, they (Arif Khan and Gujral) would reply, "We didn't know this!"[13] What Gujral didn't like he would pretend not to have heard, tapping his hearing aid. Arif would say something and Gujral would say, "*Kya kaha aapney* (What did you say)?"' Arif Khan claimed he spent all day thereafter in the guest-house room he had been given, doing nothing, while Gujral worked on Farooq and finally had him agree to the swap. The jailed terrorists were set free in the late afternoon of the same day near the Jama Masjid in Srinagar and given time to disappear,[14] after which Rubaiya was escorted home by the negotiating intermediaries.

Srinagar burst into applause, with joyous crowds and exploding firecrackers everywhere—not over Rubaiya's rescue, but over the terrorists' success in making the government genuflect to them. The uprising that followed over the next few years surpassed Farooq's fears, even resulting in the Hindu residents of the Kashmir Valley, the Kashmiri Pandits, being terrorized into leaving en masse, with the government powerless to stop their exodus. The national press flayed the government's capitulation, but VP stood by it to the end. 'None of the people we released had been charged with any heinous crime, according to my information,' he said later.

'Even today I believe that considering the kind of prisoners we let off to save Rubaiya's life, we did the right thing.'[15]

Despite the deal Raza and Dulat had nearly worked out, it is hard to say for sure if Rubaiya could have been saved without freeing all the five terrorists. Following strong criticism of the government's decision, VP's cabinet soon resolved that from then on, kidnappers' demands would never be met. Accordingly, when Mushirul Huq, vice chancellor of Kashmir University, was kidnapped along with his personal assistant four months later, and an exchange similar to that in the Rubaiya case sought by the abductors, the demand was ignored. The same day, 7 April 1990, M.L. Khera, the general manager of the Srinagar unit of the government-owned Hindustan Machine Tools (HMT) also had his car stopped on the road by armed men and was taken away; again, the government refused to negotiate his release. Three days later, all three men were found murdered.

—❦—

VP's term as Prime Minister panned out much the way he had feared, with the Janata Dal breaking up after he had ruled for just eleven months, leading to his government's collapse. It was not his ideologically opposed supporting parties or his regional partners that caused him any trouble, at least for the first nine months. Both the communist parties and the BJP, anxious to keep the Congress out of power, cooperated with him, refraining from insisting that he follow their disparate agendas.

VP instituted a weekly dinner at his residence on Tuesdays with leaders of the CPI, CPI (M) and BJP, as well as all the National Front parties, where he kept them informed of the government's plans and resolved through discussion whatever differences rose between them. 'The National Front manifesto has been endorsed by both the Left parties and the BJP,' he said, five months into his prime ministership. 'There is agreement on a wide area. There are no pressures and cross pressures. I do what I have to.'[16]

Indeed, the communist parties did not protest the 1990 Union budget Finance Minister Madhu Dandavate presented, which, while it had its populist features, also carried forward the liberalization efforts VP had begun in his historic 1985 budget. They did grumble at his new industrial policy, which offered incentives to private industry and sought to encourage foreign investment, but after it had been tweaked a bit, concurred with it. Similarly, though the VHP kept harping on building the Ram temple at Ayodhya, setting and postponing various dates for starting construction, the BJP initially rarely mentioned it. Rarely too did its leaders disagree with the communist parties' suggestions—and vice versa.

So too were the regional parties in the National Front always supportive. Though the TDP, the DMK and the AGP had contributed only 2 seats among them to the National Front's tally, VP included one leader from each party in his cabinet, to make his government a genuine coalition, giving them important portfolios. 'I got the full support of the regional parties,' he said. 'I must say that though their influence was regional, confined to a single state, their thinking on national issues was national.'[17]

Often, all the leaders of the allied parties wanted was not major policy initiatives but appointments of friends and followers in various positions in the bureaucracy, judiciary and public-sector enterprises. As UP chief minister, or later as commerce and then finance minister, armed with a large party majority, VP had always resisted such pressures, but now he was forced to be more accommodating. 'At times people would suggest, but they never insisted,' he said. 'They never asked a second time.'[18]

All the instability VP had to contend with, and which eventually destroyed his government, stemmed from the actions of his own Janata Dal colleagues. The manner of his elevation to Prime Minister had clearly shown that though voters regarded him the Janata Dal's foremost leader, many of the party MPs did not, and this pattern continued through his tenure. Of the five parties that had merged to form the Janata Dal—the Lok Dal (A), the Lok Dal (B), the Janata Party, the Congress (S) and the Jan Morcha—his Jan Morcha had been the last to be formed and thus had limited outreach. As a result, the number of MPs belonging to his faction among the 143 elected was also the lowest.

The other factions continued to owe first loyalty to their earlier leaders, emboldening some of these leaders to defy him. Their example rubbed off on some former Jan Morcha members, who too began working at cross purposes with him. There was little VP could do except try to reason with them, as any disciplinary step could have led to that faction breaking away and bringing down his fragile majority.

In the event, Chandra Shekhar, despite his inveterate hatred for VP, did not trouble him much once VP became Prime Minister, though he disdained accepting any position in the cabinet or the Janata Dal organization. VP, too, snubbed him by including only one of his close supporters, Yashwant Sinha, in his initial list of eighteen ministers, and that too as a minister of state. Sinha considered it an insult and, having learnt of his impending status only on arrival at Rashtrapati Bhavan for the swearing-in, left promptly without taking the oath.[19]

Still, Chandra Shekhar did make some moves that bruised VP politically. The first, embarrassing VP greatly, came in early April 1990 when, in a magazine interview, he alleged that his home had been bugged and that his telephone was being tapped. But strangely, the CBI inquiry VP promptly ordered found no evidence of it; indeed, the CBI complained that Chandra Shekhar did not cooperate with the investigation.[20] Chandra Sekhar was also the prime mover behind a bizarre idea, floated in May–June 1990, of a political realignment, which he called a 'national government', which would leave out the BJP but include the Congress and the CPI (M) along with the Janata Dal, with VP obviously being replaced as Prime Minister.[21] VP reacted just as he had to the dissidents opposing him as UP chief minister ('I'm ready to quit; the heavens will not fall if V.P. Singh steps down,' he said[22]) but with the CPI (M) refusing to play along, the proposal came to nothing.[23]

But it was Chandra Shekhar's third intervention that may have been the most fateful, terminating VP's modest economic-liberalization efforts. At a press conference in July 1990, Chandra Shekhar castigated the new industrial policy announced in May much more strongly than the communists had, especially the decision to ease foreign direct investment (FDI) norms, as well as other liberalizing steps VP had earlier taken. This was just when reports of a paper VP had sought and obtained from his special secretary in the Prime Minister's Office, Montek Singh Ahluwalia, had begun to appear in the newspapers. The paper, pointing to the dire state of the economy, thanks to reckless spending by the previous government and three consecutive years of drought (1986–88), had advocated taking free-market reforms much further as the only remedy. Among other proposals, it suggested curbing subsidies, further liberalizing foreign trade and disinvesting profitable public-sector enterprises while closing down loss-making ones.[24]

The paper was already being officially discussed by secretaries of the concerned ministries, and had its ideas been implemented, would have been an even more radical departure from India's socialistic economic path than VP's 1985 budget. Chandra Shekhar's remarks—though he never mentioned the document directly—were widely seen as a move to scuttle it early.[25] He succeeded. Aware of Chandra Shekhar's support among Janata Dal MPs, VP too did not pursue the 'M document', as it came to be called, any further. (But karma bit back strongly the following year for Chandra Shekhar, when, after becoming Prime Minister—with the country's economic position having worsened in the interim—

he was forced to seek the very IMF loan the paper had advocated, and which he had all along opposed.)[26]

Even so, much more than Chandra Shekhar, it was Devi Lal who troubled VP. To start with, within hours of having helped VP's ascent by deceiving Chandra Shekhar, he revealed that the renunciatory stance in his speech backing VP for Prime Minister had been a charade. He demanded to be made deputy prime minister alongside VP, without waiting until the other ministers were also sworn in. (Though still Haryana chief minister, he had also contested and won the 1989 Lok Sabha election from both Rohtak in Haryana and Sikar in Rajasthan.)

VP, still grateful to him, felt he had no choice but to agree. It also led to Devi Lal committing a gratuitous impropriety during the swearing-in ceremony the next day, to emphasize his importance. Though India has had several deputy prime ministers, starting with Sardar Vallabhbhai Patel right from 15 August 1947, there is no constitutional provision for one, and in the past all candidates had taken their oaths of office and secrecy as 'ministers', being designated deputy prime ministers subsequently. But Devi Lal insisted on spelling out that he was deputy prime minister even while taking his oath.

The oath-taker is required merely to repeat whatever the president, who administers the oath, says. But Devi Lal ignored the nicety, much to the embarrassment of both VP and President R. Venkataraman, who had succeeded Zail Singh. Venkataraman recalled in his memoir, *My Presidential Years*,

When I administered the oath saying '*mantri*' (minister), Devi Lal insisted on saying it as '*Up pradhan mantri* (deputy prime minister)'. 'I corrected him, saying '*mantri*' again, but a second time also he said '*Up pradhan mantri.*' I did not want to create an ugly scene and therefore allowed Devi Lal to proceed as he wished.[27]

Required to now relinquish his chief ministership of Haryana, Devi Lal summoned the state's governor and all his MLAs to Delhi the same day and had his eldest son, Om Prakash Chautala, take his place, holding the swearing-in ceremony at Delhi's Haryana Bhavan, never once informing VP. 'I learnt about it from others even as the swearing-in was taking place' said VP.[28]

After Devi Lal, it was the turn of Ajit Singh, who headed the Lok Dal (A) faction in the Janata Dal. Once the results of the UP assembly elections—held simultaneously with the 1989 Lok Sabha poll—were known (with the Janata Dal winning comfortably), Ajit Singh grew hell-bent on taking over as the state's chief minister. This was an embarrassment for VP as he had already promised the job to someone else—Mulayam Singh Yadav (see Part 3, Chapter 3).

Mulayam's relations with VP had always been hostile. His had been the loudest voice in the Opposition parties' campaign accusing VP of killing innocents in his drive against dacoits as UP chief minister. He had also made much of the allegations against the Daiya Charitable Trust and VP's alleged links with it when the latter was finance minister, delivering fiery speeches against him in the UP assembly. One of Charan Singh's most trusted followers, he was desolate when Charan Singh preferred to anoint son Ajit Singh as his successor and had naturally joined the Lok Dal (B). Yet, when the matter of forming the Janata Dal arose and his party president Bahuguna refused to join it, Mulayam—who, by then, commanded the loyalty of most of the Lok Dal (B) MLAs in UP—allowed himself to be cajoled into deserting Bahuguna and plumping for Devi Lal, who was enthusiastically supporting VP. In return, VP had assured him that if the Janata Dal won UP in the coming election, Mulayam would be made chief minister. VP wanted to keep his word.

Thus, around 4 p.m. on 2 December 1989, the very day VP was sworn in as Prime Minister, Som Pal got a telephone call summoning him to VP's home immediately. The Prime Minister met him at his doorstep. 'Ajit Singh is sitting inside; just convince him not to insist on becoming UP chief minister,' he said. 'Tell him not to get into that mess. *Agar Mulayam Singh ko isney roka, mere aur Devi Lal ke beech mein* wedge *ho jayega, aur aageki party, aage ki government ki naash ho jayegi* (If he stops Mulayam Singh from becoming chief minister, it will drive a wedge between me and Devi Lal, and the future of our party and our government will be doomed).'[29] Som Pal didn't see how he could change Ajit Singh's mind if VP had failed, but VP insisted he had great faith in Som Pal's persuasive powers.

Som Pal did his best, arguing for five long hours, joined towards the end by two other senior Janata Dal leaders whom VP had summoned[30] and VP himself, all four pleading with Ajit Singh. 'At one stage, V.P. Singh even held his hand and appealed to Ajit Singh that he would not be able to run the Central government without him,' Som Pal recalled. He noted to Ajit that Mulayam would contest anyway, and if Ajit stood against him instead of allowing a consensus in his favour, it would create a fresh rift in the party; besides—though this was not entirely certain—Mulayam had more supporters among the elected MLAs than Ajit did, and Ajit would probably lose the fight. 'V.P. Singh will soon make you a minister at the Centre, and you can get as many of your supporters into the UP cabinet as you like,' Som Pal added. 'Why do you want to go to UP?' He talked for so long that Ajit Singh missed his evening train to Lucknow, but all the latter said in the end was, 'I'll think about it.'[31]

For all of VP's efforts, he began getting urgent calls the next morning from Lucknow MLAs close to him, revealing that Ajit Singh had arrived in the city by an early-morning flight and announced his intention to contest the party leadership in the state. The MLAs wanted to know who they should vote for. 'V.P. Singh had his own style,' said Som Pal. 'He told them, "As Prime Minister, I won't say a word." I told him that I was getting calls too. He told me, "You are an independent, thinking human being. Ours is a democracy. You tell your callers whatever you feel they should do."'[32]

Som Pal suggested to all the MLAs hailing from the Jan Morcha—they numbered barely fifteen or twenty of the 208 Janata Dal MLAs—to assemble at the residence of the senior-most among them, Sachidananda Bajpai. 'I explained to Bajpai on telephone that if Mulayam Singh lost the election, the government at the Centre could well collapse,' said Som Pal. Separately, VP also briefed Mufti Sayeed, who was among the three Central leaders sent to Lucknow to ensure that the election of the UP leader was conducted fairly. 'I gave him the names of a couple of MLAs close to me and told him to speak to them, saying I wanted all Jan Morcha MLAs to support Mulayam Singh. They would take care of the rest,' said VP.[33]

The election was duly held and Mulayam Singh won, though by a surprisingly narrow margin of only nine votes.[34] 'It was the Jan Morcha MLAs' votes that made the difference,' said Som Pal. But VP got no thanks for it. On the contrary, Mulayam firmly believed that he had overcome VP's attempt to sabotage his rise to chief minister. 'That election vitiated the atmosphere within the UP Janata Dal,' said Som Pal. Mulayam, furious that Ajit Singh had been allowed to contest at all, often ignored VP's directions thereafter.

VP made it clear early on that under his dispensation, no individual should hold more than one position. Accordingly, once he became Prime Minister, he resigned as president of the Janata Dal. (This was again to emphasize the Janata Dal's democratic character, contrasting it with the Congress's, where, ever since Indira Gandhi split the party a second time to form the

Congress (I), she was both party president and the country's Prime Minister, and Rajiv had continued the tradition.) Many of those he chose as ministers already held organizational positions in the Janata Dal. Devi Lal, for instance, was also chairman of the party's parliamentary board, while Ajit Singh—whom VP soon made minister for industry despite his defiance over the UP leadership—was Janata Dal secretary general. Unlike him, they were loath to relinquishing their party posts, but eventually did.

Mulayam, however, did not. Having become chief minister, he continued to remain UP Janata Dal president too. When persuasion failed to move him, VP unilaterally appointed an old acquaintance, Ram Pujan Patel, as interim UP Janata Dal president (pending an election to choose a permanent one) in mid-March, and sent him to Lucknow to take charge.[35]

Mulayam refused to even acknowledge Patel. He saw to it that when Patel stepped off the train from Delhi at Lucknow's Charbagh station, there was no one to receive him. When he arrived at the Janata Dal headquarters, it was deserted. He was boycotted by his own party and spent most of his time in his room in Lucknow's State Guest House before quietly returning to Delhi.[36] There was nothing VP could do. 'Humility is fine, but V.P. Singh should not have tolerated such humiliation,' said Arif Khan.[37]

On Kashmir, even Mufti Sayeed sought to bypass VP, often in cahoots with Arun Nehru[38] (commerce minister in the new cabinet), another Kashmiri, who, like him, had been elected to the Lok Sabha from UP. (Both of them seemed to believe that they understood the state much better than the Prime Minister.) It started following an early, controversial decision of the V.P. Singh cabinet about a month after Rubaiya Sayeed had been brought back safely home. It figured that many of the then state governors, all appointees of the previous Congress government, were likely to be partisan and ill-disposed towards the new one, and hence should be replaced. Among them was Kashmir's governor, General K.V. Krishna Rao.[39] Though the choice of governor is entirely the Centre's prerogative, Farooq Abdullah was informally sounded out on three possible successors;[40] he said he was okay with all of them.

There was only one person he did not want as governor, claiming that it would be impossible for them to work together. This was General Krishna Rao's predecessor, Jagmohan, who had been governor for five years before him; Farooq had reason to believe that, soon after his taking over in April 1984, Jagmohan had connived with the Congress and opponents in his own party to bring down his government four months later.[41] It could well be that Farooq's antipathy towards Jagmohan was precisely what led Mufti Sayeed to ignore the three names Farooq had okayed and reappoint Jagmohan as General Rao's successor.

VP had no particular view on Jagmohan, but as the buzz about his impending reappointment grew—and Farooq began frantically working the phone lines to his Delhi contacts to prevent it[42]—he had an unusual visitor, Chandra Shekhar. Chandra Shekhar had stayed studiedly aloof from the government until then, but was sufficiently alarmed by the national consequences of Kashmir being mishandled to set aside his pride. As VP later narrated,

> Chandra Shekhar came to meet me and said, 'Don't send Jagmohan to Kashmir; it will make the situation there worse.' I told Mufti sahib about it and said, 'Let's send someone else.' He agreed. Then I got busy with other work and suddenly, on the afternoon of 17 January, Mufti sahib announced Jagmohan's name as governor. Once he had done so, heading a new government, I could hardly overrule the home minister.[43]

Mufti Sayeed was dismissive of the fear many expressed to him that Farooq might resign if Jagmohan were sent back, claiming that the man loved the perks of office too much to do so. Farooq quit the very day Jagmohan was appointed. With General Krishna Rao also having done the same, Kashmir, for a day, was left without a government head. 'At midnight on 18 January 1990, I asked him (Jagmohan) to immediately take charge of the state,' writes Gujral.[44]

For no fault of his, Jagmohan's second stint as Kashmir governor began disastrously. Unbeknownst to him, the very day he reached Srinagar, the state police chief had ordered a cordon-and-search operation in the city's Chota Bazaar area, a separatists' ghetto. The next day saw a frenzied crowd protesting the operation, which led to firing by security forces, killing at least fifty-three people—the incident forever etched in the annals of Kashmiri victimhood as the Gawkadal massacre. There were more police firings, leading to more killings, on subsequent days, as Kashmir's turmoil grew far worse than it had been under Farooq.

But as he struggled to regain control, Jagmohan also took an arbitrary decision, which alienated VP, who had been uneasy about his appointment from the start. After Farooq quit and Jagmohan took charge, the state assembly was placed in suspended animation. On 19 February 1990, without taking either VP's or Sayeed's consent, Jagmohan dissolved it, destroying any chance of reinstalling a chief minister again without fresh elections. He was able to do so since Jammu and Kashmir's separate constitution—framed following the autonomy granted to it under Article 370 of the Indian Constitution—gave him such powers.[45]

In his memoirs, *My Frozen Turbulence in Kashmir*, Jagmohan acknowledges that while he had suggested the dissolution to both VP and Sayeed, he did not wait for them to agree. He had given press interviews stating his intention and written to Sayeed as well, and he maintained that should have been indication enough. He writes,

By the end of January 1990, I had put the item of dissolution of the state assembly at the top of my agenda for action. An overwhelming majority of the people believed that the assembly elections of March 1987 had been rigged ... There was anger on the faces of the people, fire on their lips and frenzy in their hearts. I was convinced that a good part of the anger, fire and frenzy would be taken away by the dissolution of the assembly. It would take away the justification for the cult of the gun.[46]

In fact, the cult of the gun carried on in Kashmir for decades thereafter.

VP, away in Gujarat that day, was furious when he heard. He said later,

How could a man appointed by the Centre take such a big political decision without informing the Centre? I was keen that the assembly not be dissolved so that the political process could be revived. I had not expected Farooq Abdullah to resign. I wanted a representative government in Kashmir. I told Mufti sahib (on telephone), 'Ask Jagmohan to resign tomorrow. No, make that today.'[47]

But on his return to Delhi, Sayeed and Arun Nehru prevailed upon him to change his mind. 'They said it would make the militants feel triumphant,' VP added. 'It would raise their morale. Had I still insisted, it would have meant openly clashing with my home minister. Those supporting Jagmohan put things in such a way that I acquiesced.'[48]

But VP hit back in his own way. In March, soon after an all-party team of MPs visited Kashmir (and quarrelled repeatedly with Jagmohan during their interactions), he appointed one of them, George Fernandes,[49] who was already railways minister, as minister for Kashmir affairs as well, claiming that the situation in the state warranted full-time ministerial attention. He insisted that his step was not, in any way, intended to dilute Sayeed's authority over Kashmir as home minister—though of course, that was precisely the intention.

But the move proved short-sighted, further complicating the Kashmir situation, as Fernandes and Sayeed (along with Jagmohan) pursued diametrically opposed policies, each ignoring—and indeed often sabotaging—the other's efforts. While Jagmohan sought to crush the separatists and win the people's support through corruption-free governance, Fernandes tried to negotiate with the separatists, hoping to persuade some groups to drop their independence demand while marginalizing the others.

Neither approach worked, with Jagmohan even claiming later that Fernandes's impetuosity proved fatal for some of those who responded to Fernandes, as the more intransigent insurgents retaliated by murdering them. In his book, he mentions, in particular, the assassination of Mirwaiz Moulvi Farooq, the revered hereditary head preacher at Srinagar's Jama Masjid, whose forefathers had held the same position for centuries and who was shot dead in his study by two visitors on 21 May 1990. His death also finally cost Jagmohan his job. '[The murder was] a tragedy in which they [Fernandes and his team of advisers] themselves played, albeit unwittingly, no small part, by initiating the so-called political process prematurely, and creating an impression among pro-Pakistan terrorist groups ... that the Moulvi was having talks with George Fernandes or his emissary,' Jagmohan writes in *My Frozen Turbulence in Kashmir*.[50]

A vast, hysterical crowd assembled at Mirwaiz Farooq's funeral the next day and, convinced that Indian intelligence was behind the murder, advanced threateningly on security forces nearby, who retaliated with firing, killing at least twenty-four. With that, VP had had enough. 'I said, "I'm not going to take this—Jagmohan has to go,"' he said later. But he also realized the political cost—across the country, the Kashmir turmoil was being widely seen as a Hindu–Muslim confrontation, and if Jagmohan were removed for his bludgeoning style of dealing with it, Hindus would be upset with the government and the BJP would benefit. He said later,

> My principal secretary, B.G. Deshmukh, said to me, 'Sir, if he is removed at this stage, you will turn him into a martyr. You offer him a Rajya Sabha seat. If he accepts, the BJP won't be able to exploit him.' I told him to speak to Jagmohan, who agreed. I found Deshmukh very wise and often took his advice.[51]

Deshmukh had been principal secretary in the PMO under Rajiv as well, and though he offered to resign when the government changed, VP retained him throughout his tenure.

Fernandes, too, had his Kashmir charge shortly taken away. But contrary to VP's hopes, strife in Kashmir increased so much that governor's rule—with Girish Chandra Saxena, a former chief of India's external intelligence agency, the Research and Analysis Wing (RAW), succeeding Jagmohan—had to be continued for another six years, with no representative government being formed.

―――∞∞∞―――

Even before he carried out his large-scale change of governors, VP had removed one of them within days of being sworn in— Punjab Governor Siddhartha Shankar Ray.

In the five years since Indira's assassination, Punjab had gone through many more upheavals. Rajiv's keenness to end the confrontation there had led him to sign the Punjab Accord with then Akali Dal President Harchand Singh Longowal in July 1985, which he hoped would address all the state's grievances. But implementing some of its key clauses ran into unexpected difficulties, while Longowal himself was soon after shot dead by extremists, who termed the accord a sell-out. (The only beneficiary of the accord seems to have been Devi Lal, who won his massive victory against the Congress in Haryana's June 1987 assembly election by claiming it ripped off Haryana.)

Despite Longowal's assassination, Rajiv insisted on holding assembly elections soon after (the state had been under President's Rule since October 1983, when its then Congress government was dismissed for failing to contain the terrorists), which the Akali Dal won. But its government's unwillingness to confront the extremists led to increased killings and their fresh takeover of the Golden Temple complex. As chaos returned, the Akali Dal government was also dismissed in May 1987 and President's Rule imposed again, which remained in force when VP became Prime Minister.

VP, anxious to convince the state of his government's goodwill towards it, travelled to Amritsar on 7 December 1989, within a week of becoming Prime Minister, driving through the city in an open Jeep despite the danger it posed, often stopping to speak to people in the crowd that gathered to welcome him, praying at the Golden Temple as well as at a number of other Sikh and Hindu shrines. 'Some of the lanes we ventured into were narrow, with tall buildings on either side,' he remembered. 'I know how difficult ensuring my security must have been for the police. But I felt we needed to send out the message that we trusted the Sikhs, so I took the risk.'[52]

The only early irritant was the behaviour of Governor Ray.[53] 'Ray was a close friend of my elder brother [Sant Bux Singh] and I had a good relationship with him,' said VP. 'But he began playing politics.' Within the first three days of VP taking over, he sent him four telex messages, seeking instructions on how to handle various sensitive matters.[54] VP said later,

When an alleged terrorist was caught, he sent a message asking if the man should be prosecuted or released. This is not decided at the Prime Minister's level. The police decide, not even the governor. I realized that if I said he should be prosecuted, he would tell people I was responsible for the arrest, and if I said release him, he would say I was setting terrorists free. I decided this could not go on.[55]

With President's Rule in Punjab set to complete three years in May 1990—the maximum period permitted by the Constitution—VP was keen to conduct elections and instal a popular government there. (He had also promised to do so during his 7 December 1989 visit.) But with terrorist killings as rampant as ever, in a rare consensus, both the communist parties and the BJP opposed him. Their fear was the same as that evoked by the MUF in Kashmir in the 1987 polls—that parties close to the extremists could win a majority. 'The BJP and the Left both went to the extent of saying they would reconsider their support if I held elections in Punjab,' said VP. 'I realized I'd have to wait until I convinced them.'[56] He reluctantly extended President's Rule for another six months, getting a constitutional amendment passed—which all parties supported—to allow breaching the three-year limit.

———⊶∞⊷———

The other gubernatorial changes, carried out en masse, evoked much media debate on whether such a sweeping step was justified. VP maintained that it was. 'Governors are appointees of the party in power at the Centre, and when the government changes, they should resign, but they don't,' he said.[57] In fact, the idea of making all the governors resign was not his, but President Venkataraman's. (It is the President who formally appoints and removes governors.) Venkataraman wrote in his memoirs,

> Home Minister Mufti Sayeed ... showed me a list of governors he wanted to remove and hinted that I might convey this information to them. I felt ... it might create an impression that I wanted some to go and some to stay. We then discussed the issue with the Prime Minister and decided that resignations of

all governors might be sought, but only those accepted whom
the government wanted to change.[58]

VP graciously agreed, silently absorbing the press criticism that
followed. 'I didn't want friction with the President from the
start, having seen how the Rajiv–Zail Singh feud had escalated,'
he said.[59]

Eventually, twelve resignations were accepted (of the twenty-
three submitted—Ray's and General Krishna Rao's had come in
earlier; there were twenty-five states at the time), while two more
governors were shifted to other states. Among the new appointees,
one was notable—D.P. Chattopadhyaya, who had been VP's
boss in the commerce ministry when he had first become deputy
minister in 1974. Chattopadhyaya, who had developed major
differences with Rajiv, had always got along well with VP. He was
made Rajasthan governor on 1 February 1990, having quit the
Congress just the previous day.[60]

2

'GOING NUCLEAR WOULD HAVE BEEN A SELF-GOAL'

At the Rashtrapati Bhavan get-together after V.P. Singh's swearing-in as Prime Minister on 2 December 1989, Ajeya Singh made it a point to introduce himself to Rajiv Gandhi. 'He wouldn't look me in the eye,' he remembered. 'I realized that he must have known the St. Kitts charge against me was utter falsehood, but still allowed it to be pursued.'[1]

Once he was Prime Minister, VP promptly got the CBI to investigate the matter. The CBI got the documents used as evidence of Ajeya's account in Saint Kitts's First Trust Corporation Bank examined by the Central Forensic Science Laboratory, whose handwriting experts established that both his and VP's signatures on them were forgeries, copied from their signatures on their passport applications. The probe led to the filing of forgery charges in May 1990 against an extraordinary roster of names: Rajiv's External Affairs Minister P.V. Narasimha Rao (who would become Prime Minister from June 1991), his Minister of State K.K. Tewari (the same Tewari who had called VP a CIA agent for hiring Fairfax), the chief of the Enforcement Directorate at the time and some of his senior officials, Indian embassy staffers in

the US and Trinidad, along with George Maclean of the First Trust
Bank and the controversial godman Chandraswami (known to be
close to Narasimha Rao).

But with the unexpected death of an important accused-turned-
approver—the Enforcement Directorate's A.P. Nanday, the man
who had travelled to the US and St. Kitts purportedly to gather the
bank-account documents that were later found to be spurious—
and the case carrying on well after VP's government fell, all the
accused were eventually exonerated.[2]

The inquiries into the HDW and Bofors kickbacks, which also
VP entrusted to the CBI, went the same way. Soon after taking
charge, VP blacklisted both companies, shutting off any future
Indian defence deals with them; the blacklisting remained in force
for the next decade. But identifying and prosecuting the agents
involved, or those in the government who had colluded with
them, proved much more difficult. In the HDW case, in early
March 1990, the CBI filed criminal conspiracy charges against the
agent in question, as well as six officials of the defence ministry
and the PMO, and even sought the help of the West German
government. But court hearings were few, especially after the VP
government fell, and the case was ultimately buried in the early
2000s for lack of evidence.

In the case of Bofors, VP was especially anxious to nail the
commission takers, having harped on the scam endlessly during
his election campaign, even rashly promising in one of his speeches
to expose the guilty within twenty-four hours of the Janata Dal
winning the election. On taking over, however, he found the
task much complicated by confidentiality laws in both Sweden
and Switzerland; though the CBI filed a first information report
(FIR) on the matter by late January 1990 against fourteen Indian
officials, agents and Bofors executives, it failed to make much
headway thereafter. Indian officials went to Geneva and managed
to freeze the six accounts—which had been unearthed by then—

into which the Bofors commissions were paid, but identifying the account holders took much longer. The Swiss authorities refused to transfer the concerned papers until objections to their doing so raised by the account holders had been disposed of.

Bofors was pressured too but remained uncooperative. 'I'd hoped the threat of blacklisting would compel Bofors to reveal the names of their agents,' said VP. 'Two Bofors officials did indeed come to Delhi and meet the home secretary and the defence secretary. But some people then advised them that our government was unlikely to last long; they needn't worry and shouldn't give away anything.'[3]

The CBI also left gaps in the first request letter (called letter rogatory) it sent to the relevant Swiss court seeking information, which was turned down. It had to draft a second one, leading to more time being wasted; it erred by failing to get the papers it was provided properly attested, which led to the Delhi court initially rejecting them.

'The CBI achieved nothing,' said VP. 'It was a Swiss court, which at the request of the Delhi High Court, agreed that bank secrecy could be waived and the requisite papers handed over, but the CBI messed up that too.'[4] (Many years later, there were reports that the largest chunk of the payoffs could well have gone to Rajiv's family friend Ottavio Quattrocchi,[5] but the criminal case against him eventually ran aground, with Quattrocchi being discharged by the Delhi High Court in 2011.)

With Reliance Industries, VP, for reasons unclear, made no effort to probe its dubious overseas links again or even the forged letters that had ended his career in the Congress. However, he did reopen the case related to smuggling of additional capacity for its polyester fibre plant and underpaying customs duty, even though the collector of customs, Bombay, at the time—whom VP promptly transferred—had by then exonerated the company, cancelling the fine the department had imposed in February 1987.

In May 1990, customs officials also raided Reliance's PTA-making plant at Patalganga—up and running by then—and once again claimed to have found excess capacity on which customs duty had been evaded.[6] But again, as with the St. Kitts forgery or the HDW scam, neither case was seriously pursued once VP demitted office.

VP also ensured that Vinod Pande and Bhure Lal, who had been shifted to unimportant positions after he had left the finance ministry and much harassed by the Thakkar Natarajan Commission, were rehabilitated. He made Vinod Pande his cabinet secretary and brought Bhure Lal into the PMO—it was Bhure Lal who led the team to Geneva that got the Swiss accounts frozen.[7] (Once more, as he'd done on becoming UP chief minister or Union finance minister, VP handpicked the most honest and diligent of officials for his PMO team; they included Prabhat Chaturvedi, the Allahabad district magistrate who had withstood much pressure from UP Chief Minister Bir Bahadur Singh to rig the 1988 Allahabad by-election VP had contested.)[8]

In their fresh stint with him, however, anxious not to appear vengeful, VP cautioned both Pande and Lal against excessive zeal in pursuing the old cases. 'The Prime Minister has not allowed anyone to go the whole hog after a particular target,' Vinod Pande observed in an interview in July 1990. 'Otherwise, look at our record in the finance ministry ... If we took shortcuts, we would appear to be vindictive ... (I just hope) the remorseless chariot of the law will trample them (the wrongdoers) eventually.'[9]

Where VP did succeed was in torpedoing Reliance Industries' audacious attempt to take over the engineering conglomerate Larsen & Toubro (L&T). Begun in 1938 by the two Dutchmen after whom it was named, L&T had since acquired a diversified ownership, with public-sector financial institutions such as Life Insurance Corporation (LIC) and Unit Trust of India (UTI) being its largest shareholders, together holding around 42 per cent. Initially invited by L&T's then managing director—who was trying to stave off another corporate raider—to buy a chunk of the company's shares, Reliance Chief Dhirubhai Ambani soon felt it would be a good fit in his own corporate empire, and began steadily increasing Reliance's shareholding in it.

By early 1989, Reliance's ownership of L&T had touched around 20 per cent, while that of the financial institutions had dropped to around 37 per cent,[10] since the bulk of Reliance's share purchases were made from UTI and BoB Fiscal Services, as the investment arm of Bank of Baroda was then called. In April 1989, Dhirubhai Ambani was named L&T chairman, while three other Reliance executives—including his sons Mukesh and Anil Ambani—became, in due course, board members.

The redoubtable Swaminathan Gurumurthy surfaced again, with reports in the *Indian Express* alleging serious irregularities in the way Reliance had acquired its 20 per cent L&T shareholding. Many of the old shareholders of the company also began to feel that some of Ambani's decisions as chairman were aimed more at advancing Reliance's interests than L&T's. They were particularly peeved about a Rs 820-crore debenture issue L&T had planned, of which Rs 760 crore was subsequently invested in Reliance, rather than used for L&T's own expansion or consolidation.[11]

VP got LIC—still L&T's largest shareholder—to summon an extraordinary general body meeting, at which Dhirubhai Ambani was forced to resign as chairman, exactly one year after he had taken over; soon after, under a new chairman, L&T withdrew its Reliance investment. Ambani thereafter gave up on L&T, selling off Reliance's shares to the Aditya Birla Group. (In later years, the Aditya Birla Group, too, tried to make L&T part of its stable, but was again thwarted, this time with company employees setting up the L&T Employees' Welfare Fund, which bought up its shares.)[12]

Most UP politicians take pride in their security trappings—the more elaborate, the better. Upcoming ones feel validated if they can convince their local police that their lives are threatened and get even a single armed constable to follow them around. It was the opposite with VP—never having forgotten the embarrassment of his father's armed guards accompanying him to class and back during his high school years, he hated the rings of protection that descended on him as soon as he became Prime Minister (way more than in his previous ministerial assignments) and strove to reduce them.

After Indira Gandhi's assassination, it had been widely felt that the country's Prime Minister needed better protection than provided until then, which led to the setting up of a fresh unit of exceptionally well-trained commandos called the Special Protection Group (SPG), solely for that purpose. At first, VP declined SPG security, wanting the unit wound up or reassigned, but the home ministry pointed out that under existing rules, the choice was not his. Still, he managed to get the number of personnel protecting him cut from 400 to 15; he reduced his convoy while travelling by road from over a dozen vehicles to three; and refused to wear a bulletproof vest as his predecessor did.[13]

Indeed, at his insistence, in his early days as Prime Minister, while still at his old home at 28, Lodhi Estate (he had been allotted the house on vacating his ministerial quarters at 1, Teenmurti Marg, once he had resigned as defence minister), the protective shield around him was so laidback that once, a group of children on their way home from a nearby school strolled on to the premises without an appointment and—finding VP at home—chatted him up.[14] But with Punjab and Kashmir in flames, the terror threat was real and security gradually became more rigorous, especially after VP moved into the Prime Minister's official residence at 7, Race Course Road in April.[15] Yet VP never ceased to chafe at it, often accusing those safeguarding him—who were merely doing their job—of keeping him 'away from the people'.

VP's voluntary cutback in his own security, however, made fewer headlines than the supposed reduction in Rajiv's. Under the terms of the SPG Act passed in 1988, only the incumbent Prime Minister was entitled to the unit's protection, not former Prime Ministers. Hence, Rajiv's SPG cover was withdrawn in February, and the responsibility for his safety reverted to the Delhi police.[16] Though Rajiv himself remained silent, senior Congress leaders— obviously with his encouragement—ferociously attacked VP for the decision. Many even complained to President Venkataraman. Venkataraman recalled in his memoirs,

> The Congress people mounted a campaign on the issue of security and a number of delegations, including some former ministers, met me. They urged that Rajiv Gandhi's security should not be measured in terms of expenditure, and added that the (new) government was deliberately exposing their leader to risk ... Nothing short of SPG deployment would satisfy them.[17]

The expenditure amounted to Rs 75 lakh a year and included 125 security personnel and four bulletproof cars.[18]

This charge against VP was utterly unfair, as, for all the history of acrimony between them, he was anxious to ensure that Rajiv got the best possible personal protection. Years later, his principal secretary, the wise B.G. Deshmukh (as VP described him), confirmed in a newspaper column that VP had told him that 'he might have sharp and fundamental differences with Rajiv Gandhi on the political front, but he still had personal obligations to the Gandhi family and would not tolerate any criticism of the expenditure required to be incurred for Rajiv's protection'.[19]

But with both his cabinet and the legal advice he sought insisting there was no way the SPG cover for Rajiv could remain, he was forced to discontinue it. Yet VP found a way out—after meeting Rajiv, they decided that the same SPG personnel who had been guarding him could be deputed to the Delhi police and could thus continue doing the same job. Rajiv was satisfied.[20]

With Rajiv becoming leader of the Opposition in the Lok Sabha, he repeatedly clashed with VP on numerous matters—which was only to be expected—but VP was a mite upset when he also carried their rivalry overseas. 'Once we leave the borders of our country, we are all Indians,' he observed.[21] This happened on VP's first overseas trip as Prime Minister, when he visited Windhoek, Namibia, on the historic occasion of the country gaining formal Independence from South Africa on 21 March 1990.

Instead of just his officials, VP invited all the leading political parties, including the Congress, to send a representative to join his delegation, but Rajiv preferred to travel separately. K. Natwar Singh, who, after a long diplomatic career, had joined the Congress and had been a minister in Rajiv's cabinet, arranged a separate invitation for him through Zambian President Kenneth Kaunda; Rajiv arrived in Windhoek via Lusaka along with Kaunda, aboard his state plane. 'I telephoned President Kaunda at Lusaka and the invitation reached within twenty-four hours,' Natwar Singh writes in his memoirs.[22]

VP's delegation turned up a little late for the main function, enabling Rajiv, who had already arrived, to corner all the applause for India. 'The name of each leader was announced,' writes Natwar Singh. 'When Rajiv's name was called, there was clapping. Before him, the name of Prime Minister V.P. Singh had been called, but there was no response. The Prime Minister had failed to arrive on time.'[23] At every subsequent stage, Rajiv used his lineage and his previous contacts with African leaders while Prime Minister to upstage VP.

Many world leaders attended the Namibia event, but the man who garnered the most attention was one who held no official position at the time—Nelson Mandela, who had been released only a month earlier from a South African prison after twenty-seven years behind bars. VP met Mandela by appointment with his delegation and was overwhelmed ('He is the world leader I admire the most,' he said),[24] but once again Rajiv preferred to meet him separately. At VP's invitation, Mandela visited India later that year in October, when he was also awarded the Bharat Ratna.

———◦∞∞◦———

VP travelled abroad four times in his eleven months as Prime Minister. His second trip was to Kuala Lumpur, Malaysia, in early June 1990, for the first meeting of the then newly created 'Group of 15', a forum to foster cooperation between developing countries. The third was to Malé, Maldives, in late June, on the occasion of its twenty-fifth anniversary of independence. And the last one was to the USSR at end of the July, to reaffirm India abiding ties with that country as it shrank to become the 'Russian Federation' soon after. (Of these, it was the one to Kuala Lumpur that seemed to make the greatest impression on him. He was so struck by the transformational improvement the city had undergone since he last visited in 1975 as deputy commerce minister that he asked Montek Ahluwalia, who was part of his delegation, what was holding India back from prospering similarly. Ahluwalia noted that this was because Malaysia had been pursuing reforms towards a free-market economy vigorously, unlike India. It was this exchange that led to Ahluwalia preparing his thirty-four-page 'M document'.[25])

Overall, however, bogged down by domestic difficulties, VP took few fresh foreign-policy initiatives. He did, however, tackle two unexpected crises admirably and resolve a third he had inherited.

The inherited crisis was a standoff with Nepal over the trade and transit treaties between the two countries, which had existed since the 1950s and which were periodically renewed, until India refused to do so after their expiry in March 1989. The ostensible reason was India's insistence on a single treaty for both trade and transit, while Nepal wanted dual treaties as before; the actual reason, however, was India's annoyance at Nepal's increasing closeness to China and its import of Chinese arms.

Nepal, in turn, resenting Indian domination as well as the support India had been giving parties such as the Nepali Congress, which sought democratic rule in the country—Nepal was then still an absolute monarchy—refused to back down. It claimed that, as a landlocked country, transit rights through Indian ports were its due under international conventions and were not to be confused with trade. With India closing eleven of the thirteen transit routes on the India–Nepal border once the treaties expired, Nepal was crushed, its shortages growing dramatically and its GDP growth rate falling to 1.5 per cent in 1989 from 5 per cent the previous year.[26]

Once the Janata Dal government took over, VP and Foreign Minister I.K. Gujral moved carefully, trying to remain equidistant between Nepal's King Birendra Bir Bikram Shah and the Nepali Congress—much to the annoyance of Chandra Shekhar, who had strong links with the Nepali Congress leaders and even attacked his own government's Nepal policy in the Lok Sabha.[27] VP and Gujral, however, simultaneously pressured Nepal to loosen its China ties. In the end, VP's caution proved needless, as, in early April 1990, King Birendra—after facing months of street demonstrations—agreed to allow the Nepali Congress to form an interim government. The last glitches were overcome at a meeting between VP and the new Nepal Prime Minister K.P. Bhattarai in June 1990, after which all the closed transit points were reopened. (In due course, in December 1991, after VP's government had fallen, Nepal and India signed fresh, separate treaties on trade and transit.)

VP's first external crisis was the threat of war with Pakistan—a spin-off from the Kashmir upsurge. Through most of the 1980s—and despite Pakistan's covert support for the Khalistan movement in Punjab—India–Pakistan relations had been placid, but with the cry for azaadi (freedom) starting to resound in the Kashmir Valley in 1989, Pakistan again began considering if an armed attack could enable it to annex the state. Just as India had done with its Operation Brasstacks exactly three years ago, Pakistan, too, conducted its biggest-ever military exercise close to the India–Pakistan border in December 1989.

But its intention, unlike India's earlier, was not innocent—its army did not withdraw to former positions after the exercise ended. As VP explained,

> Instead of returning to their barracks, the Pakistani army began digging trenches and dumping top-grade ammunition in them. This is done only if an army is preparing for war, because ammunition left exposed to the elements starts losing its potency. Its air force began strengthening its radars close to the border, increasing its sorties near the border and improving its airfields there. It was all a bit too much.[28]

Further evidence of Pakistan's fresh designs on Kashmir came the following month, when Pakistani Foreign Minister Sahibzada Yaqub Ali Khan arrived in Delhi, ostensibly to discuss matters related to the South Asian Association for Regional Cooperation (SAARC), of which both India and Pakistan were members. But his attitude during his meetings clearly showed he had confrontation, not cooperation, in mind. Hailing from Rampur in UP and related to former President Fakhruddin Ali Ahmed's wife, Yaqub Khan was an old friend of Gujral's, but this time, Gujral remembered that he 'avoided looking into my eyes while delivering the message that ... the situation in Kashmir was "risky and could lead to perilous consequences"'. Gujral added in his memoirs, 'He did not use words such as "ultimatum" or "war" but the tone of the hard message was clearly to that effect.'[29]

Gujral sought to remain diplomatic, but eventually had to be blunt. 'I hope you realize and appreciate that my pleas for peace are not out of weakness,' he said. 'Do not underestimate the strength and tenacity of the Indian state.'[30] Unmoved, Yaqub Khan, at a later meeting with VP, repeated his threat. Soon after, Pakistani Prime Minister Benazir Bhutto—in power since December 1988, after her party won the first election held in Pakistan in eleven years after the death of Zia-ul-Haq in a plane crash in August—began holding meetings all over her country, reiterating the Kashmiri right to self-determination and Pakistan's determination to fight for it, if required, for a thousand years.[31]

VP—who also held the defence portfolio—and Gujral decided that demonstrating India's superior military numbers would be the best means to check Pakistani recklessness. If Pakistan was amassing troops at the border, so could India. 'We assessed that as long as the ice was frozen on the passes in Kashmir, Pakistan would not be able to attack,' said VP. 'That gave us about forty-five days to two months' time.'[32]

Following the Tamil insurgency in Sri Lanka, led by the Liberation Tigers of Tamil Eelam (LTTE), which broke out in 1983, Rajiv had sent Indian troops to help the Sri Lankan government quell it. But the move proved extremely controversial, as the Sri Lankan populace resented the Indian presence, more so because India was said to have trained the LTTE in guerrilla combat in the first place. Towards the end of his tenure, Rajiv had begun to withdraw the Indian Peace Keeping Force (IPKF), but the process had not been completed when the government in India changed. VP sped up the departure, with the last troops leaving Trincomalee in Sri Lanka by ship on 24 March 1990, well before the deadline, and rushed them all to the India–Pakistan border.

A great many troops were also deployed on the eastern border with China, following the border dispute that had led to the India–China war in 1962. VP and Gujral, working through the Chinese embassy in Delhi, suggested that deployment on both sides of the border could be reduced. 'We started a dialogue with China,' said VP. As it progressed, the then Chinese Foreign Minister Qian Qichen visited India in March 1990. VP added,

> I said to him, 'Look, you have no intention of attacking us and neither have we any of fighting you, so why have we amassed so many soldiers at the border? We can keep up our patrolling strength, but let us withdraw the rest of the troops.' He agreed. It was a major breakthrough.[33]

Four divisions were promptly moved from the eastern to the western border—three to Kashmir and one to Punjab.[34]

By then, the US, too, was worried about the rising tension on the India–Pakistan border, particularly because it knew—though neither India nor Pakistan had acknowledged it yet—that both were already nuclear-capable.[35] Its fears had been reinforced when VP inducted Raja Ramanna, former director of the Bhabha Atomic Research Centre and the key person behind India's successful testing of a small nuclear device in May 1974 (and someone who had never been in politics before), as his minister of state for defence in January. This stemmed entirely from VP's admiration for physicists—he had once aspired to be one himself—but the US was not to know that. (VP included another physicist too, also apolitical, in his cabinet—M.G.K. Menon, former director of the Tata Institute of Fundamental Research, as minister of state for science and technology.)

VP acknowledged later that India could have officially gone nuclear during his tenure but that he decided against it. 'Our scientists told me, "We can conduct an explosion any time, we just need a signal from you,"' he said. 'But I realized it would needlessly attract sanctions from Western countries. With Punjab and Kashmir in flames, it would not have been politically wise to alienate the West. It would have inclined Western countries towards Pakistan. It would have been a self-goal.'[36]

US President George W.H. Bush Sr (who had succeeded Ronald Reagan) sent Robert Gates, then his deputy national security adviser, to both India and Pakistan in May 1990 to talk them out of starting a fight. VP assured Gates that India would never do so, but would defend itself robustly if attacked. He said,

> I pointed out to the US delegation that we had been to war with China too and believed China was still occupying our territory, but our relations with China were improving, while those with Pakistan were not. It was because China did not interfere in our internal matters, while Pakistan was encouraging terrorism in India. If my neighbour keeps stoning my house, I'll repair the damage and take it quietly for a while, but one day I might pick up a stone or two and hurl them back.[37]

Gates went to Islamabad next—though Benazir Bhutto was away, still inciting anti-India sentiment across her country—and told Pakistani President Ghulam Ishaq Khan that every US military analysis had shown that if an India–Pakistan war occurred, India would win. That warning, coupled with the size of the army India had amassed near Pakistan's border, convinced Pakistan to restrain its aggressive impulse.

———— ∞ ————

The second crisis struck on 2 August 1990, when Iraq invaded Kuwait on its south-eastern border and, despite worldwide condemnation of its move, rapidly annexed it. Almost 10 per cent of Kuwait's 2.2 million residents were expatriate Indians working there, and their families. While they were not in any life-threatening danger, since India had cordial relations with Iraq (quite unlike the 3,500-odd British and US residents, who were held hostage), they did face, like all Kuwaitis, severe shortages of money, food, medicine and other essentials, and began clamouring to return to India.

VP's initial response may have been a trifle slow, but by 21 August 1990, after visits to Moscow, Washington and Amman for support, Gujral landed in Baghdad, met Iraqi dictator Saddam Hussein and secured his consent to take all Indians who wanted to leave out of Kuwait.[38] (The purported callousness and indifference of Indian officials to the fate of Indians in Kuwait following the attack, as depicted in the 2017 Hindi film *Airlift,* is utter misrepresentation.[39])

Complications arose, however, following a US blockade of the waters around Kuwait, which prevented India from evacuating its citizens as it had originally intended, by ship, as well as due to Saddam Hussein's insistence that only aircraft bearing food and other necessities would be allowed to land in Kuwait or Baghdad. Ultimately, about 120,000 Indians were transported in buses through the blazing desert of southern and western Iraq— with temperatures at 45–50 degree Celsius—to Jordan, housed in makeshift camps and flown back to Bombay from Amman.

Requisitioned Air India planes made four round trips a day to Amman until late October that year, in an operation that has been called the biggest airlift in world history.[40] It was an extraordinary logistical feat pulled off by VP and Gujral, with able support from Civil Aviation Minister Arif Khan. 'Never were so many human beings moved by aircraft in such a short time,' noted VP. 'Much credit should go to Gujral for managing everyone and representing India's case very well before all the countries involved.'[41]

Kuwait's annexation, and the war that followed to liberate it (the country was finally freed at the end of February 1991), had another vital fallout for India. Global oil prices soared, since supplies from both Kuwait and Iraq had all but stopped, leading to the country's oil-import bill escalating dramatically. The economy, already staggering under the weight of excessive government expenditure and short-term borrowings through the late 1980s, thereby reached the verge of collapse by mid-1991, forcing the economic liberalization that came thereafter.

———— ∞∞∞ ————

VP took many initiatives as Prime Minister, which, if brought to full fruition, would have been historic, but his term proved too brief for him to do so. For decades, there had been widespread public grumbling about the news bulletins of All India Radio and Doordarshan, which were heavily slanted in favour of the ruling party, since both entities were directly controlled by the Ministry of Information and Broadcasting. (It was a time when no private channels were allowed either.) In his first speech as Prime Minister on 3 December 1989, VP promised to make them autonomous[42] and, sure enough, in September 1990, he had the relevant Bill passed by Parliament, creating the public broadcaster Prasar Bharati to run them both.

But with his government falling soon after, Prasar Bharati was eventually set up only in November 1997. Similarly, though it was VP's government that passed the Act setting up the National Commission for Women as a statutory body, the first such commission began working only from January 1992, well after VP had quit.

The Right to Information Act was finally passed after many agitations in 2005, but the first effort to formulate one had been by VP's government. In that same first address of 3 December 1989, he had said, 'Right to information will be enshrined in our Constitution ... If the government functions in full public view, wrongdoings will be minimized ...'[43] Soon after, he sent officials to Sweden and Finland, which already had similar laws, to study their models. 'Some parties in our coalition government strongly resisted bringing such a law,' said VP.

Apparently, so did the very officials he had entrusted to prepare a draft for the proposed law. 'The draft I got left so much to the discretion of the government that no information would have been obtained quickly, had it been passed,' he said. 'Any information given out would be superficial—no sensitive matter would ever be revealed. I asked for another draft, but after that our government fell.'[44] In his pursuit of transparency, VP also directed the law ministry to examine whether the Official Secrets Act, 1923 (which had been used to harass Gurumurthy during the Fairfax brouhaha), a colonial-era law, was worth retaining, but once again nothing came of it.

So too did VP try to pass a law akin to the National Rural Employment Guarantee Act (NREGA), also enacted subsequently in 2005 by the United Progressive Alliance (UPA) government. (No doubt, the wisdom of doing so—given the additional expenditure it would entail—at a time when the fiscal deficit was already alarmingly high, can be debated.[45]) There had been several employment-guarantee schemes in the past, including the wide-ranging Jawahar Rozgar Yojna started by the Rajiv Gandhi government in 1989, but VP's was the first attempt to give the right to work constitutional status. However, as he explained,

> The cabinet passed the draft bill of the act, which proposed that funding of the employment guarantee programme that would follow the law should be shared equally between the Centre and the states. Before taking it to Parliament, I held a meeting of all chief ministers. They insisted that states' finances did not permit them to take on the burden. They wanted the Centre to fund it fully.[46]

VP then suggested raising the Centre's contribution to 75 per cent. 'We set up a committee, which included a number of chief ministers, to prepare a fresh draft, but before it was ready, our government was out,' he added. (In the Mahatma Gandhi National Rural Employment Guarantee Scheme, which followed the NREGA Act, the Centre covers the entire payout to unskilled workers, while payouts for semi-skilled and skilled workers are shared with the states in the ratio of 75:25.)

It was the same with VP's push for the Lok Pal Act (which would appoint an ombudsman to probe corruption cases against public servants, including the Prime Minister). In this case, though, his was not the first attempt—earlier, too, some governments had tried and failed for different reasons. (The Act was finally passed in 2013.) The story was repeated with the 'One Rank, One Pension' (OROP) scheme for defence personnel, which would provide them with the same pension based on rank and length of service, irrespective of how long ago they had retired. Bureaucrats opposed it strongly, demanding a similar scheme for themselves too, finally preparing a proposal so shoddy that VP had to ask them to work on it again.[47] (The scheme was implemented at last in September 2015.)

So too was the case with VP's pet concern—electoral reforms. The eleven-member all-party committee he had appointed to recommend some, especially on how to achieve transparency in funding, never produced the report it was expected to.[48] In his pursuit of greater federalism, VP also set up the Inter-State Council in May 1990 for better dispute resolution and coordination between states, but since he left office, it has met only eleven times in thirty years.[49] He started a National Security Council as well in August 1990, to collate security inputs from different agencies and formulate holistic security policies, but it became non-functional after his departure and was only revived after the BJP came to power in 1998.

Tackling the hoary, complicated problems of Indian agriculture was another priority for VP, but once again, his time in office was too fleeting for him to take remedial steps. He did, however, set up three government committees, chaired by experts, to identify these problems—a high-powered committee on agricultural policies and programmes under a former agriculture minister, Bhanu Pratap Singh; a standing advisory committee on agriculture under the Planning Commission, headed by Sharad Joshi, a prominent

Maharashtra-based farmers' leader; and a national commission on rural labour under eminent economist C.H. Hanumantha Rao. 'The reports of these committees, all submitted in mid-to-end 1990, became Bibles on Indian agriculture for subsequent governments,' said Som Pal, who was himself agriculture minister in 1998–99.[50]

For Delhi, specifically, VP began an ambitious effort to re-house its jhuggi-jhopdi residents in better conditions, and though, once more, his tenure proved too short to do so, even the preliminary steps he took made a big difference to them. He ordered the city's first comprehensive slum survey—completed in three months—during which all the 900-odd such clusters at the time were registered, and every family living in them issued both ration and identity cards. The identity cards, which came to be called in time the 'V.P. Singh cards', became the basis of all slum-rehabilitation schemes over the next decade in the city, as those possessing them now had proof of being residents of the city prior to 1990. During a visit to a south Delhi slum on New Year's Day 1990, he also promised that no jhuggi would be demolished without first providing alternative accommodation, and passed a government order to that effect.[51]

One far-reaching step VP did effect was that of amending the Standard of Weights and Measures Act 1976, which made it mandatory for all packaged goods to have their maximum retail price (MRP) printed on them, providing immense protection to consumers from profiteering retailers. (Even today, India is among just a handful of countries to have such a law.) But altogether, his prime ministership was a sorry tale of promise cut short. Som Pal's observation, though hyperbolic, has some truth to it. 'If V.P. Singh had had a full five years as Prime Minister, unfettered by fractious colleagues,' he said, 'he would have changed the face of the country.'[52]

3

'I HAVE LEARNT A LESSON. I THINK I MUST BE MORE FIRM'

V.P. Singh's government began unravelling barely two and a half months after he had taken charge, all due to a controversy over a routine by-election. The constituency was Meham, one of the nine in Haryana's Rohtak district, about 100 km north-west of Delhi. It was from Meham that Devi Lal had been elected to the Haryana assembly three times—in both the 1982 and the 1987 assembly elections, as well as in 1985 (after he rashly resigned to protest the Punjab accord, but finding the move had little impact, contested again when the by-election was held).

After his election to the Lok Sabha in the November 1989 election and becoming deputy prime minister (he also got the agriculture portfolio), Devi Lal naturally quit the seat. His son Om Prakash Chautala, who, though president of the Haryana Janata Dal at the time, hadn't fought the 1987 assembly election and wasn't an MLA, decided to contest it when a fresh election was announced for 27 February 1990. (Already sworn in as chief minister on 2 December 1989, he had to become an assembly member before 2 June 1990.)

Meham was not the only seat contested that day. Assembly elections to UP, Karnataka and Andhra Pradesh had been held along with the November 1989 Lok Sabha election, but eight others—Rajasthan, Himachal Pradesh, Madhya Pradesh, Bihar, Orissa, Gujarat, Maharashtra and Arunachal Pradesh—were also close to completing their terms, and elections for all of them were also held at the same time. There followed a repeat of the pattern that had set in since 1977, when the Janata Party had won the Lok Sabha polls and then proceeded to win most of the state elections that came soon after. So too had the Congress, after winning the 1980 and 1985 Lok Sabha elections, won the bulk of the assembly elections held in the next three months.

Before the 1990 elections, all eight states had had Congress governments ruling since 1985. With the Janata Dal in power, in six of them the Congress was now routed, with the Janata Dal, the BJP or a coalition of the two forming the government. (In the November 1989 Lok Sabha polls, the Janata Dal and the BJP sought to put up common candidates, succeeding in reaching a consensus in some areas and failing in others.) The only states that returned the Congress to power were Maharashtra and Arunachal Pradesh.

In all, 1,619 seats were contested,[1] but with the other outcomes turning out much as expected, the only individual seat that made national headlines was Meham. Chautala's election should have been a cinch; as VP had found while contesting the Tindwari by-election as UP chief minister, voters, whichever the constituency, are usually keen to have an incumbent chief minister representing them and often bury political differences to support him, knowing he can bring them development goodies at a pace no other MLA can. Chautala also stood to benefit from his father's legacy, as well as the fact that about 60 per cent of Meham's voters belonged to his Jat caste. But in their arrogance, father and son messed up the campaign.

Though Devi Lal had won Meham three times, he did not hail from the area, his village—also called Chautala—being located about 200 km further north-west in Sirsa district, close to Haryana's border with Rajasthan and Punjab. The second and third times he stood from Meham, there had been an undercurrent of resentment that his monopolizing the Meham seat was thwarting local ambition to enter the Vidhan Sabha and that he ought to fight from where he belonged. The sentiment was strong enough for Devi Lal to declare, while announcing his candidature for the June 1987 assembly poll at a rally in Meham attended by thousands, that if he left Meham for any reason, he would back a local candidate.

'*Agar maine kabhi yeh seat chhodi aur kahin aur gaya, to agli baar panchayat jiska naam degi, usi ummeedwar ko ladawoonga yahan se* (If I ever quit this seat and go elsewhere, I will back whichever candidate from here the panchayat chooses in the next election),' he had said then.[2] The panchayat—called Meham Chaubisi, comprising one representative from each of the twenty-four villages making up the constituency—was an extremely influential traditional local institution, as it is in most Jat areas.

'In our villages we say, "*Pancho ke samne koi baat keh di, to Ishwar uska sakshi hota hai, aur agar us par woh wapas jata hai, to Ishwar usey kabhi maaf nahi karta* (If a person says something before the panchayat, then God is his witness, and if he reneges on it, God will never forgive him),"' said Som Pal. 'But Devi Lal did renege, nominating his son as candidate, and the panchayat was furious. I reminded Devi Lal of this, but for him such a promise meant nothing. He said, "*Ke panchayat? Kya hoti hai panchayat* (Panchayat? What's a panchayat)?"'[3] Worse, Devi Lal had fallen out with his chief election manager in all the three Meham polls he had won—a local named Anand Singh Dangi. Dangi now decided to contest against Chautala as an independent, strongly backed by the Meham Chaubisi and somewhat tepidly by the Congress too.

Nearly all of Chautala's ministers campaigned for him in Meham, making extravagant promises, as did many Janata Dal Central leaders, but the Chaubisi's influence was formidable. Polling day proved fateful for VP, as Meham saw a repeat of the Garhwal by-election of June 1981. Goons—allegedly Devi Lal's private army, the Green Brigade—protected and assisted by local policemen,[4] stuffed ballot papers stamped in Chautala's favour into ballot boxes across hundreds of polling stations. In twelve booths,[5] the rigging was so flagrant that the Election Commission ordered re-polling in them the next day. Once again, violence followed as locals resisted the Green Brigade, leading to police firing, in which six people were killed. A few days later, after receiving the relevant report from its observers, the Election Commission countermanded the entire poll.[6]

All through VP's efforts to marshal a united front against Rajiv Gandhi's Congress, Devi Lal had been his strongest supporter. But passing up the chance to become Prime Minister in VP's favour, even though he had done so voluntarily, seemed to rankle greatly with him, especially after he quickly realized that the consolation prize of deputy prime minister he had sought and obtained was no prize at all, since the position was bereft of constitutionally defined powers. In practice, he remained largely confined to his agriculture ministry while all other important matters were decided by VP with the concerned minister. His behaviour towards VP changed drastically. 'From Day 1, there was hardly any issue on which the two [VP and Devi Lal] responded as colleagues,' wrote Gujral in his memoirs later. 'Even the civil courtesies normally extended to a rival, were denied by Devi Lal to the leader of the party.'[7]

The 'mayhem in Meham'—a favourite press headline at the time—and its aftermath took the relationship between the two several notches lower, adding Devi Lal to VP's long list of friends-turned-enemies. VP realized that the events in Meham would severely dent his image, since the Janata Dal had been elected on the plank of providing ethical and corruption-free governance, and decided that the only damage control possible was to get Chautala to resign as chief minister.

Fortunately, most of his cabinet colleagues, led by Industries Minister Ajit Singh—Devi Lal's old rival—agreed with him, but Devi Lal wouldn't hear of it. Soon after the Meham clashes, Chautala had announced a judicial inquiry into them, which he felt should be enough to satisfy those complaining. (A year later, the inquiry report, by Chautala's hand-picked judge S.S. Grewal, exonerated him of any involvement in the rigging.[8])

At a 16 March 1990 meeting of the Janata Dal's Political Affairs Committee (PAC), at VP's 28, Lodhi Estate home—he was yet to move to the Prime Minister's residence—Devi Lal and his critics clashed so bitterly that the deputy prime minister stormed out, declaring he was quitting the government. His written resignation reached VP an hour later by courier.[9] VP was half inclined to accept it but was persuaded not to. ('My instinct, honed from watching Indira Gandhi at work, told me to do so; once he had resigned, making his differences public, there was nothing left to discuss,' he said later.[10]) Over the next two and a half days, Janata Dal leaders pleaded with Devi Lal to take it back and finally got him to do so.

But the Chautala issue remained. Reluctant, perhaps, to rile Devi Lal again and risk—given Devi Lal's substantial support among the Janata Dal's MPs—destroying his government, VP avoided directing Chautala to resign, though he continued to maintain that he should. Meanwhile, a fresh election in Meham was announced for 27 May 1990, for which both Chautala and Dangi again filed their nominations. But this time Chautala also created a fallback option for himself by getting the Janata Dal female MLA from Darba Kalan—an assembly seat in his Sirsa home district—

to resign, promising her a Rajya Sabha seat in its lieu, and contesting from there as well.

It was lucky for him that he did, because, on 17 May 1990, ten days before the polling, an independent candidate from Meham, Amir Singh, was found murdered, leading to the election again being countermanded. Who committed the crime was never established, but at the time, the development gave the demand for Chautala's resignation a fresh impetus, both in the media and among Devi Lal's detractors in the Janata Dal. They openly accused Chautala, claiming that he wanted the election countermanded to avoid loss of face, since he knew he was set to lose, while being fairly certain of getting elected from the Darba Kalan seat. Chautala, on the contrary, held Dangi responsible, claiming that Amir Singh and he had been long-time enemies. Indeed, he sent a police team to arrest Dangi the next day, but the Meham Chaubisi intervened, its volunteers attacking the police, who opened fire and killed three of them, further fuelling the resentment against Chautala.[11]

By then, after VP had quit the post on becoming Prime Minister, a new Janata Dal president had been chosen too. This was S.R. Bommai, once a trusted colleague of Ramakrishna Hegde's, who had succeeded Hegde as Karnataka chief minister. (Hegde, who had been VP's second-most-enthusiastic backer while the Janata Dal was being formed—after Devi Lal—was forced to resign as chief minister in August 1988, having been caught tapping the telephones of associates and rivals.) However, Bommai's tenure as chief minister lasted only a few months, ending with his dramatic dismissal by the governor after defections from his party in April 1989[12]—but it was long enough for him to develop major differences with Hegde and grow close to Devi Lal instead. In his NMML interview, VP confirmed that Bommai would never have been chosen as party president but for Devi Lal's support.

Yet, within two days of being elected unanimously on 19 May 1990, Bommai took the decisive step VP had been shying

away from for weeks—he personally told Chautala that he would
be expelled from the Janata Dal unless he resigned forthwith.
Chautala complied; a new chief minister, Banarsi Das Gupta, taking
his place.[13] 'When Bommai came to pay his respects after getting
elected, I told him, "You have to get Chautala's resignation,"'
said VP. 'Despite Devi Lal's support in making him president,
he did a complete U-turn and got me the resignation letter that
very evening.'[14]

Devi Lal was incensed but chose not to respond at once. Instead,
he sought to leverage his undoubtedly large rural support (at least
in Haryana) to embarrass his own government, accusing it of not
doing enough for farmers, writing a letter to VP demanding to
know how many bureaucrats came from rural backgrounds, and
one to Gujral asking how many of India's 103 ambassadors did, and
why there were so few of them.[15] Then, five days after Chautala's
resignation, the election to the other seat he was contesting, Darba
Kalan, was held as scheduled, and passed peacefully, with Chautala
winning by a huge margin.

The victory convinced Devi Lal—obsessed with securing his
son's political future and yearning to get even with his opponents
in the party—that there was no reason now, with Chautala having
become an MLA at last, that he shouldn't be made chief minister
again. But how to get VP to agree? By then, the Prime Minister and
his deputy were virtually not on speaking terms.

Som Pal felt that such estrangement made the future of the
government untenable. He asked VP if he should try and set up a
private meeting between the two, where they could sort out their
differences by themselves; VP said he had no objection. Devi Lal,
seventy-six at the time, with various geriatric afflictions, had taken
time off for a sojourn at the Institute of Naturopathy and Yogic
Science on the outskirts of Bangalore (since renamed the Jindal
Naturecure Institute, after the industrialist Sitaram Jindal, who set
it up). On 26 June 1990, Som Pal travelled there to meet him,

accompanied by another of Devi Lal's sons, Ranjit Singh (power minister in the Haryana cabinet at the time of writing). He found Devi Lal agreeable to the idea as well. The meeting, which turned out to be ruinous for the Janata Dal, was held over dinner at the Prime Minister's residence on 8 July 1990.

Som Pal remembered briefing VP shortly before it. 'I knew Devi Lal's nature,' he said. 'I knew he would bring up all kinds of superfluous issues he didn't really care about before casually slipping in, towards the end, the only thing that mattered to him— making Chautala chief minister again.' He accordingly suggested a response to VP. 'Tell him that what happened at Meham has led to much controversy, but feelings and perceptions fade as time passes,' he said. 'Tell him he should wait a month or two. If you do so, he will listen to you.'

The next morning, Som Pal visited VP and asked if his hunch had been correct. VP confirmed it had been. 'What did you say?' Som Pal asked.

'I told him, "Chaudhary sahib, Haryana is your state. You can do what you like,"' VP replied.[16]

In his memoirs, Gujral put it slightly differently. 'According to V.P. Singh, just when Devi Lal was getting up after dinner did he ask for the reinstalling of Chautala as chief minister of Haryana,' he wrote. 'To this request, the Prime Minister replied: "We have never nominated chief ministers from here (i.e. Delhi)."'[17]

Som Pal was appalled, realizing that Devi Lal would interpret the reply as carte blanche for bringing back Chautala as Haryana chief minister immediately. Sure enough, Devi Lal soon telephoned, calling him over, chortling with delight. 'He said, *"Bahut badhiya kaam kiya tumne. Eh toh bahut hi bhala aadmi hain. Mera dimaag aise hi kharab kar rakha tha logon ne. Jo maine kaha usne sari baat maan li* (You did a very good thing. He's a very nice man. People had given me a wrong impression about him. He agreed to everything I said),"' said Som Pal. 'When I met him, I asked,

"*Om bhaisaab ko CM banane ke bare mein aapki kuch baat hui* (Did you talk about making Om chief minister)?" He nodded emphatically. I said, "What have you decided?" He said, "I'll go today or tomorrow, get Banarsi Das Gupta to resign and make Om Prakash CM again.""[18]

It was just what Som Pal had feared. He sought to dissuade Devi Lal, knowing that the media and many of his cabinet colleagues would be outraged. 'I told him, "*Main sahmat nahi hoon aapki baat se, kyunki is baat ko aap nibha nahi payenge* (I don't agree with your decision, because you will not be able to see it through)." The party could break up,' he said. Devi Lal was enraged. 'He said, "*Main to janta hoon, tu uski phooti aankh dekhna nahi chahta* (I know you can't stand Chautala),"' recalled Som Pal. Som Pal denied the charge and departed coldly, but as he was driving off in his car, he saw the security guard at the gate of Devi Lal's bungalow come running behind him. He stopped. The guard said that Devi Lal wanted him to return. When they met again, Devi Lal urged him to explain himself better.

Som Pal did and thought he had almost convinced Devi Lal. 'This is something I didn't want to say, Mamaji, but now I'm forced to,' he said. 'You are a ruffian Jat. V.P. Singh is an astute and polished politician. I suspect that with the offer he made you, he wants to trap you. If Om Prakash becomes the chief minister again, you will be dependent on V.P. Singh to save you, because there will be a big onslaught on you. If Chautala is forced to quit again, your reputation will suffer.' As Som Pal elaborated, Devi Lal seemed to understand.

Som Pal's mother-in-law was then visiting him, and Devi Lal rang again in the evening, saying he was flying to Sirsa the next day using the Haryana state plane—there had been floods in the area with the Ghaggar river overflowing, which he wanted to inspect—and would like to take her back to their village with him. Som Pal feared that Devi Lal's extended family in the village, the members of which he would naturally meet during his visit, could instigate him to push again for Chautala as chief minister right away. 'While dropping my mother-in-law at the airport, I warned Devi Lal,' he said. 'His reply was, "*Bawla hai tu? Jab maine teri baat samajh li, befikar rahe* (Are you an idiot? I've understood you, don't worry)."'[19]

Two days later, on 12 July 1990, Devi Lal summoned Som Pal to his Krishi Bhavan office and pushed a sheet of paper before him, saying, 'Read this.' It was Banarsi Das Gupta's resignation as chief minister. 'I read it and said to him, "You didn't listen to me. *Ab dekhna tamasha khada hoga* (Now watch the circus that unfolds),"' said Som Pal. 'He said, "Go and give this letter to V.P. Singh." I said, "Mamaji, I'm not your postman," and left.'

Reaching home, he called VP at his office, but VP's secretary wouldn't put him through. 'The Prime Minister is in a cabinet meeting,' he said.

'Very soon, there may be no cabinet left to meet,' Som Pal replied. 'Just call him out.' But the secretary was too meek to interrupt a cabinet meeting, so Som Pal then called another of VP's secretaries, who proved bold enough, enabling him to finally speak to the Prime Minister. He remembered VP's reaction to his revelation as strangely phlegmatic. 'About Devi Lal, all he said was, "He is in the cabinet meeting, sitting right next to me. He hasn't said a word about this,"' recalled Som Pal. 'He asked me to meet him after the cabinet meeting. When I did so in his office, he again did not seem at all perturbed. I suspect he had expected it; it was perhaps part of some strategy of his to corner Devi Lal.'[20]

If it indeed was a strategy, it had consequences VP would never have imagined. The 'tamasha'—though it was all dead serious— Som Pal had predicted began the very next day. (Already, on the evening of 12 July 1990, within hours of Banarsi Das Gupta resigning, Chautala had been elected leader of Haryana's Janata Dal legislature party; as in December, party MLAs were directed to rush post-haste to Delhi and duly obeyed, after which Haryana's governor, also summoned to Delhi, swore Chautala in as chief minister for a second time.) On the morning of 13 July 1990, Arun Nehru, who had been away in London, returned, having already been briefed over telephone by Ajit Singh and Arif Khan. After confabulating all day, they decided they would resign as ministers in protest.[21]

Eventually, Ajit Singh opted out, but Arif Khan and Arun Nehru—along with Satyapal Malik (governor of Meghalaya at the time of writing), who had been made a minister of state in a cabinet expansion VP carried out in April—wrote out near-identical resignation letters. The letters called Chautala's return as chief minister 'a flagrant violation of all norms of democratic behaviour and decent values in public life'.[22] 'We cannot let the party become a laughing stock,' Nehru told Gujral on telephone, as the latter was away in Nairobi at the time, explaining his reasons for quitting.[23]

'Arun Nehru and Arif Khan believed I had struck some sort of deal with Devi Lal and agreed to Chautala becoming chief minister again,' said VP. 'It was a misunderstanding, which I cleared up when we met.'[24] But they still insisted that VP accept the resignation letters, at which VP declared he would quit as well. He promptly drafted his own resignation letter and sent it off both to party president Bommai and the chairman of the National Front, N.T. Rama Rao.[25] 'The rationale of my being in office was the trust of the people,' he wrote. 'The developments of the last few days show I have lost that trust.'[26]

Unlike his earlier resignations as UP chief minister or Union defence minister, however, whether he was serious about this one can be questioned. No doubt his reason for sending it to Bommai and NTR instead of President Venkataraman (which he should have done if he truly intended it to be accepted), has been well explained by Venkataraman himself. The former President wrote,

The Prime Minister met me (on 14 July 1990) and briefed me on the events leading to his sending his resignation letter to the party president. He explained that if he had sent it to me, there would have been no one to take over the government immediately, and therefore he wanted the party president to elect another leader first.[27]

But Venkataraman did not believe him entirely, and with good reason. 'During the conversation, I asked him if his proposed visit to the Soviet Union was not too short,' Venkataraman added. 'V.P. Singh did not say that since he had resigned, the question did not arise. On the contrary, he said four days were quite enough.'[28]

The resignation was obviously intended to pressure Devi Lal into getting Chautala to quit again, VP having gauged that neither his own party and nor his BJP and communist allies would accept his resignation. Its impact was just as he had hoped—the Janata Dal, the BJP and the communists all began insisting that Chautala should go while VP should stay on.[29] Finally, on 16 July 1990, even as Haryana MLAs were staging a sit-in outside 7, Race Course Road, demanding Chautala be retained, he resigned again, after just four days as chief minister. At first, Devi Lal sought a deal, demanding that Arun Nehru's and Arif Khan's resignations also be accepted if Chautala was to submit his, but VP turned him down.

Thwarted and humiliated, Devi Lal plotted revenge, especially against Arun Nehru and Arif Khan. 'One day, while all this was happening, Ranjit Singh [Devi Lal's third son who had accompanied Som Pal to Bangalore in end-June], who was a good friend of mine, brought along this person to meet me,' said Som Pal. 'His name was Nand Kishore Sharma and he claimed to be some kind of tantric. Though a wretched, slimy sort of fellow, he had contacts with many Congress leaders, whose names he kept dropping.'

Sharma brandished a telex he had brought with him before Som Pal, claiming its contents were so sensational, they could bring down the government. 'I took Ranjit aside and told him, "Why are you giving this sort of person so much importance?" He said, "No, no, you take a look at the telex."' Som Pal did and found that though the telex sender's identity was unclear, it had come from London and charged both Arun Nehru (then commerce minister) and Arif Khan (then power minister) with taking kickbacks from companies it named—Arun Nehru while importing phosphoric acid and a fertilizer called di-ammonium phosphate (DAP), and Arif Khan while ordering power turbines. 'I was very dismissive of the whole thing, but, in fact, that fellow was proved right,' said Som Pal.[30]

He was proved right not because the allegations were confirmed—quite the contrary, they were soon exposed as absurd[31]—but because Devi Lal chose to repeat them in a letter to VP soon after. VP wrote back immediately, seeking proof within three days, at which Devi Lal maintained that he had none but was only passing on received information. In the same reply, he added that he had learnt even VP had had his suspicions about Arun Nehru's role in the Bofors scam and had written to the President saying so. VP replied that he had never written any such letter, whereupon Devi Lal sent him a purported copy, which had both VP's letterhead and seemingly genuine signature, and which indeed indicted Arun Nehru.[32]

VP requested President Venkataraman to check if any such letter existed in the Rashtrapati Bhavan records, but none was found. Besides, the letter had distinct factual errors, the most obvious being that while dated 26 November 1987, it gave VP's address as 28, Lodhi Estate, though at the time he was yet to move there and was still staying at 1, Teenmurti Marg.[33] 'It is very easy to forge signatures,' said VP later. 'I even showed the CBI officer who visited me how it could be done, using my office scanner.'[34]

As in the case of the Fairfax letters to Gurumurthy, who sent the telex or forged the letter was never established.

With his accusations backfiring, Devi Lal lost it. In an interview to *The Illustrated Weekly of India*, a popular magazine then published by the Times of India Group (it was shut down in 1993), while justifying making his son chief minister again ('The Haryana MLAs wanted no one other than Om Prakash') and seemingly supportive of VP ('I respect him. I got him elected as Prime Minister. Without me, would he be sitting on that chair?'), he still called the Prime Minister 'spineless' and the colleagues who were opposing him 'nalayaks' (useless, unworthy) and 'wimps'.[35] Not surprisingly, after VP's return from the USSR, the 29 July 1990 meeting of the Janata Dal's PAC saw member after member tearing into Devi Lal for his accusations and indiscreet comments. On 1 August 1990, VP sacked Devi Lal from his cabinet. Asked about his takeaway from the entire drama, VP replied, 'I think I have learnt a lesson. I have to be more firm. Maybe I was too quiet and tolerant (before).'[36]

Part 7

MANDAL AND MANDIR

1

'AFTER MANDAL, IT WAS AS IF I WAS A DIFFERENT PERSON'

Though he had resigned as defence minister on 11 April 1987, it was only three months later—on 15 July 1987, infuriated by Arun Nehru, Arif Khan and V.C. Shukla's expulsions—that V.P. Singh quit the Congress. During the months when he was hesitating to do so, S. Jaipal Reddy,[1] spokesperson for the Janata Dal for most of its brief existence, recalled once asking him why he remained with the party—having fallen out so bitterly with Rajiv Gandhi that his future in it was doomed. Reddy maintained that VP replied with great candour. 'If I join the Opposition, I'll have to abandon the social groups I've always been close to and embrace others with which I've had little to do so far,' he said.[2]

By social groups, of course, VP meant castes—though he would never have realized at the time how crucially the new groups he was about to embrace would shape his political legacy. As many political scientists have noted, and as VP himself found out in all the elections he fought as a Congress candidate, the Congress's electoral base in north India comprised a 'coalition of extremes'[3]—the bulk of its voters were either upper castes (Brahmins, Kshatriyas and Vaishyas) or Scheduled Castes (the Dalits or traditional untouchables), apart from the Muslims. This odd combination of upper castes and the lowliest castes had been forged in pre-Independence times. While the far-better-educated upper castes naturally dominated the freedom movement and were the Congress's main supporters, the Scheduled Castes were attracted to it mainly due to Mahatma Gandhi's crusade against untouchability.

The group left out of the Congress fold in north India were the Shudras—the bulk of peasants and rural service providers who form the mainstay of rural society, many of whom (though, importantly, not all) came to be classified as the OBCs. Historically, they, too, had been discriminated against by the upper castes, but to a lesser extent than the Dalits. Though the peasants among them were big gainers from the Congress's land-reform drive—the abolition of zamindari and the imposition of ceilings on large landholdings—in north India they still stayed away from the party, partly because the reforms were not implemented rigorously enough but mainly because the upper-caste leaders who dominated the Congress organization resisted sharing power with them. Even in the breakaway parties Indira Gandhi formed after splitting the Congress in 1969 and again in 1977–78, the upper caste–Scheduled Caste combination remained her bulwark of support in north India.

Though their numbers were formidable—their nationwide population estimated at different times between 35 and 52.4 per cent[4]—the OBCs, especially in north India, due to poor political awareness, would initially scatter their votes, which, in turn, enabled the Congress to keep winning elections, despite the fact that the Brahmins, Kshatriyas and Vaishyas together averaged merely 20 per cent of the population, with Dalits about 15 per cent and Muslims another 13–15 per cent.[5] The personal popularity of Jawaharlal Nehru and Indira also helped the Congress garner votes, irrespective of caste.

The politicized sections of the OBCs, however, mostly supported the Socialist Party and its successor, the SSP, as VP had vividly observed while fighting his first election from Soraon in 1969. The socialists' main appeal for OBCs stemmed from their avowal that if elected to power, they would reserve 60 per cent of all government jobs for them, embodied in a slogan much heard in the SSP's (abbreviated to 'Sasopa' in Hindi) heyday, *'Sasopa ne baandhi gaant/Pichhdey pawey sau mein saat'* (The SSP has pledged amen/ for backwards, it's six out of ten)'. No doubt the OBCs realized that such reservation would only benefit a minuscule number among them, since government jobs comprised a very small slice of the total number of available jobs. But with OBC representation in government services extremely low—in the Central government, when VP took over, it was 14.5 per cent[6]—and such jobs providing prestige, security and power, even as private industry in the north Indian states remained moribund, the slogan resonated strongly with them.[7]

The scenario differed considerably in south and west India, where, unlike in the north, the Congress drew sizeable support from the leading peasant castes. In these states, upper castes are even fewer than in north India, their population as a per centage of the total mostly in single digits. They thus matter far less electorally, leaving the Congress no choice but to woo other castes as well. Yet, here too, as in the north, the upper castes—especially the Brahmins—given their millennia-old tradition of education, held the bulk of government jobs. But with the OBCs being in greater numbers and better organized than in the north, they had long ago begun protesting this imbalance. In response, even before Independence, the British governments of the Bombay and Madras presidencies, as well as the princely states of Kolhapur (the first to introduce job reservations of any kind, in 1902), Mysore, Cochin and Travancore, acknowledging the validity of the protests, had begun setting aside quotas in government jobs for them.

Post-Independence, the Congress governments in these states had continued with the quotas. In most north Indian states, however, the only reservations were for Dalits and the tribals; the Congress saw no reason to extend them to the OBCs, who didn't vote for them anyway. They also knew that doing so would surely annoy their upper-caste supporters, whose job opportunities would shrink.

But on the recommendation of an advisory committee to the constituent assembly, the Indian Constitution had included an article—Article 340—which authorized appointing a commission 'to investigate the conditions of socially and educationally backward classes ... and the difficulties under which they labour, and to make recommendations as to the steps that should be taken ... to remove such difficulties and improve their condition'. Accordingly, in January 1953, such a commission was set up, chaired by former freedom fighter, social reformer and writer Dattatreya Balakrishna (Kaka) Kalelkar, which submitted its report two years later, listing 2,399 castes countrywide that it considered OBCs and recommending 25–40 per cent reservation for them in different categories of Central government service.

Yet its recommendations were never implemented, partly because, in a bizarre afterthought, Chairman Kalelkar undermined his own report, adding to it a twenty-three-page covering letter pointing to its several purported shortcomings,[8] but also because the Congress feared upsetting its upper-caste voters in north India. Yet, anxious to not lose the OBC votes it drew in the south and the west (which it might have if it dismissed the report entirely), the Congress found a middle path, declaring that while there would be no OBC quota in Central government jobs, state governments were free to set up their own commissions to identify state-level OBCs and reserve jobs for them if they wanted.

Thereafter, over the next two decades, ten state governments (including some of those that already had OBC reservations dating from before Independence) set up fifteen such commissions, all of which acknowledged that reservations for OBCs was necessary and set varying quotas for them, ranging from 5 per cent (Punjab) to 50 per cent (Karnataka), which their state governments mostly accepted.[9] Significantly, these ten included all the southern and western states—Tamil Nadu, Karnataka, Kerala, Andhra Pradesh, Maharashtra and Gujarat—but only two of the north Indian, Hindi-speaking ones—Bihar and UP.[10] Even in Bihar, it was not a Congress government but one of the half a dozen governments that ruled during the political flux of 1967–72 that took the step, setting up the Mungeri Lal Commission—named after its chairman, a state Vidhan Parishad MLC at the time—in June 1971.[11]

Though the bickering of its leaders destroyed the SSP—as it did the other socialist party, the PSP—the OBC reservation idea long outlived it. Some former socialists joined the Congress, especially in the 1960s; others—once Charan Singh quit the Congress and made another political alternative available—preferred to join him, since his electoral base comprised mainly farmers, many of whom were also OBCs. They continued to keep the OBC reservation demand alive.

When the Janata Party was formed after the Emergency, both Charan Singh's BLD and the remnants of the socialist parties joined it, cooperating closely thereafter, further consolidating the OBCs politically. Thus, while the Janata Party's victory in the March 1977 general elections was no doubt a reassertion of democracy against Indira's dictatorship, it was also seen in north India as a victory of the OBCs over the upper-caste–Scheduled Caste combine.[12]

The Janata Party's election manifesto had promised to implement the Kalelkar Commission report's proposals, but eventually, in January 1979, given the report's shortcomings and the tussles within the party, it decided to set up a new commission to repeat the effort. As chairman of the commission, it appointed Bindeshwari Prasad Mandal, who had been Bihar's chief minister for a fleeting forty-seven days during the political churn of 1967–72. In its report, which proved seminal in VP's career, the five-member Mandal Commission listed 3,743 castes across the country as OBCs and made a host of recommendations for their uplift—the most important of them being reserving for them 27 per cent of jobs across all categories of Central government service and in all Central government-run technical and professional educational institutions.

Why 27 per cent? The Mandal Commission report maintained that according to its calculations based on the last caste census held in 1931 (the censuses thereafter avoided enumerating specific castes), the country's OBC population was 52.4 per cent and, ideally, the community's share of government jobs should match that figure. But it also noted a crucial legal impediment—the 1963 Supreme Court judgment in the case of *Balaji versus the State of Mysore*, which had ruled that reserved quotas had to be less than a total of 50 per cent. Since, at the Central level, the Scheduled Castes had already been allotted a 15 per cent quota and the Scheduled Tribes another 7.5 per cent, the OBCs could not be given more than 27 per cent.[13]

The Balaji judgment had also decreed that OBCs should not be identified by caste alone, though caste could be one of the yardsticks defining backwardness. Accordingly, the Mandal Commission used levels of education and income as indicators too, to determine which castes to list as backward, though in computing the final 'backwardness' score of each caste, social backwardness—being looked down upon by other castes and such—was given more weight than educational backwardness or economic deprivation.[14]

The Mandal Commission was set up on the first day of 1979 and submitted its report on the last day of 1980. Momentous political changes had taken place in those two years, with the Janata government collapsing and the Congress returning to power at the Centre, so it was no surprise that the report was ignored both by Indira and Rajiv, when he succeeded her. The former SSP members in Charan Singh's party—by then called the Lok Dal—would not, however, allow it to be forgotten and kept periodically bringing it up, even holding a rally (roping in a few other Opposition parties too) at Delhi's Boat Club on 18 February 1982 to demand its implementation.[15] Within a few weeks of the rally, the government tabled the Mandal report in Parliament, following which it was discussed in the Lok Sabha[16] and sent off to the chief ministers of all states for their views, without any further step being taken. (As UP chief minister then, VP, too, must have received a copy. His response, if any, is not known.)

Naturally, the Janata Dal—of which the Lok Dal and the Janata Party were the main constituents—included implementing the Mandal Commission's recommendations in its manifesto for the November 1989 elections. Its leaders also referred to it in some of their campaign speeches, but with VP's crusade against the Congress's corruption dominating campaign discourse, few among the castes that stood to lose from such a step even noticed. In north India—110 of the Janata Dal's 143-seat Lok Sabha tally came from there—its win was thus a second victory of the OBCs over the upper-caste–Scheduled Caste alliance. But the vocal sections of VP's supporters during the election campaign—the middle classes, especially students, all largely upper-caste—remained blithely unaware of it.

'Implementing the Mandal report was never V.P. Singh's brainchild,' said Som Pal. 'It was a Janata Party commitment he inherited.'[17] But as Prime Minister, VP promptly began taking preliminary steps towards enforcing it, including the task in his government's 'action plan' announced on 25 December 1989; setting up a committee the same month, chaired by Devi Lal, to oversee the process (their relations were then excellent);

and directing the social welfare ministry to match the Mandal report's list of OBC castes for each state with the lists already in use by many of them, to iron out anomalies.

Yet, VP knew well that he had to tread cautiously. The parties on which his government depended heavily for its slim majority—the BJP and the communists—were both lukewarm to the report's recommendations. The BJP wasn't enthused because, like the Congress, its supporters were mainly upper-caste, while the communists maintained on principle that caste was 'false consciousness' and only class differences mattered. VP knew, too, that enforcing the report's 27 per cent proposal could lead to strong protests from the castes adversely affected—at least three efforts in the past fifteen years at bringing in or expanding OBC reservations in different states, on the basis of their own commissions' suggestions, had all shown so.

In Bihar, the Mungeri Lal Commission's report, seeking 26 per cent OBC reservation in government jobs, had been ignored by the Congress government when it was submitted in mid-1976, but once the Janata Party won the June 1977 assembly elections and one of the prominent leaders of the former SSP, Karpoori Thakur,[18] became chief minister, it had been enforced within a little over a month. It had immediately sparked a violent agitation by upper-caste students, lasting over a year, in which 118 people were killed in police firings and group clashes, until Thakur, negotiating with the agitators, reduced the quota from 26 to 20 per cent, adding other categories instead, such as 3 per cent reservation for women across all castes.[19]

In Gujarat, where, unlike in north India, the Congress drew much support from some of the OBC castes, it was a Congress government that appointed a second commission on OBCs in 1981. Headed by a retired Supreme Court judge, C.V. Rane, the commission suggested increasing the OBC quota—at 5–10 per cent then at different levels of government, as recommended by an earlier commission—to 28 per cent. Implementing the suggestion sparked one of the most violent agitations in Gujarat's history across the first half of 1985, causing 275 deaths and forcing Madhavsinh Solanki, the chief minister who took the step, to resign, after which his successor withdrew the increase.[20]

So too was the case in Andhra Pradesh. In July 1986, Chief Minister N.T. Rama Rao, fearing that the Congress was making inroads into his OBC support, used the recommendations of an OBC commission's report submitted four years earlier[21] to raise the state's OBC quota from 25 to 44 per cent. Protests began immediately but were short-lived as, with the total reserved quota having surpassed 50 per cent due to the order, the Andhra Pradesh High Court struck it down.

Indeed, the upper castes had grown so restive over reservations by then that even the quotas for Scheduled Castes—which had remained unchanged since 1951—were drawing protests. There had been one such in Gujarat in January–March 1981, which had led to fifty people being killed, but the Congress government there resisted the pressure.[22] The quotas had initially been valid for forty years from 1950, according to Article 334 of the Constitution, and thus, soon after the Janata Dal came to power in December 1989, needed to be extended through a constitutional amendment. Upper-caste students in Bihar and UP demonstrated strongly, opposing any such amendment, demanding that the concession be allowed to lapse, but an unmoved VP had it passed,[23] which continued the reservations for another ten years.[24]

But there was also an important fault line running through the Janata Dal's peasant support base inherited from Charan Singh. Though the bulk of it comprised OBCs, it did not include all small and middle farmers[25] and thus not all backed the Mandal report's recommendations. In particular, the Jats—a vital part of this base who comprised around 9 per cent of the population of western UP, 20–25 per cent of Haryana and 17 per cent of Rajasthan—

were regarded as an 'intermediate caste' and had been left out of the Mandal Commission's list.

Barring some districts of Rajasthan (where indeed they were disadvantaged), Jat farmers inhabited areas where zamindari had largely been absent—and where small and mid-sized holdings (or the ryotwari system) were the norm—and had thus prospered far more than their counterparts from other north Indian peasant castes, rising socially and educationally as well.[26] They had been further empowered by the Green Revolution of the 1970s, when the introduction of high-yielding varieties of seeds increased their wheat-production manifold.[27] Thus Devi Lal, a Jat, showed little interest in the eight-member Mandal report implementation committee VP had made him chairman of,[28] his indifference even provoking another member, Ram Pujan Patel, who belonged to an OBC caste and was anxious to see the recommendations implemented, to resign in protest.[29]

―――∞∞―――

Except for the Meham issue, on which, too, he briefly wavered, VP did his best to accommodate Devi Lal. In all the positions he had held—and even as Prime Minister, when his political position was weakest—he had been reluctant to dispense patronage and had incurred the resentment of many MPs and MLAs by refusing to do them undue favours.[30] But with Devi Lal, he compromised repeatedly.

I.K. Gujral, for instance, recalled VP telephoning him while he was in Nairobi, at the height of the Meham crisis in July 1990, and suggesting that the Indian envoy in Switzerland be replaced by an acolyte of Devi Lal's. Gujral tried to defer the matter by saying he would attend to it on returning to Delhi, whereupon, a little later, his foreign secretary called saying that VP wanted the acolyte's immediate posting to 'the Seychelles, Botswana or anywhere in Africa'.[31]

But once he had dismissed Devi Lal from his cabinet on 1 August 1990, VP steadfastly refused, despite immense pressure from party leaders, to take him back. (He later said that he regretted having done so even in March.[32]) He may well have recalled the experience of Janata Party Prime Minister Morarji Desai a decade ago, who, clashing repeatedly with Charan Singh, his deputy prime minister—just as VP had done with Devi Lal—had forced him to resign in mid-1978, only to bring him back into the cabinet as finance minister in January 1979. It had not improved relations between them—instead, it had helped Charan Singh strengthen his position and finally led to him splitting the party six months later.

A major reason for Desai's rethink—apart from the pressure of Charan Singh's supporters in the party—was Charan Singh's demonstration of his popular appeal by organizing an 800,000-strong farmers' rally at Delhi's Boat Club on 23 December 1978, his seventy-seventh birthday.[33] So too did Devi Lal seek to repeat history, immediately after his expulsion, announcing a similar rally for 9 August 1990. (It was not his birthday, but the anniversary of the start of the Quit India movement.)

Many more Janata Dal MPs owed their nominations to Devi Lal than to VP. If he was unwilling to reconcile with Devi Lal, VP knew he would have to find some means of preventing them from attending the farmers' rally. Their choice would indicate where their loyalty lay and which side they would back if Devi Lal sought to split the party, as surely he soon would.

Som Pal tried hard to get Devi Lal to compromise, but without success. 'Many people, including me, tried, but Devi Lal would not budge,' he said. 'With V.P. Singh's consent, I even drafted a letter for Devi Lal to sign, which broadly said that the events of the past few days had been regrettable but they should be blanked out and everyone should come together in the interests of the party and the nation. V.P. Singh would have accepted it. Devi Lal read it and put it under a paperweight on his office table, where it stayed for days.

Every morning and evening I kept going to him, urging him to sign it, but he didn't.'[34]

But once Devi Lal had been dropped, Som Pal felt that VP's best option lay in quitting and seeking fresh elections, since his government was now doomed anyway. 'I said to him, "Until now, you were the party's tallest leader and all the others were dependent on you,"' he said. 'After this, you will be at their mercy, always having to placate them to prevent them from leaving you. Your authority will be seriously compromised. If you resign tomorrow, your integrity will remain intact. It will be seen as a great sacrifice and you will win the next election hands down.' VP nodded, but, Som Pal said, he wouldn't look him in the eye.[35]

As his crafty response to the earlier Meham crisis—when Arun Nehru and Arif Khan had resigned—had shown, VP was not willing to sacrifice his prime ministerial position as insouciantly as he had renounced his earlier jobs of UP chief minister or Union defence minister. Possibly, as when Rajiv had sought to defame him, his fighting instinct had also been aroused; he had, against his inclinations, tried earnestly to placate Devi Lal, only to face further bullying, and now wanted to hit back. Perhaps he also feared, given his modest record as Prime Minister (and especially his failure to reinforce his corruption-buster image acquired during his finance ministry years and campaign thereafter), that if he did call another election, he might well lose.

Whatever his reasons, VP decided to implement the Mandal report's recommendations instead, which he felt would make it impossible for his OBC MPs to desert him and join Devi Lal.

⟐

Three people[36] played crucial supporting roles in VP's historic decision to adopt the Mandal Commission report, sustaining him through the storm that followed. The first was Sharad Yadav, minister for textiles and food processing in his cabinet, himself an OBC Yadav by caste, who still smarted from the caste humiliation he had faced from teachers at his village school in the Hoshangabad district of Madhya Pradesh, despite his father being a grain merchant and fairly wealthy.[37]

'V.P. Singh telephoned me in the evening (of 1 August 1990) and said he was finding it difficult to work with Devi Lal,' said Sharad Yadav. 'I said, "Don't be hasty; don't ask him to resign or any such thing."' VP then revealed that he had already removed Devi Lal from the cabinet. They agreed on a breakfast meeting the next morning, at 7, Race Course Road, which lasted over three hours. 'We were both committed to the Mandal Commission report, but V.P. Singh was not too enthusiastic about implementing it immediately,' Yadav added. 'I told him, "If you want the Lok Dal [B] MPs to stay with you, you have no choice. You either bring it in or we go with Devi Lal." *Gardan pakad ke karwaya unsey* (I held him [figuratively] by the neck and got him to do it).'[38]

VP proposed announcing the decision in his Independence Day speech, due in a fortnight. Sharad Yadav suggested he do it sooner. 'I said, "That might be too late. It should be announced before Devi Lal holds his 9 August rally,"' he recalled.[39] Both of them realized that Devi Lal, for all his earlier indifference to the report, could well declare at his rally that he had been keen to enforce it but that VP had been obstructing him. Their announcing its implementation thereafter would be politically fruitless.

The second was Ram Vilas Paswan, minister for social welfare,[40] who, though a Dalit and not an OBC, was much influenced by the SSP, which he had joined in his early youth, and was thereby a strong advocate of OBC reservation. In March 1990, when VP found the Devi Lal-chaired committee inactive, he had turned to Paswan for the preparatory spadework, whose ministry, in any case, was vital to the report's implementation.

The third was P.S. Krishnan, secretary in the social welfare ministry, to whom Paswan entrusted the task. Krishnan was a

1956-batch IAS officer from the Andhra Pradesh cadre, who combined exhaustive knowledge of the legislative and judicial history related to Dalit and OBC reservations, with a marked bent in their favour. 'On taking over in January 1990, I prepared an agenda of things to get done, among which implementing the Mandal report was foremost,' he said. 'I knew, given the nature of the government, that it would not last long. So there was no time to lose.'[41]

He submitted a note on the Mandal report to the cabinet on 1 May 1990, placing it in historical and legislative perspective, pointing out that enforcing it needed no parliamentary approval but a mere executive order. Other senior bureaucrats, who had to acquiesce before it reached the cabinet, raised objections, but Krishnan rebutted all their arguments. 'Cabinet Secretary Vinod Pande told me, "We have to find a way out of the Mandal problem for V.P. Singh,"' he said. 'I said, "Problem? That's not what he told me. V.P. Singh wants to enforce Mandal."'[42]

Krishnan estimated that the note reached VP by the end of May 1990, after its passage through the law ministry. VP wrote to all the state chief ministers, seeking their opinion, in June 1990—only the chief ministers of UP and Bihar replied, both supporting its prompt enforcement[43]—but it was brought before the cabinet only on 2 August 1990, the day after he axed Devi Lal.

Barring Sharad Yadav and Paswan, most ministers were surprised. '*Pehle se koi* build-up *nahi tha, pata bhi nahi tha kisiko* (There was no previous build-up, no one knew it was coming),' said Arif Khan.[44] But with the report's implementation having been promised in the Janata Dal manifesto, no one dissented on that day either. Arif Khan, however, presciently worried about how their supporting parties—the BJP and the communists—would respond, though he realized that no party would risk opposing the decision publicly, given the size of the OBC vote bank.

At the next cabinet meeting the following day, when the report was discussed again, he maintained he was the only one to demur. 'Arun Nehru, Ajit Singh and I had met earlier and decided to raise objections together, but at the meeting I was the only one to speak up,' he said. 'I had nothing against the Mandal proposals. *Lekin maine ek imandari ki baat ki, aap ek nayi cheez karna chahte hain, hamari majority nahi hai, aap BJP aur CPM ke sahyog se sarkar chala rahein hain* (I brought up a matter of probity. You want to introduce something new. We don't have a majority. We are running the government with the support of the BJP and the CPI [M]). Why not involve them?'[45] But VP knew that since neither party favoured it, trying to convince them would lead to further delays, while 9 August 1990 loomed.

Between the two cabinet meetings, on the evening of 2 August 1990, there was also a boisterous National Front parliamentary party meeting in the Parliament Annexe, which Som Pal, having been elected to the Rajya Sabha by then, attended. The MPs were overwhelmingly supportive of introducing the Mandal recommendations; indeed, the meeting also offered evidence of VP's slipping prime ministerial authority, as some of them openly admonished him for the delay in doing so until then.

'The meeting went on for four hours, with twenty-seven MPs speaking,' said Som Pal. 'One of the MPs, an OBC belonging to Chandra Shekhar's faction, had the temerity to say sarcastically, "*Jab tak iss desh ka PM savarn hoga, Mandal Commission lagoo nahi ho sakta* (As long as the country's Prime Minister is an upper-caste individual, the Mandal Commission report will never be implemented.)" That really provoked V.P. Singh. He gave a chronology of all that had been done until then, saying, "The Mandal list of OBCs and the state lists need to be reconciled; I've put a dozen joint secretaries on the job."

"*Bahaneybaji* (Excuses)," some MPs yelled back.

V.P. Singh stood up and said, "Let's decide the date to introduce it right now."[46]

The meeting chose 7 August 1990, the day Parliament would reopen for a fresh session. On the evening of 6 August 1990, Krishnan, Paswan and VP met for a final discussion at 7, Race Course Road, where Krishnan drafted the brief speech enforcing the Mandal report that VP had to make in the Lok Sabha the next day.[47] It was only then that VP also made brief calls to top leaders of the BJP, the CPI and the CPI (M), informing them of his decision.[48] BJP President Lal Krishna Advani tried hard to dissuade him, suggesting that the subject could be discussed at length at their weekly Tuesday dinner, only two days away. 'V.P. Singh's reply was, "No I cannot wait. I have to announce it tomorrow,"' Advani recalled in his memoirs.[49]

The official notification was issued on 13 August 1990, with the government listing only those castes as OBCs that were common to the Mandal Commission's and the state governments' lists—about 1,200 of them.[50]

<hr />

More than the adoption of the Mandal report, it was the frenzied agitation against the step that made its impact memorable. Though the Central government recruited barely 100,000 people a year at the time, its total employment accounting for just 1 per cent of the country's jobs, and though state governments in twelve of the then-twenty-five states already had job quotas for OBCs, the response of the castes adversely affected was near-hysterical. Student protests began in Patna within a day of VP's Lok Sabha announcement,[51] reaching Delhi by 10 August 1990.[52] Within a fortnight they had engulfed towns in all the north Indian states and spread beyond, stretching from Chandigarh to Calcutta.

So intense and widespread was the fury evoked that sections rarely seen protesting publicly joined the students—teachers' and doctors' associations; schoolchildren in uniform (with the obvious support of the school authorities); wives of government employees (as proxies for their husbands who could not risk losing their jobs).[53] While the outrage sprang mainly from the feeling of being discriminated against, some of the slogans and actions of the protesters also gave away their caste prejudice. In Lucknow, for instance, students set up cobbler stalls and washed cars to imply that these would be the only jobs available to them once OBC reservations set in, tacitly suggesting that these were the only sort of employments OBCs were fit for.[54]

A fierce debate on the merits and demerits of quota-based affirmative action in general, and on the strengths and weaknesses of the Mandal Commission report in particular, raged in the press, but with OBCs generally lacking in education and media access, detractors of both heavily outnumbered supporters. Among the urban—and largely upper-caste—middle classes, who had once been VP's loudest supporters, his image underwent a metamorphosis; he was now reviled for starting a caste war for political gain. 'After Mandal, it was as if I was a different person,' he said later.[55]

He offered two concessions immediately—he would defer implementing the Mandal report's suggestion of reserving an equal proportion of seats in technical and professional educational institutions (as in government jobs) for OBCs; he was also prepared to reserve another 10 per cent of such jobs for the poor, regardless of caste.[56] Neither concession made any difference to the protesters, whose agitation intensified, while VP refused to budge on the job-reservation quota.

Feelings ran so high that some Janata Dal leaders were put to personal risk. Yashwant Sinha, for instance, no fan of VP but forced to defend his government's decision, accepted an invitation to address Delhi University students on the subject, only to find himself trapped by hostile students on his way to the venue.

'We came out of our car and tried to reason with them, but they were in no mood to listen,' he writes in his autobiography. 'The crowd started pushing and shoving me roughly. Someone poured black ink on my white kurta, while others tried to hit me. I felt like a hunted animal.'[57]

Even VP's school-going granddaughters, Richa and Adrija, then aged eight and six, respectively—Ajeya Singh's daughters, who studied in Calcutta and stayed with their maternal grandparents, though their parents were in the US—faced the sting of the animosity he had attracted. 'The teachers taunted us in class; the children would make up scurrilous rhymes about V.P. Singh and sing them before us in the playground,' said Richa Singh. 'Our art teacher flung my drawing book into the dustbin, saying, "You can't draw, you're about as good at it as your grandfather is at governance,"' recalled Adrija. 'In revenge, a friend and I emptied a bottle of Fevicol into her handbag when she wasn't looking.'[58]

For VP, who cared so deeply about his image, its transformation must have been galling, but he expected the much larger constituency of OBCs he had aimed at to make up for it electorally. Aware of the previous protests against OBC reservations in Bihar, Gujarat and Andhra Pradesh, he maintained he had been prepared for them. 'I had expected an even bigger reaction,' he said later. 'I expected it in the villages, but nothing happened there, except in some areas of Bihar. I'd thought caste feelings were greater in rural areas.'[59]

Thereafter 'social justice' became the dominant theme of his speeches, just as combating corruption had once been, which he linked to his implementation of the Mandal report, as in his 1990 Independence Day address. 'Bureaucracy is an important organ of the power structure,' he said. 'We wanted to give an effective share in the power structure and running of the country to the depressed, downtrodden and backward people.'[60] He justified remaining impervious to the protests. 'History has shown that any real change has come through an element of ruthlessness or it has not come at all,' he said.[61]

Curiously, the beneficiaries of his move, the OBCs, refrained from publicly demonstrating any support for him or countering the protesters—except in Bihar, where they did organize a few rallies affirming the Mandal report (one of which VP too attended, in Patna on 8 October 1990).[62] Supporters and opponents of his move clashed in several Bihar towns, engaging in gun battles in some cases.[63] But as became evident in the years that followed, the very vehemence of the protests had the effect of accelerating the politicization of the OBCs, making them a much more powerful composite pressure group in north India than they were before, giving them political clout on par with what their counterparts in the south had already achieved. (The induction of more OBCs in the bureaucracy, however—the main objective of the Mandal report's recommendations—does not seem to have made any difference to its nature or functioning.)

Politically, too, at least at first, VP's gambit seemed a success. No doubt, his closest advisers changed, with his early Jan Morcha associates—Som Pal, Santosh Bhartiya, Arun Nehru and Arif Khan—disapproving of his decision and distancing themselves from it (though Som Pal and Bhartiya claimed that their personal relations with him remained the same). Their place was taken by Sharad Yadav and Paswan.[64] But Devi Lal's farmers' rally at Delhi's Boat Club, though mammoth in size, was successfully neutralized—very few Janata Dal MPs or MLAs attended it. (VP's old enemy Chandra Shekhar did.)

In his speech, Devi Lal was forced to endorse the adoption of the very Mandal report he had been apathetic towards, while claiming his ouster from the cabinet was due to 'a conspiracy' against him that he would soon 'expose' (he never did, and in any case, was hardly believed). Similarly, despite their dependence on upper-caste support, neither the BJP nor the Congress—as VP had anticipated—risked supporting the students or opposing the Mandal report's enforcement publicly.

VP had correctly guessed that however upset the BJP—or even the communists—might be, they would not endanger his government by withdrawing support, for fear of bringing the Congress back to power if fresh elections were held once it fell. All the BJP leaders said was that they should have been consulted in advance. The Congress dithered for three weeks before issuing its official response that merely criticized the manner in which the report had been introduced—and which it blamed for the severe backlash—and not the enforcing of the report itself. On 3 September 1990, VP held a meeting of all political parties, including the ones in Opposition, and got them all to endorse his decision, Congress representatives merely adding that economic criteria should have been given greater emphasis.[65] (Indeed, the only politicians to criticize the Mandal report decision openly were some upper-caste leaders from VP's own party.[66])

With VP unbending, the agitation seemed to be shedding momentum when it was unexpectedly revived by a single incident, which set off a trend and, in turn, maimed his government irreparably. On 19 September 1990, almost six weeks after VP's initial Mandal report announcement, Rajeev Goswami, a third-year humanities student in south Delhi's Deshbandhu College, who had been on a hunger strike for days with his friends to protest the Mandal report's adoption without garnering any media attention, decided to set himself on fire to get it, summoning photographers in advance and drenching himself in kerosene outside his college.[67]

There are conflicting versions of his motives and intentions—whether he wanted to be martyred, or merely create a spectacle and douse the fire immediately afterwards (but failed to do so), or whether local workers of any political party had egged him on.[68] What is known is that though he was rushed to a hospital with 65 per cent burns and eventually survived (he died in

February 2004[69]), he became the protest's icon, with his example being regularly repeated for another four weeks.

Agitations in India, both before and after Independence, have employed many outlandish means for impact, but self-immolation had been resorted to only once earlier—when the question of whether to make Hindi the sole official language or continue with English as well arose in 1964–65. With campuses across north India agitating to get English, a colonial inheritance, abolished, some Tamil Nadu protesters—with their deep-rooted dread of Hindi being imposed on them—had countered them by setting themselves ablaze, insisting that English be retained, and the Centre had acquiesced. But they were a handful—this time, 152 young people followed Goswami's example, including some thirteen-to-fourteen-year-olds, sixty-three of them dying of their burns.[70]

VP was appalled, though he later insisted that the toll was exaggerated. 'I was prepared for the protests, not the self-immolations,' he said. 'I was very unhappy about them. But many of them were suicides unconnected to the Mandal report. Someone may have killed himself over a love affair but the family, wanting to conceal that, attributed it to the Mandal report.'[71]

He appealed plaintively to the students. 'Even to fight me, you have to live,' he said. But the attempts kept multiplying.[72] He set up a committee to negotiate with the students, which he had resisted doing until then, but the students refused to meet its members.

Yet he remained unyielding about implementing the Mandal report. By then, a number of petitions questioning the constitutional validity of the report had been filed in the Supreme Court, and Gujral, who was in New York at the time, proposed to him over the telephone that the agitation could perhaps be defused if he announced he would defer adopting the report until the court gave its verdict. Gujral later recalled in his memoirs,

The prime minister did not even respond to my suggestion (the first time). I spoke to him thrice (on a single day) ... He believed that such a step would indicate a retreat on his part and could trigger another agitation by the pro-Mandal sections. 'Once this were to happen, it would be impossible to hold any ground ... It would be better to go out of office standing for some principles rather than be pushed out losing support from both sides,' he asserted.[73]

Later, Gujral also spoke to VP's Principal Secretary Deshmukh, who said he had already 'transgressed the bureaucratic code by making earnest pleas to the cabinet, but the poor fellow (i.e. VP) is unable to act, since Sharad Yadav and Paswan are not willing to compromise'.[74] Ultimately, after refusing to do so at the first two hearings of the case on 11 and 21 September 1990, it was the Supreme Court which, on 1 October 1990, directed that the 13 August 1990 order implementing the Mandal report be 'kept in abeyance'—as its interim order put it—until it decided on the cases.[75] Even so, sporadic self-immolation attempts continued for another fortnight, each fresh death further undermining VP's reputation and authority.

The big boost the anti-Mandal report agitation got from the suicides had two other consequences. First, it rejuvenated the demonstrators, making them more aggressive and violent, while political forces opposed to VP, both within his party and without, began encouraging them more openly. The main instigators were Devi Lal and his son Chautala, still smarting from their humiliation, who used the pliant Haryana Chief Minister Hukam Singh—chosen by Chautala, after he was forced to quit a second time—to encourage protests in Haryana, as well as send members of their infamous Green Brigade to participate in the Delhi demonstrations and provoke the police.[76] Between mid- and end September, agitators burnt so many Delhi Transport Corporation buses that the service was withdrawn for a few days.

A heavily attended rally of reservation opponents at Delhi's Boat Club on 2 October—ironically Mahatma Gandhi's birthday—despite the Supreme Court having already stayed the Mandal report's implementation the previous day, turned particularly destructive, with participants smashing windscreens and windows of nearby vehicles and firing at the police. The police naturally retaliated, with three demonstrators being killed.[77] At the end of September 1990, VP sent the Haryana government an official warning, saying it would be dismissed and President's Rule imposed in the state unless it reigned in its goons.[78]

But the police were also excessively brutal with the protesters at times, especially during an attempt by the latter on 24 August 1990 to besiege Parliament House. On another occasion, they needlessly thrashed a group of women demonstrators.[79] VP appealed to the police to remain as restrained as possible, but it was yet another sign of his diminishing control that, with Home Minister Mufti Sayeed strangely quiescent during the crisis,[80] his deputy, Subodh Kant Sahay, a Chandra Shekhar supporter then,[81] told VP off, saying he preferred 'strict action'.[82] Gujral noted that by the time he returned to India on 3 October 1990, 'the internal situation had moved into the orbit of helplessness'.[83] Santosh Bhartiya confirmed that though the National Front's parliamentary majority was still intact, the government was wobbling by then. 'Its cohesiveness had been destroyed,' he said. 'All the ministers felt they knew better than the Prime Minister.'[84]

Secondly, VP's old foe, Chandra Shekhar, quiet for some time until then, now saw an opportunity in his discomfiture—a chance to bid for the Prime Minister's position again—and set his men, led by Yashwant Sinha, to challenge VP's leadership of the Janata Dal. Sinha, reviving a hoary tradition in Indian politics, began holding 'dissident dinners' to assess their strength—which, ominously for VP, kept increasing with each successive dinner. At the next National Front parliamentary party meeting on

30 September 1990, Sinha sought to move a no-confidence motion against VP for 'his all-round failure in running the government'. But VP's supporters, citing constitutional provisions, prevented him from doing so, whereupon Sinha and his supporters stormed out, while the meeting expressed 'full faith' in VP.[85] (Chandra Shekhar did not attend at all.)

Following the meeting, Sinha and Chandra Shekhar—who had also, by then, teamed up with Devi Lal—decided that if VP could not be removed from his position, they would rather split the party. Their hopes of doing so, and thereby making Chandra Shekhar Prime Minister, were raised by Rajiv Gandhi, who, archly observing in a tabloid interview that VP had proven his own prediction correct—that he would be a disaster as Prime Minister—added that the Congress would favourably consider supporting a Janata Dal government under a new leader.[86] The anti-defection law specified that party splitters needed at least a third of the party's Lok Sabha MPs to join them to be recognized separately—thus Sinha knew he required a minimum of forty-seven of the Janata Dal's 140 Lok Sabha MPs (the number had fallen slightly from the 143 elected for different reasons) to back him.

'We identified the MPs who were likely to come over to our side and assigned hardcore Chandra Shekhar supporters the task of approaching each of them personally,' writes Sinha in his autobiography. 'At one point, I thought we had reached the magic figure. However, at the last moment, some of the MPs deserted us ...'[87] The letter he drafted, criticizing VP strongly, had twenty-two MPs signing it (and another seven from the Rajya Sabha), though a few later dissociated themselves from it. Since their number was well short of the one-third of MPs needed for a split, VP promptly hit back by getting Bommai to expel them all from the Janata Dal, which cost them their Lok Sabha memberships too, enabling VP—still supported by the BJP and the communists—to hold on to his slender majority.

The much-awaited Supreme Court judgment, after amalgamating all the petitions filed against the Mandal report's adoption into one—the case of *Indra Sawhney, etc. versus the Union of India and Others*—came two years later, on 16 November 1992. It found the adoption perfectly valid constitutionally, adding only one caveat—that OBCs with family incomes above a specified threshold (a section it called the 'creamy layer') should be excluded from reservations. It left it to the government to decide the threshold, which was initially set at Rs 100,000 per annum and is presently Rs 800,000.

The caveat was also based on judicial precedent—the V.K. Vishwanathan Commission set up by the Kerala government way back in 1961, in its report, which the state adopted, had recommended such a 'means test'. When it was challenged, in the case of *K.S. Jayashree versus the State of Kerala*, the Kerala High Court had dismissed the appeal and upheld the means test. The judgment also directed the Centre and the states to set up separate and permanent Backward Classes Commissions to guide them in all OBC-related matters henceforth.

On that evening of 16 November 1992, VP telephoned Krishnan. 'If I die now, I'll die a satisfied man,' he said.

'There was sincerity in the man, which is not very common in politicians,' Krishnan observed.[88]

The relevant government order was issued on 10 September 1993, with the first IAS aspirants under the new quota being inducted in 1995.

2

'I WAS NOT CLINGING
TO POWER'

BJP President Lal Krishna Advani[1] had publicly welcomed the V.P. Singh government's decision to adopt the Mandal report. But within the party, there was much disquiet over his announcement. Even more than the Congress, which, besides the upper castes, had the bulk of Dalit and Muslim voters behind it too, the BJP—until the 1989 Lok Sabha election—had depended solely on the upper castes, especially the Vaishyas of north India, for its support. (It had little following elsewhere in the country then.) Many in the party now feared that by propping up a government that had so enraged the upper castes as VP's had, the BJP was destroying its own electoral base, which would shift to the Congress in the next election, since the Congress was at least the Janata Dal's political opponent.

But the BJP could not afford to stop backing the Janata Dal government citing the Mandal report decision as reason, since its avowed objective was to unite all castes—including the Mandal report's beneficiaries, the OBCs—behind its key tenet of Hindu nationalism. In the 1989 election, thanks to its seat-sharing arrangements with the Janata Dal, it had drawn a fair share of

OBC votes for the first time, which it naturally wanted to retain. Advani needed some other conflict with the Janata Dal to set his party apart and justify, if necessary, withdrawing support to the government, one which would also highlight the BJP's distinct nature as a champion of Hindus.

Emphasizing the BJP's position on the Ayodhya Ram temple controversy was the obvious choice. At its Palampur national executive meeting in mid-1989, the party had already endorsed the VHP's resolve to build a new Ram temple at the disputed spot in Ayodhya (See Part 5, Chapter 3) without waiting for the court verdict on the site's ownership. It had constantly harped on the issue during its November 1989 election campaign, winning many votes for doing so. But once V.P. Singh formed his government, the BJP had hardly ever mentioned the subject in discussions between them, seeking to downplay differences with the Janata Dal. 'Whenever I spoke to the BJP leaders about Ayodhya, hoping to get them to rein in the VHP, they would say, "That's on the VHP's agenda. You settle it with them,"' said VP. 'They didn't help me at all.'[2]

Despite the succession of crises he had to cope with as Prime Minister, which took up most of his time and energy, VP had been trying his best to resolve the Ayodhya dispute as well. At a two-day meeting it held on the banks of the Sangam in Allahabad, during the annual Magh Mela event in late January 1990, the VHP announced that it would start building the Ram temple from 14 February 1990. VP met its leaders on 8 February 1990 and persuaded them to postpone their plan by four months, the most they were willing to concede, during which he promised to try and overcome their legal hurdle.

Helped by the then Karnataka governor Krishan Kant,[3] he sought out Hindu religious leaders, including the Shankaracharya of Kanchi; with similar assistance from the then Bihar governor Yunus Saleem,[4] he drew in their Muslim counterparts and arranged meetings between the two groups. He hoped they would evolve a consensus that would lead to the cases filed over the disputed spot being withdrawn. 'I hoped the dialogue would bring about a mutually acceptable solution, but it did not,' he said. 'The main obstacle was the attitude of the VHP. The gist of what its leaders kept saying to me was, "You solve the problem. We'll not compromise an iota, we'll not wait for the court's verdict or abide by it if it goes against us, but you please solve the problem."'[5]

In mid-June 1990, with the matter still unresolved, the VHP gave him a further four and a half months, setting the date for the start of its kar seva—as its temple-building programme was called—for 30 October 1990. 'It used the time to make better preparations for the kar seva,' said VP.[6] From its start in 1984, the VHP's Ram-temple-building campaign had been steadily fuelling Hindu–Muslim hostility. The announcement of a firm date for the start of construction, which the VHP leaders insisted they would not postpone on any account, exacerbated it.

It was against this backdrop that Advani decided to make the BJP's first direct intervention in the VHP's campaign by embarking on a 10,000-km-long circuitous journey across west, central and north India to garner support for the kar seva. 'A voice inside me said, "Do it,"' he writes in his memoirs, never once mentioning the Mandal report in this context.[7] 'It would give me an opportunity to meet people, including villagers, and explain to them the significance of the Ayodhya movement.'[8] But the timing made the connection apparent—he announced his decision, knowing well it would lead the BJP to openly clash with the Janata Dal, at a press conference on 11 September 1990, about five weeks after VP's Mandal report bombshell.

If Advani had any doubts that continuing support to the Janata Dal government was damaging the BJP, they were quelled on 20 September 1990, the day after Rajeev Goswami's self-immolation bid, when he tried to visit Goswami in hospital to express sympathy and concern. Goswami's supporters, who had blocked the road leading to the hospital, insisted that he denounce the Mandal report before he was allowed in. When he baulked at doing so, as he had openly supported it before, he was physically attacked. While the agile Advani, running hard, managed to get away, his companion, the somewhat portly Madan Lal Khurana,[9] could not, was manhandled and had his clothes torn.[10]

Advani had originally intended a shorter journey on foot—a walkathon, or padyatra—but was persuaded by his colleague Pramod Mahajan[11] that motorized travel would enable him to cover much more ground and thus address many more people. It was Mahajan (who also travelled with Advani) who suggested commencing a rath yatra (chariot journey) instead (using a van with its exterior remodelled to resemble a chariot), which would invoke public memory of ancient times and the Ramayana.

The rath yatra had been popularized by N.T. Rama Rao in 1982, when he entered politics and used a chaitanya ratham (chariot of awakening), as he called it, for his travels during his election campaign in Andhra Pradesh. But while the chaitanya ratham was simply a Chevrolet van fitted with loudspeakers and a hatch in the roof, with a device enabling NTR to climb on top to address gatherings, and eschewed any religious motifs, Advani's Toyota rath stressed the latter. 'My initial reaction to the idea was that it was too theatrical as I felt it did not suit my temperament,' writes Advani.[12] But he soon concurred.

The rath set off on 25 September 1990—the birth anniversary of one of the Jana Sangh's ideologues, Deendayal Upadhyaya—from Somnath on the Gujarat coast, taking a diversionary route through half a dozen states, intending to reach Ayodhya on 30 October 1990, the day the kar seva was to begin. The significance of starting from Somnath was unmistakeable—it was the site of the Somnath temple, of immense significance to Hindus as the spot where one of the twelve jyotirlingas of Shiva was located. The ancient temple there had been pillaged and destroyed by the medieval invader Mahmud of Ghazni, who attacked India seventeen times between 1001 and 1025, but a new one had been built after Independence by the Indian government. Its similarities with the proposed Ram temple in Ayodhya were obvious. But there were important differences too—no mosque had ever stood on the remains of this broken temple as at Ayodhya, nor had the spot where the temple was rebuilt been under litigation.

Advani himself was surprised by the rapturous reception he got from the start. 'I was truly overwhelmed,' he writes. 'In villages, towns and even along roads, people from nearby hamlets would gather under trees eagerly waiting for the rath to arrive. The response reached a crescendo in the bigger towns and cities, where it would take hours for us to reach the venue of our meetings.'[13] But the larger the crowds he got, the more insecure Muslims grew and the more belligerent their leaders and the political parties supporting them. Many pointed out that Advani's exhortations to Hindus to participate in building the Ram temple amounted to inciting them to break the law, for which he deserved to be arrested.

UP Chief Minister Mulayam Singh Yadav, in particular, who, unlike VP at the Centre, enjoyed a near-majority on his own and did not need the BJP's support to keep his government in power, realized he would be politically unassailable if he could consolidate the Muslim vote, adding it to the OBC support he already enjoyed, thanks to his Yadav lineage and the Centre's decision to implement the Mandal report. He began holding sadbhavana (harmony) rallies across his state, stressing the importance of goodwill between Hindus and Muslims, and vowing he would never allow either the kar seva to be held in Ayodhya or Advani to get anywhere near it, ensuring he would be jailed the moment he set foot in UP. At the same time, the VHP began organizing Ram Jyoti yatras (processions of people carrying lighted torches, akin to its

Ram Shila Pujan yatras a year earlier) countrywide in support of building the Ram temple, often deliberately routing them through Muslim-dominated areas.[14]

With the rising Hindu–Muslim standoff, and the fresh provocations of Advani and the Ram Jyoti yatras, communal riots were inevitable and duly occurred—at Karnailganj (in Gonda district of UP), in Hyderabad and across several districts of Karnataka. VP was in a quandary, knowing that if he got Advani arrested or detained, the BJP would immediately withdraw support, bringing down his government. At the same time, the VHP could not be allowed to mock the court order expressly seeking status quo at the disputed spot. Failing to stop the VHP would be politically damaging too, losing him most of his Muslim support at a time when, given how unstable his government had grown, fresh Lok Sabha elections seemed inevitable.

The only way out lay in getting the VHP to defer or abandon its kar seva, whereby Advani, too, would naturally give up his rath yatra midway. Reports of the crowds besieging Advani growing larger as the yatra progressed were reaching him daily. Indeed, following the euphoria witnessed in Gujarat, which the yatra toured for its first four days, Mahajan had warned Advani not to expect the same in the next state, Maharashtra. 'Pramod (Mahajan) was wrong, totally wrong,' writes Advani. 'The response was as big, even bigger in Maharashtra as well as in all the subsequent states we travelled through.'[15]

Having failed with the VHP and the BJP, VP decided, as a last-ditch measure, to turn to their parent organization, the RSS. Having had little to do with the RSS in his political career, however, he knew no one there he could trust—save one person, Swaminathan Gurumurthy, a long-time member of the RSS, with whom he had worked closely during his finance ministry stint to try and nail Reliance Industries. On 15 October 1990, VP requested him to fly down to Delhi from Chennai, where he lived; on that day and the next, VP held long discussions with him.[16]

It so happened that by then, Advani was in Delhi too. Diwali that year fell on 16 October, and Advani had worked a four-day Diwali break from his yatra into his itinerary, arriving in the capital on the evening of 14 October 1990—to another rapturous reception—having travelled, after Maharashtra, through Andhra Pradesh (the part that is now Telangana), Madhya Pradesh, Rajasthan and Haryana. He would resume the yatra from Dhanbad on 20 October 1990, travelling there by train, with the rath having already been transported beforehand.

Gurumurthy, after conferring with RSS and BJP leaders, informed VP that while they were unwilling to postpone the start of the kar seva beyond 30 October 1990, they were ready to perform just a 'symbolic' kar seva that day, conducting a puja and laying a few bricks without actually starting construction, and stopping thereafter, holding the ceremony at a spot close to the disputed structure while leaving the structure untouched. But that, too, amounted to flouting the court-ordered status quo. To get over this impediment, the RSS had proposed a three-point formula—first, that the government use the Land Acquisition Act 1894, which gave it blanket powers to acquire any land it chose for a 'public purpose', to take over the disputed site and its surroundings; next, that it hand over the surroundings to the VHP while holding on to the disputed site, so that any kar seva there would be legally sound; and finally, that it ask the Supreme Court to determine if indeed a temple had been razed to build the mosque in 1528.[17]

The formula was not really a solution to the dispute, since it skirted its most vital aspect—the structure, though built as a three-domed mosque, had been functioning as a temple since December 1949, when the idols of Ram and Sita were smuggled into it and installed right under its central dome. The VHP had always insisted that Ram's birthplace was the precise spot where the idols had been placed and that the new temple it would build would have to encompass it, with the idols remaining in the same spot. It would never agree to merely building a Ram temple in the vicinity of the disputed structure and shifting the idols there.

In his NMML interview, VP maintained, however, that an informal proposal to resolve even this core issue had been mooted, though it was never stated officially. 'It was suggested that the Muslims retain the portion of land under one of the domes, ceding the rest, including the area under the central dome, to the Hindus,' he said. 'A temple and a mosque could both be built cheek-by-jowl with their entrances from different directions.'[18]

Many marathon meetings followed over the next four days between government representatives, the RSS, the BJP, the VHP and various Hindu and Muslim leaders, with intermediaries rushing back and forth, but they all came to nothing. On the telephone, VP urged Advani to delay his Delhi departure to resume his rath yatra by a day so that the formula could be finalized. Advani, who was to leave on the evening of 18 October 1990, agreed.[19] (He'd intended to spend a day in Calcutta before resuming his yatra from Dhanbad on 20 October, but cancelled the visit.) On the morning of 19 October 1990, as agreed earlier, VP duly brought an ordinance before the cabinet, seeking to take over 70 acres of land in Ayodhya, with the disputed structure at its centre, explaining to his ministers the formula evolved. Arif Khan was sceptical. 'Muslims will never agree to this,' he said.

'They have already agreed,' VP replied.[20]

Arif Khan was proved right, though he himself maintained that the Muslim leaders had indeed acquiesced at one stage but later changed their minds. 'They had all come to Delhi from different parts of the country to accept the proposal and checked into hotels, which the government had arranged for them,' he said. 'I heard from an extremely reliable source that they were incentivized to take a different position at their meeting with V.P. Singh.

Who persuaded them? Forces that didn't want a solution to the dispute, is all I can say.'[21]

VP was shocked at the volte-face. 'I had taken Syed Shahabuddin [the most vocal of the Muslim representatives—see also Part 5, Chapter 2], into confidence myself, and he was willing, but at my meeting with the Babri Masjid Action Committee leaders, they all opposed the idea vehemently,' he said later.[22] Along with the Muslims, UP Chief Minister Mulayam Singh Yadav too—whom VP had not consulted in advance—furiously objected to the plan when he was informed, claiming it was a sell-out to the VHP and that his government would not let it take possession of the area around the disputed structure.[23]

The same day, 19 October 1990, NTR, who had also arrived in Delhi to help resolve the crisis—he was no longer Andhra Pradesh chief minister, having lost the 1989 assembly elections, but remained National Front chairman—met Advani at his home and pleaded with him to give up his yatra entirely. When Advani refused, he staged a sit-in outside Advani's house until cardiac complications forced him to be hospitalized. VP, too, telephoned, requesting Advani to stay put in Delhi for another day—this time to no avail. In his memoirs, I.K. Gujral quotes George Fernandes telling him that Advani, too, had rejected the three-point formula, saying 'Mujhe aapki neeyat par shaq hai (I don't trust your intentions),' and resumed his yatra, but in his own memoirs Advani claims that he had welcomed the formula but that there was never any question of stopping his yatra.[24] He left for Dhanbad in the evening by the Rajdhani Express.

The ordinance was duly issued, but after the adverse responses, VP began reconsidering it within hours. It was apparent that if he transferred the Babri Masjid's surroundings to the VHP, as he had earlier agreed to, doing so against the wishes of both the Muslim leaders and Mulayam, his own Muslim support would ebb drastically. Besides, neither of his original objectives had

been achieved—the VHP had not agreed to stop its kar seva, nor
Advani his yatra. Indeed, though the VHP had agreed, following
RSS pressure, to holding a symbolic kar seva, it had been largely
indifferent to the formula, insisting that what it really wanted was
the disputed structure—which it would demolish to build a proper
temple—and that the kar seva date was inviolable.

VP had summoned Gurumurthy, who had returned to Chennai,
to Delhi again on 19 October 1990, but when Gurumurthy, soon
after his arrival, spoke to him on telephone, VP's tone was markedly
different from before. 'He said that not just the disputed structure,
but all the land taken over would remain with the government
and would not be handed over to the Ayodhya movement,' said
Gurumurthy.[25]

By the morning of 21 October 1990, VP had decided that
there was no point to the government keeping the land either, and
called another cabinet meeting to get its consent to take back his
own ordinance. 'I thought, "What is the point of the ordinance if
neither Hindus nor Muslims are happy about it, when it has not
built confidence on either side?"' he said later. 'So I withdrew it.
That raised a lot of controversy.'[26]

At the meeting, Arif Khan reminded him of his earlier warning.
'V.P. Singh didn't reply,' said Arif Khan. 'He rarely replied to
inconvenient questions.'[27]

With negotiations failing, VP knew he had to enforce the
law, whatever its consequences for his government—he had to
forcibly stop both the kar seva and Advani's yatra. Already, on the
evening of 19 October 1990, immediately after Advani left Delhi,
Mulayam had telephoned to say he was set to halt the *Rajdhani
Express* at Rura, 55 km short of Kanpur, which it would reach
around 8.30–9 p.m., and detain Advani forthwith, but VP, still
mulling his alternatives, had dissuaded him.[28] Advani duly arrived
in Dhanbad the next morning (it was still part of Bihar then, with

Jharkhand state yet to be carved out) and restarted his yatra, once again attracting a huge crowd of raucous supporters.

Bihar Chief Minister Lalu Prasad Yadav,[29] as keen as his UP counterpart Mulayam to forge a winning electoral combination of OBCs and Muslims, claimed later that he'd wanted to arrest Advani immediately but that the Dhanbad district authorities hesitated, fearing the crowd's reaction, and allowed the yatra to leave the city.[30]

In his autobiography, Lalu claims that he telephoned VP twice, seeking his consent to detain Advani, but receiving no reply, later went ahead anyway.[31] In his NMML interview (given more than a decade before Lalu wrote his autobiography), VP maintained that he first asked Lalu to make all preparations for Advani's detention, without actually taking the step, and then called him again the next day (22 October 1990) directing him to go ahead, advising only that the arrest be executed after 2 a.m. (In that pre-internet age, with TV state-controlled, VP hoped thus to prevent news of the arrest from appearing in the morning's newspapers, since all newspapers would have closed their editions by then. This would give state governments enough time to make security arrangements to meet possible protests before RSS/BJP/VHP supporters got to know and reacted.)[32]

Lalu followed his counsel, with the desired results. Soon after 2 a.m. on 23 October 1990, the Bihar police stopped Advani as his yatra was approaching Samastipur town, taking him away immediately by helicopter to a guesthouse on the Bihar–Bengal border. Street protests, which began only in the late afternoon, were not as large as VP had feared and were quickly contained. But the BJP had already decided, at a meeting of its national executive in Delhi on 17 October 1990—which Advani had attended—to withdraw support to the V.P. Singh government if Advani was arrested, and promptly did so in the evening.

VP said later that he had wanted to resign immediately thereafter, but other party leaders insisted he do so only after losing his vote of confidence in the Lok Sabha, which would give him a chance to underscore during the debate on the vote that he was sacrificing his position to uphold OBC and minority interests. 'It was a matter of tactics decided by the party,' he said. 'I was not clinging to power.'[33] But Som Pal maintained that VP had also hoped that his having implemented the Mandal report would lead to OBCs from across parties supporting his government, enabling it to survive. 'Sharad Yadav and Paswan had somehow convinced V.P. Singh that Mandal was such a potent issue that it would split Parliament in two,' he said. 'OBC MPs from the Congress would defect and support him. I had registered my doubts. I told him, *"Aap Congress mein rahein hain. Congress ke aadmi ko muddon se kuch lena dena nahi hai* (You've been in the Congress. Congressmen have no concern for issues or principles). They are brute power brokers. *Koi aapke saath aane wala nahin hai* (None of them will join you)."'[34]

Indeed, what occurred was the opposite of what VP had expected—with his government doomed, and Rajiv Gandhi offering Congress backing to any Janata Dal ministry without VP in it, his own party MPs began deserting him to support Yashwant Sinha and his dissidents, who were rooting for Chandra Shekhar as Prime Minister. Even his old Jan Morcha colleague V.C. Shukla shifted allegiance, as did his nephew-in-law Sanjay Singh; contrary to Sharad Yadav's prediction, some OBC Janata Dal MPs, too, allowed their old loyalty to Chandra Shekhar and various inducements on offer to override their gratitude to VP for implementing the Mandal report. There was much talk at the time of MPs being bribed, of deals being sealed in a Delhi five-star hotel, with certain businessmen who still feared and hated VP for his raid raj helping out, though Yashwant Sinha in his memoirs denied it. 'While we did promise ministerships in our government to some of the MPs, in case it was formed, there was never any monetary exchange for a change of loyalty,' he wrote.[35]

Whatever the truth, eventually, fifty-eight MPs—crossing the all-important one-third mark of 47 out of 140—broke away from the Janata Dal to form the Janata Dal (Samajwadi), later renamed the Samajwadi Janata Party (SJP), on 5 November 1990. Five days later, on 10 November 1990—after the no-confidence vote had been held on 7 November and VP's government predictably voted out—Chandra Shekhar was sworn in as the new Prime Minister. His own party—with sixty-three MPs by then—was still minuscule, but with the 197-MP Congress and some regional parties providing outside support, he managed a slender majority. Devi Lal, having teamed up with Chandra Shekhar, returned as deputy prime minister in the new government. Yashwant Sinha became finance minister, V.C. Shukla got external affairs and Sanjay Singh communications.

With the BJP further withdrawing its support to the Janata Dal's state governments, and the state units splitting between VP loyalists and Chandra Shekhar supporters, these governments lost their majorities as well. But unlike VP's government, they survived the upheaval. In Bihar, Chief Minister Lalu Prasad Yadav stuck by VP, putting together a shaky majority with the help of the two communist parties and some smaller ones. But in Haryana, Gujarat and UP, the chief ministers transferred their loyalties to Chandra Shekhar, thereby comfortably surviving, since the state Congress legislature parties backed them in return.

While Haryana's shift was anticipated (with Devi Lal in the new cabinet) and Gujarat's near-inevitable (the government had been heavily dependent on the BJP), UP Chief Minister Mulayam Singh Yadav's decision was not. He neither needed the BJP's support, nor had his party initially split, but he seemed to allow his personal animus towards VP to cloud his political judgement. (His most recent grouse was not having been permitted to arrest Advani, which had enabled Lalu to corner all the plaudits for doing so from those opposed to the BJP–VHP's Ayodhya campaign.) Once he chose Chandra Shekhar, however, nearly half his MLAs broke away, preferring to stay with VP.

Mulayam's efforts to prevent the 30 October 1990 kar seva also proved a fiasco. He imposed a curfew in Ayodhya, closed all its entry points, stopped all trains and buses from travelling there and arrested over 100,000 prospective kar seva participants (or kar sevaks) from different parts of UP before they could reach the town. On 29 October 1990, all of Ayodhya's streets were being heavily patrolled but were otherwise deserted. Yet, on the morning of 30 October 1990, thousands of kar sevaks, who had still somehow managed to enter the town—they are believed to have been surreptitiously helped by sections of the police, which, predominantly Hindu, succumbed to their religious bias—storm its streets and subsequently the disputed structure complex, climbing on top of the domes and damaging them, scorning the legal status quo. Having failed to stop them with tear gas and lathi blows (there were suggestions in the press at the time that given their divided sympathies, they did not try hard enough), the police, losing control, eventually fired at them, killing half a dozen but getting them off the domes.

On 2 November 1990, the savage drama was repeated with the kar sevaks making a second attempt, once again breaking police barriers with ease and mounting the Babri Masjid domes, once again inviting police firing, which killed another half a dozen of them, after which the VHP temporarily called off its programme. The firing and resultant deaths enraged Hindus, leading to a rash of Hindu–Muslim riots across UP and Gujarat, with a body count far higher than in those earlier in the year, but also enhancing the BJP's popularity and the Janata Dal's corresponding notoriety among Hindus.[36]

Advani was soon released and allowed by the new Chandra Shekhar government to drive his rath triumphantly into Ayodhya on 19 November 1990. As the VHP launched yet another round of processions, this time with urns carrying the ashes of those killed in Ayodhya's police firings on 30 October and 2 November 1990, more riots followed across the country, including a particularly vicious one in Hyderabad, which killed more than 200 people.

Part 8

THE LONG GOODBYE

1

'I'M LIKE A ROCKET THAT BURNS AWAY AFTER PUTTING THE SATELLITE INTO ORBIT'

If V.P. Singh's political rise was rapid—from MLA-aspirant to Prime Minister in a little over twenty years—his decline was even more so.

Chandra Shekhar's government was not expected to last, and it didn't. Rajiv Gandhi beguiled Chandra Shekhar much the way his mother had done Charan Singh in 1979—withdrawing the Congress's support within four months on a specious plea, which forced Chandra Shekhar to resign on 6 March 1991. Rajiv had soon begun chafing at the oddity of his party of 197 Lok Sabha MPs enabling Chandra Shekhar's sixty-three-MP SJP to rule the country, and decided to try and lure some of those sixty-three MPs to the Congress, so as to get a majority on his own and form the government. While he was at it, two Haryana policemen in plainclothes were caught keeping unauthorized watch on his home to see which MPs visited him. Rajiv considered it outrage enough to break the alliance. President R. Venkataraman, realizing that no further combination of parties could achieve a majority, dissolved

Parliament, leading to fresh Lok Sabha elections being scheduled for the third week of May 1991 in three phases.

With the announcement of elections came VP's biggest triumph—his rivals adopted his agenda. Both the Congress and the BJP decided that they, too, needed to woo the OBCs, and promised, in their manifestos, to adopt the Mandal report's recommendations if they formed the government. (And, indeed, the 27 per cent OBC quota was implemented promptly by the Congress government [which was in power by then], once the Supreme Court upheld its constitutional validity in November 1992.) But this also weakened VP to an extent, as with a political consensus on the report having been achieved, the issue lost much of its vote-drawing potential for his party.

Indeed, an opinion poll at the time indicated that the upper caste swing away from the Janata Dal— holding it responsible for exhuming the near-buried Mandal report in the first place—would be more than four times the OBC swing in its favour for adopting it.[1] Even so, with his National Front alliance—with the TDP, the DMK and the AGP—still intact, as also his electoral understanding with the Left parties—and the fact that his meetings, as he toured the country extensively, were sizeably attended—VP hoped to do well. 'There was much appreciation everywhere of what my government had achieved in its short span,' he said later.[2]

No doubt the falling out with the BJP would hurt the Janata Dal's electoral prospects, as also the Chandra Shekhar split. In the November 1989 election, VP had bested the Congress essentially by collating all the votes against it and thus ensuring direct contests across the majority of Lok Sabha seats; this time the contests would be four-cornered, giving the Congress a big advantage. The SJP's breaking away was also bound to divide the core vote bank of the Janata Dal—OBCs and Muslims—especially in UP, where Mulayam Singh Yadav's pugnacious support for the Mandal report and opposition to the Ayodhya kar seva had won him a substantial, individual following among these two groups. Hindu annoyance—across castes—at the Janata Dal's insistence on enforcing the law in Ayodhya was also expected to cost it votes.

But as it happened, the biggest factor that went against the National Front–Left Front combine and led to the Congress winning the election was Rajiv's shocking assassination while on the campaign trail. On 21 May 1991, at Sriperumbudur in Tamil Nadu, a day after the first phase of polling for 190 constituencies had already been held, he was blown up by a female LTTE suicide bomber, who, strapped with explosives, came close to him, ostensibly to greet him, and detonated the bombs.

It led to a flood of sympathy for the Congress, and though this was less intensely manifested than in the December 1984 election following Indira Gandhi's killing, it was enough to enable the party to perform much better in the second and third rounds of polling—postponed by two weeks to mid-June following the assassination[3]—winning 232 of 521 seats overall (no elections were held in the troubled states of Punjab and Jammu and Kashmir).[4] The Congress still fell 30 seats short of a majority, but being way ahead of the National Front–Left Front combine, which got 129 seats, and the BJP, which had 120, it formed the next government.

VP, contesting for a second time from Fatehpur, won easily, polling more votes than all his opponents together, achieving a victory margin slightly higher than in November 1989. 'Due to Mandal, the Brahmins of Fatehpur had abandoned us completely, while the Thakurs cursed us but still voted for my father,' said Ajeya Singh, who, as in 1989, took a break from his career to help out in the constituency while VP was mostly absent, campaigning in the rest of the country. 'But the OBCs blindly supported us. There is a large population of Kurmis in Fatehpur, and their leaders essentially told me, "Don't waste your time campaigning, your dad will win by more than 200,000 votes."'[5] His most vivid memory of the election was the May heat. 'In Fatehpur, the temperature often crossed 50 degree Celsius,' he said. 'I was drinking three buckets of water a day and yet hardly ever peed. Even back in my room at night, I dared not switch on the AC for fear that the great difference of temperature within and without would make me ill.'[6]

But many among VP's close associates were defeated, including Sharad Yadav from UP's Badaun seat. After Chandra Shekhar's break with it, the Janata Dal's Lok Sabha tally had shrunk from 140 seats to 76; it now fell further to 59. (Of the remaining seats in the National Front–Left Front count, it was the latter that contributed fifty-six, about the same as in 1989; for a second time, the regional parties in the National Front—the TDP, the DMK and the AGP—fared poorly.)

Unlike in most of the country, however, in UP, Rajiv's killing made little difference to the vote. It was the Ayodhya row that provoked the electorate, raising the BJP's tally from 8 seats in 1989—and that too after seat adjustments with the Janata Dal—to 52 of the 85 seats. (The Congress got just 5 seats; the Janata Dal 22.)[7] Following the SJP–Congress break-up, the latter withdrew support to the SJP state governments in Haryana and UP too, leading to assembly polls in both states. While the Congress won Haryana, crushing the SJP, the BJP got a clear majority in UP in the assembly election—221 of the 425 seats—and for the first time, set up its government in the state.

The Janata Dal's electoral performance, while disappointing, was by no means deplorable (unlike that of Chandra Shekhar's SJP, which, contesting 349 Lok Sabha seats, won only 5; while Chandra Shekhar retained his seat, even as Devi Lal lost his). But the internecine quarrels and power struggles that had been part of the party from the time it had been launched increased after the defeat, with more and more leaders eventually either leaving or being expelled.

Even before the May–June 1991 general election, following the Ayodhya flare-up, Arun Nehru had argued for lowered hostility towards the Congress, the party's principal opponent until then, so as to more effectively check the 'communal forces'—as the BJP was increasingly called—from growing stronger, but most others in the Janata Dal opposed him. So too did Arif Khan begin to publicly criticize VP's deference to Muslim leaders he considered regressive and fundamentalist. Arun Nehru and Arif Khan were both expelled in April 1991.[8] After the general election, Ajit Singh took the same stance as Arun Nehru earlier, going on to even challenge VP's leadership, which led to him being expelled as well, along with his followers, in January 1992.

Over the next decade, the Janata Dal did have a few unexpected successes. It won the next assembly elections in Karnataka and Bihar, in December 1994 and April 1995, respectively, and, the biggest triumph of all, performed well enough in the April–May 1996 Lok Sabha election to form, through an unlikely alliance, the government at the Centre. But its long-range trend remained towards contraction, not expansion. It shrank and shrank and ultimately dwindled to nothing, as most of its leaders, following some difference or other with the rest, departed to set up their own outfits. George Fernandes launched his Samata Party, which soon allied with the BJP; Ajit Singh, after a stint in the Congress, set up the Rashtriya Lok Dal; Sharad Yadav began the Janata Dal (United); Ram Vilas Paswan the Lok Janashakti Party; Lalu Prasad Yadav the Rashtriya Janata Dal; Mufti Sayeed the Progressive Democratic Party; and Ramakrishna Hegde the Lok Shakti Party. At first, VP, playing neutral referee most of the time, tried hard to stop the exodus, but soon his deteriorating health forced him to give up.

—◆◆◆—

Resisting the Ayodhya Ram temple movement and its fallout cost VP not only his prime ministerial position but also, to an extent, his life. The apogee of the movement was reached on

6 December 1992, when the VHP organized yet another kar seva at the disputed spot. This time, however, it was not Mulayam running the state but a BJP government, and its response was the opposite of Mulayam's—far from thwarting the kar sevaks, it facilitated their travel to Ayodhya.

Both the Centre and the Supreme Court, worried over the kar sevak influx, warned the state government that whatever the BJP's stance on the Ayodhya controversy, it was bound as a government to uphold the law—to ensure that the status quo at the disputed spot continued, and allow, at worst, another symbolic kar seva. The BJP's UP chief minister, Kalyan Singh—an OBC from the Lodh caste, who owed his job largely to VP's Mandal report adoption, as the BJP felt it needed to overly promote the few OBCs within its ranks or else lose this section's votes entirely—assured them he would obey.

But on the appointed day, with lakhs of kar sevaks gathered around the disputed structure, a few hundred among them managed—once again, as in October–November 1990—to breach the elaborate security that had been put in place and climb on top of the domes. Only this time, with the state police remaining inactive and the central forces deployed barred by the state government from reaching the area, the kar sevaks demolished the structure completely over six hours, using pickaxes, hammers, spades and iron rods they had brought along. Kalyan Singh resigned the same day and the Centre imposed President's Rule in the state, but by then, the Babri Masjid had been flattened.

Once again, Hindu–Muslim riots broke out all over the country, several notches worse and more widespread than the ones two years ago, with major eruptions in Bombay, Bhopal, Ahmedabad, Surat and Kanpur. The most barbarous riot, however, was yet to come—a second round of killings in Bombay in the first half of January 1993, which was a near-pogrom against Muslims, with more than 500 being killed over three days.

Both the demolition and the riots tormented VP,[9] but being out of the government, there was little he could do. When the second round of rioting began in Bombay, however, possibly recalling Mahatma Gandhi's example in Delhi soon after Partition, he decided to go on a fast-unto-death at Bombay's Hutatma Chowk from 15 January 1993 to restore peace. 'We all felt helpless; the government seemed quite ineffective. Some Janata Dal colleagues and I decided to fast to exert moral pressure for restraint,' he wrote later.[10] He carried on until 17 January 1993, when, with his blood sugar level falling to a life-threatening 22 mg/dL,[11] he was arrested, hospitalized and force-fed.[12]

He recovered over two months but while abstaining from solid food, he had made the mistake of not drinking enough fluids too. 'Foolishly, I had cut down on my intake of water so that I would not have to urinate often as there was no proper arrangement (nearby),' he wrote later.[13] Released from hospital, he returned to Delhi. 'Before starting his fast, he had undergone a check-up at Bombay's Breach Candy hospital and been found perfectly healthy,' said Sita Kumari Singh. 'But once he got back, within days the creatinine levels in his blood began to rise, and the doctors we consulted said his kidneys were permanently damaged.'[14]

For a while, his kidney function was kept at tolerable levels with drugs, but by March 1997, he had to start dialysis at Delhi's Indraprastha Apollo hospital. The dialysis continued until his death, on 27 November 2008. 'He was one of the longest-surviving dialysis patients, from 1997 to 2008, but dialysis cannot go on forever,' said Ajeya. His father's ailment led to an important life change for him as well. 'After we learnt what had happened, I spoke to my brother Abhay, who was also in the US, and we agreed that one of us should go back to Delhi, as our parents were likely to need our help in the coming years,' he revealed. 'I decided I would do so.'

He joined the US investment firm Lehmann Brothers (whose collapse in November 2008 would later trigger the global financial crisis) and opened its Delhi office in 1996, but after India conducted nuclear tests in May 1998 and the US imposed sanctions on it for doing so, Lehmann decided to withdraw and transferred him back to New York. He finally returned to India with another leading investment firm, Credit Suisse, in 2004.[15]

VP's kidney impairment also activated earlier, dormant ailments; indeed, his indefinite fast seemed to have broken his health. 'He had this problem of aneurysm in his right eye,' said Sita Kumari.[16] 'It had been under control but got worse through 1993. He underwent treatment at a leading eye hospital in Bombay, including laser treatment, but it didn't help much. He proved allergic to the dye that was injected to examine the eye, which made things worse. At one stage, when he couldn't see half his face in the mirror, we got really worried.'

It was then that Parliament Speaker Shivraj Patil[17]—whom, a decade back in 1983, VP had succeeded as commerce minister in Indira Gandhi's cabinet—suggested that he seek treatment overseas at government cost. Accordingly, VP and Sita Kumari left for London and later New York in January 1994 on a trip that, a few months later, raised needless controversy over the expense the state had been put to, of around Rs 1 crore.[18] 'It was not his fault—costs increased because of the eleven SPG officers who accompanied him,' said Dr Shishir Ray, large and avuncular with a shock of snow-white hair, a general physician who practised on London's Harley Street for decades and was attached to the Indian High Commission.[19] He was the first doctor to examine VP on that trip, and remained among his physicians until his death.

Following Rajiv's assassination, the matter of his SPG security having been removed once he ceased to be Prime Minister had been raised again, with the Congress blaming VP once more, seeking a review of how it had been allowed. VP dismissed their gripe as 'all humbug',[20] but the renewed debate led to the SPG Act being amended to extend protection to former Prime Ministers as well for five years after demitting office. 'V.P. Singh told me he didn't even want the SPG with him, but he had no choice in the matter,' said Dr Ray. 'I explained this to the Union health secretary, who came some months later to probe if the expense had been justified. I told him the government could have asked Scotland Yard to provide the security for a fee, which would have cost it less and been less obtrusive too.'

The retinal aneurysm, the main reason for the trip, was successfully treated. 'I put V.P. Singh through to a leading London ophthalmologist, Dr Hamilton, and his treatment worked,' said Dr Ray. As for the kidney ailment, Dr Ray, examining his records, told him that dialysis was inevitable. He mentioned the option of a kidney transplant, but VP was unwilling, saying that the only matching kidney found had been that of his son Ajeya, which he refused to consider.[21]

But a shock awaited VP in New York, the next leg of his trip—his blood sample, subject to a protein electrophoresis test, revealed an abnormal spike in the resulting graph, which doctors said indicated the beginnings of multiple myeloma, a cancer of the plasma cells in the bone marrow. (Myeloma's causes are still unknown; it remains incurable and is invariably fatal.) 'Going through his old medical records, we found that he had that spike even in the 1980s,' said Sita Kumari. 'I was present when a leading Delhi doctor told him looking at the report, "Some will say you have myeloma, but don't worry about it." Now the New York doctors were saying he indeed had myeloma.'[22]

Soon after, VP was also invited for a lecture tour of the US, one of the venues being Rochester—600 km north of Washington, DC—where the world-renowned Mayo Clinic is located. 'People suggested that since we were going to Rochester, he should get himself checked at the Mayo Clinic, and so he did,' said Sita Kumari.

'The doctors confirmed the myeloma diagnosis. But they also said there was no need to start chemotherapy immediately, as long as he got himself tested every year.' Chemotherapy eventually began only in 2004.

On his return from London and New York—with his energy flagging and doctors having warned him against excessive travel— VP decided he had no choice but to withdraw from politics until his health improved, if at all it did. He wrote later,

> [But] I did not want to back out when things were in bad shape for the Janata Dal and the National Front. It would look like (I was) running away. So I had to bide my time. Failure binds one as much as success. The much-awaited time came with the victories in the assembly elections of Karnataka and Andhra Pradesh.[23]

In Karnataka, the Janata Dal captured 115 of the 224 seats to form the government; in Andhra Pradesh, it was its National Front partner, N.T. Rama Rao's TDP, which made a comeback, winning 216 of the 294 seats. The same month, in December 1994, VP resigned his Fatehpur Lok Sabha seat and announced his retirement from politics.

He maintained that he would decide after five years whether to return, but that, in any case, with the Mandal report upheld by the Supreme Court and implemented thereafter, his chief purpose had been achieved. 'I'm like a rocket that burns away after putting the satellite into orbit,' he said.[24] He stuck to his retirement decision even when, in an unexpected political turn following the next Lok Sabha polls in April–May 1996, he was offered the Prime Minister's position all over again.

The BJP's role in encouraging the Babri Masjid's demolition[25] had led to a radical shift in political fault lines—while earlier, the Congress, as the ruling party in most states, was seen by all other parties as their principal opponent, against which they sometimes fought together and sometimes separately, post 6 December 1992, it was the BJP that was similarly isolated, while the Congress and its former non-BJP foes began to warily cooperate. Indeed, among political parties, the BJP became a near-pariah, though that did not affect its popularity with Hindu voters, which continued to increase.

In the 1996 general election, the BJP's seat tally, for the first time, surpassed the Congress's, reaching 161 of the 543 seats while the Congress's fell to 140 and the Janata Dal managed 46. The Janata Dal's National Front partners, however, unlike in the last two Lok Sabha polls, performed admirably this time in their respective states, bringing in another 58 seats. The DMK in Tamil Nadu, in particular, after failing to get any seats in the 1989 and 1991 general elections, captured (in alliance with another regional party) 37 of the state's 39 constituencies. With the Left Front adding another 48 seats, the total National Front–Left Front tally, too, surpassed the Congress's.

Most of the other unaffiliated smaller parties that had won the remaining seats also disdained backing the BJP. Within days of the poll results being declared on 10 May 1996, all of them thus bandied together to expand the National Front–Left Front into a thirteen-party United Front, which among them held a total of 192 seats. To keep the BJP out of power, the Congress also added its 140-seat tally to the United Front's, agreeing to support the alliance from outside, giving it an obvious majority of 332 out of 543 seats.

But who would be Prime Minister if this hybrid combination took over? Very few among the elected MPs of the United Front had national stature. Some of the better-known chief ministers of states were considered, but they either refused or their parties' other leaders would not let them shift to the Centre. By the night of 13 May 1996, the United Front leaders reached a consensus—

though he had neither contested the 1996 election nor campaigned in it, VP was the only possible candidate.

After he left 7, Race Course Road, having quit as Prime Minister, VP had moved back into the 1, Teenmurti Marg bungalow he had earlier occupied as finance minister (and where he would stay for the rest of his life), which the MP occupying it obligingly vacated for him. On the morning of 14 May 1996, two chief ministers were at his door, insisting he become Prime Minister again. (All the chief ministers of the parties supporting the United Front had arrived in Delhi to finalize their government.) VP refused. The two chief ministers said they would be back at 4 p.m. with more persuaders.[26]

But VP's mind was made up. 'I was determined to refute those who had called me power-hungry when I had agreed to become Prime Minister (in December 1989), after having said during the election campaign that I wouldn't accept the position,' he said. 'I had taken up the job then only because I was pressured.'[27]

Recalling the day's drama, Sita Kumari was more matter-of-fact. 'I, too, didn't want him to become Prime Minister again, as I knew his health could not take the strain,' she said. 'Besides, everyone knew the Congress's record of supporting other parties—the support would inevitably be withdrawn sooner rather than later.'[28]

VP decided that he did not want to meet (or even speak to) the United Front leaders again, until they had chosen someone else as their new Prime Minister—he would find it impossible to resist if they all pressured him together. Pure farce followed as, soon after lunch, he left home, while a whole posse of the leaders—including eight chief ministers—arrived barely an hour later, looking for him.

VP first went to the Kailash Colony apartment he owned for his vital post-lunch nap but realized he could easily be tracked there. He visited a close friend in east Delhi, a bureaucrat uninvolved in politics, hoping he could remain untraced at his home, but by then, the Opposition leaders had alerted the police and their journalist friends, who had also begun searching for him. With his SPG escort staff required to continuously update their bosses of their movements on wireless, VP's whereabouts were soon established. 'My friend made tea, but I had barely taken my first sip when the press was at his door,' he said. 'I left in a hurry and told my driver to simply keep the car moving along Delhi's Ring Road.'[29]

The few among VP's SPG security men, who had been left behind at his home, got in touch with their counterparts travelling with him via wireless, saying that the Opposition leaders were urging them to find out where he was. 'You can tell them,' VP said. He figured that if the car kept moving, they would still not be able to catch him.

'It was a weird situation, with the chief ministers, their security staff and hangers-on all over the place,' said Sita Kumari. 'My servant boy had such a hard time, endlessly serving tea and biscuits. The SPG people kept telling me, "Madam, *unko bol do na, ban jaye pradhan mantri* (Madam, please tell him to become Prime Minister)."'[30]

VP hinted later that she had been quite annoyed. 'I spoke to her and she said, "I don't know what you are doing. Everyone's asking where you are and I'm unable to tell them anything,"' he recalled. 'I said, "Tell them I'll return very late." She said, "I won't do it. You tell them." But I didn't want to speak to them.'[31]

He eventually went to Delhi airport, hoping to mislead the other leaders into thinking he was flying out, and thence to Sohna in Haryana, checking into a guest house close to the sulphur springs. Eventually, giving up, the United Front leaders left his home and, holding another meeting, chose the Karnataka Chief Minister H.D. Deve Gowda—a farmers' leader little known outside his state at the time—as their candidate for Prime Minister. It was only after he heard this on the news on TV in his room at the Sohna guest house that VP checked out and returned home.

Briefly, it seemed as if the United Front leaders had left their decision too late. They had taken so long to choose their leader that President Shankar Dayal Sharma—who succeeded President R. Venkataraman in July 1992—had already invited the BJP (since it was the single-largest party) to form the government. But with only three small parties supporting it, raising its total strength from 161 to 195 seats, still much lower than the 272 seats (out of 543) needed for a majority, the BJP government was forced to resign after thirteen days, enabling the United Front to form the government and Deve Gowda to become Prime Minister.

As Sita Kumari had predicted, the Congress allowed Deve Gowda's rule to last a mere eleven months, after which it sought a change of leader. The United Front obliged and I.K. Gujral replaced Deve Gowda, but after another eleven months, more differences arose and the Congress withdrew support. It led to another general election in February–March 1998, after which the Janata Dal—beset by more splits by then, down to only 6 Lok Sabha seats after the poll—disintegrated completely.

In three decades, from 1964 to 1994, VP had completed only two paintings—one of them while he was immobilized by a broken toe in 1982, soon after he had quit as UP chief minister. After he returned to Allahabad from Pune in 1962—he had been sketching and painting regularly until then—his interest seemed to temporarily wane; from 1969, politics left him no time. In 1994, however, two of his school-going grand-nieces, who were visiting him in Delhi, urged him to 'draw something' for them. He produced two identical sketches of flowers ('so they would not quarrel'), simply copying from a book of Chinese paintings. But doing so rekindled his interest.[32]

Once he had announced his political retirement, confined mostly to home by his health problems, he began drawing and painting furiously. 'As in the lower classes (in school), one studies every subject, I, too, tried every medium—oil, water, acrylic, gouache, charcoal, pencil, ink and even sand and glue,' he wrote.[33]

He was not sure if his work had any merit, but validation soon came. One of the cabinet colleagues he had chosen while Prime Minister had been Maneka Gandhi, Sanjay Gandhi's widow and Indira Gandhi's estranged daughter-in-law, who had earlier wound up her Rashtriya Sanjay Manch party to join the Janata Party and thence the Janata Dal. Maneka Gandhi had also forged a parallel career as an animal rights advocate and pioneer environmentalist in India and, having seen his paintings, arrived one day to declare that she was organizing an exhibition of animal sketches and paintings and wanted one of his she remembered.

'*Raja sahib, hum aapki billi le ja rahein hain* (I'm taking away your cat),' she said.[34] VP said he would prefer she take his goat instead—told by well-wishers that goat's milk could delay the progress of myeloma, he had kept a she-goat as a pet for some years (the sprawling lawns of 1, Teenmurti Marg afforded enough space), and made some sketches and paintings of her too. As he wrote later,

> Maneka rang in the evening and said the painting had been lying in the (exhibition) hall to be put up, when a lady turned up and offered Rs 50,000 for it, without knowing who had painted it. I did not want to part with the painting and declined. However, the incident gave me great encouragement that my work was being recognized for its artistic content and not because of my signature.[35]

His failing kidneys forced him to take many breaks. 'By early 1997 ... I became very weak,' he wrote. 'After 15 minutes at the canvas, I would get exhausted. I would lie down staring at the canvas knowing what to do but without the strength to do it. It was very depressing to be so helpless.'[36]

Dialysis, which began soon afterwards, caused its own problems. 'Haemodialysis in India was primitive in those days,' said Dr Ray. 'There were no guidelines on quality. I requested V.P. Singh to write about it in the newspapers and he did.'[37]

VP even shifted briefly to London for his dialysis, but after Apollo Hospital acquired better machines, he returned to Delhi. 'My efforts to paint became erratic,' he wrote. 'For months I could not pull myself up to paint.'[38] But he did, persisting through all kinds of physical discomfort his dialysis, and later his chemotherapy, brought him. 'During his chemo, he became an insomniac, but he used it to often paint all night,' recalled Sita Kumari.[39]

His efforts were rewarded. Soon his paintings were part of other exhibitions; he also held several solo shows—in London at the Nehru Centre in 1998; in Delhi at the Academy of Fine Arts and Literature in 1999, 2003 and 2005; in Bombay at the Jehangir Art Gallery in 1999, 2004 and 2005; and elsewhere, drawing much praise from critics and fellow artists. ('Of course, there were some adverse reviews too,' VP said.[40])

Initially averse to selling his paintings, VP started doing so after participating in a Bombay exhibition organized by industrialist and art connoisseur Harsh Goenka (the son of Rama Prasad Goenka, the same person who had publicly complained to Rajiv about VP's 'raid raj' as finance minister), who convinced VP that his attitude was 'snobbish'.[41] Characteristically, while getting art experts to set his prices, he urged them to go by artistic worth alone, without attaching any value to his signature.

Unlike his painting, VP had never entirely stopped writing poetry, but after renouncing politics, he wrote much more, publishing his solitary book of poems, *Ek Tukda Dharti, Ek Tukda Akash* (A Piece of Earth, a Piece of Sky), in 1997. He insisted that there was no political thrust to either his paintings or his poetry. 'I have so many avenues through which to express my political views,' he said. 'I can write in newspapers, I can hold press conferences or public meetings. Some political content may seep in subconsciously, but I would never use my paintings or poetry to extend my politics.' To the end he remained modest about his work. 'Both painting and literature call for a lifetime of devotion to achieve anything worthwhile,' he said. 'That is too late for me now. I just do what I can.'[42]

———— ∞∞∞ ————

'It is very hard for a tiger not to hunt,' said Ajeya Singh.[43] He was explaining his father's decision to return to politics, despite his poor health, after the five-year break he had set himself ended in 1999. VP began his second foray, however, with a different kind of politics, unaffiliated to any party, only advocating causes he cared about—slum dwellers' rehabilitation, farmers' interests, legislation on the right to information and the right to employment—through an NGO he set up called the Jana Chetna Manch. It caught public attention when he took the dramatic step of spending a night in a 30,000-strong slum cluster in Wazirpur, west Delhi, on 25 March 2000, to stop the bulldozers that had been assembled there from razing it.[44]

The jhuggis had encroached on land belonging to the railways, and after a long legal battle, the court had ordered their demolition. One of VP's notable achievements as Prime Minister had been to provide every slum-dwelling family in Delhi a ration card and an identity card, thanks to which the city's slum population venerated him. Unsurprisingly, the Wazirpur slum residents sought his help, and he agreed with them that if at all they were to be evicted, they should be given someplace else to stay.

'We held a meeting at the site, to which I brought the Railway Board chairman and other officials, which went on for three days,' said VP. 'When the meeting continued beyond the first day, I decided to stay the night there, as I feared bulldozers might be used to raze the slum at night before we had finished the meeting. I got some bedding and a blanket, and slept on the very platform where the meeting had been held. Though it was March, it was quite cold. Next morning, I had to leave as I had dialysis scheduled.'[45]

Ultimately, VP got the urban development ministry—then headed, curiously enough, by the same Jagmohan he had appointed and later sacked as Jammu and Kashmir governor earlier—to issue a government order that no slum evictions should be carried out in Delhi without providing alternative accommodation. (VP's own government had also passed a similar order, but with various judicial developments thereafter, it had become infructuous.) He then convinced the railways' top officials, who feared setting a precedent that could lead to railway land encroachers across the country seeking similar rehabilitation, to follow the order.

VP's status as former Prime Minister and access to ministers and senior officers in the government, most of whom he knew personally, obviously helped him settle the Wazirpur slum case, as in many other instances. As social activists Aruna Roy and Nikhil Dey, who were vital to the movement to bring in both the Right to Information (RTI) Act and the National Rural Employment Guarantee Act (NREGA), noted in their obituary of VP, 'History will remember V.P. Singh, among many other things, for his contribution to what we now call peoples' politics, and his crafting of methods for its engagement with mainstream political structures.'[46]

VP mined his contacts freely for his causes, particularly in getting the RTI Act and NREGA—both of which had been initiated by his government and were dear to him—eventually passed in 2005. Roy and Dey wrote,

As a former prime minister, he gave us a sense of what was in the realm of the possible, without losing the capacity to fashion a dream. He would get involved in the planning of events; he would try and ensure the presence of other people crucial to its success, and come to meetings, demonstrations, and press conferences as long as his body allowed it.[47]

But, eventually, he was persuaded to get into electoral politics again; he restarted the Jan Morcha in April 2006. 'My father was totally against doing so, but with people surrounding him insisting on it, he succumbed,' said Ajeya. The Jan Morcha highlighted the perfidy of successive UP governments that had been acquiring agricultural land dirt-cheap from farmers, while selling (or leasing) it dear for industrial projects, insisting farmers should be compensated better or their lands returned. It focused particularly on land thus taken for a proposed power project in Dadri, 60 km south-east of Delhi. (In Dadri, about 2,500 acres across seven villages had been acquired at Rs 135 per square metre, while the market rate at the nearest urban centre was around Rs 15,000 per square metre at the time;[48] the acquisition was later annulled by a court verdict.) In the April–May 2007 UP assembly polls, however, in which the revived Jan Morcha set up 118 candidates and VP campaigned to the extent he could, it won only 1 seat. (After VP's death, Ajeya ran the party briefly before merging it with the Congress in July 2009.)

VP's revived Jan Morcha may not have made any impact, but individually he continued to wield immense political influence right up to his death, especially with former United Front colleagues. This was vividly seen after the 2004 general elections, in which neither the Congress (with 145 seats) nor the BJP (with 138) came anywhere close to achieving a majority in the 543-strong Lok Sabha. Implacably opposed to the BJP by then, VP played a vital role in convincing the communist parties, the regional parties and most of the multifarious groups his Janata Dal had split into (including old frenemies such as Chandra Shekhar and Mulayam), to back the Congress, which led to the formation of the

United Progressive Alliance (UPA), which would rule the country for the next decade.[49]

⸎

'I know I'm not going to be cured,' VP told noted journalist Shekhar Gupta on NDTV's *Walk the Talk* show in July 2005. 'I know my days are not many. But if I spend them with a long face, whatever I have is also lost. If you don't feel oppressed by your disease, it's gone. The major part of a disease is the mental impact it has.'[50]

To the end, VP remained active and curious, but ultimately, the physical impact overcame him. He was admitted to Apollo Hospital in late November 2008—'Of all things, for backache,' said Dr Ray[51]—and deteriorated rapidly.

Both Ajeya and Dr Ray maintained that his anguish over a family property dispute hastened his end. Once his ailments had become known, VP had made his will, dividing up his assets between his sons and his wife. 'Broadly, he left his Allahabad properties to Ajeya, his Dehradun properties to Abhay, both of which were inherited, and whatever few properties he had personally bought in Delhi to me,' said Sita Kumari.

VP's younger son Abhay Singh—who had also returned to India from the US in the early 2000s and joined AIIMS—and his wife Niharika divorced in 2004. As part of the settlement, Niharika Singh received a sizeable alimony and maintenance for her two children, Akshay and Aditi, and, indeed, for many months after the divorce, continued to stay at 1, Teenmurti Marg. 'I told my dad, "This is ridiculous, she has to go,"' Ajeya recalled. 'But he said, "Her children are my grandchildren, leave her alone."'

On 23 November 2008, Niharika's lawyer met the family to claim that VP's will had short-changed Abhay, and that he would be moving court on behalf of Abhay's son Akshay for a larger property share. 'We tried to keep this development from my father, but he got to know,' said Ajeya. 'He loved all his grandchildren dearly, but Akshay was his favourite. It broke his heart. Soon after, doctors said, he stopped eating. He had lost the will to live.'[52] (The case, filed days later, like most property-related cases, dragged on for years.)

<hr />

With the nation riveted by the drama of the 26/11 terror attacks in Mumbai, which had begun the night before and lasted four days, VP's passing on 27 November 2008 received far less media attention than it would have in normal times. His body was flown by special plane to Allahabad and cremated on the banks of the Ganga. Though the crowd at his funeral was vast, political representation was limited, as, in his political life, he had managed the rare feat of being equally hated by both the main contesting forces of the Indian political system—the BJP and the Congress. No BJP leader attended, while only state-level Congress leaders did. But many of his Janata Dal colleagues, now scattered across different parties, were present, including frenemy Mulayam Singh Yadav.

Summing up his father's career, Ajeya recalled the words of one of VP's long-time political associates from Meja, 'He said, "Your dau (father) was a madari (magician). He could put his hand inside a bag full of snakes and scorpions, pull out a snake by the neck, put his hand in again and take out a scorpion, without being harmed. If you or I tried to do that, we would be finished. He managed to work with people with ideologies and value systems completely opposed to his own, and yet retained his integrity."'[53]

VP's own assessment was completely different. 'One of my granddaughters asked me, "Are you satisfied with your political life?"' he said to an interviewer. 'I told her, "I'm not satisfied with my *life*. I should have become a scientist and pursued painting on the side."'[54]

ACKNOWLEDGEMENTS

My foremost thanks are to Som Pal, V.P. Singh's closest associate in the latter part of his political career. Som Pal gave me enormous amounts of his time across several sessions to freely share his views and memories of V.P. Singh. I am fortunate that he is blessed with extraordinary recall, a near-eidetic memory, and was able to narrate events from long ago in more vivid detail than I had ever expected, which has contributed greatly to the book. He was also kind enough to go through the entire manuscript twice over after it was completed, pointing out factual inaccuracies, which I promptly corrected. The opinions expressed in the book, of course, are entirely my own.

I would also like to thank the Nehru Memorial Museum and Library, New Delhi, for giving me permission to quote extensively from the 900-page unpublished transcript of its interview with V.P. Singh, conducted during his last years and looking back on his entire life, which is preserved in its Oral History section. This transcript is truly the foundation on which the book rests.

My sincere thanks as well to Kunwar Pragy Arya and Aryan Art Gallery, New Delhi, for sharing the photographs used in this book.

Immense thanks are further due to V.P. Singh's family, especially his wife, Sita Kumari Singh, and elder son, Ajeya Singh, for tolerating me for hours and hours and answering my innumerable probing questions. I am beholden to them for their candour and grace. I would also like to thank V.P. Singh's younger son, Abhay Singh, his sister, Vimla Devi, his granddaughters Richa and Adrija Singh, and his nephews Anand Singh, Vikram Singh and Ramendra Pratap Singh for sparing time to speak to me.

A large number of V.P. Singh's friends and former colleagues also shared their memories of him with me, for which I am truly grateful. I would like to deeply thank Arif Mohammad Khan, Sharad Yadav, Atul Anjaan, Bhure Lal, Janardhan Pratap Singh, Somansh Prakash, Swaminathan Gurumurthy (who laboriously wrote out detailed answers at my behest and emailed them from Chennai), Colonel Ranamata Singh (retd), Jagdish Mathur, Harikesh Bahadur, Santosh Bhartiya, Shekhar Singh and Dr Shishir Ray.

I would also like to thank V.P. Singh's Allahabad (Prayagraj) associates Ramesh Pande, Vijay Chaturvedi and T.B. Singh (especially Pande) for the details they shared about working with V.P. Singh. From Koraon, similarly, I would like to thank Rudra Narayan Bajpai, Udit Narayan Singh, Prabha Shankar Tiwari and Mohammed Shabir Ali; and from Daiya, Ram Kripal Singh.

Regrettably, a few of those who spoke to me at length have passed away in the six years it has taken me to finish this book and publish it. I am indebted to S. Jaipal Reddy, P.S. Krishnan, Wasim Ahmed and Manohar Subramanyam, though they are now beyond thanking. Rest in peace.

I would like to thank my wife, Radhika Ramaseshan, for her support, as also for providing a number of initial contacts. I must also thank a host of friends who helped out in small but vital ways—Pradeep Kapoor (who also shared his Lucknow memories of V.P. Singh as UP chief minister), Somnath Batabyal,

K.S. Sachidananda Murthy, Rashmi Saksena, Nandini Iyer, Manini Chatterjee, Krishan Saith, Vijaylakshmi Vardan, Uddalok Bhattacharyya, Shekhar Ghosh and Shekhar Hattangadi.

I would also like to thank Ujjaini Dasgupta for her meticulous editing of my manuscript and Siddhesh Inamdar for his guidance and support.

NOTES

Introduction

1. V.P. Singh transcripts, Oral History section, Nehru Memorial Museum and Library (NMML), translated (from Hindi) by the author.
2. Interview with Sita Kumari Singh.
3. There were originally 85 Lok Sabha seats in UP and 54 in Bihar. In 2000, Uttarakhand was carved out of UP, with 5 Lok Sabha seats, while UP retained 80. In the same year, Jharkhand was separated from Bihar, with 14 Lok Sabha seats, while Bihar kept the remaining 40.
4. Interviews with Sharad Yadav and Som Pal.
5. See press reports at the time. For instance, Prabhu Chawla, 'Finance to Defence: PM Rajiv Gandhi Removes V.P. Singh from the Limelight', *India Today*, 15 February 1987, https://www.indiatoday.in/magazine/cover-story/story/19870215-finance-to-defence-pm-rajiv-gandhi-removes-v.p.-singh-from-the-limelight-798500-1987-02-15; also V.P. Singh transcripts, NMML; also Seema Mustafa, *The Lonely Prophet: VP Singh, A Political Biography* (New Delhi: New Age International [P] Ltd, 1995), p. 67.
6. Seema Mustafa, *The Lonely Prophet*, pp. 77–78; V.P. Singh transcripts, NMML.
7. Ibid., pp. 75–76; also V.P. Singh transcripts, NMML.
8. V.P. Singh transcripts, NMML.

9.   Aruna Roy and Nikhil Dey, 'The Raja of Small Things', *The Indian Express*, 12 December 2008, http://archive.indianexpress.com/news/the-raja-of-small-things/397312/2

10. The first 'electoral system' was that of 'Congress dominance', from the first Lok Sabha election to the fourth in 1967; the second that of 'increasing opposition to the Congress at the state level', from the 1967 Lok Sabha election to the one in 1989. See Yogendra Yadav, 'Electoral Politics in a Time of Change—India's Third Electoral System 1989-99', *Economic and Political Weekly*, Vol. 34, Issue 34–35, 21 August 1999, https://www.epw.in/journal/1999/34-35/special-articles/electoral-politics-time-change.html

11. Milan Vaishnav and Jamie Hintson, 'The Dawn of India's Fourth Party System', Carnegie Endowment for International Peace, 5 September 2019, https://carnegieendowment.org/2019/09/05/dawn-of-india-s-fourth-party-system-pub-79759

12. Ibid.

13. V.P. Singh transcripts, NMML.

PART 1: THE MAKING OF AN IDEALIST

Chapter 1: 'I was insecure, very insecure'

1.   Interview with Jagdish Mathur.

2.   Reconstructed from accounts by V.P. Singh himself (as recalled by Ajeya Singh) and Jagdish Mathur, and from Seema Mustafa, *The Lonely Prophet: V.P. Singh, A Political Biography* (New Delhi: New Age International [P] Ltd, 1995), pp. 10–11.

3.   Interviews with Ajeya Singh and Jagdish Mathur.

4.   Interview with Sita Kumari Singh.

5.   Interview with Ram Kirpal Singh, Daiya estate accountant.

6.   Nurul Hasan Siddiqi, *Landlords of Agra and Oudh* (Lucknow: The Pioneer Press, 1950), p. 50; figures given in H.R. Nevill, *Allahabad, a Gazetteer,* published in 1928 (Vol. 23, p. 279), are different—'Raja Digvijay Singh of Daiya owns 67 villages and portions of 44 others, assessed at Rs 33,678.' Village areas and rents must have been periodically revised.

7.   Nurul Hasan Siddiqi, *Landlords of Agra and Oudh,* p. 50.

8.   Vinod Sharma, 'Sant Bux Singh: My Brother VP', *Hindustan Times*, 24 June 1990.

9. Vijaya Lakshmi Pandit, *The Scope of Happiness: A Personal Memoir* (New Delhi: Speaking Tiger, 2018), p. 154. The author mistakenly calls him the raja of Manda.

10. Interview with Ajeya Singh.

11. Seema Mustafa, *The Lonely Prophet*, p. 3. This was also reiterated by Sita Kumari Singh and Ajeya Singh in their interviews.

12. Interview with Sita Kumari Singh.

13. Jagdish Prasad (ed.), *Manual of Titles, United Provinces of Agra and Oudh*, seventh edition (Allahabad: Government of India Press, 1929), p. 99, https://archive.org/stream/in.ernet.dli.2015.63142/2015.63142. Manual-Of-Titles-United-Provinces-Of-Agra-Amp-Oudh_djvu.txt

14. V.P. Singh transcripts, Oral History section, Nehru Memorial Museum and Library (NMML), translated (from Hindi) by the author.

15. Interview with Sita Kumari Singh.

16. V.P. Singh transcripts, NMML.

17. Nurul Hasan Siddiqi, *Landlords of Agra and Oudh*, p. 48.

18. Ibid.; H.R. Nevill in *Allahabad, a Gazetteer*, published in 1928 (Vol. 23, p. 279), has different figures—'The raja of Manda is by far the largest landowner in the tehsil, holding 207 villages and 45 mahals, assessed at Rs 85,854.'

19. Daiya was bigger in size, but large parts of it were unpopulated wasteland.

20. H.R. Nevill in *Allahabad, a Gazetteer*, Vol. 23, 1928, p. 104; along with family accounts.

21. Esha Basanti Joshi, *Uttar Pradesh District Gazetteers: Allahabad* (Lucknow: Department of District Gazetteers 1968), p. 34, https://indianculture.gov.in/gazettes/uttar-pradesh-district-gazetteers-allahabad

22. Thomas R. Metcalf, *Land, Landlords, and the British Raj: Northern India in the Nineteenth Century* (New Delhi: Oxford University Press, 1979), pp. 3–4.

23. Janardhan Thakur, *V.P. Singh: The Quest for Power* (New Delhi: Warbler Books, 1989), p. 19.

24. Thomas R. Metcalf, *Land, Landlords, and the British Raj*, pp. 5–6.

25. Nurul Hasan Siddiqi, *Landlords of Agra and Oudh*, p. 47.

26. Jagdish Prasad (ed.), *Manual of Titles, United Provinces of Agra and Oudh*, p. 96, https://archive.org/stream/in.ernet.dli.2015.63142/2015.63142. Manual-Of-Titles-United-Provinces-Of-Agra-Amp-Oudh_djvu.txt

27. The 'law of rent' was outlined in David Ricardo's book *On the Principles of Political Economy and Taxation*, published in 1809.

28. Thomas R. Metcalf, *Land, Landlords and the British Raj*, p. 64.

29. Ibid., pp. 55–56.

30. Ibid., Chapter 5, pp. 105–35.

31. H.R. Nevill, *Allahabad, a Gazetteer*, Vol. 23, p. 278.

32. Popular verse forms in Hindi/Urdu. Dohas are couplets and chaubolas four-liners with rhyming pattern 'a-a-b-a', both with twenty-four matras per line.

33. H.R. Nevill, *Allahabad, a Gazetteer*, Vol. 23, p. 105.

34. Thomas R. Metcalf, *Land, Landlords, and the British Raj*, pp. 86–104.

35. Jagdish Prasad (ed.), *Manual of Titles, United Provinces of Agra and Oudh*, p. 98, https://archive.org/stream/in.ernet.dli.2015.63142/2015.63142. Manual-Of-Titles-United-Provinces-Of-Agra-Amp-Oudh_djvu.txt; also, Nurul Hasan Siddiqi, *Landlords of Agra and Oudh*, p. 49.

36. Seema Mustafa, *The Lonely Prophet*, p. 2.

37. It was the Sixth Regiment Native Infantry stationed in Allahabad town that revolted, killing its British officers, forcing all British families to barricade themselves in Allahabad's fort. But within five days, Brigadier General James Neill, with his First Madras Europeans, arrived there and won the town back in a week, wreaking much gratuitous violence.

38. Chhatarpal Singh's troops even clashed with Maulvi Liaqat Ali's—the best known among Allahabad's rebels, later caught, tried and sentenced to the Andamans for life—in a crucial battle at Khaga, 100 km north-west of Allahabad town. They guarded the British treasury at Meja, 40 km south-east of Allahabad town, on the outskirts of the two estates, from the rebels. See Nurul Hasan Siddiqi, *Landlords of Agra and Oudh*, p. 47. 'The rajas of Manda and Daiya [were] actively loyal. The first took charge of the treasury and the district police ... Raja Tejbal Singh of Daiya [who succeeded Dhaukal Singh] saved the Drummondganj post in Mirzapur and assisted the Banda fugitives on their way from Nagod ...' From H.R. Nevill, *Allahabad, a Gazetteer*, Vol. 23, p. 188.

39. Jagdish Prasad (ed.), *Manual of Titles, United Provinces of Agra and Oudh*, p. 95.

40. C.A. Bayly, *The Local Roots of Indian Politics: Allahabad (1880–1920)* (New Delhi: Oxford University Press, 1975), p. 50.

41. Janardhan Thakur, *V.P. Singh*, p. 18.

42. Jagdish Prasad (ed.), *Manual of Titles, United Provinces of Agra and Oudh*, p. 94.

43. Nurul Hasan Siddiqi, *Landlords of Agra and Oudh*, p. 48.

44. 'Khairagarh: Princely State', Indian Rajputs, http://www.indianrajputs. com/view/khairagarh

45. Janardhan Thakur, *V.P. Singh*, pp. 22–23; Seema Mustafa, *The Lonely Prophet*, p. 4; interview with Sita Kumari Singh.
46. Interview with Sita Kumari Singh.
47. Ibid.
48. Ibid.
49. Seema Mustafa, *The Lonely Prophet*, p. 4.
50. Ibid.; also see Malini Parthasarathy, 'Vishwanath Pratap Singh: Person of the Year, Man behind the Legend', *Frontline*, 24 December 1988.
51. Ibid.; V.P. Singh transcripts, NMML.
52. Ibid.
53. Malini Parthasarathy, 'Vishwanath Pratap Singh: Person of the Year, Man behind the Legend', *Frontline*, 24 December 1988.
54. Seema Mustafa, *The Lonely Prophet*; interview with Sita Kumari Singh.
55. V.P. Singh transcripts, NMML.
56. Seema Mustafa, *The Lonely Prophet*, p. 5.
57. Rambahadur Rai, *Vishwanath Pratap Singh – Manzil Se Zyada Safar* (New Delhi: Rajkamal Prakashan, 2006), p. 29.
58. V.P. Singh transcripts, NMML; Seema Mustafa, *The Lonely Prophet*, p. 8.
59. Seema Mustafa, *The Lonely Prophet*, pp. 7–8.
60. Khushwant Singh, 'Profile of V.P. Singh', *Malicious Gossip* (New Delhi: HarperCollins India, 2004), p. 97; Seema Mustafa, *The Lonely Prophet*, p. 9; interview with Jagdish Mathur.
61. Seema Mustafa, *The Lonely Prophet*, p. 9; Janardhan Thakur, *V.P. Singh*, p. 24; Khushwant Singh, *Malicious Gossip*, p. 98.
62. Khushwant Singh, *Malicious Gossip*, p. 98; interview with Jagdish Mathur.

Chapter 2: 'I studied at the pace of a roadroller, but whatever I read, I ingested'

1. Seema Mustafa, *The Lonely Prophet: V.P. Singh, A Political Biography* (New Delhi: New Age International [P] Ltd, 1995), p.7; Malini Parthasarathy, 'Vishwanath Pratap Singh: Person of the Year, Man behind the Legend', *Frontline*, 24 December 1988.
2. Janardhan Thakur, *V.P. Singh: The Quest for Power* (New Delhi: Warbler Books, 1989), p. 24.
3. Interview with Vimla Devi.
4. V.P. Singh transcripts, Oral History section, Nehru Memorial Museum and Library (NMML), translated (from Hindi) by the author.

5. 'College' in the name merely denoted that it offered classes up to intermediate—the equivalent of today's Class XII.

6. Jagdish Prasad (ed.), *Manual of Titles, United Provinces of Agra and Oudh*, seventh edition, Allahabad, 1929, p. 243, https://archive.org/stream/in.ernet.dli.2015.63142/2015.63142.Manual-Of-Titles-United-Provinces-Of-Agra-Amp-Oudh_djvu.txt

7. Interview with Colonel Ranamata Singh (retd).

8. Ibid. (Records—see http://www.upcollege.org/college.html—indicate that Udai Pratap Singh also funded an orphanage in Varanasi and made donations to institutions such as the King George Medical College, Lucknow, but Ranamata Singh was accurate in noting that all of these were towards the end of his life.)

9. Interview with Colonel Ranamata Singh (retd); V.P. Singh transcripts, NMML.

10. V.P. Singh transcripts, NMML; Rambahadur Rai, *Vishwanath Pratap Singh – Manzil Se Zyada Safar* (New Delhi: Rajkamal Prakashan, 2006), p. 35.

11. V.P. Singh transcripts, NMML.

12. Ibid.; Rambahadur Rai, *Manzil Se Zyada Safar*, p. 36.

13. Ibid.; Rambahadur Rai, *Manzil Se Zyada Safar*, p. 31.

14. Interview with Colonel Ranamata Singh (retd).

15. Interview with Sita Kumari Singh.

16. V.P. Singh transcripts, NMML; Rambahadur Rai, *Manzil Se Zyada Safar*, p. 31.

17. Ibid., p. 32.

18. Seema Mustafa, *The Lonely Prophet*, p. 12.

19. Vinod Sharma, 'Sant Bux Singh: My Brother VP', *Hindustan Times,* 24 June 1990.

20. Interview with Vimla Devi.

21. V.P. Singh transcripts, NMML.

22. Rambahadur Rai, *Manzil Se Zyada Safar*, p. 32.

23. Interview with Colonel Ranamata Singh (retd).

24. V.P. Singh transcripts, NMML.

25. Rambahadur Rai, *Manzil Se Zyada Safar*, p. 33.

26. V.P. Singh transcripts, NMML.

27. Malini Parthasarathy, 'Vishwanath Pratap Singh: Person of the Year, Man behind the Legend', *Frontline*, 24 December 1988.

28. V.P. Singh transcripts, NMML.

29. Seema Mustafa, *The Lonely Prophet*, p. 14; V.P. Singh transcripts, NMML; Rambahadur Rai, *Manzil Se Zyada Safar*, p. 33; Malini Parthasarathy,

'Vishwanath Pratap Singh: Person of the Year, Man behind the Legend', *Frontline*, 24 December 1988.

30. V.P. Singh transcripts, NMML; Rambahadur Rai, *Manzil Se Zyada Safar*, p. 33.
31. Ibid.; Rambahadur Rai, *Manzil Se Zyada Safar*, p. 34.
32. Ibid.; Rambahadur Rai, *Manzil se Zyada Safar*, pp. 35–36.
33. Ibid.

Chapter 3: 'This man is something else'

1. Esha Basanti Joshi, *Uttar Pradesh District Gazetteers, Allahabad* (Lucknow: Department of District Gazetteers 1968), p. 11, https://indianculture.gov.in/gazettes/uttar-pradesh-district-gazetteers-allahabad
2. Rambahadur Rai, *Vishwanath Pratap Singh – Manzil Se Zyada Safar* (New Delhi: Rajkamal Prakashan, 2006), p. 38.
3. Ibid.
4. Seema Mustafa, *The Lonely Prophet: V.P. Singh, A Political Biography* (New Delhi: New Age International [P] Ltd, 1995) p. 17; interview with Sita Kumari Singh.
5. V.P. Singh transcripts, Oral History section, Nehru Memorial Museum and Library (NMML), translated (from Hindi) by the author.
6. W. Beran Wolfe, *How to Be Happy though Human* (London: Penguin Books, 1932).
7. Khushwant Singh, 'Profile of V.P. Singh', *Malicious Gossip* (New Delhi: HarperCollins India, 2004), p. 103; see too Rambahadur Rai, *Manzil Se Zyada Safar*, p. 50.
8. For various reasons, the term is little used in modern-day psychology; 'lack of self-esteem' is preferred.
9. Mark Tully and Gillian Wright, 'A Tale of Two Brothers', *India in Slow Motion* (New Delhi: Penguin Books India, 2002), p. 226.
10. V.P. Singh transcripts, NMML.
11. Rambahadur Rai, *Manzil Se Zyada Safar*, p. 41.
12. Interview with Sita Kumari Singh.
13. Rambahadur Rai, *Manzil Se Zyada Safar*, p. 41.
14. Ibid.
15. Neelum Saran Gour, *Three Rivers and a Tree: The Story of Allahabad University* (New Delhi: Rupa Publications India, 2015), p. 53.
16. Ibid., p. 169.

17. L.H. Naqvi, 'V.P. Singh: Adopted Son of a Raja', *Hindustan Times*, 10 June 1980.
18. Seema Mustafa, *The Lonely Prophet*, p. 16.
19. Ibid.; interview with Ajeya Singh.
20. Neelum Saran Gour, *Three Rivers and a Tree*, p. 91.
21. Ibid., pp. 118–146.
22. V.P. Singh transcripts, NMML; Neelum Saran Gour, *Three Rivers and a Tree*, p. 94.
23. In the Mahabharata, during the Kurukshetra war, Yudhishthira, eldest of the Pandava brothers and known for never telling a lie, tricked the Kaurava army chief Dronacharya into submission by uttering the words '*Ashwatthama hata* (Ashwatthama is dead)'. Ashwatthama was the name of Dronacharya's son, and Dronacharya was so distraught at the news he gave up fighting. But Yudhishtira was referring to an elephant named Ashwatthama that had been killed in battle, not Dronacharya's son, who was very much alive.
24. Seema Mustafa, *The Lonely Prophet*, p. 16.
25. V.P. Singh transcripts, NMML.
26. Neelum Saran Gour, *Three Rivers and a Tree*, p. 298.
27. V.P. Singh transcripts, NMML.
28. Ibid.
29. Census of India, 1951, Chapter 6, 'State of Literacy', http://censusindia.gov.in/2011-prov-results/data_files/india/Final_PPT_2011_chapter6.pdf
30. Interview with Prabha Shankar Tiwari, former block pramukh, Koraon.
31. V.P. Singh transcripts, NMML.
32. Interview with Udit Narayan Singh.
33. Interview with Rudra Narayan Bajpai.
34. V.P. Singh transcripts, NMML.
35. Rambahadur Rai, *Manzil Se Zyada Safar*, p. 37.
36. Both Sant Bux Singh—quoted in Janardhan Thakur, *V.P. Singh: The Quest for Power* (New Delhi: Warbler Books, 1989), p. 27—and Sita Kumari Singh (author's interview) gave the same figure.
37. Khushwant Singh, *Malicious Gossip*, p. 104.
38. Interview with Sita Kumari Singh.
39. Vinod Sharma, 'Sant Bux Singh: My Brother VP', *Hindustan Times*, 24 June 1990.
40. Interview with Sita Kumari Singh.
41. Ibid.; Seema Mustafa, *The Lonely Prophet*, p. 17.
42. Interview with Anand Singh.
43. Interview with Sita Kumari Singh.

44. Vinod Sharma, 'Sant Bux Singh: My Brother VP', *Hindustan Times*, 24 June 1990.
45. Bipan Chandra, Aditya Mukherjee and Mridula Mukherjee, *India since Independence* (New Delhi: Penguin Books, 2008), p. 15.
46. Hallam Tennyson, *Saint on the March: The Story of Vinoba* (London: Victor Gollancz Ltd, 1955), pp. 54–93.
47. Ibid., pp. 201–05.
48. Ibid., pp. 43, 53–60.
49. Arthur Koestler, *The Lotus and the Robot* (London: Hutchinson, 1960), p. 19. Most historians, however, put the total land collected through the Bhoodan movement at 'over 4 million acres'. See Ramachandra Guha, *India after Gandhi: The History of the World's Largest Democracy* (New Delhi: Picador, 2008), p. 219.
50. Ramachandra Guha, *India after Gandhi*, p. 219.
51. Interviews with Prabha Shankar Tripathi and Udit Narayan Singh.
52. V.P. Singh transcripts, NMML.
53. Ibid.; Rambahadur Rai, *Manzil Se Zyada Safar*, pp. 48–49.
54. Interview with Sita Kumari Singh.
55. Janardhan Thakur, *V.P. Singh*, p. 18.
56. Interview with Sita Kumari Singh.
57. Rambahadur Rai, *Manzil Se Zyada Safar*, p. 49.
58. Janardhan Thakur, *V.P. Singh*, p. 18.
59. Ibid.
60. V.P. Singh transcripts, NMML.
61. Interview with Sita Kumari Singh.
62. Ibid.
63. Ibid.
64. Interview with Colonel Ranamata Singh (retd).
65. Ibid.
66. Seema Mustafa, *The Lonely Prophet*, p. 16.
67. V.P. Singh transcripts, NMML; Rambahadur Rai, *Manzil Se Zyada Safar*, p. 43.
68. Interview with Colonel Ranamata Singh (retd).
69. Interview with Sita Kumari Singh.
70. Ibid.
71. V.P. Singh transcripts, NMML.
72. Ibid.
73. L.H. Naqvi, 'V.P. Singh: Adopted Son of a Raja', *Hindustan Times*, 10 June 1980.
74. Interview with Sita Kumari Singh.

75. Interview with Colonel Ranamata Singh (retd).
76. Interview with Sita Kumari Singh.
77. Interview with Colonel Ranamata Singh (retd).
78. L.H. Naqvi, 'V.P. Singh: Adopted Son of a Raja', *Hindustan Times*, 10 June 1980.
79. V.P. Singh transcripts, NMML; Rambahadur Rai, *Manzil Se Zyada Safar*, p. 31.
80. Seema Mustafa, *The Lonely Prophet*, p. 18.
81. Ibid.; interview with Sita Kumari Singh.
82. Seema Mustafa, *The Lonely Prophet*, p. 18; V.P. Singh transcripts, NMML.
83. Interview with Colonel Ranamata Singh (retd).
84. Seema Mustafa, *The Lonely Prophet*, p. 18.
85. Interview with Anand Singh.
86. Kunwar Pragy Arya and Suneet Tandon, *Vishwanath Pratap Singh* (New Delhi: Aryan Art Gallery, 2006), pp. 8–12.
87. Ibid., pp. 12–13.
88. Interview with Abhay Singh.

PART 2: LOYALTY DILEMMAS

Chapter 1: 'One may or may not crave wealth, but everyone craves recognition'

1. V.P. Singh transcripts, Oral History section, Nehru Memorial Museum and Library (NMML), translated (from Hindi) by the author; Rambahadur Rai, *Vishwanath Pratap Singh – Manzil Se Zyada Safar* (New Delhi: Rajkamal Prakashan, 2006), p. 41.
2. Three decades after the collapse of communism, the festival is still organized sporadically in the capitals of countries with left-leaning governments. See, for instance, Choe Sang-Hun, 'North Korea's Would-Be Olympics: A Tale of a Cold War Boondoggle', *The New York Times*, 4 February 2018, https://www.nytimes.com/2018/02/04/world/asia/north-korea-olympics.html
3. V.P. Singh transcripts, NMML.
4. Ibid.
5. Ibid.
6. Ibid.
7. Alexander Lipkov and Thomas J. Mathew, 'India's Bollywood in Russia', *India International Centre Quarterly*, Vol. 21, Nos 2–3, 1994.

8. V.P. Singh transcripts, NMML.
9. K.P.S. Menon, *The Flying Troika: Extracts from a Diary by K.P.S. Menon, India's Ambassador to Russia, 1952-61* (London: Oxford University Press, 1963), p. 228.
10. V.P. Singh transcripts, NMML.
11. Ibid.
12. Interview with Sita Kumari Singh.
13. Ibid.
14. Election Commission of India, 'Second General Elections, Vol. I (1957)', https://eci.gov.in/files/file/7452-second-general-elections-vol-i-1957/
15. Election Commission of India, 'Third General Elections, Vol. I (1962)', https://eci.gov.in/files/file/7455-third-general-elections-vol-i-1962/
16. Rambahadur Rai, *Manzil Se Zyada Safar,* p. 44.
17. V.P. Singh transcripts, NMML.
18. Ibid.
19. Anil Shastri and Pavan Choudary, *Lal Bahadur Shastri: Lessons in Leadership* (Gurgaon: Wisdom Village Publications, 2014), p. 146.
20. Rambahadur Rai, *Manzil Se Zyada Safar,* p. 40; V.P. Singh transcripts, NMML.
21. Interview with Lalita Shastri, *Illustrated Weekly of India,* 12 June 1988. V.P. Singh, however, had no recollection of such a reaction. 'He may have said so to her later,' he told his NMML interviewer (V.P. Singh transcripts, NMML).
22. The meeting was arranged by the then Soviet premier Alexei Kosygin, with the USSR successfully interceding between the two countries to end the war. The circumstances of Shastri's unexpected death remain controversial.
23. Rambahadur Rai, *Manzil Se Zyada Safar,* pp. 40–41.
24. Paul Brass, *An Indian Political Life: Charan Singh and Congress Politics, 1957 to 1967, Vol. 2* (New Delhi: Sage Publications, 2014), pp. 263–86, 373–401.
25. Election Commission of India, 'Fourth General Elections, Vol. I (1967)', https://eci.gov.in/files/file/7449-fourth-general-elections-vol-i-1967/
26. Vinod Sharma, 'Sant Bux Singh: My Brother VP', *Hindustan Times,* 24 June 1990.
27. V.P. Singh transcripts, NMML; interview with Sita Kumari Singh.
28. This was the same B.V. Keskar who, as information and broadcasting minister, had banned film music from All India Radio for many years and sought to do the same with cricket commentary as well, claiming they were too frivolous for a national broadcaster.
29. Interview with Rudra Narayan Bajpai, who lives in Fatehpur.

30. V.P. Singh transcripts, NMML.
31. Ibid.
32. Election Commission of India, 'Fourth General Elections, Vol. I (1967)', https://eci.gov.in/files/file/7449-fourth-general-elections-vol-i-1967/

Chapter 2: 'If not now, when?'

1. V.P. Singh transcripts, Oral History section, Nehru Memorial Museum and Library (NMML), translated (from Hindi) by the author; Rambahadur Rai, *Vishwanath Pratap Singh – Manzil Se Zyada Safar* (New Delhi: Rajkamal Prakashan, 2006), p. 82.
2. V.P. Singh transcripts, NMML.
3. Unlike most rajas, Dinesh Singh's grandfather had been a strong supporter of Mahatma Gandhi and the Congress. As a result, after Independence, Dinesh Singh became Jawaharlal Nehru's private secretary, and later, on joining politics, was made deputy minister. When Indira Gandhi became Prime Minister, he thrived initially but later fell out of favour. See Katherine Frank, *Indira: The Life of Indira Nehru Gandhi* (New York: HarperCollins Publishers, 2001), pp. 294–95; also see Kuldip Singh, 'Obituary: Dinesh Singh', *The Independent*, 2 December 1995, https://www.independent.co.uk/news/people/obituary-dinesh-singh-1523677.html
4. Bahuguna had participated in the Quit India movement as a student and been jailed for more than three years. After Independence, he had been a deputy minister in UP and also held various organizational positions in the Congress. He would go on to become UP chief minister from November 1973 to November 1975, and Union minister in the Janata Party and Janata Party (S) governments holding important portfolios (1977–79).
5. V.P. Singh transcripts, NMML; Seema Mustafa, *The Lonely Prophet: V.P. Singh, A Political Biography* (New Delhi: New Age International (P) Ltd, 1995), p. 21.
6. Paul Brass, *An Indian Political Life: Charan Singh and Congress Politics, 1967 to 1987, Vol. 3* (New Delhi: Sage Publications, 2014), pp. 3–17; also 'Charan Singh Quits as CM', *Hindustan Times*, 18 February 1968.
7. Interview with Sita Kumari Singh.
8. H.R. Nevill, *Allahabad, a Gazetteer*, 1928, p. 308.
9. A.P. Bhatnagar, *Maulvi Liaqat Ali: Icon of 1857 Uprising at Allahabad* (Gurgaon: Shubhi Publications, 2009), p. 66 and p. 68.
10. Hailing from the Lakhimpur Kheri town in UP's Terai area, Chandra Bhanu Gupta had begun his career as a lawyer defending both Congressmen

and revolutionaries in cases filed against them by British authorities. He later jumped into agitations against the British rule and was imprisoned during the Quit India movement. He held several portfolios in successive UP ministries after Independence (health, industries, chemicals and fertilizers), before becoming chief minister in December 1960.

11. Paul Brass, *An Indian Political Life: Charan Singh and Congress Politics, 1957 to 1967, Vol. 2* (New Delhi: Sage Publications, 2014), p. 164.

12. Ibid., pp. 411–16.

13. V.P. Singh transcripts, NMML; Rambahadur Rai, *Manzil Se Zyada Safar*, p. 51.

14. Ibid.; Seema Mustafa, *The Lonely Prophet*, p. 21.

15. Ibid.; Rambahadur Rai, *Manzil Se Zyada Safar*, p. 51.

16. Interview with Abhay Singh.

17. V.P. Singh transcripts, NMML; also Seema Mustafa, *The Lonely Prophet*, p. 21; here, he called it a 'terrible experience'.

18. V.P. Singh transcripts, NMML.

19. Ibid.; also Seema Mustafa, *The Lonely Prophet*, pp. 21–22; Rambahadur Rai, *Manzil Se Zyada Safar*, p. 52.

20. Janardhan Thakur, *V.P. Singh: The Quest for Power* (New Delhi: Warbler Books, 1989), pp. 29–30.

21. V.P. Singh transcripts, NMML; also Rambahadur Rai, *Manzil Se Zyada Safar*, p. 52; Seema Mustafa, *The Lonely Prophet*, p. 22—the wordings vary, but the gist is the same.

22. V.P. Singh transcripts, NMML; also Rambahadur Rai, *Manzil Se Zyada Safar*, p. 52.

23. Katherine Frank, *Indira*, pp. 295–96.

24. V.P. Singh transcripts, NMML; Rambahadur Rai, *Manzil Se Zyada Safar*, p. 52.

25. Interview with Som Pal, former Janata Dal MP (Rajya Sabha) and agriculture minister in the first National Democratic Alliance government (1998–99).

26. V.P. Singh transcripts, NMML.

27. Paul Brass, Chapter 5, 'Leadership Conflict and the Disintegration of the Indian Socialist Movement: Personal Ambition, Power and Policy', *Caste, Faction and Party in Indian Politics,* Vol. 1 (New Delhi: Chanakya Press, 1984), pp. 155–63; also Bipan Chandra, Aditya Mukherjee and Mridula Mukherjee, *India since Independence* (New Delhi: Penguin Books, 2008), pp. 252–56.

28. Ibid., pp. 155–63; also see 'Uttar Pradesh Assembly Election Results in 1962', http://www.elections.in/uttar-pradesh/assembly-constituencies/1962-election-results.html; and 'Uttar Pradesh Assembly

Election Results in 1967', http://www.elections.in/uttar-pradesh/assembly-constituencies/1967-election-results.html

29. V.P. Singh transcripts, NMML; Rambahadur Rai, *Manzil Se Zyada Safar*, p. 54.

30. In his earlier years, people often addressed V.P. Singh as 'VN' or 'Vishwanath'.

31. V.P. Singh transcripts, NMML; interview with Vijay Chaturvedi.

32. The youth wing of the Samajwadi Party in UP is also called 'Samajwadi Yuvjan Sabha', but this is a different SYS. The original SYS has long been dissolved, after the Socialist Party ceased to exist.

33. Interview with Vijay Chaturvedi.

34. Rambahadur Rai, *Manzil Se Zyada Safar*, p. 52.

35. V.P. Singh transcripts, NMML.

36. Interview with Vijay Chaturvedi.

37. Election Commission of India, 'Uttar Pradesh 1969', https://eci.gov.in/files/file/3247-uttar-pradesh-1969/

38. V.P. Singh transcripts, NMML.

39. Ibid.

40. The Muslim Majlis was started by a leading Lucknow doctor, Abdul Jalil Faridi, to specifically promote Muslim interests—in particular, to get Urdu recognized as the second official language of UP, after Hindi. Though most UP Muslims had been unquestioningly voting for the Congress since Independence, Dr Faridi, who had a particularly sour personal relationship with C.B. Gupta, had always opposed the party, starting his career with the PSP and then launching the Muslim Majlis. See Paul Brass, *Language, Religion and Politics in North India* (Cambridge: Cambridge University Press, 1974), pp. 136–40; also see N.A. Ansari, 'Dr Faridi – A Forgotten Giant', http://www.milligazette.com/Archives/01072002/0107200270.htm

41. V.P. Singh transcripts, NMML; Rambahadur Rai, *Manzil Se Zyada Safar*, pp. 55–56.

42. Ibid.

43. Ibid.

44. Election Commission of India, 'Uttar Pradesh 1969', https://eci.gov.in/files/file/3247-uttar-pradesh-1969/

45. Seema Mustafa, *The Lonely Prophet*, p. 23.

46. Election Commission of India, 'Uttar Pradesh 1969', https://eci.gov.in/files/file/3247-uttar-pradesh-1969/

47. Paul Brass, *An Indian Political Life, Vol. 2*, pp. 48–52.

48. Election Commission of India, 'Uttar Pradesh 1969', https://eci.gov.in/files/file/3247-uttar-pradesh-1969/

49. However, the BKD's success hurt the two other major Opposition parties, the Jana Sangh and the SSP, much more than it did the Congress. Most of the seats it won had been held by these two parties previously, with the Jana Sangh's tally in particular falling to half that of its 1967 peak of 98 seats.

Chapter 3: 'You can't force anyone to do what he doesn't want to'

1. V.P. Singh transcripts, Oral History section, Nehru Memorial Museum and Library (NMML), translated (from Hindi) by the author.
2. V.P. Singh transcripts, NMML; Rambahadur Rai, *Vishwanath Pratap Singh – Manzil Se Zyada Safar* (New Delhi: Rajkamal Prakashan, 2006), p. 57.
3. Ibid.; Seema Mustafa, *The Lonely Prophet: V.P. Singh, A Political Biography* (New Delhi: New Age International [P] Ltd, 1995), pp. 23–24.
4. Ibid.
5. V.P. Singh transcripts, NMML.
6. Ibid.
7. V.P. Singh transcripts, NMML; Seema Mustafa, *The Lonely Prophet*, p. 24.
8. Ibid.
9. V.P. Singh transcripts, NMML.
10. Paul Brass, Chapter 4, 'Factionalism and the Congress Party in Uttar Pradesh', *Caste, Faction and Party in Indian Politics*, Vol. 1 (New Delhi: Chanakya Press, 1984), pp. 142–43.
11. Rambahadur Rai, *Manzil Se Zyada Safar*, p. 58.
12. Katherine Frank, *Indira: The Life of Indira Nehru Gandhi* (New York: HarperCollins Publishers, 2001), pp. 289–90.
13. K. Kamaraj, hailing from the Virudhunagar district in Tamil Nadu, was a veteran freedom fighter, having been imprisoned six times by the British for his role in various agitations. After Independence, he was chief minister of Madras state from 1954 to 1963, during which he introduced the midday-meal scheme for schoolchildren, which is now enforced across the country and has contributed substantially to enhancing school enrolment. In the early 1960s, recognizing the Congress's declining popularity, he formulated the 'Kamaraj plan'—as it came to be known—by which certain chief ministers (with Kamaraj being the first) resigned their offices to try and rejuvenate the party organization. Impressed, Jawaharlal Nehru made him national Congress president in 1964.

14. Morarji Desai, who would go on to become India's fourth Prime Minister, from 1977 to 1979, came from Gujarat's Valsad district. Like Kamaraj, he was also a long-time freedom fighter, who had been repeatedly jailed by the British. After Independence, he was chief minister of the undivided Bombay state from 1952 to 1956, when it was divided into Maharashtra and Gujarat. Desai fiercely opposed creating a separate Maharashtra state, and the police firing he ordered on those demanding one—leading to more than a hundred deaths—proved a watershed moment for the movement. He later became finance minister in Nehru's cabinet, but refused—after Nehru's death—to join Shastri's.

15. Katherine Frank, *Indira,* p. 302.

16. Kuldip Nayar, *India after Nehru* (New Delhi: Vikas Publishing House, 1975), p.126. Indira Gandhi won by over 90,000 votes.

17. Sanjeeva Reddy, too, had participated in the Quit India movement. He was the first chief minister of Andhra Pradesh after the state was created in 1956, and later a Union cabinet minister.

18. Kuldip Nayar, *India after Nehru,* p. 150.

19. Ibid., pp. 149–50.

20. V.V. Giri had been an influential trade union leader under British rule, a founder member of the All India Railwayman's Federation and twice president of the All India Trade Union Congress. He was Union labour minister in Nehru's cabinet, and thereafter governor of different states before being elected vice president in 1967.

21. Vice President S. Radhakrishnan took over after India's first President Rajendra Prasad retired; so too Vice President Zakir Husain had been made President after Radhakrishnan retired.

22. V.P. Singh transcripts, NMML; Kuldip Nayar, *India after Nehru,* p. 150.

23. Ibid.

24. Paul Brass, *An Indian Political Life: Charan Singh and Congress Politics, 1957 to 1967,* Vol. 2 (New Delhi: Sage Publications, 2014), p. 428.

25. V.P. Singh transcripts, NMML; Rambahadur Rai, *Manzil Se Zyada Safar,* p. 59; Seema Mustafa, *The Lonely Prophet,* p. 26.

26. Ibid.

27. Initially, the Indira Gandhi group was mostly referred to as 'Congress (N)' in the press, where 'N' merely stood for 'new', while the 'O' in the Congress (O)'s name stood for 'old'. Congress (Requisitionists) and Congress (Organization) became popular only after the 1971 general election.

28. V.P. Singh transcripts, NMML.

29. Kuldip Nayar, *India after Nehru,* p. 157.

30. These were annual retainers—costing the exchequer around $6 million annually at the time (Katherine Frank, *Indira,* p. 323)—paid to the former rulers in lieu of their having merged their kingdoms in the Indian union after Independence.
31. Hailing from Varanasi, T.N. Singh was a Rajya Sabha member at the time, who had stayed with the Congress (O) following the split.
32. V.P. Singh transcripts, NMML.

Chapter 4: 'I may be a dhok (scarecrow), but I don't give dhoka'

1. Janardhan Thakur, *V.P. Singh: The Quest for Power* (New Delhi: Warbler Books, 1989), p. 31.
2. V.P. Singh transcripts, Oral History section, Nehru Memorial Museum and Library (NMML), translated (from Hindi) by the author.
3. Janardhan Thakur, *V.P. Singh,* p. 31.
4. Ibid., p. 32; V.P. Singh transcripts, NMML.
5. Janeshwar Mishra, a former Allahabad University student leader, was an SSP stalwart with a state-wide reputation for oratory and combativeness. India's tallest socialist leader had been Ram Manohar Lohia—who died unexpectedly early in 1967, aged just fifty-seven—but Mishra showed such early promise that he used to be called 'Chhote Lohia' (Lohia Junior) by SSP supporters.
6. Seema Mustafa, *The Lonely Prophet: V.P. Singh, A Political Biography* (New Delhi: New Age International [P] Ltd, 1995), p. 27; Rambahadur Rai, *Vishwanath Pratap Singh – Manzil Se Zyada Safar* (New Delhi: Rajkamal Prakashan, 2006), p. 82.
7. V.P. Singh transcripts, NMML; Rambahadur Rai, *Manzil Se Zyada Safar,* p. 83.
8. Katherine Frank, *Indira: The Life of Indira Nehru Gandhi* (New York: HarperCollins Publishers, 2001), p. 326.
9. Seema Mustafa, *The Lonely Prophet,* p. 28.
10. Hari Krishna Shastri lost the Meerut seat by more than 80,000 votes to the Congress (R)'s Shahnawaz Khan in 1971.
11. V.P. Singh transcripts, NMML.
12. Ibid.
13. Ibid.
14. Ibid.
15. Ibid.

16. Election Commission of India, 'General Election, 1971 (Vol I, II)', https://eci.gov.in/files/file/4115-general-election-1971-vol-i-ii/
17. Ibid.
18. V.P. Singh transcripts, NMML.
19. Ibid.
20. Ibid.
21. Ibid. Pande was duly made a member of the legislative council (MLC).
22. 'Uttar Pradesh Assembly Election Results in 1969', http://www.elections.in/uttar-pradesh/assembly-constituencies/1969-election-results.html

Chapter 5: 'I began making my presence felt'

1. V.P. Singh transcripts, Oral History section, Nehru Memorial Museum and Library (NMML), translated (from Hindi) by the author; Rambahadur Rai, *Vishwanath Pratap Singh – Manzil Se Zyada Safar* (New Delhi: Rajkamal Prakashan, 2006), pp. 85–86.
2. V.P. Singh transcripts, NMML.
3. Ibid.
4. Ibid.
5. Rambahadur Rai, *Manzil Se Zyada Safar*, pp. 412–13.
6. 'MPs Raise Sky-high Victorious PM', *Hindustan Times*, 19 December 1971.
7. Katherine Frank, *Indira: The Life of Indira Nehru Gandhi* (New York: HarperCollins Publishers, 2001), p. 349.
8. Ajit Bhattacharjee, *Unfinished Revolution: A Political Biography of Jayaprakash Narayan* (New Delhi: Vikas Publishing House, 1975), p. 181
9. 'Delhi Rally Seeks a New Deal', *Hindustan Times*, 7 October 1974.
10. 'Top Party Aides Join Government', *Hindustan Times*, 11 October 1974.
11. 'Union Ministry of 36 Installed; Raj Bahadur, Ray, Kumaramangalam, Gokhale, Huq in; Nanda, Dinesh, VKRV Rao, Sen among Seven Dropped', *Hindustan Times*, 19 March 1971.
12. Kuldip Singh, 'Obituary: Dinesh Singh', *The Independent*, 2 December 1995, https://www.independent.co.uk/news/people/obituary-dinesh-singh-1523677.html
13. Mark Tully and Gillian Wright, 'A Tale of Two Brothers', *India in Slow Motion* (New Delhi: Penguin Books India, 2002), p. 212.
14. Ibid., p. 221.
15. Ibid.
16. Ibid.; also Janardhan Thakur, *V.P. Singh: The Quest for Power* (New Delhi: Warbler Books, 1989), p. 32. The story was narrated to both

Mark Tully and Thakur by Devendra Nath Dwivedi, quoting Kamalapati Tripathi.

17. Mark Tully and Gillian Wright, *India in Slow Motion*, p. 222.
18. Ibid., pp. 212–23.
19. Interview with Abhay Singh.
20. V.P. Singh transcripts, NMML.
21. Seema Mustafa, *The Lonely Prophet: V.P. Singh, A Political Biography* (New Delhi: New Age International [P] Ltd, 1995), p. 29.
22. V.P. Singh transcripts, NMML.
23. Ibid.
24. Janardhan Thakur, *V.P. Singh*, p. 33.
25. Interview with Anand Singh.
26. Mark Tully and Gillian Wright, *India in Slow Motion*, p. 226.
27. V.P. Singh transcripts, NMML.
28. Interview with Colonel Ranamata Singh (retd).
29. Interview with Sita Kumari Singh.
30. Interview with Ajeya Singh
31. Ibid.
32. V.P. Singh transcripts, NMML.

Chapter 6: 'Chaprasis salute the chair I occupy, not me'

1. Interview with Sita Kumari Singh.
2. Interview with Ajeya Singh.
3. V.P. Singh transcripts, Oral History section, Nehru Memorial Museum and Library (NMML), translated (from Hindi) by the author.
4. Ibid.
5. Ibid.
6. Katherine Frank, *Indira: The Life of Indira Nehru Gandhi* (New York: HarperCollins Publishers, 2001), p. 400, quoting Amnesty International.
7. The election was made necessary by the student agitation in the state the previous year, which got the earlier assembly prematurely dissolved.
8. Ramachandra Guha, *India after Gandhi: The History of the World's Largest Democracy* (New Delhi: Picador, 2008) p. 489.
9. V.P. Singh transcripts, NMML.
10. Katherine Frank, *Indira*, p. 379.
11. Pranab Mukherjee, *The Dramatic Decade: The Indira Gandhi Years* (New Delhi: Rupa Publications India, 2015), p. 44.
12. V.P. Singh transcripts, NMML.
13. Ibid.

14. Vinod Mehta, *The Sanjay Story: From Anand Bhavan to Amethi* (Bombay: Jaico Publishing House, 1978), p. 86.
15. Ibid., p. 100.
16. Ibid., p. 125.
17. V.P. Singh transcripts, NMML.
18. Katherine Frank, *Indira*, p. 409.
19. V.P. Singh transcripts, NMML.
20. Ibid.
21. Ibid.
22. Mark Tully and Gillian Wright, 'A Tale of Two Brothers', *India in Slow Motion* (New Delhi: Penguin Books India, 2002), p. 223.
23. Seema Mustafa, *The Lonely Prophet: V.P. Singh, A Political Biography* (New Delhi: New Age International [P] Ltd, 1995), p. 31.
24. Interview with Sita Kumari Singh.
25. V.P. Singh transcripts, NMML; also Seema Mustafa, *The Lonely Prophet*, p. 31. Indira Gandhi was, however, perfectly aware of her party's dismal prospects in the 1977 election. Inder Kumar Gujral recounts in his autobiography, 'Then all of a sudden, she [Indira Gandhi] asked me what I thought would be the result of the (March 1977) elections. When I replied that it seemed she would win comfortably, she turned irritable and retorted, "*Ab aapne bhi jhoot bolna shuru kar diya hai? Main haar rahi hoon* (Now you too have started lying? I'm losing!).'" – Inder Kumar Gujral, *Matters of Discretion: An Autobiography* (New Delhi: Hay House India, 2011), Kindle edition: Loc 1551.
26. V.P. Singh transcripts, NMML.
27. Election Commission of India, 'General Election, 1977 (Vol I, II)', https://eci.gov.in/files/file/4116-general-election-1977-vol-i-ii/
28. Ibid.
29. Bipan Chandra, Aditya Mukherjee and Mridula Mukherjee, *India since Independence* (New Delhi: Penguin Books, 2008), p. 331.
30. Interview with Sita Kumari Singh.

Chapter 7: 'If we shared power with her, we should also share defeat with her'

1. Pranab Mukherjee, *The Dramatic Decade: The Indira Gandhi Years* (New Delhi: Rupa Publications India, 2015), p. 111.
2. Interview with Sita Kumari Singh.
3. The same Lakshmi Kumari Chundawat who had insisted on Sita Kumari being sent to school, making her the first girl in her family to get this privilege (see Part 1, Chapter 3).

4. Janardhan Thakur, *V.P. Singh: The Quest for Power* (New Delhi: Warbler Books, 1989), p. 33.
5. V.P. Singh transcripts, Oral History section, Nehru Memorial Museum and Library (NMML), translated (from Hindi) by the author.
6. Ibid.
7. Ibid.
8. Interview with Sita Kumari Singh.
9. 'Vinoba Denies Political Talks with Mrs Gandhi', *The Indian Express*, 27 July 1977; many other contemporaneous reports.
10. Pranab Mukherjee, *The Dramatic Decade,* pp. 150–51.
11. V.P. Singh transcripts, NMML.
12. 'People Regret Voting against Indira Gandhi in Rae Bareli', *India Today*, 15 September 1977, https://www.indiatoday.in/magazine/cover-story/story/19770915-people-regret-voting-against-indira-gandhi-in-rae-bareli-823883-2014-09-02
13. Paul Brass, *An Indian Political Life: Charan Singh and Congress Politics, 1967 to 1987*, Vol. 3 (New Delhi: Sage Publications, 2014), pp. 240–43.
14. Ibid.
15. V.P. Singh transcripts, NMML.
16. Interview with Ramesh Pande.
17. Interview with Sita Kumari Singh.
18. V.P. Singh transcripts, NMML.
19. Ibid.
20. Ibid.
21. 'Violence in Lucknow Provides Ready Ammunition to Janata Party against Congress(I)', *India Today,* 15 April 1978, https://www.indiatoday.in/magazine/states/uttar-pradesh/story/19780415-violence-in-lucknow-provides-ready-ammunition-to-janata-party-against-congressi-822929-2014-12-29
22. V.P. Singh transcripts, NMML.
23. Interview with Sita Kumari Singh.
24. V.P. Singh transcripts, NMML.
25. 'Violence in Lucknow Provides Ready Ammunition to Janata Party against Congress(I)', *India Today,* 15 April 1978, https://www.indiatoday.in/magazine/states/uttar-pradesh/story/19780415-violence-in-lucknow-provides-ready-ammunition-to-janata-party-against-congressi-822929-2014-12-29
26. The Maharashtra coalition, however, did not last long. A section of the Congress (R), led by Sharad Pawar, broke away to form another coalition government with the Janata Party, with Pawar as chief minister.
27. V.P. Singh transcripts, NMML.

28. Katherine Frank, *Indira: The Life of Indira Nehru Gandhi* (New York: HarperCollins Publishers, 2001), p. 433.

29. Ibid., pp. 435–36; 'Ex-PM Held Guilty of Contempt by Lok Sabha Panel', *Hindustan Times*, 22 November 1978.

30. '428 Agitators Arrested in Capital', *Hindustan Times*, 21 December 1978; 'All Congress (I) MPs to Court arrest', *Hindustan Times*, 21 December 1978; 'Bogie Set on fire', *Hindustan Times*, 23 December 1978; '30,000 Congress (I) Workers under Arrest in UP', 25 December 1978.

31. 'Boeing Hijackers Summon CM to Varanasi; Commandos Flown in; Some Passengers Released', *Hindustan Times*, 21 December 1978; 'Boeing Hijackers Surrender, Police Arrest Tripathi Son "Brain behind Incident"', *Hindustan Times*, 22 December 1978.

32. V.P. Singh transcripts, NMML.

33. Ibid.

34. Interview with Ramesh Pande.

35. 'Fury of Flood Sweeps through Haryana, Delhi, Uttar Pradesh, Bihar and West Bengal; Leaves a Trail of Death, Destruction and Disease', *India Today*, 30 September 1978, https://www.indiatoday.in/magazine/cover-story/story/19780930-fury-of-flood-sweeps-through-haryana-delhi-uttar-pradesh-bihar-and-west-bengal-818688-2015-04-21

36. Interview with Ramesh Pande.

37. 'Janata Party Wins Samastipur Seat by 27,000 Votes', *Hindustan Times*, 30 November 1978; 'Janata Wins Fatehpur Lok Sabha Seat By over 30,000 Votes', *The Indian Express*, 6 December 1978; 'Khandwa Seat Stays with Janata', *Hindustan Times*, 8 February 1979.

38. Seema Mustafa, *The Lonely Prophet: V.P. Singh, A Political Biography* (New Delhi: New Age International [P] Ltd, 1995), pp. 33–34; V.P. Singh transcripts, NMML.

39. Paul Brass, *An Indian Political Life*, Vol. 3, p. 257; 'Charan Singh Meets President, Stakes Claim to Form Government', *The Indian Express*, 17 July 1979; many other similar contemporaneous reports.

40. Seema Mustafa, *The Lonely Prophet*, p. 33; Rambahadur Rai, *Vishwanath Pratap Singh – Manzil Se Zyada Safar* (New Delhi: Rajkamal Prakashan, 2006), p. 95.

41. Rambahadur Rai, *Manzil Se Zyada Safar*, p. 100.

42. Ibid., p. 100; Seema Mustafa, *The Lonely Prophet*, p. 35.

43. V.P. Singh transcripts, NMML; Seema Mustafa, *The Lonely Prophet*, p. 37.

44. Ibid.

45. Interview with Atul Anjaan.

46. Election Commission of India, 'General Election, 1980 (Vol I, II)', https://eci.gov.in/files/file/4117-general-election-1980-vol-i-ii/
47. Not to be confused with the well-known Communist Party of India leader Sarjoo Pandey, who also fought the 1980 poll from the Ghazipur seat in east UP and lost.
48. Interview with Ramesh Pande.
49. Election Commission of India, 'General Election, 1980 (Vol I, II)', https://eci.gov.in/files/file/4117-general-election-1980-vol-i-ii/

PART 3: UP AND ITS DISCONTENTS

Chapter 1: 'Singing praises of the leader is part of Congress culture'

1. 'Mrs Gandhi, 21 Ministers Sworn In', *Hindustan Times*, 15 January 1980.
2. V.P. Singh transcripts, Oral History section, Nehru Memorial Museum and Library (NMML), translated (from Hindi) by the author.
3. Ibid.; Seema Mustafa, *The Lonely Prophet: V.P. Singh, A Political Biography* (New Delhi: New Age International [P] Ltd, 1995), pp. 38–39.
4. Election Commission of India, 'Uttar Pradesh 1980', https://eci.gov.in/files/file/3254-uttar-pradesh-1980/
5. Prabhu Chawla, 'Uttar Pradesh: The Making of a Chief Minister', *India Today*, 30 June 1980, https://www.indiatoday.in/magazine/cover-story/story/19800630-uttar-pradesh-the-making-of-a-chief-minister-821230-2014-01-25; Seema Mustafa, *The Lonely Prophet*, p. 38; V.P. Singh transcripts, NMML; Janardhan Thakur, *V.P. Singh: The Quest for Power* (New Delhi: Warbler Books, 1989), p. 36.
6. Prabhu Chawla, 'Uttar Pradesh: The Making of a Chief Minister', *India Today*, 30 June 1980, https://www.indiatoday.in/magazine/cover-story/story/19800630-uttar-pradesh-the-making-of-a-chief-minister-821230-2014-01-25
7. Janardhan Thakur, *V.P. Singh*, pp. 36–37.
8. 'Uttar Pradesh Mein 15 Sadasya Mantra Mandal Dwara Shapath Grahan', *Hindustan*, 10 June 1980.
9. V.P. Singh transcripts, NMML.
10. Interview with Sita Kumari Singh.
11. Election Commission of India, 'Uttar Pradesh 1980', https://eci.gov.in/files/file/3254-uttar-pradesh-1980/

12. 'A Look at the New Chief Ministers and Their States after the Assembly Poll', *India Today*, 30 June 1980, https://www.indiatoday.in/magazine/cover-story/story/19800630-a-look-at-the-new-chief-ministers-and-their-states-after-the-assembly-polls-821207-2014-01-25

13. *Illustrated Weekly of India*, 5–11 May 1985, quoted by Janardhan Thakur in *V.P. Singh*, p. 35.

14. Janardhan Thakur, *V.P. Singh*, p. 35.

15. Mark Tully and Gillian Wright, 'A Tale of Two Brothers', *India in Slow Motion* (New Delhi: Penguin Books India, 2002), p. 223.

16. Katherine Frank, *Indira: The Life of Indira Nehru Gandhi* (New York: HarperCollins Publishers, 2001), p. 445; Seema Mustafa, *The Lonely Prophet*, p. 43.

17. Seema Mustafa, *The Lonely Prophet*, p. 43; V.P. Singh transcripts, NMML.

18. V.P. Singh transcripts, NMML.

19. Katherine Frank, *Indira*, p. 449.

20. H.K. Dua, 'Functioning of Congress (I) to Undergo Change', *The Indian Express*, 26 June 1980.

21. Minhaz Merchant, *Rajiv Gandhi: The End of a Dream* (New Delhi: Penguin Viking, 1991), p. 87.

22. Janardhan Thakur, *V.P. Singh*, p. 39.

23. 'A Mixed Reception', *India Today*, 31 December 1980, https://www.indiatoday.in/magazine/indiascope/story/19801231-indira-gandhi-arun-kumar-nehru-sanjay-gandhi-harijan-congress-vishwanath-pratap-singh-rajiv-gandhi-773646-2013-12-02

24. 'Moderate to Low Turnout in 29 By-Elections', *Hindustan Times*, 15 June 1981.

25. 'Amethi Parliamentary Constituency Election and Results Update', http://www.elections.in/uttar-pradesh/parliamentary-constituencies/amethi.html

26. 'Rajiv Gandhi Promises to Complete All Sanjay Projects in Amethi', *India Today*, 15 June 1981, https://www.indiatoday.in/magazine/indiascope/story/19810615-rajiv-gandhi-promises-to-complete-all-projects-sanjay-in-amethi-772974-2013-11-20

27. 'Moderate to Low Turnout in 29 By-Elections', *Hindustan Times*, 15 June 1981.

28. Mark Tully and Gillian Wright, *India in Slow Motion*, p. 225.

29. 'Uttar Pradesh Assembly Election Results in 1980', http://www.elections.in/uttar-pradesh/assembly-constituencies/1980-election-results.html

30. Seema Mustafa, *The Lonely Prophet*, p. 47; Mark Tully and Gillian Wright, *India in Slow Motion*, p. 225.

31. V.P. Singh transcripts, NMML; Seema Mustafa, *The Lonely Prophet*, p. 47.
32. Seema Mustafa, *The Lonely Prophet*, p. 47.
33. Ibid.
34. 'Rajiv Gandhi Wins by Record Margin, Congress (I) Captures Four Lok Sabha and Fourteen Assembly Seats', *Hindustan Times,* 16 June 1981.
35. 'Bahuguna Quits Party, Seat in Lok Sabha, PM Accused of Stifling Democracy', *The Indian Express,* 20 May 1980.
36. 'Kamla Bahuguna Also Quits Congress (I)', *The Indian Express,* 20 May 1980; 'Two More Congress (I) MPs Quit Party', *The Indian Express,* 21 May 1980; subsequent reports.
37. 'Bahuguna Quits Party, Seat in Lok Sabha, PM Accused of Stifling Democracy', *The Indian Express,* 20 May 1980.
38. V.P. Singh transcripts, NMML.
39. 'Elections in Garhwal Ranked Among the Worst in the History of India's Parliamentary Polls', *India Today*, 15 July 1981, https://www.indiatoday. in/magazine/indiascope/story/19810715-elections-in-garhwal-ranked-among-the-worst-in-the-history-of-indias-parliamentary-polls-773040-2013-11-19
40. Ibid.; V.P. Singh transcripts, NMML; Seema Mustafa, *The Lonely Prophet*, p. 46.
41. V.P. Singh transcripts, NMML.
42. Ibid.
43. Ibid.
44. Ibid.
45. Seema Mustafa, *The Lonely Prophet*, p. 45; 'Garhwal Repoll Put Off Indefinitely', *Hindustan Times*, 15 November 1981.
46. 'Uttar Pradesh Assembly Election Results in 1980', http://www.elections.in/uttar-pradesh/assembly-constituencies/1980-election-results.html

Chapter 2: 'I think I should be replaced'

1. V.P. Singh transcripts, Oral History section, Nehru Memorial Museum and Library (NMML), translated (from Hindi) by the author; 'Uttar Pradesh Mein 15 Sadasya Mantra Mandal Dwara Shapath Grahan', *Hindustan*, 10 June 1980.
2. Seema Mustafa, *The Lonely Prophet: V.P. Singh, A Political Biography* (New Delhi: New Age International [P] Ltd, 1995), p. 39; Janardhan Thakur, *V.P. Singh: The Quest for Power* (New Delhi: Warbler Books, 1989), pp. 37–38.
3. Janardhan Thakur, *V.P. Singh*, p. 37.

4. Prabhu Chawla, 'On an Average, Congress(I) Chief Ministers Spend One Day Out of Three in Delhi', *India Today*, 15 October 1980, https://www.indiatoday.in/magazine/indiascope/story/19801015-on-an-average-congressi-chief-ministers-spend-one-day-out-of-three-in-delhi-821516-2014-01-06

5. Ibid.

6. Seema Mustafa, *The Lonely Prophet*, p. 40; V.P. Singh transcripts, NMML.

7. Seema Mustafa, *The Lonely Prophet*, p. 41.

8. Ibid., pp. 39–40.

9. 'Two UP Ministers Dropped', *Hindustan Times*, 13 December 1980; 'Three UP Ministers Resign', *Hindustan Times*, 17 August 1981. Of these latter three, only two were actually dropped. The third, K.P. Tiwari, resigned because he had contested and won the Allahabad Lok Sabha seat, which V.P. Singh vacated on becoming chief minister.

10. V.P. Singh transcripts, NMML.

11. Janardhan Thakur, *V.P. Singh*, p. 42.

12. Prabhu Chawla, 'Uttar Pradesh CM Vishwanath Pratap Singh Has a Reputation for Being Scrupulously Honest', *India Today*, 30 September 1980, https://www.indiatoday.in/magazine/indiascope/story/19800930-uttar-pradesh-cm-vishwanath-pratap-singh-has-a-reputation-for-being-scrupulously-honest-821465-2014-01-14

13. S. Premi and Prabhu Chawla, 'Several Hospitals in Uttar Pradesh Raided, Scandal Involving Purchase of Medicines Unfolds', *India Today*, 31 August 1980, https://www.indiatoday.in/magazine/indiascope/story/19800831-several-hospitals-in-uttar-pradesh-raided-scandal-involving-purchase-of-medicines-unfolds-821395-2014-01-14

14. Prabhu Chawla, 'Uttar Pradesh CM Vishwanath Pratap Singh Has a Reputation for Being Scrupulously Honest', *India Today*, 30 September 1980, https://www.indiatoday.in/magazine/indiascope/story/19800930-uttar-pradesh-cm-vishwanath-pratap-singh-has-a-reputation-for-being-scrupulously-honest-821465-2014-01-14

15. Janardhan Thakur, *V.P. Singh*, p. 42.

16. Interview with Somansh Prakash.

17. Ibid.

18. V.P. Singh transcripts, NMML.

19. Ibid.; Seema Mustafa, *The Lonely Prophet*, p. 44.

20. Seema Mustafa, *The Lonely Prophet*, p. 45.

21. Ibid., p. 40.

22. 'UP Ke Mantriyon Ka Vibhagon Ka Vitaran', *Hindustan*, 10 June 1980; 'UP Mein Kuch Aur Mantralayaon Ka Vitharan', *Hindustan*, 18 June 1980.

23. '20 MLAs Seek Leadership Change', *Hindustan Times*, 24 July 1981. The replacements suggested were Rajiv Gandhi himself, and failing that, Arun Nehru; or, if they were both unwilling, Sheila Kaul, then MP from Lucknow and a relative of Indira Gandhi's.

24. '20 MLAs Seek Leadership Change', *Hindustan Times*, 24 July 1981.

25. Janardhan Thakur, *V.P. Singh*, p. 42.

26. V.P. Singh transcripts, NMML; 'Anti CM Legislators in UP Served Show-Cause Notices', *Hindustan Times*, 24 July 1981.

27. Interview with Virendra Dixit.

28. Interview with Manohar Subrahmanyam.

29. Interview with J.P. Singh.

30. Interview with Bhure Lal.

31. Interview with Manohar Subrahmanyam.

32. Ibid.

33. Interview with J.P. Singh.

34. Janardhan Thakur, *V.P. Singh*, p. 40.

35. Interview with J.P. Singh.

36. V.P. Singh transcripts, NMML.

37. Interview with Sita Kumari Singh.

38. V.P. Singh transcripts, NMML.

39. This was a popular picnic spot on the edge of the Kukrail reserve forest, where a crocodile breeding centre had been set up in 1978.

40. Interview with Sita Kumari Singh.

41. Interview with Janardhan Pratap Singh.

42. V.P. Singh transcripts, NMML.

43. Ibid.

44. Interview with Som Pal.

45. V.P. Singh's government also financed the Muzaffar Ali-directed feature film *Aagman*, highlighting cane farmers' exploitation by the mills, and suggesting farmer-owned cooperatives set up their own mills as a solution. But the film, though an artistic success, was a commercial failure.

46. V.P. Singh transcripts, NMML.

47. Ibid.

48. Ibid.; Seema Mustafa, *The Lonely Prophet*, p. 45.

49. V.P. Singh transcripts, NMML.

50. Ibid.

51. 'UP to Have 12 Regional Ministers', *Hindustan Times*, 20 August 1981.

52. V.P. Singh transcripts, NMML.
53. Interview with Udit Narayan Singh.
54. Ibid.

Chapter 3: 'In senior positions, one must take responsibility for others' errors'

1. See 'Inflation, Consumer Prices (annual %) – India', The World Bank, https://data.worldbank.org/indicator/FP.CPI.TOTL.ZG?locations=IN
2. 'Flood Fury in North India Unabated', *Hindustan Times,* 20 July 1980; 'Many Lucknow Areas Flooded', *Hindustan Times,* 23 July 1980; 'IAF Alerted to Combat Floods in UP', *Hindustan Times,* 24 July 1980; and many more.
3. 'Were Baghpat Victims Dacoits?', *Hindustan Times,* 28 June 1980; also, Bulbul Pal, 'D.P. Gaur Is Famous for Terrorizing Everyone: Maya Tyagi', *India Today,* 31 July 1980, https://www.indiatoday.in/magazine/special-report/story/19800731-d.p.-gaur-is-famous-for-terrorising-everyone-maya-tyagi-821317-2014-01-17; and many other contemporaneous reports.
4. The judicial commission that enquired into the incident rejected the police's version. Ten policemen were arrested, of which six were sentenced to death and four to life imprisonment by a Bulandshahr court in January 1988. The Allahabad High Court, however, in September 1988, reduced the sentences to life imprisonment for the first six, and shorter prison terms for the other four. See *Sheo Kumar Gupta and Others vs the State of UP,* https://www.casemine.com/judgement/in/56b49278607dba348ffffe1c
5. V.P. Singh transcripts, Oral History section, Nehru Memorial Museum and Library (NMML), translated (from Hindi) by the author; Rambahadur Rai, *Vishwanath Pratap Singh – Manzil Se Zyada Safar* (New Delhi: Rajkamal Prakashan, 2006), p. 123.
6. Rambahadur Rai, *Manzil Se Zyada Safar*, p. 124.
7. Ibid., p. 123.
8. V.P. Singh transcripts, NMML; Rambahadur Rai, *Manzil Se Zyada Safar*, p. 124.
9. All details about the Moradabad riots are from *Hindustan Times* and *India Today* archives; V.P. Singh transcripts, NMML; Seema Mustafa, *The Lonely Prophet: V.P. Singh, A Political Biography* (New Delhi: New Age International [P] Ltd, 1995); and Paul Brass, *The Production*

of Hindu-Muslim Violence in Contemporary India (Delhi: Oxford University Press, 2003), pp. 101–04.

10. The M.P. Saxena Commission of Enquiry into the riots rubbished the claim that a pig had got into the idgah premises at all. But its report was widely called one-sided, as it absolved the police and Hindu organizations of all blame and indicted only local Muslims for provoking the initial attack on the police. It was never tabled in the UP assembly.

11. Seema Mustafa, *The Lonely Prophet*, p. 42.

12. The novel *Shehr Mein Curfew* (English translation, *Curfew in the City* [New Delhi: Penguin Random House India, 2016]) by Vibhuti Narain Rai is a fictionalized account of the 1980 Allahabad riots. Rai was Allahabad's senior superintendent of police at the time. *The Production of Hindu-Muslim Violence in Contemporary India* by Paul Brass has a detailed account of the 1980 Aligarh riots, pp. 101–04.

13. Seema Mustafa, *The Lonely Prophet*, p.43; 'UP Chief Minister Offers to Quit', *Hindustan Times*, 15 September 1980.

14. 'UP Chief Minister Offers to Quit', *Hindustan Times*, 15 September 1980.

15. 'Mrs Gandhi's Asks V.P. Singh Not to Quit Office', *Hindustan Times*, 17 September 1980.

16. Kapal Verma, 'Lucknow under Curfew after Shia-Sunni Riots', *Hindustan Times,* 14 December 1980.

17. 'Lucknow Quiet but Tense as Curfew Continues', *Hindustan Times,* 17 December 1980.

18. 'Lucknow Students on Rampage', *Hindustan Times*, 17 December 1980; 'BHU, Gorakhpur University Closed Indefinitely', *Hindustan Times,* 2 April 1981.

19. Interview with Atul Anjaan.

20. Interview with Vijay Chaturvedi.

21. 'West UP Bandh Today', *Hindustan Times,* 16 March 1981; 'UP Lawyers Told to Call off Strike', *Hindustan Times,* 12 April 1981, are representative news reports.

22. Prabhu Chawla, 'Uttar Pradesh CM V.P. Singh's Penchant for Taking Quick Decisions Lands Him in Trouble', *India Today*, 15 April 1981, https://www.indiatoday.in/magazine/indiascope/story/19810415-uttar-pradesh-cm-v.p.-singhs-penchant-for-taking-quick-decisions-lands-him-in-trouble-772848-2013-11-23

23. '275 Jail Employees Arrested in UP', *Hindustan Times*, 1 November 1981.

24. '1000 UP Townships in Darkness', *Hindustan Times*, 6 July 1981; L.H. Naqvi, 'UP Power Situation at Critical Low', *Hindustan Times*, 23 July 1981.

25. Ibid.

26. Interview with Sita Kumari Singh.

27. Interview with Som Pal.

28. Richard Shears and Isobelle Gidley, *Devi: The Bandit Queen* (London: George, Allen and Unwin, 1984), p. 20.

29. Ibid., pp. 21–29.

30. 'Dacoits Massacre 22 in UP Village', *Hindustan Times*, 16 February 1981.

31. 'Dacoits Gun Down 21 in Etah', *Hindustan Times*, 4 May 1981.

32. '24 Massacred in Mainpuri', *Hindustan Times*, 20 November 1981; V.P. Singh transcripts NMML; Seema Mustafa, The *Lonely Prophet.*, pp. 48-49.

33. V.P. Singh transcripts, NMML; Rambahadur Rai, *Manzil Se Zyada Safar*, p. 115.

34. Prabhu Chawla, '30 Undertrials in Gazipur District Brutally Disabled by Uttar Pradesh Police', *India Today*, 28 February 1981, https://www.indiatoday.in/magazine/investigation/story/19810228-30-undertrials-in-ghazipur-district-brutally-disabled-by-uttar-pradesh-police-772697-2013-11-27

35. M.Z. Khan, *Dacoity in Chambal Valley* (New Delhi: S. Chand Publishers, 1981), p. 80.

36. Ibid., p. 80–81.

37. V.P. Singh transcripts, NMML.

38. Seema Mustafa, *The Lonely Prophet*, p. 48; Prabhu Chawla, 'Uttar Pradesh CM V.P. Singh's Penchant for Taking Quick Decisions Lands Him in Trouble', *India Today*, 15 April 1981, https://www.indiatoday.in/magazine/indiascope/story/19810415-uttar-pradesh-cm-v.p.-singhs-penchant-for-taking-quick-decisions-lands-him-in-trouble-772848-2013-11-23

39. V.P. Singh transcripts, NMML.

40. Chaitanya Kalbag, 'Fake Encounters by Uttar Pradesh Police: Five Brutal Tales', *India Today*, 31 January 1982, https://www.indiatoday.in/magazine/special-report/story/19820131-alleged-dacoits-killed-by-uttar-pradesh-police-in-fake-encounters-771478-2013-10-22

41. Janardhan Thakur, *V.P. Singh: The Quest for Power* (New Delhi: Warbler Books, 1989), p. 44.

42. '10 Harijans in UP Massacred, Second Carnage in 6 Weeks', *Hindustan Times*, 1 January 1982.

43. '21 Killed in Fake Police Encounters', *Hindustan Times,* 11 April 1981.

44. Mulayam Singh Yadav began his political career in the early 1960s, winning his first election to the UP assembly in 1967 as an SSP candidate at the age of twenty-seven, later joining (after the SSP disintegrated) Charan Singh's BLD, the Janata Party and the Janata Dal, before starting his own Samajwadi Party in 1992. He was elected MLA another seven times over the next four decades and had three stints as UP chief minister—from 1989 to 1991, from 1993 to 1995, and from 2003 to 2007. He has also been elected to the Lok Sabha seven times and was Union defence minister from 1996 to 1998.

45. Janardhan Thakur, *V.P. Singh*, pp. 43–44.

46. For instance, Chaitanya Kalbag, 'Fake Encounters by Uttar Pradesh Police: Five Brutal Tales', *India Today,* 31 January 1982, https://www.indiatoday.in/magazine/special-report/story/19820131-alleged-dacoits-killed-by-uttar-pradesh-police-in-fake-encounters-771478-2013-10-22

47. Interview with Atul Anjaan.

48. Interview with J.P. Singh.

49. V.P. Singh transcripts, NMML.

50. Ibid.

51. Ibid.; Seema Mustafa, *The Lonely Prophet*, p. 48.

52. Interview with Col. Ranamata Singh (retd).

53. Interview with Vikram Singh.

54. The account combines inputs from interviews with Vikram Singh and Sita Kumari Singh; V.P. Singh transcripts, NMML; Seema Mustafa, *The Lonely Prophet*, pp. 50–51; and Anand Sagar, 'Senior Judge of Allahabad High Court, 15-Year-Old Son Killed by Dacoits', *India Today*, 15 April 1982, https://www.indiatoday.in/magazine/indiascope/story/19820415-senior-judge-of-allahabad-high-court-15-year-old-son-killed-by-dacoits-771682-2013-10-16

55. Interview with Vikram Singh.

56. V.P. Singh transcripts, NMML.

57. Interview with Vikram Singh.

58. Ibid.

59. Interview with Sita Kumari Singh.

60. V.P. Singh transcripts, NMML.

61. Interview with Sita Kumari Singh.

62. Seema Mustafa, *The Lonely Prophet*, pp. 51–52.

63. V.P. Singh transcripts, NMML.

64. Ibid.; Anand Sagar, 'Brother of Dacoit Mustaqueem Avenges His Death, Hunts Down 10 Members of a Family', *India Today,* 31 July 1982, https://www.indiatoday.in/magazine/indiascope/story/19820731-brother-of-

dacoit-mustaqueem-avanges-his-death-huns-down-10-members-of-a-fimily-772027-2013-10-16

65. V.P. Singh transcripts, NMML.
66. Interview with Sita Kumari Singh.
67. V.P. Singh transcripts, NMML.
68. V.P. Singh, 'Maine Mukhyamantri Pad Se Istifa Kyun Diya (Why I Resigned as Chief Minister)', *Ravivar*, 11 July 1982 (translation by the author).
69. Ibid.
70. Interview with Pradeep Kapoor.
71. Ibid.
72. V.P. Singh transcripts, NMML.
73. Anand Sagar and Prabhu Chawla, 'Dacoits Gun 21 People in Uttar Pradesh, CM Vishwanath Pratap Singh Resigns', *India Today*, 31 July 1982, https://www.indiatoday.in/magazine/indiascope/story/19820731-dacoits-gun-21-people-in-uttar-pradesh-cm-vishwanath-pratap-singh-resigns-772003-2013-10-15#ssologin=1#source=magazine; Janardhan Thakur, *V.P. Singh*, p. 46.
74. Mark Tully and Gillian Wright, 'A Tale of Two Brothers', *India in Slow Motion* (New Delhi: Penguin Books India, 2002), p. 225.

Chapter 4: 'You won't be asked to collect funds for the party'

1. 'Nainital Talks on CM Crucial', *Hindustan Times*, 4 July 1982.
2. Seema Mustafa, *The Lonely Prophet: V.P. Singh, A Political Biography* (New Delhi: New Age International [P] Ltd, 1995), p. 54; V.P. Singh transcripts, Oral History section, Nehru Memorial Museum and Library (NMML), translated (from Hindi) by the author.
3. V.P. Singh transcripts, NMML.
4. 'Congress (I) Strongholds Crumble, NTR Party Sweeps Andhra', *Hindustan Times*, 7 January 1983; also see Election Commission of India, 'Karnataka 1983', https://eci.gov.in/files/file/3777-karnataka-1983/
5. 'V.P. Singh, V.B. Reddy Join Union Cabinet', *Hindustan Times*, 30 January 1983.
6. V.P. Singh transcripts, NMML.
7. Janardhan Thakur, *V.P. Singh: The Quest for Power* (New Delhi: Warbler Books, 1989), p. 47.
8. V.P. Singh transcripts, NMML.
9. Ibid.

10. Interview with Som Pal (incident narrated to him by V.P. Singh).
11. Subramanian would go on to becoming UP chief secretary from December 1992 to July 1996, and cabinet secretary thereafter, until March 1998.
12. T.S.R. Subramanian, *Journeys through Babudom and Netaland: Governance in India* (New Delhi: Rupa Publications India, 2004), pp. 156–57.
13. Ibid.
14. V.P. Singh transcripts, NMML.
15. Abid Hussain was later a Planning Commission member (1985–90) and India's ambassador to the US (1990–92).
16. V.P. Singh transcripts, NMML.
17. T.S.R. Subramanian, *Journeys through Babudom and Netaland*, pp. 160–66.
18. It rose from Rs 4,295 crore in 1982–83 to Rs 5,951 crore in 1983–84. See Palakunnathu G. Mathai, 'Record Deficit Raises Questions about Wisdom of Relaxed Foreign Trade Policy', *India Today*, 31 August 1984, https://www.indiatoday.in/magazine/economy/story/19840831-record-deficit-raises-questions-about-wisdom-of-relaxed-foreign-trade-policy-803702-1984-08-31
19. V.P. Singh transcripts, NMML; also see Prabhu Chawla, 'Beef Tallow Controversy Gets Fresh Lease of Life as Opposition Parties Make It an Election Issue', *India Today*, 30 November 1983, https://www.indiatoday.in/magazine/investigation/story/19831130-beef-tallow-controversy-gets-fresh-lease-of-life-as-opposition-parties-make-it-an-election-issue-771228-2013-07-15
20. V.P. Singh transcripts, NMML; Prabhu Chawla, 'Parliament Rocked by Reports of Beef Tallow Being Blended into Vanaspati', *India Today*, 15 September 1983, https://www.indiatoday.in/magazine/economy/story/19830915-parliament-rocked-by-reports-of-beef-tallow-being-blended-into-vanaspati-771004-2013-07-15
21. Prabhu Chawla, 'To the Opposition Every Vanaspati Tin Appears to Be a Ballot-Box: V.P. Singh', *India Today*, 30 November 1983, https://www.indiatoday.in/magazine/investigation/story/19831130-to-the-opposition-every-vanaspati-tin-appears-to-be-a-ballot-box-v.p.-singh-771235-2013-07-17
22. V.P. Singh's friend Dharam Vir, whom Sanjay Gandhi had made UP Congress president, had long been shifted out; he was a minister in Shripat Mishra's cabinet.
23. Prabhu Chawla, 'Prime Minister Indira Gandhi Sacks Uttar Pradesh CM Sripat Misra', *India Today*, 31 August 1984, https://www.indiatoday.

in/magazine/indiascope/story/19840831-prime-minister-indira-gandhi-sacks-uttar-pradesh-cm-sripat-misra-803684-1984-08-31

24. Narayan Dutt Tiwari, hailing from Nainital, began his political career by participating in the Quit India movement. After Independence, he was a PSP MLA for two terms before defecting to the Congress in 1963. He had already been UP chief minister once before, replacing Bahuguna in November 1975 and ruling until the Congress (R) was crushed in the June 1977 assembly elections, during which he had outdone most other party chief ministers in his slavish deference to Sanjay Gandhi. He had two more stints as UP chief minister through the 1980s, held several important portfolios in the Union cabinet in the 1980s and the 1990s, and was also chief minister of Uttarakhand (after the state was carved out of UP in 2000) from 2002 to 2007. As Andhra Pradesh governor thereafter, he was also embroiled in a much-publicized sex scandal.

25. V.P. Singh transcripts, NMML.

26. Ibid.

27. Interview with Ramesh Pande.

28. In none of his interviews, including the one with NMML, does V.P. Singh elaborate on his feelings following Indira Gandhi's assassination.

29. Election Commission of India, 'General Election 1984', https://eci.gov.in/files/file/4118-general-election-1984-vol-i-ii/

30. V.P. Singh transcripts, NMML.

31. Ibid

32. Ibid.

33. Election Commission of India, 'General Election, 1984 (Vol I, II)', https://eci.gov.in/files/file/4118-general-election-1984-vol-i-ii/

34. Minhaz Merchant, *Rajiv Gandhi: The End of a Dream* (New Delhi: Penguin Viking, 1991), pp. 174–76.

35. V.P. Singh transcripts, NMML.

PART 4: RAID RAJ

Chapter 1: 'Clothes stitched for a five-year-old cannot be worn by a thirty-five-year-old'

1. The MRTP Act was abolished in 2002 and replaced by the Competition Act in the same year.

2. FERA was replaced by the considerably more liberal Foreign Exchange Management Act (FEMA) in 1999.

3. V.P. Singh transcripts, Oral History section, Nehru Memorial Museum and Library (NMML), translated (from Hindi) by the author.

4. 'No section of our vast and diverse population should feel forgotten. Their neglect is our collective loss', Speech of Shri Vishwanath Pratap Singh, Minister of Finance, Introducing the Budget for the Year 1985–86, https://www.indiabudget.gov.in/doc/bspeech/bs198586.pdf

5. The highest rate of income tax as well as that of corporate tax has since come down to 30 per cent, while wealth tax has been abolished.

6. Suman Dubey, 'Vishwanath Pratap Singh's Budget Makes a Clean Break with the Past', *India Today*, 15 April 1985, https://www.indiatoday.in/magazine/cover-story/story/19850415-vishwanath-pratap-singh-budget-makes-a-clean-break-with-the-past-769934-2013-12-04

7. The BIFR continued until the end of 2016, when the Insolvency and Bankruptcy Code (IBC) was adopted and the BIFR was replaced by the National Company Law Tribunal.

8. Suman Dubey, 'Vishwanath Pratap Singh's Budget Makes a Clean Break with the Past', *India Today*, 15 April 1985, https://www.indiatoday.in/magazine/cover-story/story/19850415-vishwanath-pratap-singh-budget-makes-a-clean-break-with-the-past-769934-2013-12-04

9. 'Towards a New Era' editorial, *The Times of India*, 17 March 1985.

10. Suman Dubey, 'Vishwanath Pratap Singh's Budget Makes a Clean Break with the Past', *India Today*, 15 April 1985, https://www.indiatoday.in/magazine/cover-story/story/19850415-vishwanath-pratap-singh-budget-makes-a-clean-break-with-the-past-769934-2013-12-04

11. 'We Want Competition in the Economy: Vishwanath Pratap Singh', *India Today*, 15 April 1985, https://www.indiatoday.in/magazine/cover-story/story/19850415-we-want-competition-in-the-economy-vishyvanath-pratap-singh-769973-2013-12-04

12. 'Deviation from Socialism Denied: V.P. Singh Defends Budget', *Hindustan Times*, 28 March 1985.

13. 'Congress for Socialism', *Sunday*, 19 May 1985; also Sumit Mitra, 'Mood Less than Festive at AICC(I) Session in Delhi', *India Today*, 31 May 1985, https://www.indiatoday.in/magazine/indiascope/story/19850531-mood-less-than-festive-at-aicci-session-in-delhi-770087-2013-12-13

14. Speech of Shri Vishwanath Pratap Singh, Minister of Finance, Introducing the Budget for the Year 1985–86, https://www.indiabudget.gov.in/doc/bspeech/bs198586.pdf

15. Reserve Bank of India, 'Select Fiscal Indicators of the Central Government (as Percentage of GDP)', *Handbook of Statistics on Indian Economy 2014–15*.

16. 'Price Rise: Ministers under Fire', *Sunday,* 16–24 August 1985.

17. Reserve Bank of India, *Handbook of Statistics on Indian Economy, 2014–15.*

18. Speech of Shri Vishwanath Pratap Singh, Minister of Finance, Introducing the Budget for the Year 1986–87, https://www.indiabudget.gov.in/doc/bspeech/bs198687.pdf; 'Budget Thrust to Anti-Poverty Plans', *Hindustan Times,* 1 March 1986.

19. The complete concept spelt out by V.P. Singh was as follows, 'In excise taxation, a vexatious question which has been often encountered is the taxation of inputs and the cascading effect of this on the value of the final product. Our Long-Term Fiscal Policy had stated that the best solution would be to extend the present system of proforma credit to all excisable commodities with the exception of a few sectors like petroleum, tobacco and textiles. The scheme which has been referred to as the Modified Value Added Tax scheme (MODVAT)—I shall stress MODVAT, not MADVAT—allows the manufacturer to obtain instant and complete reimbursement of the excise duty paid on components and raw materials', in VP Singh's 1986 budget speech, https://www.indiabudget.gov.in/doc/bspeech/bs198687.pdf

20. Ibid.

21. Shaji Vikraman, 'Looking Back at GST's Journey: How an Idea Is Now Near Reality', *The Indian Express,* 31 March 2017, https://indianexpress.com/article/explained/looking-back-at-gsts-journey-how-an-idea-is-now-near-reality-arun-jaitley-4593103/

22. 'Speech of Shri Rajiv Gandhi, Prime Minister, and Minister of Finance, Introducing the Budget for the Year 1987–88', https://www.indiabudget.gov.in/doc/bspeech/bs198788.pdf

23. V.P. Singh transcripts, NMML.

24. The administered price mechanism was dismantled in stages, being finally abolished in July 2017.

25. One example: VP's predecessor as finance minister, Pranab Mukherjee—trying to reduce the backlog in the income tax department as well as the harassment income tax payers sometimes faced over trifling amounts—had ruled that tax returns on incomes of less than Rs 100,000 a year should not be scrutinized, barring a few chosen randomly by computer. Enquiring into whether this was being complied with, VP found that the department had indeed passed such an order but had added eighteen conditions, and only those returns that fulfilled all the conditions (apart from being for incomes less than Rs 100,000) were being accepted at face value. 'Hardly any return was able to meet all eighteen conditions,' VP said, in V.P. Singh transcripts, NMML.

26. 'Finance Minister V.P. Singh Only Minister to Get a Note of Congratulation from the PM', *India Today*, 15 January 1986, https://www.indiatoday.in/magazine/economy/story/19860115-finance-minister-v.p.-singh-only-minister-to-get-a-note-of-congratulation-from-the-pm-800510-1986-01-15#ssologin=1#source=magazine

27. 'GDP at Factor Cost at 2004-05 Prices, Share to Total GDP and % Rate of Growth in GDP (31-10-2014)', https://niti.gov.in/planningcommission.gov.in/docs/data/datatable/data_2312/DatabookDec2014%202.pdf

28. In later years, Bimal Jalan was finance secretary, Reserve Bank of India chairman and Rajya Sabha member.

29. V.P. Singh transcripts, NMML.

30. Other factors were also responsible for the 1991 economic crisis, notably the spike in oil prices caused by Iraq's Kuwait invasion and the subsequent Gulf War.

31. Arjun Singh, his counterpart in Madhya Pradesh when VP was UP chief minister. He joined the Union cabinet after a short stint as governor of the then-much-troubled state of Punjab.

32. 'Export-Import Policy Liberalised for Three Years', *Hindustan Times*, 13 April 1985.

33. T.S.R. Subramanian, *Journeys through Babudom and Netaland: Governance in India* (New Delhi: Rupa Publications India, 2004), p. 164.

34. 'India Rejects US Demand on Trade Services', *Hindustan Times*, 17 September 1986.

35. T.S.R. Subramanian, *Journeys through Babudom and Netaland,* p. 166.

36. Ibid.

37. In the early 1990s, a fresh 'Dunkel Draft' on the same issues of agriculture, textiles and service would generate enormous controversy in India.

38. Juan A. Marchetti and Petros C. Mavroidis, 'The Genesis of GATS (General Agreement on Trade in Services)', *European Journal of International Law*, Vol. 22, Issue 3, 2011, pp. 18–19, https://scholarship.law.columbia.edu/cgi/viewcontent.cgi?article=3389&context=faculty_scholarship

39. V.P. Singh transcripts, NMML; an abridged version of the incident is also narrated in Seema Mustafa, *The Lonely Prophet: V.P. Singh, A Political Biography* (New Delhi: New Age International [P] Ltd, 1995), pp. 59–60.

40. Ibid.

41. 'India Vindicated at GATT Meet', *Hindustan Times*, 21 September 1986.

42. Juan A. Marchetti and Petros C. Mavroidis, 'The Genesis of GATS', p. 21, https://scholarship.law.columbia.edu/cgi/viewcontent.cgi?article=3389&context=faculty_scholarship

43. Ibid., p. 15.

44. V.P. Singh transcripts, NMML.
45. Ibid.
46. Ibid.; Seema Mustafa, *The Lonely Prophet,* p. 61.
47. Ibid.
48. Ibid.
49. 'General Agreement on Tariffs and Trade (GATT): Punta del Este Declaration', 15 September 2002, https://www.iatp.org/documents/general-agreement-on-tariffs-and-trade-gatt-punta-del-este-declaration
50. V.P. Singh transcripts, NMML.
51. In India, the controversy was particularly intense over the 1991 'Dunkel Draft', related to the same issues of trade in services, along with agriculture and textiles.
52. Juan A. Marchetti and Petros C. Mavroidis, 'The Genesis of GATS', pp. 50–54; World Trade Organization, 'The General Agreement on Trade in Services: Objectives, Coverage and Disciplines', https://www.wto.org/english/tratop_e/serv_e/gatsqa_e.htm
53. V.P. Singh transcripts, NMML; Seema Mustafa, *The Lonely Prophet*, pp. 55–56.
54. V.P. Singh transcripts, NMML.
55. Ibid.
56. Ibid.; Seema Mustafa, *The Lonely Prophet*, p. 56.
57. See, for instance, Minhaz Merchant, *Rajiv Gandhi: The End of a Dream* (New Delhi: Penguin Viking, 1991), pp. 184–85. or Kewal Verma, 'Centenary Celebrations: Congressmen Came Confused, Returned Confounded', *Sunday,* 12–18 January 1986.
58. 'Premium on Youth and Clean Image', *Hindustan Times,* 1 February 1985; 'Campaign for Assembly Elections Hots Up, Dice Heavily Loaded in Congress(I) Favour', *India Today,* 28 February 1985, https://www.indiatoday.in/magazine/cover-story/story/19850228-campaign-for-assembly-elections-hots-up-dice-heavily-loaded-in-congressi-favour-769804-2013-11-27
59. 'Campaign for Assembly Elections Hots Up, Dice Heavily Loaded in Congress(I) Favour', *India Today,* 28 February 1985, https://www.indiatoday.in/magazine/cover-story/story/19850228-campaign-for-assembly-elections-hots-up-dice-heavily-loaded-in-congressi-favour-769804-2013-11-27
60. V.P. Singh transcripts, NMML.
61. 'V.P. Singh, Tiwari Gheraoed', *Hindustan Times,* 6 February 1985; V.P. Singh transcripts, NMML.
62. V.P. Singh transcripts, NMML.

63. Sumit Mitra, 'Rajiv Gandhi's New-Look Congress(I) Back Again to Its Original Dimension', *India Today*, 31 March 1985, https://www.indiatoday.in/magazine/nation/story/19850331-rajiv-gandhis-new-look-congressi-back-again-to-its-original-dimension-769929-2013-12-03

64. V.P. Singh transcripts, NMML.

65. Interview with Som Pal.

66. The Central Industrial Security Force (CISF) took over the security of commercial airports much later, in 2007.

67. Election Commission of India, 'Uttar Pradesh Assembly Election Results in 1985', http://www.elections.in/uttar-pradesh/assembly-constituencies/1985-election-results.html

Chapter 2: 'Theft can't be business'

1. Pranab Mukherjee had a fifty-year long career in Indian politics, culminating in becoming the country's President from 2012 to 2017. Starting his career with a Congress splinter group in West Bengal, the Bangla Congress, in 1967, he moved into the Congress after Bangla Congress merged once more with its parent group in 1969, becoming a Rajya Sabha member the same year and deputy minister in 1973. He rose rapidly under Indira Gandhi to becoming finance minister in 1982, but was unable to hit it off with Rajiv Gandhi and quit the Congress in 1986. He returned to the party in 1989 and again held top ministerial positions in Congress governments in the 1990s and 2000s.

2. M.J. Akbar, interview with Rajiv Gandhi, 'The Assassination Was Done not to Kill Mrs Gandhi, It Was Done for the Reaction', *Sunday*, 10–16 March 1985.

3. V.P. Singh transcripts, Oral History section, Nehru Memorial Museum and Library (NMML), translated (from Hindi) by the author.

4. Kumkum Chadha, interview with Vinod Pande, *Hindustan Times*, 29 July 1990.

5. Prabhu Chawla, 'Reward Money Earned by Tax Officials Exceeds Their Total Salaries Drawn Over Last 10 Years', *India Today*, 15 October 1986, https://www.indiatoday.in/magazine/special-report/story/19861015-reward-money-earned-by-tax-officials-exceeds-their-total-salaries-drawn-over-last-10-years-801343-1986-10-15

6. 'Chiefs of Three Nationalized Banks Dismissed', *Hindustan Times*, 18 February 1985; 'Government Sacks Three Bank Chiefs', *The Times of India*, 19 February 1985; Prabhu Chawla, 'Finance Ministry Gives Three Banking Chiefs Marching Orders before Their Time Gets Up', *India*

Today, 15 March 1985, https://www.indiatoday.in/magazine/economy/story/19850315-finance-ministry-gives-three-banking-chiefs-marching-orders-before-their-time-gets-up-769885-2013-12-02

7. K.N. Malik, 'Indian is Britain's Biggest Bankrupt', *The Times of India,* 22 January 1985; Prabhu Chawla, 'Rajendra Sethia, Biggest Bankrupt in British History, Finally Nabbed', *India Today*, 31 March 1985, https://www.indiatoday.in/magazine/economy/story/19850331-rajendra-sethia-biggest-bankrupt-in-british-history-finally-nabbed-769925-2013-12-03

8. V.P. Singh transcripts, NMML; Seema Mustafa, *The Lonely Prophet: V.P. Singh, A Political Biography* (New Delhi: New Age International [P] Ltd, 1995), p. 57.

9. Raju Santhanam, 'CBI Raids I-T Officers Suspected of Having Assets Disproportionate to Their Earnings', *India Today*, 31 October 1985, https://www.indiatoday.in/magazine/indiascope/story/19851031-cbi-raids-i-t-officers-suspected-of-having-assets-disproportionate-to-their-earnings-802110-2014-01-14

10. Now called the Central Board of Indirect Taxes and Customs.

11. Prabhu Chawla, 'Finance Minister V.P. Singh Undertakes Comprehensive Shake-Up of Revenue Department', *India Today,* 31 July 1985, https://www.indiatoday.in/magazine/economy/story/19850731-finance-minister-v.p.-singh-undertakes-comprehensive-shake-up-of-revenue-department-770271-2013-12-27

12. Prabhu Chawla, 'STC Chairman Luthar Lands in Trouble for Controversial Basmati Rice Deal', *India Today,* 15 August 1985, https://www.indiatoday.in/magazine/economy/story/19850815-stc-chairman-luthar-lands-in-trouble-for-controversial-basmati-rice-deal-770299-2013-12-31

13. Seema Mustafa, *The Lonely Prophet*, p. 57; V.P. Singh transcripts, NMML.

14. Ibid.

15. Suman Dubey, 'Vishwanath Pratap Singh's Budget Makes a Clean Break with the Past', *India Today*, 15 April 1985, https://www.indiatoday.in/magazine/cover-story/story/19850415-vishwanath-pratap-singh-budget-makes-a-clean-break-with-the-past-769934-2013-12-04

16. Interview with Bhure Lal.

17. Ramesh Menon and Prabhu Chawla, 'Entrepreneur Mrugesh Jaikrishna Arrested on Charges of Attempting to Smuggle Foreign Currency', *India Today*, 30 April 1985, https://www.indiatoday.in/magazine/investigation/story/19850430-entrepreneur-mrugesh-jaikrishna-arrested-on-charges-of-attempting-to-smuggle-foreign-currency-770001-2013-12-07; Prabhu

Chawla, 'Major Foreign Exchange Racket Busted in Bombay Estimated at a Staggering Rs 1,200 Crore', *India Today*, 15 August 1985, https://www.indiatoday.in/magazine/economy/story/19850815-major-foreign-exchange-racket-busted-in-bombay-estimated-at-a-staggering-rs-1200-crore-770304-2013-12-30

18. 'Massive Raids on City Builders', *The Times of India*, 22 February 1985.

19. 'Spate of Income Tax Raids across India Anger Business Community', *India Today*, 15 January 1986, https://www.indiatoday.in/magazine/investigation/story/19860115-spate-of-income-tax-raids-across-india-anger-business-community-800499-1986-01-15

20. T.N. Ninan, 'From Tax Raids to Price Rise, V.P. Singh Is at the Centre of Several Converging Storms', *India Today*, 15 September 1985, https://www.indiatoday.in/magazine/economy/story/19850915-from-tax-raids-to-price-rise-v.p.-singh-is-at-the-centre-of-several-converging-storms-801947-2014-01-06

21. Gita Piramal, *Business Maharajas* (New Delhi: Penguin Books India, 2000), Kindle edition: Loc 1665.

22. The Kirloskar group was accused of seemingly divesting half its ownership of a Hamburg-based engineering goods company to another company in Liechtenstein soon after the FERA was passed in 1973, so that the Act would not apply to it. The charge was that it clandestinely owned the Liechtenstein-based company as well. The Thapar group was accused of not repatriating to India its overseas earnings, as the FERA required, and setting up an overseas subsidiary without the Reserve Bank of India's permission. Voltas was booked for breaking up the cost of its air conditioners fraudulently, overpricing the compressor on which excise duty was low and underpricing the other parts on which duty was higher, so as to pay less overall duty. Bata India was accused of using synthetic rubber on the soles of footwear it exported while claiming to use natural rubber, on which duty was lower. From V.P. Singh transcripts, NMML; 'Spate of Income Tax Raids across India Anger Business Community', *India Today*, 15 January 1986, https://www.indiatoday.in/magazine/investigation/story/19860115-spate-of-income-tax-raids-across-india-anger-business-community-800499-1986-01-15; also Interview with Bhure Lal.

23. With Bajaj Auto's production of autorickshaws forever short of demand, there had always been a premium on their selling price. The DRI claimed that part of the premium charged by dealers was being unofficially routed back to the company. See V.P. Singh transcripts, NMML; also Jagannath Dubashi, 'Bajaj Auto Gets Embroiled in Premium Racket

Three-Wheelers Sale', *India Today*, 15 January 1986, https://www.
indiatoday.in/magazine/investigation/story/19860115-bajaj-auto-gets-
embroiled-in-premium-racket-three-wheelers-sale-800470-1986-01-15

24. T.N. Ninan and Prabhu Chawla, 'We Are Not Attacking Business, We
Are Attacking Theft: V.P. Singh', *India Today*, 30 November 1985,
https://www.indiatoday.in/magazine/cover-story/story/19851130-
we-are-not-attacking-business-we-are-attacking-theft-v.p.-
singh-802225-2014-01-20

25. 'Political Competence: Rajiv Gandhi Emerges at the Top of Readers'
Preferences', *India Today*, 31 August 1986, https://www.indiatoday.in/
magazine/nation/story/19860831-political-competence-rajiv-gandhi-
emerges-at-the-top-of-readers-preferences-801167-1986-08-31

26. 'Orkay Silk Mills Chairman Kapal Mehra's Arrest Shakes Business
Community', *India Today*, 30 November 1985, https://www.indiatoday.
in/magazine/cover-story/story/19851130-orkay-silk-mills-chairman-
kapal-mehras-arrest-shakes-business-community-802182-2014-01-20

27. Interview with Bhure Lal.

28. V.P. Singh transcripts, NMML.

29. V.P. Singh transcripts, NMML; interview with Bhure Lal.

30. Interview with Bhure Lal.

31. The UB Group was accused of secretly teaming up with Dubai-based
businessman Manu Chhabria through a Hong Kong-based company it
owned, to acquire a large stake in a rival liquor company, the Calcutta-
headquartered Shaw Wallace. The case fell through two years later and
Chhabria acquired control of Shaw Wallace. Much later, in 2005, in a
completely changed business setting, Mallya finally bought the company
and merged it with UB.

32. 'Thapar Held, Granted Bail by Supreme Court', *Hindustan Times*, 6
September 1986; 'Amnesty Scheme for FERA Violators Soon', *Hindustan
Times*, 18 October 1986.

33. V.P. Singh transcripts, NMML.

34. Prabhu Chawla, 'Finance Ministry Blacklists 21 Leading Business
Houses for Central Excise Dues', *India Today*, 31 July 1986, https://
www.indiatoday.in/magazine/economy/story/19860731-finance-
ministry-blacklists-21-leading-business-houses-for-central-excise-
dues-801102-1986-07-31

35. In their profile of Sant Bux Singh and V.P. Singh, 'A Tale of Two Brothers',
Mark Tully and Gillian Wright maintain they asked V.P. Singh about this
and that V.P. Singh replied very candidly. 'I would not take money myself,'
he said. 'But I would say, "If you want, give to the party." Politicians start

from hypocrisy by making false declarations to the election commissioner about their expenses. After all, it's not much to say you don't take money yourself. You can't stand on a high pedestal yourself as long as elections are funded by non-accounted money. Perhaps you don't use that money yourself, but you know it is being used.' From Mark Tully and Gillian Wright, 'A Tale of Two Brothers', *India in Slow Motion* (New Delhi: Penguin Books India, 2002), p. 224.

36. V.P. Singh transcripts, NMML.

37. Ibid.

38. Hamish McDonald, *Ambani and Sons: The Making of the World's Richest Brothers and Their Feud* (New Delhi: Roli Books, 2010), Kindle edition: Loc 366–510.

39. T.N. Ninan and Jagannath Dubashi, 'Dhirubhai Ambani Emerges as India's Most Outstanding Businessman of the Last Two Decades', *India Today*, 30 June 1985, https://www.indiatoday.in/magazine/cover-story/story/19850630-dhirubhai-ambani-emerges-as-indias-most-outstanding-businessman-of-the-last-two-decades-770192-1999-11-30

40. The first partially convertible debenture was for Rs 7 crore, the second for Rs 10.8 crore, the third for Rs 24 crore and the fourth for Rs 50 crore.

41. Rambahadur Rai, *Vishwanath Pratap Singh – Manzil Se Zyada Safar* (New Delhi: Rajkamal Prakashan, 2006), p. 194.

42. Gita Piramal, *Business Maharajas*, Loc: 731–745.

43. Ibid., Loc: 685. All details in the account that follows are taken from Hamish McDonald, chapters 8–11, 'The Great Polyester War', 'Paper Tigers', 'Sleuths' and 'Letting Loose a Scorpion', *Ambani and Sons,* Kindle edition, Loc: 1538–2651; Gita Piramal, 'Dhirubhai Ambani' in *Business Maharajas,* LoC:228–1347; relevant reports in *India Today* (1985–87); and interview with Swaminathan Gurumurthy.

44. Reliance Industries denied this, putting out 'lengthy written explanations as to why its import contracts in May had coincidentally preceded the policy change'. From Hamish McDonald, *Ambani and Sons*, Kindle edition: Loc 1271.

45. Hamish McDonald, *Ambani and Sons*, Kindle edition: Loc 1193.

46. Ibid., Loc 1964–1978, 1993–2048.

47. Ibid., Loc 2103–2116.

48. Ibid.

49. Interview with Swaminathan Gurumurthy.

50. The two experts were Jamnadas Moorjani, then president of the All India Crimpers' Association, and Perez Chandra, a freelance journalist.

The crimpers (or texturizers) of polyester yarn had been badly hit by the increase of duty on imported polyester (allegedly to help Reliance gain market share once it began manufacturing polyester filament yarn locally) and Moorjani had been campaigning against Reliance on every available forum. 'Moorjani was my guru. He educated me on every aspect of Reliance's polyester business. He was virtually a one-man army against Reliance until *The Indian Express* exposés began. He even faced a murderous attack at the time, narrowly escaping death.' From interview with Swaminathan Gurumurthy.

51. Interview with Swaminathan Gurumurthy.
52. Ibid.
53. Hamish McDonald, *Ambani and Sons*, Kindle edition: Loc 2131–43.
54. Interview with Bhure Lal.
55. V.P. Singh transcripts, NMML.
56. Michael Hershman had also been an investigator on the US Senate committee investigating the Watergate case in the mid-1970s, and was later the deputy auditor general with the US Agency for International Development (USAID).
57. Interview with Swaminathan Gurumurthy.
58. Interview with Bhure Lal.
59. Interview with Swaminathan Gurumurthy.
60. *Polyester Prince* was never published or distributed in India following a court injunction and threat of further legal action by Reliance. See Subir Ghosh and Paranjoy Guha Thakurta, *Sue the Messenger: How Legal Harassment by Corporates Is Shackling Reportage and Undermining Democracy in India* (New Delhi: Authors Upfront, 2016), pp. 12–24.
61. Hamish McDonald, *Ambani and Sons*, Kindle edition: Loc 2375–88.

Chapter 3: 'I was not outmanoeuvred because I was not manoeuvring'

1. K. Natwar Singh, *One Life Is Not Enough,* Chapter 15, 'The Rajiv Gandhi Years' (New Delhi: Rupa Publications India, 2014), p. 240.
2. V.P. Singh transcripts, Oral History section, Nehru Memorial Museum and Library (NMML), translated (from Hindi) by the author.
3. Ibid.
4. Ibid.

5. *The Telegraph*, 12 March 1986, quoted in Janardhan Thakur, *V.P. Singh: The Quest for Power* (New Delhi: Warbler Books, 1989), p. 69.

6. Prabhu Chawla, 'V.P. Singh Is No More the Bete Noire of Industrialists', *India Today*, 15 July 1986, https://www.indiatoday.in/magazine/economy/story/19860715-v.p.-singh-is-no-more-the-bete-noire-of-indus trialists-801060-1986-07-15

7. 'Amnesty Scheme for FERA Violators Soon', *Hindustan Times*, 18 October 1986.

8. V.P. Singh transcripts, NMML.

9. Ibid.

10. Paul Brass, *An Indian Political Life: Charan Singh and Congress Politics, 1937 to 1961, Vol. 1* (New Delhi: Sage Publications, 2011), pp. 115–16. The limit was further lowered in 1972.

11. Janardhan Thakur, *V.P. Singh*, pp. 57–58.

12. Interview with Sita Kumari Singh.

13. Janardhan Thakur, *V.P. Singh*, pp. 57–68; 'V.P. Singh Sure of Vindication', *Hindustan Times*, 5 September 1986; Prabhu Chawla, 'V.P. Singh Refutes Corruption Charges Made by Calcutta-Based Hindi Weekly', *India Today*, 30 September 1986, https://www.indiatoday.in/magazine/indiascope/story/19860930-v.p.-singh-refutes-corruption-charges-made-by-calcutta-based-hindi-weekly-769671-2013-04-09

14. The MPs were Lal Krishna Advani (BJP), Madhu Dandavate (Janata Party), Nirmal Chatterjee (CPI [M]), Indrajit Gupta (CPI), Virendra Verma (Lok Dal) and C. Madhav Reddy (Telugu Desam Party).

15. Janardhan Thakur, *V.P. Singh*, p. 56.

16. V.P. Singh transcripts, NMML.

17. Janardhan Thakur, *V.P. Singh*, p. 68.

18. No connection with Ramnath Goenka, the newspaper baron.

19. Gita Piramal, *Business Maharajas* (New Delhi: Penguin Books India, 2000), Kindle edition: Loc 3008–20.

20. Janardhan Thakur, *V.P. Singh*, p. 72. The author mistakenly claims V.P. Singh was in Washington.

21. Seema Mustafa, *The Lonely Prophet: V.P. Singh, A Political Biography* (New Delhi: New Age International [P] Ltd, 1995), p. 66.

22. 'Arun Nehru, Gadgil, Ghafoor dropped', *Hindustan Times*, 23 October 1986; Prabhu Chawla, 'Cabinet Reshuffle: Rajiv Gandhi Cuts to Size Powerful Men Like Arjun Singh, Arun Nehru', *India Today*, 15 November 1986, https://www.indiatoday.in/magazine/cover-story/story/19861115-cabinet-reshuffle-rajiv-gandhi-cuts-to-size-powerful-men-like-arjun-singh-arun-nehru-801445-1986-11-15

23. Hamish Macdonald, *Ambani and Sons*, Kindle edition: Loc 2389–402.

24. Seema Mustafa, *The Lonely Prophet*, p. 67; Rambahadur Rai, *Vishwanath Pratap Singh – Manzil Se Zyada Safar* (New Delhi: Rajkamal Prakashan, 2006), pp. 198–200; interview with Som Pal.

25. The Indian Army had undergone considerable modernization in the past few years. Operation Brasstacks was intended to check its level of war preparedness—whether the weapons systems, the mobility and communications equipment, etc., that had lately been acquired would actually work if a war broke out, as also if the strategies planned would be effective. About 600,000–800,000 troops were brought together in the Rajasthan desert, frightening Pakistan.

26. V.P. Singh transcripts, NMML; Seema Mustafa, *The Lonely Prophet*, pp. 58–59.

27. Ibid., p. 67.

28. 'V.P. Singh Shifted to Defence', *The Times of India,* 25 January 1987.

29. K. Natwar Singh, *One Life Is Not Enough*, pp. 276–77. The minister in question was Arun Singh, a former school friend of Rajiv Gandhi. Natwar Singh was then minister of state for external affairs. He claims that Arun Singh had concealed the magnitude of Operation Brasstacks both from Rajiv Gandhi and the external affairs ministry.

30. V.P. Singh transcripts, NMML; Seema Mustafa, *The Lonely Prophet*, p. 67.

31. 'The Lobbyists Win', editorial, *The Indian Express*, 25 January 1987.

32. Prabhu Chawla, 'Finance to Defence: PM Rajiv Gandhi Removes V.P. Singh from the Limelight', *India Today*, 15 February 1987, https://www.indiatoday.in/magazine/cover-story/story/19870215-finance-to-defence-pm-rajiv-gandhi-removes-v.p.-singh-from-the-limelight-798500-1987-02-15

33. Ibid. The leader was Atal Bihari Vajpayee.

34. Ibid.

35. Seema Mustafa, *The Lonely Prophet,* p. 67. The aide was Makhan Lal Fotedar.

36. V.P. Singh transcripts, NMML.

37. Janardhan Thakur, *V.P. Singh*, p. 87.

38. Ibid., pp. 87–88.

39. Pritish Nandy, *The Illustrated Weekly of India*, 23 February 1986.

40. Ibid.

41. Seema Mustafa, *The Lonely Prophet: V. P. Singh*, p. 71, Janardhan Thakur, *V. P. Singh, The Quest for Power*, pp. 88–89.

42. Janardhan Thakur, *V.P. Singh*, pp. 84–85. Pritish Nandy, *The Illustrated Weekly of India*, 23 February 1986; Vir Sanghvi, *Rude*

Films: Bachchan, a Life in Chapters, https://www.hindustantimes.com/brunch/rude-films-by-vir-sanghvi-bachchan-a-life-in-chapters/story-ecrYCXgsLgGOVwnLmz18yL.html

43. Brahm Dutt was an old associate of V.P. Singh, hailing from UP's Tehri Garhwal district (now part of Uttarakhand), who had been in his cabinet when he was UP chief minister.

44. Seema Mustafa, *The Lonely Prophet*, p. 72. Bhure Lal confirmed it in his interview with the author.

45. The first letter, dated 20 November 1986, purportedly from Gordon McKay to Swaminathan Gurumurthy, went as follows:

> Dear Mr Gurumurthy, Dr Harris apprised me of his useful meeting in New Delhi last week with Mr R. Goenka, Mr N. Wadia, Mr V. Pande, Mr B. Lal and yourself. Now that the group has been retained to assist Government of India, we hope to expedite end results. We received only US $300,000 arranged by Mr N. Wadia. As considerable efforts have already been made and expenditure incurred, it is advisable Mr Goenka arranges during his forthcoming visit to Geneva an additional US $200,000. We shall refund both amounts on receipt from Government of India to F. Briner, Attorney, 31 Cheminchapeau-Rogue, 1231, Onches, Geneva. We shall apprise Mr Goenka in Geneva about the progress made on source of funds for purchase of Swiss properties of Mr Bachchan. We shall contact Mr Goenka at Casa Trola, CH-6922, Marcote (Ticina) during his visit.

The second letter, undated, also from McKay to Gurumurthy, ran:

> Dear Mr Gurumurthy, Please send me the following details to continue our investigation: (i) the details of rice exports from India to the Soviet Union (ii) Documents relating to the non-resident status of Mr Ajitabh Bachchan from the records of the Reserve Bank of India. When Mr Bhure Lal visits here next time, we will make his stay pleasant.
>
> ('Dr Harris' was the pseudonym Hershman registered under at his hotel during his India visit.) From Hamish McDonald, *Ambani and Sons*, Kindle edition: Loc 2417–35; Janardhan Thakur, *V.P. Singh*, pp. 80–81.

46. In Rambahadur Rai's *Manzil Se Zyada Safar* (p. 200), V.P. Singh charges Reliance Industries with having sent this individual, hoping to thereby create problems between him and Rajiv Gandhi, and sabotage the

investigation into its own finances. He says, 'I remember Kamal Nath (former Madhya Pradesh chief minister and earlier, Union minister) telling me that this was a ploy by Reliance, which succeeded. A manager of Kamal Nath's (company) was told this by a manager in Reliance at a dinner. It happened that after a few drinks, this Reliance manager began speaking frankly. He said, "We're going to corner the finance minister. We've finalised a detective agency in Europe. We've told the agency it doesn't have to do anything. All it need do is go meet Ajitabh Bachchan and ask him a couple of questions." This agency sent a person to meet Ajitabh and tell him that he was from Fairfax and had been retained by India's finance ministry and Bhure Lal to investigate the Bachchans.' Seema Mustafa's *The Lonely Prophet* says the same, again naming Kamal Nath as the source (pp. 71–72).

47. Interview with Swaminathan Gurumurthy.
48. Ibid.
49. Ibid.
50. Ibid.
51. V.P. Singh transcripts, NMML.
52. Ibid.
53. Prabhu Chawla, 'Defence Minister V.P. Singh Quits Office with His Image in Disarray', *India Today*, 30 April 1987, https://www.indiatoday.in/magazine/cover-story/story/19870430-defence-minister-v.p.-singh-quits-office-with-his-image-in-disarray-798814-1987-04-30
54. Frank Larkins, a former army major general, and his brother Kenneth Larkins, a former air vice-marshal, were caught selling confidential documents from the defence ministry to the US in November 1983; Coomar Narain and his associates were arrested in January 1985 for passing on similar documents from numerous ministries, including the PMO, to France, Russia, Poland and East Germany; Rama Swarup was held in October 1985 for spying for the US but was later exonerated.
55. V.P. Singh transcripts, NMML; Hamish McDonald, *Ambani and Sons*, Kindle edition: Loc 2508–21.
56. V.P. Singh transcripts, NMML.
57. Seema Mustafa, *The Lonely Prophet*, pp. 15–16.
58. V.P. Singh transcripts, NMML.
59. Ibid.
60. Prabhu Chawla, 'Thakkar Commission Probing Fairfax Affair Courts Controversy', *India Today*, 15 June 1987, https://www.indiatoday.in/magazine/indiascope/story/19870615-thakkar-commission-probing-fairfax-affair-courts-controversy-798972-1987-06-15
61. Interview with Bhure Lal.

62. Pankaj Pachauri, 'Fairfax Issue: Thakkar-Natarajan Commission Report Adds Little to What Was Already Known', *India Today*, 31 December 1987, https://www.indiatoday.in/magazine/indiascope/story/19871231-fairfax-issue-thakkar-natarajan-commission-report-adds-little-to-what-was-already-known-799678-1987-12-31

63. Hamish McDonald, *Ambani and Sons,* Kindle edition: Loc 2522–36.

64. Prabhu Chawla, 'HDW Submarine Deal Assumes Centre Stage Again. An Exclusive Inside Story', *India Today*, 15 March 1990, https://www.indiatoday.in/magazine/special-report/story/19900315-hdw-submarine-deal-assumes-centre-stage-again.-an-exclusive-inside-story-812418-1990-03-15

65. Ibid.

66. V.P. Singh transcripts, NMML.

67. Ibid.

68. Ibid.

69. Prabhu Chawla, 'Defence Minister V.P. Singh Quits Office with His Image in Disarray', *India Today*, 30 April 1987, https://www.indiatoday.in/magazine/cover-story/story/19870430-defence-minister-v.p.-singh-quits-office-with-his-image-in-disarray-798814-1987-04-30

70. Rambahadur Rai, *Manzil Se Zyada Safar*, p. 224; also see V.P. Singh transcripts, NMML; and Seema Mustafa, *The Lonely Prophet*, p. 75.

71. Prabhu Chawla, 'Defence Minister V.P. Singh Quits Office with His Image in Disarray', *India Today*, 30 April 1987, https://www.indiatoday.in/magazine/cover-story/story/19870430-defence-minister-v.p.-singh-quits-office-with-his-image-in-disarray-798814-1987-04-30

72. Mark Tully and Gillian Wright, 'A Tale of Two Brothers', *India in Slow Motion* (New Delhi: Penguin Books India, 2002) pp. 229–30; Janardhan Thakur, *V.P. Singh*, pp.100–01.

73. V.P. Singh transcripts, NMML.

74. Ibid.; Seema Mustafa, *The Lonely Prophet*, p. 76.

75. Inderjit Badhwar, 'Rajiv Gandhi Has Proved to Be a Total Failure: V.P. Singh', *India Today*, 31 March 1988, https://www.indiatoday.in/magazine/cover-story/story/19880331-it-is-clear-that-anyone-who-touches-the-mighty-bachchans-will-be-in-trouble-v.p.-singh-797103-1988-03-31

76. Girilal Jain, 'A Challenge Rajiv Cannot Ignore', *The Times of India*, 13 April 1987.

77. Interview with Sita Kumari Singh.

78. Ibid.

79. V.P. Singh transcripts, NMML.

80. Interview with Sita Kumari Singh.
81. V.P. Singh transcripts, NMML.
82. Interview with Sita Kumari Singh.

PART 5: '*DESH KA TAQDEER HAI*'

Chapter 1: 'I'm going to dig in and fight'

1. Janardhan Thakur, *V.P. Singh: The Quest for Power* (New Delhi: Warbler Books, 1989), p. 107.
2. Ibid., p. 102.
3. Ibid., p. 104.
4. 'Government of the People, Slave of None: Rajiv', *Hindustan Times*, 17 May 1987.
5. Interview with Som Pal.
6. Mir Jafar was a general in the Nawab of Bengal Siraj ud-Daulah's army, who betrayed him and backed the British forces during the Battle of Plassey in 1757, leading to the British winning the battle and paving the way for the subsequent British conquest of India. Jaichand, whom family lore cites as V.P. Singh's ancestor, backed Muhammed Ghori against Prithviraj Chauhan, raja of Ajmer, setting the stage for the Islamic conquest of India.
7. Janardhan Thakur, *V.P. Singh*, pp. 106–07.
8. V.P. Singh transcripts, Oral History section, Nehru Memorial Museum and Library (NMML), translated (from Hindi) by the author; see also Mark Tully and Gillian Wright, 'A Tale of Two Brothers', *India in Slow Motion* (New Delhi: Penguin Books India, 2002), p. 229 (which quotes Uma Shankar Dikshit a little differently, though the gist is the same).
9. Ibid.
10. V.P. Singh transcripts, NMML; Seema Mustafa, *The Lonely Prophet: V.P. Singh, A Political Biography* (New Delhi: New Age International [P] Ltd, 1995), pp. 77–78.
11. 1, Safdarjung Road, where Indira Gandhi lived, had been turned into a memorial for her following her assassination.
12. Interview with Sita Kumari Singh.
13. V.P. Singh transcripts, NMML; Seema Mustafa, *TheLonely Prophet*, p. 78.
14. Ibid.
15. Ibid. p. 79.
16. Janardhan Thakur, *V.P. Singh*, p. 102; also see Prabhu Chawla, 'Defence Minister V.P. Singh Quits Office with His Image in Disarray', *India*

Today, 30 April 1987, https://www.indiatoday.in/magazine/cover-story/story/19870430-defence-minister-v.p.-singh-quits-office-with-his-image-in-disarray-798814-1987-04-30

17. Interview with Ajeya Singh.

18. Interview with Anand Singh.

19. Lok Sabha Debates, https://parliamentofindia.nic.in/ls/lsdeb/ls10/ses3/1601049206.htm

20. The file on the Bofors gun purchase had been sent to the finance ministry while V.P. Singh was minister. His officers sent it back to the defence ministry with a few queries, which were never answered. From V.P. Singh transcripts, NMML.

21. See, for instance, Chitra Subramaniam, *Bofors: The Story behind the News* (New Delhi: Penguin Viking, 1993).

22. Interview with Som Pal.

23. Interview with Santosh Bhartiya.

24. V.P. Singh transcripts, NMML.

25. Janardhan Thakur, *V.P. Singh*, pp. 38–39.

26. See Supreme Court of India, *Mohammed Ahmed Khan vs Shah Bano Begum and Others*, 23 April 1985, https://indiankanoon.org/doc/823221/

27. Interview with Arif Mohammad Khan; Som Pal maintained that the wooing was not one-sided, that Arif Khan, too, had been trying to tie up with V.P. Singh. He recalled Arif Khan complaining to common friends that he felt 'rebuffed' when he greeted V.P. Singh at the 16 May 1987 Congress rally at Delhi's Boat Club—the same one at which Rajiv Gandhi in his speech insulted V.P. Singh—but received no acknowledgement. He assumed that V.P. Singh did not want to associate politically with him. V.P. Singh had assured him through these same friends that it was inadvertent, that he had indeed not noticed Arif's greeting. It was only thereafter that Arif responded.

28. Interview with Som Pal.

29. 'V.P. Singh Launches "Clean" Campaign', *The Times of India*, 16 July 1987; 'Sue Bofors, Says VP', *Hindustan Times*, 16 July 1987.

30. Interview with Som Pal.

31. 'Nehru, Shukla, Arif Expelled', *Hindustan Times*, 16 July 1987.

32. Interview with Som Pal.

33. Interview with Somansh Prakash.

34. 'V.P. Singh Resigns from Congress, Rajya Sabha', *The Times of India*, 16 July 1987; Seema Mustafa, *The Lonely Prophet*, pp. 85–86.

35. Interview with Somansh Prakash.

36. Zail Singh was a freedom-struggle veteran from Punjab's Faridkot district—ruled in British times by its maharaja—who had been jailed for long stints and even tortured by the maharaja's police for leading agitations against him. After Independence, he was minister in successive cabinets of PEPSU state and later Punjab from 1949, becoming chief minister of Punjab in 1972, and later Union home minister and President.

37. See, for instance, Inder Kumar Gujral, *Matters of Discretion: An Autobiography* (New Delhi: Hay House India, 2011), Kindle edition: Loc 3983.

38. Giani Zail Singh, *Memoirs of Giani Zail Singh: The Seventh President of India* (New Delhi: Har Anand Publications) 1997, p. 178.

39. Ibid., p. 217.

40. Janardhan Thakur, *V.P. Singh,* p. 110; Seema Mustafa, *The Lonely Prophet*, pp. 69–70; Rambahadur Rai, *Vishwanath Pratap Singh – Manzil Se Zyada Safar* (New Delhi: Rajkamal Prakashan, 2006), pp. 239–40.

41. In his memoirs, President Zail Singh reproduces as evidence a press release he sent out on 3 May 1987. The release read, 'The President has noted with distress the reports and comments which have appeared in the press persistently speculating that the president intends to dismiss Rajiv Gandhi from the office of prime minister ... The president wishes it to be known in the clearest terms that the said reports and comments are utterly devoid of any basis.' From *Memoirs of Giani Zail Singh*, p. 271.

42. V.P. Singh transcripts, NMML; Rambahadur Rai, *Manzil Se Zyada Safar*, pp. 239–40.

43. Ibid.

44. V.P. Singh transcripts, NMML.

45. Seema Mustafa, *The Lonely Prophet*, p. 90; interview with Som Pal.

46. V.P. Singh transcripts, NMML.

47. Interview with Som Pal.

48. V.P. Singh transcripts, NMML.

49. Ibid.; interview with Som Pal.

50. Ibid.; Seema Mustafa, *The Lonely Prophet*, p. 82.

51. V.P. Singh transcripts, NMML.

52. Ibid.

53. Mark Tully and Gillian Wright, *India in Slow Motion*, pp. 230–31.

54. V.P. Singh transcripts, NMML.

Chapter 2: *'Iski to bahut hawa hai'*

1. Election Commission of India, 'Haryana 1987', https://eci.gov.in/files/file/3821-haryana-1987/
2. 'Nation-Wide Opinion Poll Reveals Rajiv Gandhi Can Win a Mid-Term Election', *India Today*, 31 August 1987, https://www.indiatoday.in/magazine/cover-story/story/19870831-nation-wide-opinion-poll-reveals-rajiv-gandhi-can-win-a-mid-term-election-799209-1987-08-31
3. In fact, the Lok Dal had split twice in the past five years. The first time was in 1982, when Charan Singh, growing increasingly erratic with age, expelled all his close lieutenants, who then formed another party. The breakaway party, however, disintegrated soon after, with some leaders going back to Charan Singh and the rest joining the Janata Party. The second split was in 1987, when Charan Singh's son Ajit Singh sought to take over from his father, who, by then, was incapacitated by a stroke. Most party veterans, resenting this, preferred to separate. Ajit Singh's party was called Lok Dal (A), and the other group, with H.N. Bahuguna as president, was called Lok Dal (B).
4. Devi Lal had joined the freedom movement as a teenager and been repeatedly imprisoned; he was twice jailed even after Independence by the Punjab state government (Haryana was part of Punjab until 1966) for leading agitations demanding security of tenure for tenant farmers and, later, zamindari abolition. Elected as a Congress MLA in the first assembly election of 1952, he was initially close to—but later fell out with—each of Punjab's chief ministers in turn, as he kept advocating the interests of the Haryana region, which he believed were uniformly neglected by them. He had resigned from the Congress in 1962 but returned in 1965; he quit once more during the political uncertainty of 1967 (Haryana had been formed the previous year), only to return a few months later, and finally left forever in February 1971, following clashes with then Haryana Chief Minister Bansi Lal (who went on to become one of Indira Gandhi's chief hatchet men during the Emergency) and joined Charan Singh's party. He led the Janata Party to victory in the Haryana state elections once the Emergency was lifted in 1977 and became chief minister, only to lose his job two years later as collateral damage in the dust-up between Charan Singh and Morarji Desai. Despite further splits, his party remained the main Opposition to the Congress in Haryana, performing well enough in the 1982 assembly elections to narrowly miss forming the government. See K.C. Yadav, *Chaudhari Devi Lal: A Political Biography* (Gurgaon: Hope India Publications, 2002).

5. Interview with Som Pal.

6. Ibid.

7. Seema Mustafa, *The Lonely Prophet: V.P. Singh, A Political Biography* (New Delhi: New Age International [P] Ltd, 1995), p. 105.

8. A term used for any group of young people who seek radical reform, originating from a reform movement in Turkey at the turn of the twentieth century.

9. Harivansh and Ravi Dutt Bajpai, *Chandra Sekhar: The Last Icon of Ideological Politics* (New Delhi: Rupa Publications India, 2019), pp. 1–99.

10. Ibid., pp. 100–53.

11. Anita Pratap, 'Karnataka CM Ramakrishna Hegde Survives Trial as Intra-Party Rift Widens', *India Today*, 31 May 1988, https://www.indiatoday.in/magazine/indiascope/story/19880531-karnataka-cm-ramakrishna-hegde-survives-trial-as-intra-party-rift-widens-797333-1988-05-31#ssologin=1#source=magazine

12. Prabhu Chawla, 'V.P. Singh Doesn't Deserve That Much Attention: Chandra Shekhar', *India Today*, 15 July 1988, https://www.indiatoday.in/magazine/cover-story/story/19880715-v.p.-singh-does-not-deserve-that-much-attention-chandra-shekhar-797439-1988-07-15

13. Prabhu Chawla, 'Unity among Leaders from Non-Communist Parties Remains Elusive', *India Today*, 15 October 1987, https://www.indiatoday.in/magazine/indiascope/story/19871015-unity-among-leaders-from-non-communist-parties-remains-elusive-799418-1987-10-15

14. V.P. Singh transcripts, Oral History section, Nehru Memorial Museum and Library (NMML), translated (from Hindi) by the author.

15. Prabhu Chawla, 'Jan Morcha Raises More Questions than Answers', *India Today*, 31 October 1987, https://www.indiatoday.in/magazine/indiascope/story/19871031-jan-morcha-raises-more-questions-than-answers-799450-1987-10-31

16. Seema Mustafa, *The Lonely Prophet*, p. 92.

17. Ibid., p. 93.

18. V.P. Singh transcripts, NMML.

19. Interview with Arif Mohammad Khan.

20. V.P. Singh transcripts, NMML.

21. Pankaj Pachauri and Prabhu Chawla, 'Opposition's Balancing Act Called Unity Begins in Deadly Earnest', *India Today*, 15 August 1988, https://www.indiatoday.in/magazine/cover-story/story/19880815-opposition-balancing-act-called-unity-begins-in-deadly-earnest-797567-1988-08-15

22. 'Would Be a Disaster as PM: V.P. Singh', *Hindustan Times*, 24 July 1988.

23. Interview with Som Pal.
24. V.P. Singh transcripts, NMML.
25. Interview with Som Pal.
26. V.P. Singh transcripts, NMML.
27. V.P. Singh transcripts, NMML.
28. Ibid.
29. Interview with Som Pal.
30. Janardhan Thakur, *V.P. Singh: The Quest for Power* (New Delhi: Warbler Books, 1989), p. 129.
31. Interview with Som Pal.
32. Janardhan Thakur, *V.P. Singh*, p. 132.
33. The exception was the Bahujan Samaj Party, still fledgling at the time, whose founder Kanshi Ram contested against V.P. Singh and Sunil Shastri at Allahabad, polling around 50,000 votes.
34. Seema Mustafa, *The Lonely Prophet,* pp. 95–96.
35. Ibid., p. 96.
36. Interview with Som Pal.
37. Interview with Udit Narayan Singh.
38. Shekhar Gupta and Dilip Awasthi, 'Allahabad By-Election a Do-or-Die Battle for V.P. Singh, Stakes High for Congress(I) Too', *India Today*, 30 June 1988, https://www.indiatoday.in/magazine/cover-story/story/19880630-allahabad-by-election-a-do-or-die-battle-for-v.p.-singh-stakes-high-for-congressi-too-797429-1988-06-30
39. Dilip Awasthi, 'Jan Morcha Leader V.P. Singh Delivers a Crushing Blow to Congress(I) in Allahabad', *India Today*, 15 July 1988, https://www.indiatoday.in/magazine/cover-story/story/19880715-jan-morcha-leader-v.p.-singh-delivers-a-crushing-blow-to-congressi-in-allahabad-797436-1988-07-15
40. Ibid.
41. He was shifted to the Centre as communications minister, but died within a year.
42. Interview with Arif Mohammad Khan.
43. Janardhan Thakur, *V.P. Singh*, p. 124.
44. Interview with Arif Mohammad Khan.
45. The rump Congress was now called Congress (Socialist). Most of its leaders had shifted allegiance to the mainstream Congress, but the party had not vanished entirely.
46. V.P. Singh transcripts, NMML.
47. Interview with Sita Kumari Singh.

48. However, Ram Dhan eventually did join the Janata Dal, contesting the 1989 Lok Sabha election from his usual seat, Lalganj, and winning it as well.
49. Seema Mustafa, *The Lonely Prophet*, p. 110; V.P. Singh transcripts, NMML.
50. V.P. Singh transcripts, NMML.
51. Ibid.
52. Ibid.
53. Ibid.

Chapter 3: 'Politics is a very uncertain profession'

1. Pankaj Pachauri, 'Dissent over Janata Dal's New Executive', *India Today*, 31 December 1988, https://www.indiatoday.in/magazine/indiascope/story/19881231-dissent-over-janata-dal-new-executive-798074-1988-12-31; Seema Mustafa, *The Lonely Prophet: V.P. Singh, A Political Biography* (New Delhi: New Age International [P] Ltd, 1995), p. 113.
2. Seema Mustafa, *The Lonely Prophet*, pp. 113–15.
3. Ibid.
4. The Haryana crisis occurred at the end of October 1988, just after the Janata Dal was finally cobbled together, and was due to the rivalry between two of Devi Lal's sons, Om Prakash Chautala and Ranjit Singh, both of whom wanted to inherit their father's mantle. Each had his own group of followers among Janata Dal ministers and MLAs. Provoked by Chautala's opposition when he wanted to dismiss a minister (a Chautala supporter) for alleged corruption, Devi Lal announced he would resign as chief minister, only to discover that if he did, the Haryana Janata Dal would split between Chautala and Ranjit Singh. Devi Lal then hastily backtracked. See Vipul Mudgal and Ramindar Singh, 'Succession Battle between Devi Lal's Sons Creates Major Crisis in Haryana Lok Dal', *India Today*, 15 November 1988, https://www.indiatoday.in/magazine/special-report/story/19881115-succession-battle-between-devi-lal-sons-creates-major-crisis-in-haryana-lok-dal-797922-1988-11-15
   The Karnataka collapse followed a ministry expansion by Chief Minister S.R. Bommai, after which nineteen Janata Dal MLAs, who had expected to be made ministers but were disappointed, withdrew their support to his government, taking away its majority support. Governor P. Venkatasubbiah promptly dismissed Bommai's government and imposed President's Rule.

5. V.P. Singh transcripts, Oral History section, Nehru Memorial Museum and Library (NMML), translated (from Hindi) by the author.

6. Younger son Abhay Singh paid for his father's politics in a different way. He had qualified in the written test to pursue a super speciality course in gastroenterology at AIIMS (after his MD) but was turned down following the interview. 'I cannot be 100 per cent sure if it was victimization,' he said. Soon after, he took the Professional and Linguistic Assessment Board (PLAB) test to practise medicine in the UK, qualified and left the country, later moving to the US. From interview with Abhay Singh.

7. 'Swamy Alleges VP Links with CIA', *Hindustan Times*, 17 November 1989; 'Swamy Document Forgery: US Embassy', 18 November 1989. The MP was Subramanian Swamy.

8. Seema Mustafa, *The Lonely Prophet*, p. 84.

9. Prabhu Chawla, 'Ajeya Singh Seizes Advantage in St Kitts Controversy, Publicly Declares His Assets', *India Today*, 15 October 1989, https://www.indiatoday.in/magazine/special-report/story/19891015-ajeya-singh-seizes-advantage-in-st-kitts-controversy-publicly-declares-his-assets-816596-1989-10-15

10. Interview with Ajeya Singh.

11. Lok Sabha Debates (English Version), Fourteenth Session - Second Part (Eighth Lok Sabha), https://eparlib.nic.in/bitstream/123456789/385/1/lsd_08_14_12-10-1989.pdf

12. Interview with Ajeya Singh.

13. Mark Tully and Gillian Wright, 'A Tale of Two Brothers', *India in Slow Motion* (New Delhi: Penguin Books India, 2002), p. 231.

14. Ibid., pp. 234–35.

15. V.P. Singh transcripts, NMML.

16. Ibid.

17. Shekhar Gupta, 'Election 1989: For Fatehpur Voters, V.P. Singh Is Potential Prime Minister', *India Today*, 30 November 1989, https://www.indiatoday.in/magazine/cover-story/story/19891130-election-1989-for-fatehpur-voters-v.p.-singh-is-potential-prime-minister-817123-1989-11-30

18. Election Commission of India, 'General Election, 1989 (Vol I, II)', https://eci.gov.in/files/file/4120-general-election-1989-vol-i-ii/

19. V.P. Singh transcripts, NMML.

20. Interview with Ajeya Singh.

21. Ibid.

22. 'Murder in VP Constituency: NF Alleges IB Bid to Disrupt Elections', *Hindustan Times,* 19 November 1989.

23. Interview with Ajeya Singh.

24. V.P. Singh transcripts, NMML.

25. See, for instance, Asghar Ali Engineer, 'The Bloody Trail – Ram Janmabhoomi and Communal Violence in UP', *Economic & Political Weekly*, Vol. 26, Issue 4, 26 January 1991, https://www.epw.in/journal/1991/4/roots-specials/bloody-trail-ramjanmabhoomi-and-communal-violence.html. The Supreme Court finally pronounced judgment on the matter on 9 November 2019, awarding the disputed land to the Hindus to build a new Rama temple.

26. 'The Origin And Growth Of Vishva Hindu Parishad', https://vhp.org/orgnization/the-origin-and-growth-of-vishva-hindu-parishad/

27. V.P. Singh transcripts, NMML.

28. Ibid.

29. Ibid.

30. Interview with Arif Mohammad Khan.

31. '43 Killed in Poll Violence', *Hindustan Times,* 23 November 1989; '32 More Killed in Violence', *Hindustan Times,* 25 November 1989.

32. 'Shots Fired at VP', *Hindustan Times,* 25 November 1989.

33. 'Sanjay Singh Shot At', *Hindustan Times,* 23 November 1989.

34. Election Commission of India, 'General Election 1989 (Vol I, II)', https://eci.gov.in/files/file/4120-general-election-1989-vol-i-ii/; https://eci.gov.in/files/file/3256-uttar-pradesh-1989/

35. V.P. Singh transcripts, NMML.

36. Seema Mustafa, *The Lonely Prophet*, p. 133.

37. Yashwant Sinha went on to join the BJP after the Janata Dal's collapse and, from 1998 to 2004, was finance minister and external affairs minister in Atal Bihari Vajpayee's NDA government. In March 2021, he quit the BJP to join the All India Trinamool Congress.

38. Yashwant Sinha, *Relentless: An Autobiography* (New Delhi: Bloomsbury, 2019), Kindle edition: Loc 3606.

39. See, for instance, Sunita Aron, 'VP Will Stay Out of Government', *Hindustan Times,* 26 November 1989.

40. I.K. Gujral, Prime Minister from April 1997 to March 1998, participated in the Quit India movement and began his political career with the Congress. He was once very close to Indira Gandhi, playing an important role in her victory against the Syndicate. But as information and broadcasting minister early in the Emergency, he lost her confidence after he baulked at gagging the media as ruthlessly as she desired. Calling

him 'credibility-crazy', she replaced him with V.C. Shukla, and after a year packed him off to Moscow as India's ambassador. On his return to India, he had joined the Opposition, going on to become external affairs minister in V.P. Singh's government. See Inder Kumar Gujral, *Matters of Discretion: An Autobiography* (New Delhi: Hay House India, 2011), Kindle edition: Loc770–85.

41. Ibid., Loc 4293–4308.
42. Interview with Ajeya Singh.
43. Yashwant Sinha, *Relentless*, Kindle edition: Loc 3619–33.
44. Om Prakash Chautala went on to become chief minister of Haryana four times, albeit for three short spells, followed by a fourth complete term from 1999 to 2005. But he was later convicted of accepting bribes to appoint government teachers in the state while chief minister and jailed for ten years.
45. Interview with Som Pal.
46. Interview with Sharad Yadav.
47. V.P. Singh transcripts, NMML.
48. Ibid.; Seema Mustafa, *The Lonely Prophet*, p. 133.
49. Ibid.
50. Yashwant Sinha, *Relentless*, Kindle edition: Loc 3619–45.
51. K.C. Yadav, *Chaudhari Devi Lal: A Political Biography* (Gurgaon: Hope India Publications, 2002), Kindle edition: Loc 499–517.
52. Ibid., Loc 518–38.
53. V.P. Singh transcripts, NMML.

PART 6: CRISIS PRONE

Chapter 1: 'I do what I have to'

1. The 1979 government with Charan Singh as Prime Minister was also a coalition government of the Janata Dal (Secular) and the Congress (Reddy). But since Charan Singh resigned without facing Parliament, it is not being counted.
2. V.P. Singh transcripts, Oral History section, Nehru Memorial Museum and Library (NMML), translated (from Hindi) by the author.
3. Ibid.
4. There are innumerable reports testifying to the flagrant rigging of the 1987 Jammu and Kashmir assembly elections. See, for instance, Inderjit Badhwar, 'Jammu and Kashmir Assembly Poll: NC-Congress

Alliance Sweeps a Massive Win', *India Today*, 15 April 1987, https://www.indiatoday.in/magazine/cover-story/story/19870415-jammu-kashmir-assembly-poll-nc-congressi-alliance-sweeps-a-massive-win-799831-1987-04-15; or David Devadas, *In Search of a Future: The Story of Kashmir* (New Delhi: Penguin Viking India, 2007), pp. 153–54 (which describes how an MUF worker, Hamid Sheikh, who later turned terrorist, was tortured by police for protesting the rigging); or Moosa Raza, *Kashmir: Land of Regrets* (Chennai: Westland Publications, 2019), pp. 198–99.

5. V.P. Singh transcripts, NMML.

6. A number of those involved in the effort to free Rubaiya Sayeed have since published their accounts of the drama. The details in this book are aggregated from the following sources: David Devadas, Chapter 15, 'One Woman's Rights', *In Search of a Future*, pp. 183–200; Aditya Sinha, Chapter 20, 'Rubaiya's Kidnapping: Opening the Floodgates', *Farooq Abdullah: Kashmir's Prodigal Son: A Biography* (New Delhi: UBS Publishers and Distributors, 1996), pp. 216–24; Moosa Raza, Chapter 12, 'The Kidnapping of Rubaiya Sayeed', *Kashmir: Land of Regrets,* pp. 186–213; A.S. Dulat with Aditya Sinha, Chapter 3, 'Two Hostage Crises', *Kashmir: The Vajpayee Years* (Noida: HarperCollins India, 2015), pp. 58–66; and Inder Kumar Gujral, Chapter 37, 'A Despicable Kidnapping', *Matters of Discretion: An Autobiography* (New Delhi: Hay House India, 2011), Kindle edition: Loc 4554–637. Also from the author's interview with Arif Mohammad Khan and V.P. Singh's own observations in his NMML transcripts.

7. V.P. Singh transcripts, NMML.

8. I.K. Gujral, *Matters of Discretion*, Kindle edition: Loc 4554–68.

9. Ibid., Loc 4583–96.

10. A.S. Dulat with Aditya Sinha, *Kashmir: The Vajpayee Years,* pp. 58–66; Moosa Raza, *Kashmir: Land of Regrets*, pp. 187–213.

11. Interview with Arif Mohammad Khan.

12. Ibid.

13. A.S. Dulat, *Kashmir: The Vajpayee Years*, p. 65.

14. Moosa Raza, *Kashmir: Land of Regrets,* pp. 205–10.

15. V.P. Singh transcripts, NMML.

16. Inderjit Badhwar and Prabhu Chawla, 'My Job as PM Is to Solve Problems, Not to Give Tutorials: V.P. Singh', *India Today*, 15 June 1990, https://www.indiatoday.in/magazine/cover-story/story/19900615-my-job-as-prime-minister-is-to-solve-problems-not-to-give-tutorials-vishwanath-pratap-singh-812707-1990-06-15

17. V.P. Singh transcripts, NMML.
18. Ibid.
19. Yashwant Sinha, *Relentless: An Autobiography* (New Delhi: Bloomsbury, 2019), Kindle edition: Loc 3648–81.
20. 'CBI Report on Phone Tapping Soon', *Hindustan Times,* 5 July 1990.
21. Arun Shourie, 'V. P. Singh and His Year', *The State as Charade: V.P. Singh, Chandra Shekhar and the Rest* (New Delhi: Roli Books, 1991), p. 79.
22. '"I Am Ready to Quit": VP for National Government if Consensus Reached', *Hindustan Times,* 6 June 1990.
23. 'Left Rejects National Government Idea', *Hindustan Times,* 6 June 1990.
24. Montek Singh Ahluwalia, *Backstage: The Story behind India's High Growth Years* (New Delhi: Rupa Publications India, 2020), pp. 107–13.
25. Ibid., p. 113.
26. However, the 'M document' was not forgotten, and indeed turned out to be a lasting contribution of the V.P. Singh government to the economic liberalization that came in the 1990s, as one of the key inputs guiding the early efforts of Prime Minister P.V. Narasimha Rao and his finance minister Manmohan Singh in this direction.
27. R. Venkataraman, *My Presidential Years* (New Delhi: Collins, 1994), p. 326.
28. V.P. Singh transcripts, NMML.
29. Ibid.
30. They were Finance Minister Madhu Dandavate and Railways Minister George Fernandes.
31. Interview with Som Pal.
32. Ibid.
33. V.P. Singh transcripts, NMML.
34. Seema Mustafa, *The Lonely Prophet: V.P. Singh, A Political Biography* (New Delhi: New Age International [P] Ltd, 1995), p. 136.
35. Patel and V.P. Singh had been elected UP MLAs for the first time in the same 1969 assembly election. Patel was then an SSP member. He had won from Kaurihar, adjoining VP's Soraon; he was the one who had turned away the Kurmi farmers, who'd sought his help after breaching a canal and facing the police's wrath—the ones VP later rescued by approaching then Chief Minister C.B. Gupta (see Part 2, Chapter 3).
36. Sunita Aron, 'VP, Mulayam Split on Party Post', *Hindustan Times,* 16 March 1990.
37. Interview with Arif Mohammad Khan.
38. Interview with Som Pal, interview with Santosh Bhartiya.

39. General K.V. Krishna Rao had been chief of the Indian army in the early 1980s and thereafter held gubernatorial positions in a few other states before taking over in Kashmir in July 1989.

40. They were Naresh Chandra, K.F. Rustamji and Krishna Kant. See Moosa Raza, *Kashmir: Land of Regrets*, p. 217.

41. Jagmohan had a reputation for both efficiency and inflexibility, acquired during his earlier career as a civil servant. His slum-clearance drive in Delhi during the Emergency, when he was vice chairman of the Delhi Development Authority, was particularly contentious, leading to police firing and several deaths when residents of the Turkman Gate slums resisted his efforts. He was made Lieutenant Governor of Delhi after Indira Gandhi returned to power in 1980. He had two stints as Jammu and Kashmir governor, from 1984 to 1989, and again in 1990. In the mid-1990s, he joined the BJP and was elected three times to the Lok Sabha from New Delhi, becoming minister for urban development in Atal Bihari Vajpayee's NDA government.

42. David Devadas, *In Search of a Future*, p. 194.

43. V.P. Singh transcripts, NMML.

44. I.K. Gujral, *Matters of Discretion*, Kindle edition: Loc 4652–66.

45. Article 370 was annulled on 5 August 2019, taking away Jammu and Kashmir's special status.

46. Jagmohan, *My Frozen Turbulence in Kashmir* (New Delhi: Allied Publishers, 1991), p. 387.

47. V.P. Singh transcripts, NMML.

48. Ibid.

49. George Fernandes was a prominent socialist and former fiery trade unionist, who had led the memorable twenty-day railways strike in May 1974, adding to the chaos Indira Gandhi was already facing with Jayaprakash Narayan's movement against her, and which she had harshly crushed. During the Emergency, he had initially evaded arrest and plotted to set off explosions in protest against it, which made him a hero once the Emergency was lifted, getting him elected to the Lok Sabha in the 1977 poll and made a minister. After serving as a minister in V.P. Singh's government too, he broke away from the Janata Dal to form the Samata Party, which allied with the BJP, leading to Fernandes becoming defence minister in Vajpayee's NDA government.

50. Jagmohan, *My Frozen Turbulence in Kashmir*, p. 541.

51. V.P. Singh transcripts, NMML.

52. Ibid.

53. Siddhartha Shankar Ray had a long history in the Congress, having won his first assembly election in 1957 and become a minister in the West

Bengal cabinet thereafter. He was chief minister of West Bengal from 1972 to 1977, and is said to have been the main persuader behind Indira Gandhi's decision to impose the Emergency after the Allahabad High Court found her guilty of electoral malpractices. Yet, after her 1977 defeat, he sided with her detractors and remained with the Congress rump when she broke away; later, of course, like many other colleagues, he, too, had found his way back into the mainstream Congress. Rajiv Gandhi made him Punjab's governor in April 1986. In the early 1990s, he was also India's ambassador to the US.

54. Kanwar Sandhu, 'Punjab Governor S.S. Ray Quits before Being Booted Out', *India Today*, 31 December 1989, https://www.indiatoday.in/magazine/special-report/story/19891231-punjab-governor-s.s.-ray-quits-before-being-booted-out-816864-1989-12-31

55. V.P. Singh transcripts, NMML.

56. Ibid.

57. Ibid.

58. R. Venkataraman, *My Presidential Years*, pp. 335–36.

59. V.P. Singh transcripts, NMML.

60. 'RV [R. Venkataraman] Appoints 14 New Governors', *Hindustan Times*, 2 February 1990.

Chapter 2: 'Going nuclear would have been a self-goal'

1. Interview with Ajeya Singh.

2. V. Venkatesan, 'The Collapse of a Forgery Case', *Frontline*, 19 November 2004, https://frontline.thehindu.com/static/html/fl2123/stories/20041119002703600.htm

3. V.P. Singh transcripts, Oral History section, Nehru Memorial Museum and Library (NMML), translated (from Hindi) by the author.

4. V.P. Singh transcripts, NMML.

5. Neeraj Mishra and Priya Sahgal, 'The Q Files', *India Today*, January 30, 2006, https://web.archive.org/web/20070817035641/http://www.hvk.org/articles/0106/112.html

6. Hamish McDonald, *Ambani and Sons: The Making of the World's Richest Brothers and Their Feud* (New Delhi: Roli Books, 2010), Kindle edition: Loc 3168–81.

7. Prabhu Chawla, 'Bofors Case: Final Battle for Uncovering the Scam to Be Fought Overseas', *India Today*, 15 March 1990, https://www.indiatoday.in/magazine/special-report/story/19900315-bofors-case-final-battle-for-uncovering-the-scam-to-be-fought-overseas-812417-1990-03-15

8. Dilip Awasthi, 'Jan Morcha Leader V.P. Singh Delivers a Crushing Blow to Congress(I) in Allahabad', *India Today*, 15 July 1988, https://www.indiatoday.in/magazine/cover-story/story/19880715-jan-morcha-leader-v.p.-singh-delivers-a-crushing-blow-to-congressi-in-allahabad-797436-1988-07-15

9. Interview of Vinod Pande by Kumkum Chadha, *Hindustan Times*, 29 July 1990.

10. Hamish McDonald, *Ambani and Sons*, Kindle edition: Loc 2761–75.

11. Ibid., Loc 2276–2789; Gita Piramal, *Business Maharajas* (New Delhi: Penguin Books India, 2000), Kindle edition: Loc 1174–1200.

12. Gita Piramal, *Business Maharajas*, Kindle edition: Loc 1135–1214.

13. Prabhu Chawla, 'PM V.P. Singh to Drive Around the City like an Ordinary Man', *India Today*, 31 December 1989, https://www.indiatoday.in/magazine/cover-story/story/19891231-pm-v.p.-singh-to-drive-around-the-city-like-an-ordinary-man-816895-1989-12-31

14. 'Group of Schoolchildren Surprises V.P. Singh with Their Visit', *India Today*, 15 March 1990, https://www.indiatoday.in/magazine/indiascope/story/19900315-group-of-schoolchildren-surprises-v.p.-singh-with-their-visit-812422-1990-03-15

15. Their new home disappointed Sita Kumari Singh. 'I had some expectations, since it was the Prime Minister's residence, after all, but it turned out to be quite claustrophobic, with just four bedrooms, which were far from large,' she said. 'I never liked that house.' From interview with Sita Kumari Singh.

16. The SPG Act has since been amended to include former Prime Ministers for five years after demitting office.

17. R. Venkataraman, *My Presidential Years* (New Delhi: Collins, 1994), pp. 346–47.

18. Ibid., p. 346.

19. Seema Mustafa, *The Lonely Prophet: V.P. Singh, A Political Biography* (New Delhi: New Age International [P] Ltd, 1995), pp. 147–48.

20. R. Venkataraman, *My Presidential Years*, pp. 346–47.

21. Dilip Bobb, 'Namibia Wins Political Freedom, but Economic Freedom Remains a Distant Dream', *India Today*, 15 April 1990, https://www.indiatoday.in/magazine/special-report/story/19900415-namibia-wins-political-freedom-but-economic-freedom-remains-a-distant-dream-812450-1990-04-15

22. K. Natwar Singh, *One Life Is Not Enough* (New Delhi: Rupa Publications India, 2014), pp. 280–81.

23. Ibid., pp. 281–82.

24. V.P. Singh transcripts, NMML.

25. Montek Singh Ahluwalia, *Backstage: The Story behind India's High Growth Years*, p. 107; also interview with Som Pal.

26. Barbara Crossette, 'India to Lift Nepal Embargo and Discuss Rift', *The New York Times*, 12 June 1990, https://www.nytimes.com/1990/06/12/world/india-to-lift-nepal-embargo-and-discuss-rift.html

27. Harivansh and Ravi Dutt Bajpai, *Chandra Sekhar: The Last Icon of Ideological Politics* (New Delhi: Rupa Publications India, 2019), p. 178.

28. V.P. Singh transcripts, NMML.

29. Inder Kumar Gujral, *Matters of Discretion: An Autobiography* (New Delhi: Hay House India, 2011), Kindle edition: Loc 4741–70.

30. Ibid., Loc 4771–84.

31. Shekhar Gupta, 'By Using the Kashmir Card Benazir Bhutto Is Playing with Fire', *India Today*, 31 May 1990, https://www.indiatoday.in/magazine/cover-story/story/19900531-benazir-played-kashmir-card-with-skill-leaving-herself-more-secure-in-the-centre-812642-1990-05-31

32. V.P. Singh transcripts, NMML.

33. Ibid.

34. Shekhar Gupta and Kanwar Sandhu, 'India and Pakistan Shore Up Their Defence Forces for Eventuality of a Showdown', *India Today*, 30 June 1990, https://www.indiatoday.in/magazine/cover-story/story/19900630-india-and-pakistan-shore-up-their-defence-forces-for-eventuality-of-a-showdown-812722-1990-06-30

35. Both officially turned nuclear states after conducting full-fledged nuclear tests in May 1998.

36. V.P. Singh transcripts, NMML.

37. Ibid.

38. See I.K. Gujral, *Matters of Discretion*, Kindle edition: Loc 5307–5422.

39. Ibid. Also see Viju Cherian, 'Ranjit Katyal Did Not Airlift Me from Kuwait', *Hindustan Times*, 28 January 2016, https://www.hindustantimes.com/bollywood/ranjit-katyal-did-not-airlift-me-from-kuwait/story-nUSJZio8HVjjVLbG6XW16O.html

40. I.K. Gujral, *Matters of Discretion*, Kindle edition: Loc 5409–45; '1990 Airlift of Indians from Kuwait', https://en.wikipedia.org/wiki/1990_airlift_of_Indians_from_Kuwait; it has even figured in the *Guinness Book of World Records*.

41. V.P. Singh transcripts, NMML.
42. *V.P. Singh: Selected Speeches and Writings, 1989–90*, Publications Division, Ministry of Information and Broadcasting, 1993, p. 5.
43. Ibid., pp. 4–5.
44. V.P. Singh transcripts, NMML.
45. Ahluwalia's 'M document' expressly opposed bringing such legislation. See Montek Singh Ahluwalia, *Backstage: The Story behind India's High Growth Years*, p. 107.
46. V.P. Singh transcripts, NMML.
47. Ibid.
48. Ibid.
49. 'The Inter-State Council Needs to Be Rejuvenated', *Mint*, 30 April 2018, https://www.livemint.com/Opinion/c9OZI4C1jO0sBdWLDbfGmJ/The-interstate-council-needs-to-be-rejuvenated.html
50. Interview with Som Pal.
51. Taringini Sriraman, 'The State Identification and Welfare Documentary Practices in India', PhD thesis, 2012, University of Delhi, http://hdl.handle.net/10603/31686; also D. Asher Ghertner, 'Calculating without Numbers: Aesthetic Governmentality in Delhi's Slums', *Economy and Society*, Vol. 39, Issue 2, 2010, pp. 185–217, http://dx.doi.org/10.1080/03085141003620147
52. Interview with Som Pal.

Chapter 3: 'I have learnt a lesson. I think I must be more firm'

1. 'Assembly Polls to Determine Direction of India's Politics for First Half of the Decade', *India Today*, 28 February 1990, https://www.indiatoday.in/magazine/nation/story/19900228-assembly-polls-to-determine-direction-of-india-politics-for-first-half-of-the-decade-813830-1990-02-28
2. Interview with Som Pal.
3. Ibid.
4. Jay Raina, 'Rigging Plagues Meham', *Hindustan Times*, 28 February 1990.
5. 'Repoll in Eight Meham Booths', *Hindustan Times*, 28 February 1990.
6. 'EC Countermands Meham By-Election', *Hindustan Times*, 8 March 1990; Harinder Baweja, 'Haryana CM Om Prakash Chautala Rigs His Own Political Future', *India Today*, 31 March 1990, https://www.indiatoday.in/magazine/special-report/story/19900331-haryana-cm-om-prakash-chautala-rigs-his-own-political-future-813783-1990-03-31

7. Inder Kumar Gujral, *Matters of Discretion: An Autobiography* (New Delhi: Hay House India, 2011), Kindle edition: Loc 4816–29.

8. Rohit Parihar, 'CBI Finds No Clue against Om Prakash Chautala Being Accused in Poll-Killing', *India Today*, 21 July 1997, https://www.indiatoday.in/magazine/nation/story/19970721-cbi-finds-no-clue-against-om-prakash-chautala-being-accused-in-poll-killing-832569-1997-07-21

9. Shekhar Gupta, Harinder Baweja and Bhaskar Roy, 'Devi Lai Determined to Ensure Om Prakash Chautala's Political Career Remains Intact', *India Today*, 15 April 1990, https://www.indiatoday.in/magazine/cover-story/story/19900415-devi-lai-determined-to-ensure-om-prakash-chautalas-political-career-remains-intact-812441-1990-04-15

10. V.P. Singh transcripts, Oral History section, Nehru Memorial Museum and Library (NMML), translated (from Hindi) by the author.

11. Jay Raina, 'Two die in firing on angry mob', *Hindustan Times*, 18 May 1990; Jay Raina, 'Armed policemen patrol Meham', *Hindustan Times*, 19 May 1990 (report adds that the death toll had risen to three).

12. S.R. Bommai was to leave an indelible mark on Indian legislative history by challenging his government's dismissal (in April 1989) by the Karnataka governor in the Supreme Court. In 1994, the court gave a historic judgment in response, much cited thereafter. It ruled that the power of the governor (acting on behalf of the President) to dismiss state governments was not absolute but could only be exercised if both Houses of Parliament agreed. It also said that a government's majority—or otherwise—could only be decided by a vote in the concerned legislature, and not by the governor, thus putting an end to arbitrary dismissals of Opposition state governments by a hostile Centre.

13. Banarsi Das Gupta had been a freedom fighter, repeatedly jailed by the British, and a Bhoodan movement volunteer. He had been Congress chief minister of Haryana during the Emergency, but later defected to the Janata Party and thence moved to the Janata Dal.

14. V.P. Singh transcripts, NMML.

15. Ibid.

16. Interview with Som Pal.

17. I.K. Gujral, *Matters of Discretion*, Kindle edition: Loc 4902–15.

18. Interview with Som Pal.

19. Ibid.

20. Ibid.

21. Seema Mustafa, H. Baweja, Bhaskar Roy and Prabhu Chawla, 'Dramatic Developments That Almost Led to the Fall of the National

Front Government', *India Today*, 15 August 1990, https://www. indiatoday.in/magazine/cover-story/story/19900815-dramatic-developments-that-almost-led-to-the-fall-of-the-national-front-government-812924-1990-08-15

22. 'Nehru, Arif, Malik Quit; More Likely to Follow', *Hindustan Times*, 14 July 1990.

23. I.K. Gujral, *Matters of Discretion*, Kindle edition: Loc 4859–72.

24. V.P. Singh transcripts, NMML.

25. Seema Mustafa, H. Baweja, Bhaskar Roy and Prabhu Chawla, 'Dramatic Developments That Almost Led to the Fall of the National Front Government', *India Today*, 15 August 1990, https://www. indiatoday.in/magazine/cover-story/story/19900815-dramatic-developments-that-almost-led-to-the-fall-of-the-national-front-government-812924-1990-08-15

26. 'Text of PM Letter', *Hindustan Times*, 15 July 1990.

27. R. Venkataraman, *My Presidential Years* (New Delhi: Collins, 1994), p. 391.

28. Ibid., pp. 391–92.

29. 'VP Told Not to Press Resignation', *Hindustan Times*, 15 July 1990.

30. Interview with Som Pal.

31. In Nehru's case, the company named 'Polisario' did not exist; in Arif Khan's, no purchases had been made from that particular firm (ABB) during his tenure. From Arun Shourie, 'The Deputy Prime Minister, Caught in a Forgery, Wriggles', *State as Charade: V.P. Singh, Chandra Shekhar and the Rest* (New Delhi: Roli Books, 1991), pp. 102–04.

32. Ibid.

33. R. Venkataraman, My *Presidential Years*, p. 394; Arun Shourie, *State as Charade*, pp. 107–08.

34. V.P. Singh transcripts, NMML.

35. Pritish Nandy, Interview with Devi Lal, *The Illustrated Weekly of India*, 29 July 1990; also quoted in K.C. Yadav, *Devi Lal: A Political Biography* (Gurgaon: Hope India Publications, 2002), Kindle edition: Loc 2264–2317.

36. Aroon Purie, 'I Have Never Felt Alone in My Political Life: V.P. Singh', *India Today*, 15 August 1990, https://www.indiatoday.in/magazine/cover-story/story/19900815-i-have-never-felt-alone-in-my-political-life-v.p.-singh-812892-1990-08-15

PART 7: MANDAL AND MANDIR

Chapter 1: 'After Mandal, it was as if I was a different person'

1. S. Jaipal Reddy began his political career with the Congress but quit to protest the Emergency, going on to join the Janata Party and later the Janata Dal; in later years, after the Janata Dal came apart, he returned to the Congress to hold various ministerial portfolios in later governments.

2. Interview with S. Jaipal Reddy.

3. See Paul Brass, *Caste, Faction and Party in Indian Politics*, Vol. 2 (New Delhi: South Asia Books, 1987), pp. 142–48.

4. 'Report of the Second Backward Classes Commission 1980', First Part, Vol. 1, Government of India, http://www.ncbc.nic.in/Writereaddata/ Mandal%20Commission%20Report%20of%20the%201st%20 Part%20English635228715105764974.pdf. The report estimates the OBCs at 52 per cent (p. 56), using the 1931 census. However, the 1999 National Sample Survey Office estimate was 35 per cent, while the 2005 estimate was 41 per cent.

5. The figures are all from the 1931 census, the last in which caste details were made public, and hence are very likely to be inaccurate. Since it was carved out of UP in 2000, Uttarakhand has become the state with the largest percentage of upper castes.

6. *V.P. Singh: Selected Speeches and Writings*, Ministry of Information and Broadcasting, 1993, p. 61.

7. 'When a backward caste candidate becomes a collector or superintendent of police, the material benefits accruing from his position are limited to the members of his family only. But the psychological spinoff of this phenomenon is tremendous; the entire community of that candidate feels elevated.' From 'Report of the Second Backward Classes Commission 1980', First Part, Vol. 1, Government of India, p. 57, http://www.ncbc. nic.in/Writereaddata/Mandal%20Commission%20Report%20of%20 the%201st%20Part%20English635228715105764974.pdf

8. Ibid., p. 3.

9. Ibid., pp. 5–11.

10. The other two states to do so were Punjab and Jammu and Kashmir.

11. UP's was the sole Congress government in a Hindi-speaking north Indian state to set up a commission for OBC uplift—the Chhedi Lal Sathi Commission in September 1975—when V.P. Singh's frenemy Bahuguna was chief minister.

12. Paul Brass, *Caste, Faction and Party in Indian Politics*, Vol. 2, pp. 256–80.

13. 'Report of the Second Backward Classes Commission 1980', First Part, Vol. 1, Government of India, p. 58, http://www.ncbc.nic.in/Writereaddata/Mandal%20Commission%20Report%20of%20the%201st%20Part%20English635228715105764974.pdf

14. Ibid., p. 52.

15. 'Sarkar par kamzor wargon ki upaksha ka aarop', *Navbharat Times*, 19 February 1982.

16. Christophe Jaffrelot, *India's Silent Revolution: The Rise of the Lower Castes in North India* (New Delhi: Permanent Black, 2003), pp. 329–30; the Mandal report was discussed in the Lok Sabha on 30 April 1982.

17. Interview with Som Pal.

18. Karpoori Thakur was a Quit India movement veteran, who had briefly been chief minister during the 1967–72 phase (of SVD rule in Bihar) too.

19. Shyama Nand Singh, 'Anti Reservation Agitations in Bihar', *The Indian Journal of Political Science*, Vol. 52, Issue 1, January–March 1991. The 20 per cent quota (in keeping with the original report) was also segmented, with 8 per cent allotted to the peasant OBC castes and 12 per cent to the substantially worse off service-provider OBC castes, who were called 'Most Backward Classes' (MBCs). In addition, 3 per cent jobs were reserved for women (of all castes) and another 3 per cent for those below an income limit among upper castes.

20. John R. Wood, 'Reservations in Doubt: The Backlash against Affirmative Action in Gujarat, India', *Pacific Affairs*, Vol. 60, Issue 3 (Autumn, 1987).

21. It was the N.V. Muralidhar Rao Commission report. See T.N. Ninan and Amarnath K. Menon, 'Anti-Reservations Stir in Andhra Pradesh Proves First Real Challenge for CM Rama Rao', *India Today*, 31 August 1986, https://www.indiatoday.in/magazine/special-report/story/19860831-anti-reservations-stir-in-andhra-pradesh-proves-to-first-real-challenge-for-cm-rama-rao-801203-1986-08-31

22. Prabhu Chawla, 'Anti-Reservation Agitation by Medicos in Gujarat Leaves 16 People Dead, Several Injured', *India Today*, 15 March 1981, https://www.indiatoday.in/magazine/indiascope/story/19810315-anti-reservation-agitation-by-medicos-in-gujarat-leaves-16-people-dead-several-injured-772762-2013-11-26

23. Philip George and Pankaj Pachauri, 'Reservation Issue Threatens to Escalate into Long-Drawn Conflict', *India Today*, 28 February 1990, https://www.indiatoday.in/magazine/special-report/story/19900228-reservation-issue-threatens-to-escalate-into-long-drawn-conflict-813753-1990-03-01

24. Since then, every ten years, fresh constitutional amendments have been passed, extending SC reservations for another ten. The last such instance was the 126th amendment passed by the BJP government in December 2019.

25. The Janata Dal's winning caste combination in the 1989 election was widely known by the acronym 'AJGAR'—Ahir (i.e., Yadav), Jat, Gujar and Rajput.

26. Jats had 'intermediate caste' counterparts in the rest of the country, though—the Patidars in Gujarat, the Marathas in Maharashtra, the Lingayats in Karnataka, the Reddys in Andhra Pradesh and more.

27. After several agitations and prolonged lobbying, the Jats have been included in the list of OBCs of several states. But the Central list of OBCs includes only the Jats of Rajasthan (barring those from the districts of Bharatpur and Dholpur).

28. Interview with Sharad Yadav.

29. This was the same Rampujan Patel who had become MLA on an SSP ticket the same year as V.P. Singh (1969) and whom V.P. Singh had briefly made UP Janata Dal president, only for Patel to be humiliated by Mulayam Singh Yadav. V.P. Singh later made him minister of state for civil supplies during his April 1990 cabinet expansion.

30. See, for instance, Prabhu Chawla, 'With Open Rebellion of Many MPs, V.P. Singh No Longer Undisputed Leader of Janata Party', *India Today*, 31 October 1990, https://www.indiatoday.in/magazine/cover-story/story/19901031-with-open-rebellion-of-many-mps-v.p.-singh-no-longer-undisputed-leader-of-janata-party-813186-1990-10-31

31. Inder Kumar Gujral, *Matters of Discretion: An Autobiography* (New Delhi: Hay House India, 2011), Kindle edition: Loc 4830–58.

32. V.P. Singh transcripts, Oral History section, Nehru Memorial Museum and Library (NMML), translated (from Hindi) by the author.

33. Arul B. Louis, 'Kisan Rally: Farmers Throng the Capital with Festive Gaiety', *India Today*, 15 January 1979, https://www.indiatoday.in/magazine/cover-story/story/19790115-kisan-rally-farmers-throng-the-capital-with-festive-gaiety-821763-2014-12-08

34. Interview with Som Pal.

35. Ibid.

36. In his memoirs, *Gopalganj to Raisina: My Political Journey*, Lalu Prasad Yadav has claimed he was the first to suggest to V.P. Singh that he implement the Mandal Commission report to counter Devi Lal. But the

account has many discrepancies and is hence not being considered in this narrative. Lalu Prasad Yadav and Nalin Verma, *Gopalganj to Raisina: My Political Journey* (New Delhi: Rupa Publications, 2019), Kindle edition: Loc 992–1017.

37. Interview with Sharad Yadav. After his hurtful school experiences, Sharad Yadav went on to become a strident student leader at Jabalpur Engineering College. Later, he was elected to the Lok Sabha for the first time (from the Jabalpur seat) in a 1974 by-election when he was just twenty-seven, as the candidate of a combined Opposition—long before the Janata Party was formed—against Indira Gandhi's Congress (R). He had aligned with the socialist faction in the Janata Party and the Lok Dal thereafter. He was, in turn, civil aviation minister, labour minister and consumer affairs minister in the first National Democratic Alliance (NDA) ministry from 1998 to 2004.

38. Interview with Sharad Yadav.

39. Ibid.

40. Now called Ministry of Social Justice and Empowerment. Paswan was railways minister, communications minister, mines minister, and fertilizers and chemical minister in later governments, allying with both the NDA and the United Progressive Alliance (UPA) ministries. He died in office as food and distribution minister on 8 October 2020.

41. Interview with P.S. Krishnan.

42. Ibid.

43. Seema Mustafa, *The Lonely Prophet: V.P. Singh, A Political Biography* (New Delhi: New Age International [P] Ltd, 1995), p. 171.

44. Interview with Arif Mohammad Khan.

45. Ibid.

46. Interview with Som Pal.

47. The speech went as follows: 'I am happy today to announce in this august house a momentous decision of social justice that my government has taken, regarding the socially and educationally backward classes on the basis of the report of the Mandal Commission. The Constitution envisaged that OBCs be identified, their difficulties removed and their conditions improved in terms of Article 340(1), read with Article 15(4) as well as Article 16(4). It is a negation of the basic structure of our Constitution that until now this requirement was not fulfilled. The Second Backward Classes Commission under the chairmanship of the late B.P. Mandal, which was appointed on January 1, 1979, submitted its report on December 31, 1980. In accordance with our commitment before the people we included this in our Action Plan. After examining various

aspects of it, my government has taken these decisions on the Mandal Commission report: 1. To avail ourselves of the benefit of a number of states in preparing lists of SEBCs, and in order to ensure harmonious and quick implementation, we have decided to adopt in the first phase the castes, common to both the Mandal list as well as the state list. 2. The percentage of reservation for the socially and educationally backward classes will be 27 per cent. 3. This reservation will be applicable to services under the government of India and public undertakings.' From Seema Mustafa, *The Lonely Prophet*, pp. 163–64.

48. Inderjit Badhwar, 'Decision to Implement Mandal Report Threatens to Tear India's Fabric Apart', *India Today*, 15 September 1990, https://www.indiatoday.in/magazine/cover-story/story/19900915-decision-to-implement-mandal-commission-report-threatens-to-tear-india-fabric-apart-812994-1990-09-15

49. L.K. Advani, *My Country, My Life* (New Delhi: Rupa Publications India, 2008), p. 446.

50. Interview with P.S. Krishnan. The list has since increased to 2,586 castes, with the states that did not have any OBC list in 1990 preparing theirs—and these being incorporated in the Central list. There were further additions following recommendations from the National Commission on Backward Classes.

51. 'Bihar Anti-Quota Stir Turns Violent', *Hindustan Times*, 10 August 1990.

52. 'Student Protestors Beaten Up', *Hindustan Times*, 11 August 1990.

53. Seema Mustafa, *The Lonely Prophet*, p. 164.

54. Saba Naqvi Bhaumik, 'Decision to Implement Mandal Commission Report Stirs Up Protests across India', *India Today*, 30 September 1990, https://www.indiatoday.in/magazine/special-report/story/19900930-decision-to-implement-mandal-commission-report-stirs-up-protests-across-india-813545-1990-09-30

55. V.P. Singh transcripts, NMML.

56. The step he put off—that of reserving seats in educational institutions for OBCs—was implemented sixteen years later, in 2006, by the Congress-led UPA government ruling then. This led to another agitation starting April 2006, which was finally ended after the UPA government agreed to increase the number of seats in the institutions where OBC reservation was being introduced, so that the number of 'open competition' seats in each institution remained the same as before. The offer he made—of reserving seats for the poor, regardless of caste—came to nothing, as it needed a constitutional amendment. V.P. Singh's government lacked the

majority or the consensus required to get it through Parliament. But it was not forgotten—it finally reached fruition under the BJP-led National Democratic Alliance government twenty-nine years later, in January 2019.

57. Yashwant Sinha, *Relentless: An Autobiography* (New Delhi: Bloomsbury, 2019), Kindle edition: Loc 3774–96.

58. Interviews with Richa and Adrija Manjari Singh.

59. V.P. Singh transcripts, NMML.

60. *V.P. Singh: Selected Speeches and Writings*, Ministry of Information and Broadcasting, 1993, p. 61.

61. Seema Mustafa, *The Lonely Prophet*, p. 174.

62. 'VP for Debate on Quota in Houses', *Hindustan Times*, 9 October 1990.

63. See, for instance, 'Pro-Reservation Leader Killed', *Hindustan Times*, 17 August 1990; 'Anti-Quota Group Fire at Opponents in Bihar, Three Killed', *Hindustan Times*, 10 September 1990; Mammen Mathew, 'Mandal Protests Spark Caste War', *Hindustan Times*, 16 October 1990.

64. Interviews with Som Pal, Santosh Bhartiya and Arif Mohammad Khan.

65. 'Consensus Eludes All-Party Meet', *Hindustan Times*, 4 September 1990; I&B Minister P. Upendra is quoted in the report, however, as saying that there was consensus on four points, despite disagreements on others: 'All parties agreed there should be reservation for OBCs in government and public sector units, that job opportunities overall should be augmented, that there should be a review of the issue after ten years, and that a joint appeal should be made to the students to maintain peace and shun violence.'

66. Notable among them were former supporters of V.P. Singh— Ramakrishna Hegde, former Karnataka chief minister and Planning Commission chairman at the time, and Biju Patnaik, Orissa's then chief minister (current chief minister Naveen Patnaik's father). Both were Brahmins. Chandra Shekhar echoed the Congress in criticizing the 'manner' of implementing the report. See, for instance, 'Patnaik Blasts Mandal Report; Cabinet to Discuss Student Protests', *Hindustan Times*, 30 August 1990.

67. 'Self-Immolation Bid by Students, DU Colleges Closed for Two Days', *Hindustan Times*, 20 September 1990.

68. Nonita Kalra, 'Rajeev Goswami Tragedy Provides Agitation a Rallying Point', *India Today*, 15 October 1990, https://www.indiatoday.in/magazine/cover-story/story/19901015-rajeev-goswami-tragedy-provides-agitation-rallying-point-813101-1990-10-15

69. Dalip Singh, 'Burnt Out in Obscurity: Forgotten Anti-Mandal Face Fades', *The Telegraph,* 24 February 2004.
70. Christophe Jaffrelot, *India's Silent Revolution*, p. 346.
71. V.P. Singh transcripts, NMML.
72. Seema Mustafa, *The Lonely Prophet*, p. 173.
73. I.K. Gujral, *Matters of Discretion,* Kindle edition: Loc 4986–99.
74. Ibid., Loc 5000–13.
75. 'Effective Stay on Quota Order', *Hindustan Times*, 2 October 1990.
76. Seema Mustafa, *The Lonely Prophet*, p. 167.
77. 'Three Killed in Delhi Firing: Boat Club Rally Turns Violent', *Hindustan Times*, 3 October 1990.
78. I.K. Gujral, *Matters of Discretion*, Kindle edition: Loc 5028–42.
79. 'Several Students Hurt in Lathi Charge', *Hindustan Times*, 25 August 1990; 'Cops Give Vent to Their Fury', *Hindustan Times*, 19 September 1990. (The latter article carries a large photo showing a young woman flat on her back on the road, with a police barricade in the background, and several policewomen attacking her.) Also see Seema Mustafa, *The Lonely Prophet,* p. 168.
80. I.K. Gujral, *Matters of Discretion,* Loc 5000–13.
81. Subodh Kant Sahay later joined the Congress and was a minister in the UPA government, before resigning over his alleged involvement in the coal blocks allotment scandal.
82. Seema Mustafa, *The Lonely Prophet*, p. 168.
83. I.K. Gujral, *Matters of Discretion*, Kindle edition: Loc 5043–55.
84. Interview with Santosh Bhartiya.
85. 'NF Parliamentary Party Reaffirms Trust in VP', *Hindustan Times*, 1 October 1990.
86. *Blitz*, 3 October 1990.
87. Yashwant Sinha, *Relentless*, Kindle edition: Loc 3819–30.
88. Interview with P.S. Krishnan.

Chapter 2: 'I was not clinging to power'

1. L.K. Advani joined the RSS as a fourteen-year-old schoolboy in 1941, moved to the Jana Sangh when the RSS founded it ten years later, and rose rapidly in the party to become information and broadcasting minister in the Janata Party government (with which the Jana Sangh had merged) from 1977 to 1979. After the erstwhile Jana Sangh regrouped as the BJP in 1980 following the Janata government's collapse, he became the party's president in May 1986. He was later home minister and deputy

prime minister in the BJP-led National Democratic Alliance government from 1998 to 2004. From Lal Krishna Advani, *My Country, My Life* (New Delhi: Rupa Publications India, 2008).

2.　V.P. Singh transcripts, Oral History section, Nehru Memorial Museum and Library (NMML), translated (from Hindi) by the author.

3.　Krishna Kant was a Quit India movement participant, who later became part of the radical 'Young Turks' brigade in the Congress (R), which Chandra Shekhar headed. He went on to become India's vice president in the late 1990s.

4.　Yunus Saleem was a renowned Urdu scholar and former minister in Indira Gandhi's cabinet.

5.　V.P. Singh transcripts, NMML.

6.　Ibid.

7.　L.K. Advani, *My Country, My Life*, p. 372. Though Advani, in his memoirs, never once suggests any link between V.P. Singh's decision to implement the Mandal Commission report and his to launch his rath yatra, Som Pal maintained that he was perfectly frank in making the connection when Som Pal approached him on behalf of V.P. Singh. According to Som Pal, Advani said, 'It was a clear understanding between the Janata Dal and the BJP that until the end of the present government's term, the Janata Dal would keep the Mandal issue on the backburner, while we would do the same with the Mandir matter. Since V.P. Singh has violated the agreement, there can be no stopping for us now.' This could not, however, be independently verified with Advani.

8.　L.K. Advani, *My Country, My Life*, p. 373.

9.　Madan Lal Khurana was then president of the Delhi BJP unit and went on to become Delhi's chief minister from 1993 to 1996.

10.　'Advani, Khurana Face Wrath of Agitationists', *Hindustan Times*, 20 September 1990.

11.　Pramod Mahajan was then one of the BJP's four general secretaries. He would go on to become communications minister and parliamentary affairs minister in the NDA government from 1998 to 2004. He died in April 2006, shot dead in a family dispute by his own brother.

12.　L.K. Advani, *My Country, My Life*, p. 374.

13.　Ibid., p. 375.

14.　See, for instance, Asghar Ali Engineer, 'The Bloody Trail – Ram Janmabhoomi and Communal Violence in UP', *Economic & Political Weekly*, Vol. 26, Issue 4, 26 January 1991, https://www.epw.in/journal/1991/4/roots-specials/bloody-trail-ramjanmabhoomi-and-communal-violence.html

15.　Ibid.

16. Interview with S. Gurumurthy.

17. Ibid.; L.K. Advani, *My Country, My Life*, pp. 380–82.

18. V.P. Singh transcripts, NMML; Bhure Lal, then a joint secretary in the PMO, also confirmed this.

19. L.K. Advani, *My Country, My Life*, pp. 382–83.

20. Interview with Arif Mohammad Khan.

21. Ibid.

22. V.P. Singh transcripts, NMML.

23. L.K. Advani, *My Country, My Life*, p. 385.

24. Inder Kumar Gujral, *Matters of Discretion: An Autobiography* (New Delhi: Hay House India, 2011), Kindle edition: Loc 5122–31; L.K. Advani, *My Country, My Life*, pp. 380–85.

25. Interview with S. Gurumurthy.

26. V.P. Singh transcripts, NMML.

27. Interview with Arif Mohammad Khan.

28. V.P. Singh transcripts, NMML; interview with Som Pal.

29. The unexpected early death of Opposition stalwart and twice chief minister Karpoori Thakur led to a fierce struggle for the leadership of the Janata Dal's Bihar unit. It was Lalu Prasad Yadav, the fifth of six sons of an impoverished cowherd in a remote village of Bihar's Gopalganj district, who triumphed in it, outmanoeuvring seniors such as Raghunath Jha and Ram Sundar Das. Lalu remained Bihar chief minister for seven years before he was undone by the fodder scam, following which he had to resign and was later convicted of embezzlement and fraud, and imprisoned. See Lalu Prasad Yadav and Nalin Verma, *Gopalganj to Raisina: My Political Journey* (New Delhi: Rupa Publications, 2019), Kindle edition: Loc 168–381, 886–908.

30. Ibid., Loc 1304–16.

31. Ibid.

32. V.P. Singh transcripts, NMML.

33. Ibid.

34. Interview with Som Pal.

35. Yashwant Sinha, *Relentless: An Autobiography* (New Delhi: Bloomsbury, 2019), Kindle edition: Loc 3890–3900.

36. See, for instance, Asghar Ali Engineer, 'The Bloody Trail – Ram Janmabhoomi and Communal Violence in UP', *Economic & Political Weekly*, Vol. 26, Issue 4, 26 January 1991, https://www.epw.in/journal/1991/4/roots-specials/bloody-trail-ramjanmabhoomi-and-communal-violence.html; or Dilip Awasthi and Prabhu Chawla, 'Machinations and Blunders of V.P. Singh Lead National Front to Disaster', *India Today*, 15 November 1990, https://www.indiatoday.in/

magazine/cover-story/story/19901115-machinations-and-blunders-of-
v.p.-singh-lead-national-front-to-disaster-813231-1990-11-15

PART 8: THE LONG GOODBYE

Chapter 1: 'I'm like a rocket that burns away after putting the satellite into orbit'

1. 'Implementation of Mandal Commission Report Lands PM V.P. Singh in "No-Win" Situation', *India Today*, 30 September 1990, https://www.indiatoday.in/magazine/special-report/story/19900930-implementation-of-mandal-commission-report-lands-prime-minister-v-p-singh-in-no-win-situation-813072-1990-09-30
2. V.P. Singh transcripts, Oral History section, Nehru Memorial Museum and Library (NMML), translated (from Hindi) by the author.
3. There were many poll analyses to this effect. See, for instance, 'Exit Poll: Rajiv Gandhi Assassination Resulted in Distinct Swing in Favour of Congress (I)', *India Today*, 15 July 1991, https://www.indiatoday.in/magazine/cover-story/story/19910715-exit-poll-rajiv-gandhi-assassination-resulted-in-distinct-swing-in-favour-of-congressi-814550-1991-07-15
4. Election Commission of India, 'General Election, 1991 (Vol I, II)', https://eci.gov.in/files/file/4121-general-election-1991-vol-i-ii/
5. Interview with Ajeya Singh. V.P. Singh eventually won by about 136,000 votes, a slightly higher margin than in 1989.
6. Interview with Ajeya Singh.
7. Election Commission of India, 'General Election, 1991 (Vol I, II)', https://eci.gov.in/files/file/4121-general-election-1991-vol-i-ii/
8. 'JD Expels Three Jan Morcha Leaders; Big Relief, Says Arif', *Hindustan Times*, 23 April 1991.
9. Interview with Sita Kumari Singh.
10. Kunwar Pragy Arya and Suneet Chopra, *Vishwanath Pratap Singh* (New Delhi: Aryan Art Gallery, 2006), p. 17.
11. Interview with Sita Kumari Singh. The normal blood sugar range is 75–100 mg/dL while fasting, 100–140 mg/dL on a full stomach.
12. 'VP Begins Fast for Peace', *The Times of India*, 16 January 1993; 'VP Admitted to Hospital', *The Times of India*, 18 January 1993.
13. Kunwar Pragy Arya and Suneet Chopra, *Vishwanath Pratap Singh*, p. 18.
14. Interview with Sita Kumari Singh. Creatinine is a chemical waste the kidneys remove from the blood.

15. Interview with Ajeya Singh.
16. Interview with Sita Kumari Singh. An aneurysm is the weakening of an artery wall, causing the organ to bulge. Occurring in the retina, it leads to partial vision loss, and if left unattended, can burst and cause brain haemorrhage.
17. Interview with Sita Kumari Singh.
18. See, for instance, 'Ministers Turn Their Stay Abroad for Medical Reasons into Frenzied Shopping Sprees', *India Today*, 15 June 1994, https://www.indiatoday.in/magazine/special-report/story/19940615-ministers-turn-their-stay-abroad-for-medical-reasons-into-frenzied-shopping-sprees-810469-1994-06-15
19. Interview with Dr Shishir Ray.
20. R. Venkataraman, *My Presidential Years* (New Delhi: Collins, 1994), p. 474.
21. Interview with Dr Shishir Ray.
22. Interview with Sita Kumari Singh.
23. Kunwar Pragy Arya and Suneet Chopra, *Vishwanath Pratap Singh*, p. 18.
24. Javed M. Ansari, 'V.P. Singh Stages Another Resignation to Propel His Political Career', *India Today*, 31 December 1994, https://www.indiatoday.in/magazine/indiascope/story/19941231-vp-singh-stages-another-resignation-to-propel-his-political-career-810074-1994-12-31
25. See, for instance, Asghar Ali Engineer, 'The Bloody Trail – Ram Janmabhoomi and Communal Violence in UP', *Economic &Political Weekly*, Vol. 26, Issue 4, 26 January 1991, https://www.epw.in/journal/1991/4/roots-specials/bloody-trail-ramjanmabhoomi-and-communal-violence.html. In September 2020, however, thirty-two BJP and VHP leaders charged with abetting the demolition of the Babri Masjid were acquitted. See, for instance, Ananya Bhardwaj and Praveen Jain, 'CBI Court Acquits Advani, Joshi, Kalyan Singh & All Others Accused in Babri Demolition Case', *The Print*, 30 September 2020, https://theprint.in/judiciary/cbi-court-acquits-advani-joshi-kalyan-singh-all-others-accused-in-babri-masjid-demolition-case/513313/
26. Interview with Sita Kumari Singh.
27. V.P. Singh transcripts, NMML.
28. Interview with Sita Kumari Singh.
29. V.P. Singh transcripts, NMML.
30. Interview with Sita Kumari Singh.
31. V.P. Singh transcripts, NMML.
32. Kunwar Pragy Arya and Suneet Chopra, *Vishwanath Pratap Singh*, p. 18.
33. Ibid., p. 27.

34. Ibid., pp. 19–21.
35. Ibid.
36. Ibid., p. 22.
37. Interview with Dr Shishir Ray.
38. Kunwar Pragy Arya and Suneet Chopra, *Vishwanath Pratap Singh*, pp. 22–23.
39. Interview with Sita Kumari Singh.
40. V.P. Singh transcripts, NMML.
41. Kunwar Pragy Arya and Suneet Chopra, *Vishwanath Pratap Singh*, p. 22.
42. V.P. Singh transcripts, NMML.
43. Interview with Ajeya Singh.
44. 'V.P. Singh Saves 30,000 Jhuggis at Wazirpur', *The Times of India*, 26 March 2000; 'Change Attitude Towards Slum Dwellers, says V.P. Singh', *Hindustan Times*, 26 March 2000; 'VP Stir Pays Off; Squatters at Azad Colony to Be Given Alternate Sites', *Hindustan Times*, 28 March 2000.
45. V.P. Singh transcripts, NMML.
46. Aruna Roy and Nikhil Dey, 'The Raja of Small Things', *The Indian Express*, 12 December 2008, http://archive.indianexpress.com/news/the-raja-of-small-things/397312/1
47. Ibid.
48. Atiq Khan, 'Dadri Farmers Protest Land Acquisition by RPL', *The Hindu*, 28 August 2009, https://www.thehindu.com/news/national/Dadri-farmers-protest-land-acquisition-by-RPL/article16877533.ece
49. See, for instance, Santosh Bhartiya, Chapter 37, 'Sonia Gandhi', *V.P. Singh, Chandra Shekhar, Sonia Gandhi Aur Main* (New Delhi: Warrior's Victory Publishing House, 2021), pp. 457–75.
50. 'Walk the Talk with V.P. Singh', NDTV, July 2005, https://www.youtube.com/watch?v=qaO49Vu-eFc
51. Interview with Dr Shishir Ray.
52. Interviews with Ajeya Singh and Sita Kumari Singh.
53. Interview with Ajeya Singh.
54. Rambahadur Rai, *Vishwanath Pratap Singh – Manzil Se Zyada Safar* (New Delhi: Rajkamal Prakashan, 2006), p. 406.

INDEX

ABOUT THE AUTHOR

Debashish Mukerji was a journalist for nearly forty years, working with numerous publications, including *Hindustan Times*, *The Week* and *Business Today*. He has written extensively on Uttar Pradesh and on national politics.